Teaching Elementary Physical Education

STRATEGIES FOR THE CLASSROOM TEACHER

PETER HASTIE
Auburn University

ELLEN MARTIN
Columbus State University

PEARSON
Benjamin Cummings

San Francisco   Boston   New York
Cape Town   Hong Kong   London   Madrid   Mexico City
Montreal   Munich   Paris   Singapore   Sydney   Tokyo   Toronto

Publisher: Daryl Fox
Senior Acquisitions Editor: Deirdre Espinoza
Project Editor: Elisa Rassen
Developmental Editor: Mark Wales
Editorial Assistant: Alison Rodal
Managing Editor: Wendy Earl
Text and Cover Design: Kaelin Chappell Broaddus
Copyeditor: Margaret Pinette
Production Services and Composition: The Left Coast Group
Proofreader: Carole Quandt
Marketing Manager: Sandra Lindelof
Senior Manufacturing Buyer: Stacey Weinberger
Cover Image: Jon Feingersh/CORBIS

Photo credits can be found on page 467.

Library of Congress Cataloging-in-Publication Data
Hastie, Peter A.
   Teaching elementary physical education: strategies for the classroom teacher / Peter A. Hastie, Ellen H. Martin.
      p. cm.
   Includes bibliographical references and index.
   ISBN 0-8053-2834-3 (alk. paper)
   1. Physical education and training—Study and teaching (Elementary)—United States.   I. Martin, Ellen H.   II. Title.
   GV365.H38 2006
   372.86'044'0973—dc22

                                                                                    2005001093

PEARSON
Benjamin
Cummings

ISBN 0-8053-2834-3

1 2 3 4 5 6 7 8 9 10—MAL—09 08 07 06 05

This book is dedicated to all those who strive to provide quality physical education experiences to children in elementary schools.

BRIEF CONTENTS

CONTENTS

PREFACE

Why should elementary schools offer physical education programs? While physical education may often seem a superfluous part of a child's educational experience, in fact it is particularly crucial for students at an elementary level. This age is an optimal period for acquiring key motor skills and developing habits and attitudes toward physical activity that will serve them well for a lifetime.

Although physical education is one of the most valuable and important vehicles for encouraging and teaching children to lead active lifestyles, numerous elementary schools are cutting back on their programs and sending classroom teachers into the gym. Many elementary classroom teachers, however, are reluctant to teach physical education. From our observations, the main reason for this reluctance is a history of unsatisfying experiences with physical education. An important goal for this text, therefore, is to help you discover the joy of physical education, perhaps for the very first time.

Elementary classroom teachers need powerful motivation and trust in their abilities to assume the responsibility of delivering a substantive physical education program. They must learn an unfamiliar curriculum and new instructional strategies, and they must also be committed to the importance of physical education in contributing to the total wellness of elementary school students. This book will help you progress in your understanding and perceptions of physical education, make you increasingly willing to teach physical education, and give you confidence in your ability to teach it effectively.

We accomplish this goal by preparing you to recognize, plan, and teach quality physical education lessons. We will guide you every step of the way as you learn about stages of development, fundamentals of movement, lesson planning, instructional and management tactics, and more. We will provide you with both overarching strategies and specific tasks and activities to help you develop the confidence and skills you need to teach physical education. Reading this text and completing and reflecting upon each chapter's challenges, however, is just the beginning. We hope that this book will stimulate you to continue learning about children and movement so you can provide your future students with experiences full of enjoyment and learning. You have our best wishes.

ORGANIZATION OF THE BOOK

This book is divided into five units. Unit I (Chapters 1 to 3) introduces you to the world of teaching physical education to children. In Chapter 1, we propose that good teaching in any setting involves doing whatever it takes to help students learn the content. As such, many of the skills you have as a classroom teacher will transfer well to the playground or gymnasium. To supplement your existing expertise, we tell you how children learn motor skills and suggest ways you can teach these skills in an appropriate progression. Furthermore, we strongly believe that the joy of engaging in physical activity isn't just for children with exceptional skills or excellent physical fitness. Nor is it just for boys or for children of a particular ethnic group. It is for everyone. While many of you may not have seen physical education as a place of joy, in Chapter 2 we give you strategies to create an inclusive and pleasurable learning environment for your students. In Chapter 3, we describe children's progression through a certain sequence in learning motor skills, and we outline a helpful teaching progression to enable them to acquire the various skill themes and movement concepts.

Unit II (Chapters 4 to 6) outlines all the features of physical education teaching you need to consider before working on the content itself. Chapter 4 lists issues you will face when creating a lesson plan to teach physical education, while Chapter 5 deals with the specific instructional strategies you can use in teaching students in an activity-based lesson. Because teachers have become increasingly accountable for student learning, in Chapter 6 we have addressed issues of assessment in accordance with physical education objectives and standards.

Unit III (Chapters 7 to 10) provides management strategies for maximizing students' time for practicing skills and minimizing such distractions as discipline problems and equipment difficulties. Chapters 7 through 10 will arm you with strategies for managing students and their behavior, organizing and coping with equipment, and creating a developmentally appropriate and safe physical education experience.

Unit IV (Chapters 11 to 14) provides the specific information you will need to develop motor skill subject matter suitable for an elementary school curriculum. These chapters give you extensive content from which you can select individual lessons or series of lessons. We begin in Chapter 11 with a wide-ranging coverage of the locomotor and nonlocomotor skill themes that make up elementary school physical education. Chapter 12 addresses manipulative skills, Chapter 13 provides extensive coverage of games, and Chapter 14 covers teaching rhythmic movement. We give numerous tasks you can use to teach all these skills, and the progressive organization of this material will allow you to easily decide on the appropriateness of each activity for your students. This flexibility will let your students both learn and appreciate as much as possible.

Unit V (Chapters 15 and 16) provides strategies for promoting physical activity and cross-disciplinary learning. We know that many American children are overweight or at risk of becoming so, and desperately need to achieve physical fitness. Unfortunately, to many of us fitness is a dirty word that connotes tedious, repetitious, and arduous activities. But done properly, getting fit can be a lot of fun, and in Chapter 15 we offer a series of definitely enjoyable activities that will give students huge gains in health-related fitness. In conclusion, as this book is intended for elementary classroom teachers, Chapter 16 focuses on integrating lessons from the classroom into physical education and provides strategies for incorporating material from physical education into other subject areas. We hope this chapter will help you create natural links across subject areas to enhance meaningful learning for all your students.

SPECIFIC CHAPTER FEATURES

Many textbooks begin their chapters with chapter objectives. In this book, however, we prefer to begin each chapter with a set of "Getting Started" questions to bring the important issues of the chapter to the foreground and provide a number of possible discussion starters.

Incorporated throughout the chapter is a feature entitled "What's Wrong with This Picture?" that offers an entertaining way to test your knowledge. This feature describes situations where developmentally appropriate practices are being violated. Your challenge is to identify these problems and suggest solutions.

We have also found that many elementary teacher education programs have extensive field experiences in which you visit schools to observe or teach children. To enhance this element of your learning process, the "Inquiring Minds" feature lists stimulus questions you might ask practicing teachers in schools during your visits. The questions ask teachers to give you real-world, practical answers to some of the key issues addressed in each chapter.

The conclusion of each chapter returns you to the initial reflection process through a feature called "Over to You." These thought-provoking questions ask you to consider how confident you feel in carrying out the applications from the chapter into the work setting.

Finally, we include in each chapter suggestions for "Portfolio Tasks." Many teacher education programs now require their students to produce portfolios as evidence of their learning and professional growth. Completing the tasks listed in each chapter will allow you to demonstrate mastery of the key factors that we consider most important for that topic. Any student who completes all the tasks in this book will have a magnificent résumé.

RESOURCES FOR INSTRUCTORS

We would like to thank Ann-Catherine Sullivan of Saginaw Valley State University who created an Instructor's Guide and Test Bank for the book. This guide includes chapter objectives, a chapter overview, the National Association for Sport and Physical Education (NASPE) standards that are appropriate for each chapter, lecture outlines which include discussion and reflection questions, in-class activities and out-of-class assignments, key terms, references, websites, and test questions which include multiple choice, true/false, matching, fill-in-the-blank, and essay questions (there are about 25 per chapter). The test questions are also available via a computerized test bank where instructors can edit existing questions or add questions of their own. Finally, a PowerPoint presentation is available via the Benjamin Cummings catalog page for this book at www.aw-bc.com. Please ask your Benjamin Cummings sales representative for more information about these supplements.

ACKNOWLEDGMENTS

The authors would like to thank the following persons, who all gave freely of their time. The reviewers of the original book proposal and those who read the chapter drafts, whose contributions certainly enhanced this text, include:

Judith Ausherman
Cleveland State University

Sarah M. Boeh
California State University–
San Bernadino

Deborah Buswell
Southwest Texas State University

Melissa A. Chase
Miami University

David Chen
California State University–Fullerton

Matthew Dell'Orso
Shepherd College

Elaine Gregory
Syracuse University

Nina Grove
York College of Pennsylvania

Tina Hall
Western Kentucky University

Donna Hester
University of Alabama at Birmingham

Christine Heusser
California State University–Fullerton

Dee Jacobsen
Southeastern Louisiana University

Alisa James
SUNY–Brockport

Grace Goc Karp
University of Idaho

Susan Kasser
University of Vermont

Joy Kiger
Otterbein College

Nancy J. Krattiger-Ziltener
University of Wisconsin–Madison

Cindy Kuhrasch
University of Wisconsin–Madison

Jewel Lehman
Greensboro College

Robyn Lock
San Francisco State University

LeaAnn Martin
Western Washington University

Brian McCullick
University of Georgia

Shauna McGhie
Utah Valley State College

Debby Mitchell
University of Central Florida

Deanne Riess
McKendree College

Cynthia Rutledge
McMurry University

Richard Samara
University of Oklahoma

Sadie B. Sanders
University of Florida

Jon A. Spaventa
University of California–Santa Barbara

Ann-Catherine Sullivan
Saginaw Valley State University

Susan Truitt
Towson

Sue Vincent
Brigham Young University

Susan Wagner
Texas A&M University

Doris Watson
University of Utah

Patricia Wilson
Otterbein College

The authors would like to thank Deirdre Espinoza, Senior Acquisitions Editor at Benjamin Cummings, who provided the approval for this project and showed great confidence in its potential; Elisa Rassen and Mark Wales of Benjamin Cummings, who adopted the considerable challenge of making this text the best it could be, provided us with many reality checks, and significantly improved the final text through their efforts; Alison Rodal and Sabrina Larson, also of Benjamin Cummings, who managed the review process and made sure the ancillary materials were of the highest quality; Walter Martin, who employed his amazing artistic skills to create the artwork and enhance the photography for this book; Deana Schnuelle of Ogletree Elementary School and Charles Cooper of Auburn Early Education Center, both model physical education teachers without peer, who most generously provided us with access to their ideas, resources, classes, and children; Gary Gibson of Columbus State University for his down-to-earth and practical advice; the editors of PE Central for permission to use resources from their website; Kaelin Chappell Broaddus for her great graphic design; and the production team at The Left Coast Group and Wendy Earl Productions for bringing it all together in book form. The authors would also like to thank those who posed for and contributed to the photographs and artwork for this book.

PETER HASTIE   ELLEN MARTIN
Auburn University   Columbus State University

ABOUT THE AUTHORS

Peter Hastie received a Ph.D. from the University of Queensland in the field of Human Movement Studies (Education). He is currently a professor at Auburn University in the Department of Health and Human Performance. His courses focus on elementary and secondary school physical education as well as the skills and concepts of sports and other activities. Peter is well known in the physical education community, mainly for his contributions to the study of Sport Education.

Peter is the author of *Teaching for Lifetime Physical Activity through Quality High School Physical Education* (Benjamin Cummings, 2003). In addition, he is co-author of *Complete Guide to Sport Education,* along with Daryl Siedentop and Hans van der Mars (Human Kinetics, 2004).

Ellen H. Martin earned her Ph.D. from Auburn University in the field of Physical Education. Currently she is an assistant professor at Columbus State University in the Department of Teacher Education. She teaches courses on assessment, elementary physical education methods, and the history of physical education, recreation, and sport.

Ellen has served for several years as the Bookmark editor for the journal *Teaching Elementary Physical Education.* She has written several articles and co-authored a chapter for the book *Resources for Developmentally Appropriate Practice: Recommendations from the Profession,* edited by Gail Perry and Mary S. Duru (National Association for the Education of Young Children, 2000).

One size fits all? Spend a few minutes showing some four-year-olds how to kick a ball, and you'll soon find yourself adapting your guidance to each child's skill level. Indeed, when it comes to teaching physical education to children, "one size fits none." In this unit you will be introduced to the world of elementary school physical education where each child will need your help to develop the motor skills and love of physical activity that will serve him or her throughout life. Chapter 1 surveys your role in physical education and candidly asks you to examine how past experience has influenced your feelings about teaching this subject. You will read, in Chapter 2, about how to foster an inclusive learning environment during physical education so that every child feels personally secure and free to participate. Finally, in Chapter 3, you will learn a motor skills–based framework for teaching physical education to children. This framework, which informs this book, is readily adaptable to the individual needs and abilities of every child in your class.

THE WORLD OF CHILDHOOD PHYSICAL EDUCATION

UNIT **I**

INTRODUCTION TO ELEMENTARY PHYSICAL EDUCATION

1. What is a "balanced curriculum," and where does physical education fit in?

2. How has your experience in physical education influenced your view of physical education?

3. If you had to implement a physical education program in your school, what would it look like?

4. How do children benefit from being physically active?

Teaching in U.S. schools today is a unique and dynamic challenge, as the student population continues to diversify and teachers' responsibilities continue to expand. As a teacher, your responsibility is no longer simply to ensure that students learn the content. Now, you are asked to play the roles of counselor, psychologist, police officer, health care provider, and mediator. Performing these duties competently can be daunting. What is even more challenging than fulfilling these roles, however, is the responsibility to teach an expanding content that includes not only reading, math, language, and writing skills, but also character education, music, social skills, and physical education. If teaching physical education is a source of concern for you, as it is for many elementary education teachers, we hope this book will alleviate your anxiety and let you face this challenge with confidence.

We believe that an individual's response to such challenges provides insight into how that person will fulfill the role of teacher. We believe that a teacher is someone who will do whatever it takes to help students learn content regardless of the circumstances. For some individuals, the challenge of teaching physical education will test this belief. You may be saying to yourself, "But I'm not even good at sports, so how can I possibly teach gym?" The question you should be asking yourself is, "Am I a teacher?" Since you are a teacher, when you find yourself outside your comfort zone and are unsure of your ability to teach the content, do you still try to do everything you can to provide students with good instruction? If this describes you, then open your mind to the content and information in this book and enjoy the learning experience.

This chapter will make you more aware of how important physical activity and physical education are to maintaining children's overall health and well-being. More specifically, it will describe your role in teaching children about how their bodies move and function so they can develop the motor skills needed to be physically active.

WHAT ARE THE BENEFITS OF PHYSICAL ACTIVITY?

Most health care experts believe that lifelong participation in physical activity greatly improves an individual's short- and long-term health and well-being. In the short term, being physically active eases daily tasks like taking out the trash, walking through a store, or cooking dinner. This is because physical activity helps people develop the basic strength and stamina to complete a day's required activities. Over time, physically active people are less likely to develop preventable conditions like heart disease, high blood pressure, or diabetes. Their cardiovascular systems work more efficiently and typically resemble those of younger people. Active people also seem to experience a better quality of life because they are more resistant to illness, weight gain, fatigue, and stress.

Children of all ages must be given opportunities to engage in purposeful physical activity, and school physical education programs are usually the best way to offer these opportunities. These programs provide children with the knowledge, skills, and attitudes to maintain an active lifestyle, and they encourage children to make physical activity a part of their daily routine. The physical education teacher bears the responsibility to ensure that children develop both the physical skills to remain active throughout their lifespans and a real appreciation of physical activity and its contribution to their health.

Ironically, as the benefits of physical activity become more apparent, the amount of physical education actually taught during the school years is steadily decreasing throughout the United States. Many schools designate the classroom teacher rather than a physical education specialist to teach physical education (NASPE, 1993). Over the years, state requirements for daily physical education have slowly eroded despite health experts' warnings about the level of inactivity and the increase in childhood obesity among the nation's youth. Physical education class is an ideal way to encourage activity and develop fitness among children. The Centers for Disease Control and Prevention (CDC), the National Association for Sport and Physical Education (NASPE), and the American Heart Association (AHA) all recommend comprehensive daily physical education for children in grades K through 12.

Health Benefits

Children today are less fit than children of a generation ago and are showing earlier signs of cardiovascular risk such as high cholesterol, inactivity, and obesity (AHA, 2004). In fact, the percentage of overweight children aged 6 to 11 and 12 to 17 has more than doubled in the past 30 years (USDHHS, 2000), with 15 percent of children and adolescents now classified as overweight. We must begin identifying ways to address this problem to ensure the future health of all children, especially because obesity has been linked to cardiovascular disease (Blair & Brodney, 2000).

Three national reports—the U.S. Surgeon General's report *Physical Activity and Health* (USDHHS, 1996), *Healthy People 2000* (USDHHS, 1991), and *Healthy People 2010* (USDHHS, 2000)—provide overwhelming evidence of the health benefits of physical activity and the role that it plays in disease prevention. Box 1.1 highlights these health benefits. The exciting news is that remaining healthy throughout one's life requires engaging in physical activities of moderate intensity, not the vigorous activities that were once thought necessary. Box 1.2 on page 9 provides examples of light, moderate, and vigorous activities.

Children especially benefit from being physically active, because activity helps them develop healthy bones, muscles, and joints, besides improving their muscular strength, flexibility, balance, and coordination. Children who are stronger

FIGURE **1.1**
Play is important in early brain development.

and more flexible are less susceptible to injury as they grow, and their better-conditioned hearts will work more efficiently during **exercise** and rest.

The Surgeon General currently recommends that elementary school children should engage in at least 60 minutes of physical activities on all or most days of the week. The exercise should be age-appropriate and varied. Teachers can assist children on the road to good health simply by helping them become physically active and motivating them to remain physically active.

exercise
Planned and structured physical activity, producing repetitive bodily movement that will improve or maintain one or more of the components of physical fitness.

BOX 1.2 ■ Examples of Physical Activities of Different Intensities[a]

Activity	Intensity Level[b]		
	Light	**Moderate**	**Vigorous**
Walking	Casual stroll	Determined	Competitive (aware of time and distance)
Biking	Leisure	Concentrated	Intense (aware of time and distance)
Jogging	Amble	Purposeful	Rigorous (aware of time and distance)
Jumping Rope	Leisure play	Sustained	Intense (aware of time and distance)
Roller Blading or Skating	Relaxed	Determined practice	Competitive (aware of time and distance)
Yard Work	Plod through	Constant	Extreme effort

a. The intensity of any activity is determined by the effort exerted by the individual and the resulting physiological changes in the body, such as increased heart rate or breathing.
b. According to NASPE, *light* physical activity is easily performed at an intensity at which the heart rate and breathing are slightly elevated; *moderate* physical activity is easily maintained and is performed at an intensity at which the heart rate and breathing are elevated; and *vigorous* physical activity can produce fatigue after short periods of time and is performed at an intensity at which the heart rate and breathing are significantly elevated. From *Active Start: A Statement of Physical Activity Guidelines for Children Birth to Five Years*, by NASPE, 2002, Reston, VA: American Alliance for Health, Physical Education, Recreation and Dance.

Cognitive Benefits

Infants learn by exploring and interacting with their environment; for example, by playing with a mobile that hangs above their crib or from touching various objects around them. This active exploration is the key to brain development, as these experiences help children create neural pathways—or connections—among the billions of neurons in the brain. These connections aid in developing future movement and intellectual skills and are represented by specific actions such as reaching, walking, or talking.

Many developmentalists today believe that when children are provided a learning environment that is hands-on, active, and interactive, they utilize more of their brains' capacity by building more neural networks. Neurons that are not used or connected early on typically fade away, so *early movement experiences* are critical to a child's cognitive development. *Play* is the vehicle that children use to explore their surroundings and to learn about the environment and how things work (Figure 1.1). Play thus helps set the stage for higher-order brain functions, such as decoding messages and problem solving (Diamond, 1998).

The Relationship of Physical Activity to Brain Function

When the body moves, circulating blood carries glucose and oxygen to the brain, where they are used to fuel brain activity. When the brain lacks the requisite supply of these nutrients, individuals may exhibit signs of stress, loss

WHAT'S WRONG WITH THIS PICTURE?

Mr. Adams has just finished a lengthy lesson with his fourth grade math class on fractions and feels as though they could let off some steam. By good fortune, it's also time for physical education. Making an effort to incorporate some revision of fractions into his physical education lesson, Mr. Adams has planned a series of "boys versus girls" relays in which students have to call out the correct answer to a math problem before they can run their turn in each relay.

of concentration, or fatigue. Physical activity feeds the brain the nutrients it needs to function optimally, thus helping children stay mentally alert and resist physical fatigue.

With the increased focus on promoting physical activity from private and government health organizations, this is an exciting time to help children learn to move and be active. Considerable information is available detailing how critically important physical activity is to improving children's cognitive functioning. It is believed that active children may develop and strengthen parts of the brain that inactive children cannot.

Social Benefits

Maslow's hierarchy of needs theory describes how an individual's desire to belong to and to be loved and accepted by others reflects a basic biological human *need* to socialize. This ability to interact with others is foundational in building relationships. Socialization is also an important aspect of physical activity. Most physical activities take place in a social environment; very few take place in isolation. For example, playing a dual sport like tennis or a team sport like soccer requires you to interact with at least one other person. Thus, physical activity provides children with the chance to interact with others and build social skills that will help keep them from feeling isolated or lonely.

Emotional Benefits

Self-esteem—the opinion one has of one's self—is influenced by demonstrating competence or mastery of a task. Children are constantly challenged to learn new things. Each time a child successfully meets a challenge, he or she benefits emotionally because it increases the feeling of self-esteem. Physical activity also has a positive impact on children's psychological well-being. For example, active children demonstrate higher levels of self-esteem and self-concept and lower levels of anxiety and stress (Calfas & Taylor, 1994). These benefits are critical in light of fostering healthy self-esteem in children and enabling them to deal with the interpersonal pressure to succeed.

self-esteem
The opinion you have of yourself.

THE SHARED MISSION OF ALL TEACHERS

Today over 50 million children attend more than 110,000 schools in the United States. Although these children are from diverse backgrounds and have unique life experiences, the educational mission is the same for all: to teach them to become healthy, productive, and responsible citizens. It is this mission that guides teachers in grades K through 12 to ensure that children can read, write, calculate, experiment, move efficiently, think critically, and interact positively with others. The shared mission of all teachers is to help the whole child develop:

- Intellectually through the acquisition and use of knowledge
- Emotionally through the awareness and expression of feelings
- Physically through the healthy functioning of the body
- Socially through the ability to interact with others and the environment
- Spiritually through the capacity to find meaning and purpose to existence in general

Teachers endeavor to instill basic knowledge and skills so that students become productive self-sustaining adults. Few would deny that every teacher is responsible for teaching students to respect themselves and others, to adhere to the rules and procedures of the school, and to interact with others in positive ways. Regardless of the subject, every teacher's mission is to teach children personal and social responsibility. Teachers should also model, demonstrate, and encourage students to strive to integrate all school experiences into a balanced lifestyle.

Living productive lives in this fast-paced, multitasking world requires a balanced curriculum throughout the school years. Future generations need these skills to have lives that are well managed in work, play, fitness, diet, and family. All content areas in a balanced curriculum contribute holistically to a child's development, so limiting time for physical education is counterproductive and neglecting it sends a conflicting message to students.

The message schools should send to students is that their health and well-being is as important as their academic success. This message becomes meaningful only if children have real opportunities to be physically active during the school day. Physical education provides a planned program to help students develop the skills that will let them enjoy the physical and mental benefits of being active—hopefully for a whole lifetime.

THE UNIQUE MISSION OF PHYSICAL EDUCATORS

While the shared mission of all teachers is the education of the whole child, the *unique* mission of the physical education teacher is to instruct the child in the physical or psychomotor domain. Physical education is the only content area in

FIGURE **1.2**
Children need to become active for a lifetime.

the school curriculum that focuses on this. To face this unique responsibility, all physical education teachers should help children develop in the following areas:

- Motor skills, for participating successfully.
- An appreciation for the different ways the body can move
- An understanding of how physical activity is beneficial to the body

Thus, the unique mission of physical educators is to teach children how to achieve the ultimate goal of remaining physically active for a lifetime (NASPE, 2000); see Figure 1.2.

Therefore, children must be exposed to a quality physical education curriculum that uses developmentally appropriate practices for content and instruction. The Council for Physical Education for Children (NASPE, 2000) describes appropriate practices as those that recognize children's development and changing movement abilities:

> Children's past psychomotor, cognitive, and affective experiences are also recognized and accommodated in developmentally appropriate instruction. A variety of individual characteristics such as developmental status, fitness and skill levels, body size, and age are considered in designing lessons and selecting instructional strategies. (p. 4)

Thus, appropriate physical education instruction recognizes children's differing levels of ability and incorporates appropriate learning experiences to maximize their success and subsequent learning potential (NASPE, 2000).

Children who are exposed to physical education programs that provide appropriate learning experiences and instruction exhibit the five characteristics of a physically educated person (NASPE, 2004; see Box 1.3). Attention to these focus areas will help teachers at all grade levels ensure that children will exhibit these characteristics by the time they leave high school. That is, a child who knows the

BOX **1.3** ■ Five Major Focus Areas

A physically educated person:

1. *Has* learned skills necessary to perform a variety of physical activities

2. *Is* physically fit

3. *Does* participate regularly in physical activity

4. *Knows* the implications and benefits of involvement in physical activities

5. *Values* physical activity and its contribution to a healthful lifestyle

Source: From *Moving into the Future: National Standards for Physical Education* (2nd ed.) by the National Association for Sport and Physical Education, 2004, Reston, VA: American Alliance for Health, Physical Education, Recreation, and Dance.

FIGURE **1.3**
Students need ample time to practice skills at an appropriate level of difficulty.

content—such as movement concepts, rules, and tactics—can apply this knowledge to regular physical activity. Such children will eventually achieve a health-enhancing level of fitness; value physical activity for its challenge, joy, and social aspects; and master a variety of motor skills that they can use to stay active (NASPE, 2004). Teachers at each level make a contribution to this overall mission.

As a teacher, what types of instructional tasks and activities will you need to reach the goal of producing a physically educated person? To design tasks that meet an individual learner's needs, you must understand a student's skill level, prior experience, and developmental status. Therefore, during a lesson, you must give students ample practice appropriate to their skill level (Figure 1.3)—and simultaneously include enough challenges to hold their interest. We will go into greater detail on how to teach a meaningful lesson in Chapter 4.

TABLE 1.1 ■ Terms Used in Physical Education

Term	Definition
Physical Activity	Any bodily movement produced by skeletal muscles and resulting in energy expenditure.
Physical Fitness	A measure of a person's ability to perform physical activities that require endurance, strength, or flexibility. It is achieved through a combination of regular exercise and genetically inherited ability.
Exercise	Planned and structured physical activity, producing repetitive bodily movement that will improve or maintain one or more of the components of physical fitness: ■ Aerobic capacity ■ Muscular strength ■ Muscular endurance ■ Flexibility ■ Body composition

Source: From *Physical Activity and Health: A Report of the Surgeon General,* by the U.S. Department of Health and Human Services, 1996, Atlanta, GA: Centers for Disease Control and Prevention.

physical fitness
A measure of a person's ability to perform physical activities that require endurance, strength, or flexibility.

physical activity
Any bodily movement produced by skeletal muscles and resulting in energy expenditure.

fundamental skills
Basic motor actions with specific movement patterns.

sports skills
Proficiency in using fundamental motor skills in specialized and often competitive situations.

physical education
A planned, sequential program of instruction designed to develop basic fundamental skills, sports skills, and physical fitness to prepare children for lifetime participation in physical activity.

When discussing the unique mission of physical education, we use terms like *physical activity, exercise,* and **physical fitness** to describe critical elements within a physical education program. When you think about these terms, does the same image appear for each? Although many people use them interchangeably, these terms have distinct meanings. Table 1.1 defines the meaning of each term.

The different definitions of the activity terms in Table 1.1 are those commonly used in the physical education context. Until you recognize these differences, it will be difficult for you to design effective programs that reflect them. To plan a comprehensive curriculum, a physical education teacher must understand that **physical activity** requires the expenditure of energy regardless of whether the activity is of moderate or vigorous intensity. Exposing children to a variety of activities prepares them to enjoy all kinds of fitness and recreational activities as adults.

However, physical education involves *more* than developing physically fit individuals; it should produce students who are knowledgeable, active, skillful, and appreciative of physical activity. A teacher who fails to make that connection will compromise the child's cognitive (what is known) and affective (what is valued) development, as well as his or her ability to develop *lifelong physical activity* and *sports-related* skills, such as balance, agility, and coordination.

Within the scope of the elementary physical education curriculum, children learn various movement patterns that require bodily action. Motor activities with specific movement patterns are referred to as **fundamental skills** (Gabbard, 2004), such as walking, throwing, and kicking. Combined and used in competitive situations, these skills are often referred to as **sports skills** (such as fielding a ground ball in softball or shooting a layup in basketball). **Physical education** is defined as a planned, sequential program of instruction designed to develop basic *fundamental skills, sports skills,* and *physical fitness* to enable a lifetime of appreciating and participating in physical activity. The physical educator's duty is to give children the requisite knowledge, motor skills, personal/social skills, and fitness level to engage in any type of physical activity they enjoy, whether it is dancing, bike riding, running, hiking, climbing, or playing sports such as basketball, tennis, and soccer.

This makes the difference between physical education and recess more obvious. Physical education involves teaching and developing fundamental motor skills. Recess is free time, apart from instruction, that gives children personal choices on how to spend their time. Those might include playing on the playground, sitting and talking with friends, or reading a book. Getting children active for a lifetime requires experiences that foster skill development, not just unstructured free time.

THE ROLE OF THE PHYSICAL EDUCATION TEACHER IN THE ELEMENTARY SCHOOL

INQUIRING MINDS

What type of hurdles have you had to overcome to ensure that physical education remains a significant part of the elementary school curriculum at your school?

Elementary school children have an innate desire to move and play. You can see this if you watch them: they love to run, chase, flee, dodge, jump, and tumble. These actions can be problematic in a school environment where rules govern student behavior. In a typical school day, teachers frequently tell students, "Stop running in the hallway!" or "Stop that horseplay before someone gets hurt!" But in the appropriate places, these actions would be a welcome sight. In physical education, we *want* children to run, jump, and tumble. So instead of squashing this desire to move, elementary physical education teachers need to help children use their varied motor skills safely. Physical education teaches children about where and how the body moves in space and the relationship of the body to self, others, and objects. These are critical skills for children to develop in order to successfully participate in physical activities that require specialized skills such as inline skating, bike riding, tennis, or soccer. With this goal in mind, part of the physical educator's job is to implement curricula and instruction that emphasize the enjoyment of lifelong participation in physical fitness and physical activity.

In addition to helping children to become more skillful in particular activities, the role of the physical educator includes the following:

- Helping children gain confidence in their motor ability
- Fostering a positive attitude in children toward physical activity and physical fitness
- Helping children respect differences among individuals in activity settings
- Promoting children's desire to engage in physical activity outside the school environment
- Managing the instructional environment to help children feel safe physically and psychologically
- Helping children demonstrate personal and social responsibility
- Providing planned sequential programs of instruction to meet national standards

To summarize, to inspire children to remain active as they age, they must be given quality physical education programs that meet their individual needs in a physically and psychologically safe environment.

THE TEACHER'S IMPACT ON CHILDREN'S PERCEPTIONS OF PHYSICAL EDUCATION

There is invariably a dichotomous dialogue in any discussion about children's physical education experiences (see Box 1.4). When discussing their elementary physical education experience, some students share fond memories of playing with their friends, climbing on the horizontal bars, or even engaging in their favorite games. But other students' faces cloud over, and their eyes take on a distant look as if caught in an unpleasant dream. These students recall the embarrassment of striking out in softball or hearing their classmates laugh when they tripped and fell during a relay race. Still others recall being picked last for a team or getting hit with a soccer ball. Some adults' attitudes toward physical activity and fitness were shaped by those kinds of negative physical education experiences.

Most negative experiences in physical education can be traced back to poor teaching practices or poor content development, which typically turn children off of physical activity and convince them that they are not good at sports or movement activities. Teachers' sarcastic comments can also cause negative feelings about physical activity. Remarks like "You should try harder," or "I can't believe you're having such trouble with this task," can make children feel inadequate to perform movement activities and deter them from trying in the future.

BOX 1.4 ■ Learning Tasks to Stimulate Class Discussion

Partner with three friends and write independent answers to each of these questions:

1. Was there a time when you were really frustrated in your elementary physical education class? What were the circumstances?

2. What was your favorite activity during your elementary physical education class?

3. If you could change one thing about your elementary physical education experience, what would it be?

4. What do you see as the greatest challenge facing you as a physical educator?

5. The contribution that physical education makes to the development of the whole child is . . .

Compare your answers. Are there consistencies across your responses? How do you think these experiences might affect the way you will teach physical education?

FIGURE **1.4**
Children need to believe that they "can" do anything. Tamara didn't think she could be successful on the balance board until her teacher helped her believe in saying, "I can."

Poor content development can also place students in distressing situations. Too-difficult tasks decrease children's success rates and frustrate them. Success rate is intricately tied to learning; successful children continue to practice, while unsuccessful ones may stop and become "learned helpless." Such children feel they lack the requisite skills to be successful, so they fail to try. This feeling is most evident when you hear a child say, "I can't." Unfortunately, children learn this behavior quickly after repeated failures at a task or after being made fun of during games, and they learn to avoid future frustration by giving up on physical activity before even trying. To avoid the negative construct of learned helplessness you need to provide learning tasks appropriate to children's own levels so they will succeed often enough to learn that they "can" (Figure 1.4).

Just as teachers can have a negative impact on children, they can have a positive impact on them as well. Think back to teachers you had in school that truly influenced your life. Remember how they made learning fun, creating a learning environment that piqued your curiosity and made you want to know more. They helped you embrace difficult content instead of fearing it, and changed your view of the subject matter, bringing positive emotions to it.

You can have the same impact on children's view of physical education by using appropriate teaching practices and content development. To do this, use encouraging language that is free of sarcasm to create a psychologically safe environment. Have children work on tasks at the appropriate difficulty level to help develop their motor skills. If you provide a positive learning experience, they will be excited about learning how high they can jump or how hard they can throw. This fosters a climate where children can shout with glee when it is time for physical education instead of moaning with despair. The teacher sets the tone for children's experience in physical education. Whether that experience is positive or negative depends on the value you place on their learning the content.

HOW PHYSICAL EDUCATION IS CHANGING

Elementary physical education is currently moving away from games of low organization such as dodgeball, red rover, and relay races. These games do not provide quality opportunities for children to develop their physical skills; additionally, they can put children in positions where they have to perform in front of others, in ways that might become embarrassing. For example, children who can't break through the arm chain in red rover are often laughed at and put down for their attempts.

In teaching physical education, you should always consider how each activity contributes to developing motor skills. You should ask yourself, "What skills are children working toward when they play these games?" Unfortunately, some teachers still think a game like red rover helps develop running or cooperative skills. But consider: Red rover is played with two lines facing each other. Players on one team join hands and wait as they challenge a player from the other team to come break through their line. One child from the other team dashes forward and tries to break the "chain." Children cannot develop running skills when one player is moving and the other 20 are stationary! Hopefully, by the time you finish this book, you will see that games like duck, duck, goose and red rover do not help anyone develop fundamental motor skills like running, throwing, or balancing. The problems with these games and other popular games used in some physical education programs are clearly outlined by Williams (1992, 1994, 1996), who puts them in physical education's "Hall of Shame." Membership in the "Hall" is based on one or more of the following elements: elimination of participants, low activity time, lack of a meaningful learning objective, lack of content progression, safety issues, and overemphasis on fun rather than skill acquisition. Games meant solely to entertain rather than develop motor skills should not be part of physical education.

Instead, there is a movement across the country to implement the "New PE," which involves creating more engaging and exciting programs for all children. The New PE steps away from games of low organization and toward fun, creative learning experiences that help children develop the important fundamental skills.

Furthermore, the New PE helps children learn about physical activity and appreciate being physically active. Children in these programs learn much more than how to crash through red rover's line. New curricula include instruction about heart rate, problem-solving, and cooperation. Teachers can provide fun learning experiences by creating fitness stations—a number of different fitness activities spread throughout the gym—that address different components of health-related fitness. Students rotating among these stations can learn the difference between the components of fitness (for example: muscular strength, flexibility, and cardiovascular endurance) and the type of activities appropriate for developing them. Students must work cooperatively as they rotate and complete the stations. Some teachers play music to motivate students as they complete the circuit, and then ask them to identify which component of health-related fitness that each activity promoted. This shows how knowledge acquisition can be a fun part of physical education.

INQUIRING MINDS

At what grade level do you typically see children lose interest in participating in physical education activities? How do you explain this phenomenon?

Ideally, the New PE will become the common standard for exposing children to worthwhile programs. While this is not yet the case, we have personally seen and been involved in a number of fun and exciting elementary physical education programs that help children develop a repertoire of motor skills they can use for recreation and enjoyment throughout their lives.

EFFECTIVE TEACHING IN THE PHYSICAL EDUCATION SETTING

Because teachers have a significant impact on students' *perceptions* of physical education and on their ability to acquire skills and knowledge and develop an appreciation for physical activity, it is essential that physical education programs are taught by effective and good teachers. As you read this section, ask yourself these questions:

- What does effective physical education teaching look like?
- Is it different from good classroom teaching?
- How does one distinguish between a good teacher and a bad one?

These are difficult questions to answer, because a complex learning environment makes prescriptive or formula-driven teaching ineffective. Yet we believe that all effective teachers in any subject area exhibit five specific characteristics that guide and inform their teaching practices. As each characteristic is presented, try to see how its application in teaching physical education compares to that of teaching in the classroom. As you make the connection and understand how each characteristic guides practice, you can better face the specific challenges of teaching physical education.

Creating a Positive Learning Environment

Effective teachers create an environment conducive to learning. Environments filled with uncertainty and conflicts rarely produce a successful learning experience. Teachers create a positive atmosphere by managing and organizing the learning environment to ensure a feeling of safety and stability for students. Rules and routines established by good physical education teachers will guide classroom procedures throughout the year. These routines usually involve the details

FIGURE **1.5**
Quality lessons engage all students by allowing children the opportunity to participate and remain active.

of entering and leaving the gymnasium, starting and stopping an activity, using equipment, working with groups, and dealing with behavioral disruptions (Graham, 2001).

Effective teachers use management skills to increase practice opportunities for children; for example, your lesson plan should account for transitions between tasks and how to retrieve and store equipment. Planning for such activities reduces time lost to poor management and increases children's practice opportunity. A well-managed class also has higher levels of student engagement. An observer in such a learning climate will not see children waiting in line, playing on large teams, or waiting too long for instruction (Figure 1.5).

Being a Good Communicator

Good relationships are based on the interactions and communications of individuals, whether verbal or nonverbal. Effective communication is rooted in understanding the intent of a statement or gesture. For example, a smile can convey either a positive or a negative message; it could mean, "You're doing fine on the task," or "I knew you couldn't do it." Communication breakdowns usually lead to misunderstandings, uncertainty, and frustration. To avoid this, make sure you send the proper message both verbally and nonverbally. Clearly communicate to students what is expected to help them stay on task. Our experience has shown that when students know what is expected and are given explicit task statements, their uncertainty and frustration diminish and classes lose less instructional time (Figure 1.6).

Two aspects of presenting tasks to students require particularly clear communication: demonstrations (discussed in depth in Chapter 5) and learning cues (discussed in Chapter 4). These two functions help children focus on the critical elements or strategies for the required task and often let them work independently of the teacher.

FIGURE **1.6**
Students need clear expectations. When the teacher made her expectations clear, these students were better able to learn and enjoy jumping rope.

Communication between teacher and students should be a two-way street. You must be able to give clear instructions, and students must feel secure enough to tell you if they do not understand them. This helps everyone work together toward the same goal with the same expectations.

Being a Knowledgeable Practitioner

Another characteristic of effective teachers is that they are **knowledgeable practitioners.** Effective teachers have a thorough understanding of the content and know how to teach it to children. This means providing meaningful explanations and connecting new information to things already familiar to the student. Effective teachers can also transmit material to students systematically enough to make it easy to understand.

Unfortunately, in an effort to meet curriculum demands teachers are often asked to teach material that they are unfamiliar with or uncomfortable with. If this happens to you, whatever the content area, you must go the extra mile and obtain the knowledge you need to feel more comfortable teaching it. Physical education is a content area identified as a weakness by many elementary school teachers. You can increase your knowledge base in this area by reading content-related journals or books, searching the Internet for relevant websites, or watching instructional videos or DVDs.

Low-organization games are an old standby for teachers who lack content knowledge in physical education. These games don't require physical education knowledge because the teacher needs to know only how to play the game, not how to develop skills or knowledge. However, the knowledgeable practitioner's classroom is much different—fun and full of valuable learning experiences.

knowledgeable practitioner
A teacher with a thorough understanding of the content who knows how to teach its content to children.

FIGURE **1.7**
Example of feedback to help children learn right from left.

Providing Meaningful Feedback

Being able to provide meaningful feedback is another characteristic of effective teachers. Think about the last time you tried to teach a new concept or skill. When your student had trouble, what did you do? You probably offered a few hints or clues to help him or her learn the information better. For example, most elementary classroom teachers instruct students in the difference between right and left. One technique is to tell students to raise the thumbs and index fingers of both hands in front of their faces to see which hand makes an L. This helps students learn which hand or body part is on the left side (see Figure 1.7).

Quantifying how feedback aids learning is a continual source of debate among teaching professionals. Although it is difficult to pinpoint the exact benefit of feedback, it *does* unquestionably influence student performance. Teachers can see this influence when children who are performing tasks are provided with information about the quality or outcome of their actions. Children will use the teacher's information to adjust subsequent practice tasks; they try to use the feedback to aid or facilitate performance.

There are numerous types of feedback teachers use: positive, negative, approval, disapproval, general, specific, supportive, and congruent. Most physical education professionals believe that the best feedback is specific and congruent. **Specific feedback** relates to an aspect or result of a performance, indicating what the student needs to correct; and **congruent feedback** relates to the learning cue or critical features of the skill identified during the task focus. See Table 1.2 for examples of specific and congruent feedback. These and additional types of feedback are discussed more extensively in Chapter 5.

Creating Stimulating Learning Tasks

One of the most important aspects of teaching is creating stimulating learning tasks. The key is to develop content well and to structure it appropriately. The process for developing content is discussed in Chapters 11 and 12. By using your knowledge of children's logical skill progression to create motivating and suitable learning tasks, you will engage students in individually appropriate activities.

specific feedback
Information given about a consistent aspect or result of a performance.

congruent feedback
Information related to the learning cue or critical feature of the task focus.

TABLE **1.2** ■ Examples of Different Types of Feedback

Feedback Type	Example
Specific	Be sure to bend your knees when you land.
	This time be sure to snap your wrist on the follow-through.
	You need to get the racket back sooner next time.
Congruent	Remember to swing your arms forward as you jump (Cue: swing arms).
	Keep your eye on your opponent's belly button (Cue: belly button).
	Try to remember to take the racket back low (Cue: low to high).

Children who are given appropriate tasks are motivated by the lesson and continue to practice their tasks longer and more successfully.

Effective teachers use various instructional strategies that allow children to work on their individual skill level. Chapter 5 focuses on how such strategies facilitate the learning process.

Being Concerned with Student Achievement

Finally, effective teaching transcends the content. Teachers concerned with overall student achievement will provide children with quality instruction and learning experiences in every lesson. This is reflected in the classroom, where a good teacher helps students who are having difficulty or seem bored. Changing the task to make it easier or more difficult will help such children continue working during the lesson.

Student achievement is often tied to opportunities to practice and can be quantified by success rates. Siedentop and Tannehill suggest (2000) that students should be at least 80 percent successful to continue a task. For example, a child would need to be able to hit a target with a ball eight out of ten times to ensure a high success rate. This rate of success is believed to keep children in a state of "flow" (Csikszentmihalyi, 1975). A state of flow occurs when children participate diligently, stay challenged and motivated, and do not become bored with a task; although some contend that specifying a universal success rate like 80 percent is shortsighted (Rink, 2002).

The unique demands of a specific task often affect the rate of success, and therefore rates can vary. For example, an expected success rate at or near 80 percent is realistic if you have children kick a ball at a stationary target; a child batting from a live pitch would most likely have a lower success rate. After all, a professional baseball player with a batting average of around 30 percent is considered a very good hitter (Figure 1.8).

Essentially, your approach to teaching has either a positive or a negative impact on your students' achievement. If you provide motivating learning experiences for children, they will continue to practice and experience success—although if you

FIGURE **1.8**
Success rates are critical to student motivation and achievement.

provide the same tasks for all children, many will become frustrated or bored and will quit practicing. Of course, children who don't practice don't improve.

Effective teachers establish sound management techniques, use appropriate feedback, structure sound and appropriate learning tasks, and engage children during instruction. These characteristics, which are all critical to teachers' success, will be reinforced throughout this book.

WHAT CLASSROOM TEACHERS BRING TO PHYSICAL EDUCATION

As a classroom teacher, you bring a unique perspective to physical education. You can influence your children to think positively about physical education by being an advocate and showing them that you are willing to try new things too. Seeing their classroom teacher performing different fundamental motor skills shows children the importance of physical activity. Your modeling in teaching physical education is more important than what you say.

FINAL WORDS

We strongly believe in physical education's important place in the school curriculum. Children must have good physical education programs with effective teachers and appropriate practice to develop their fundamental motor skills fully. Children with the requisite fundamental skills are more likely to become active adults who experience the intellectual, social, and physical benefits that being physically active provides.

1. You are attending a school board meeting where discussion centers on eliminating physical education from the curriculum. The school board opens the floor for questions and comments from the audience. Make a stand defending the importance of physical education.

2. Physical educators must play multiple roles. Identify what you feel are the three most crucial of these roles and explain your position.

3. We have suggested that effective teachers are knowledgeable, communicate well, create good learning tasks, provide appropriate feedback, and create an environment conducive to learning. Do you think additional characteristics should be included? Justify your answer. Is there a characteristic on the list that you think should be eliminated? Why?

PORTFOLIO TASKS

1. Interview one of your classmates on his or her experiences in elementary physical education and then use the information you gathered to write a one-page description of the impact those experiences had on your classmate's current view of physical education.

2. Develop a "Concept Map" or "Webbing" for physical education.

3. Research and identify three websites that could serve as a resource base to support physical education in the schools.

4. Make a commitment to engage in some form of physical activity daily for at least 30 cumulative minutes for the next 15 weeks or for the duration of this course. Keep a daily log of the duration of total activity, type of activity, and how you felt at the completion of the activity. At the end, review your log and check for any themes in how you felt physically, mentally, emotionally, socially, or spiritually.

REFERENCES

American Heart Association. (2004). *Children's need for physical activity: Fact sheet.* Retrieved on March 19, 2004, from www.americanheart.org/presenter.jhtml?identifier=771

Blair, S. N., & Brodney, S. (2000). Effects of physical inactivity and obesity on morbidity and mortality: Current evidence and research issues. *Medicine and Science in Sports and Exercise, 31*(Suppl.): S646–S662.

Calfas, K. J., & Taylor, W. C. (1994). Effects of physical activity on psychological variables in adolescents. *Pediatric Exercise Science, 6,* 406–423.

Csikszentmihalyi, M. (1975). *Beyond boredom and anxiety.* San Francisco: Josey-Bass.

Diamond, M. (1998). *Magic trees of the mind.* New York: Zephyr Press.

Gabbard, C. P. (2004). *Lifelong motor development* (4th ed.). San Francisco: Benjamin-Cummings.

Graham, G. (2001). *Teaching children physical education: Becoming a master teacher* (2nd ed.). Champaign, IL: Human Kinetics.

National Association for Sport and Physical Education. (1993). *Shape of the nation 1993: A survey of state physical education requirements.* Reston, VA: National Association for Sport and Physical Education.

National Association for Sport and Physical Education. (2000). *Appropriate practices for elementary school physical education.* Reston, VA: National Association for Sport and Physical Education.

National Association for Sport and Physical Education. (2002). *Active start: A statement of physical activity guidelines for children birth to five years.* Reston, VA: American Alliance for Health, Physical Education, Recreation and Dance.

National Association for Sport and Physical Education. (2004). *Moving into the future: National standards for physical education* (2nd ed.). Reston, VA: American Alliance for Health, Physical Education, Recreation and Dance.

Siedentop, D., & Tannehill, D. (2000). *Developing teaching skills in physical education* (4th ed.). Mountain View, CA: Mayfield.

Rink, J. E. (2002). *Teaching physical education for learning* (4th ed.). Boston, MA: McGraw-Hill.

U.S. Department of Health and Human Services. (1991). *Healthy people 2000: National health promotion and disease prevention objectives.* Washington, DC: Author.

U.S. Department of Health and Human Services. (1996). *Physical activity and health: A report of the Surgeon General.* Atlanta, GA: Centers for Disease Control and Prevention.

U.S. Department of Health and Human Services. (2000). *Healthy people 2010: National health promotion and disease prevention objectives.* Washington, DC: Author.

U.S. Department of Health and Human Services. (2000). *Prevalence of overweight among children and adolescents: United States, 1999–2000.* National Health and Nutrition Examination Survey (NHANES). Atlanta, GA: Centers for Disease Control and Prevention.

Williams, N. F. (1992). The physical education hall of shame. *Journal of Physical Education, Recreation, and Dance 63*(6), 57–60.

Williams, N. F. (1994). The physical education hall of shame, Part II. *Journal of Physical Education, Recreation & Dance 65*(2), 17–20.

Williams, N. F. (1996). The physical education hall of shame, Part III: Inappropriate teaching practices. *Journal of Physical Education, Recreation & Dance, 67*(8), 45–48.

CHAPTER 2

CREATING AN INCLUSIVE LEARNING ENVIRONMENT

1. What does the phrase "physical education is for everybody" mean to you?

2. Do girls have the same opportunities as boys to excel in physical education?

3. How might a child's religious convictions limit his or her full participation in physical education?

4. Is a child with a disability destined to a lifestyle without physical activity?

5. How do you feel about accommodating a child's religious or cultural beliefs? (Muslim children, for example, can't swim during Ramadan.) Is accommodating a child's religious beliefs sometimes a form of favoritism that other students might find to be grossly unfair?

The joy of engaging in physical activity isn't just for children with exceptional skills or excellent physical fitness. Nor is it just for boys or children of a particular ethnic group. It is for everyone. Although all educational discrimination is prohibited by federal law, many children still experience discrimination during physical education. This is partly because students themselves may act out their physical, gender, racial, and religious biases; and even well-intentioned teachers can unwittingly reinforce these biases through their physical education curricula.

You can overcome your students' biases (and your own) through inclusive physical education programs. In educational parlance, **inclusion** refers to policies and programs undertaken to accommodate students with special needs, i.e., policies that help all students participate fully despite their physical, cognitive, or emotional challenges. In this chapter, inclusion is extended to children who may face barriers in physical education because of body composition, language, or cultural background. This chapter will teach you strategies to provide an enjoyable physical education for every body—meaning every size, shape, or ability.

WHAT *INCLUSION* MEANS IN PHYSICAL EDUCATION

inclusion
A policy that lets all students successfully participate, develop skills, and have a sense of belonging in the class.

Inclusion is a policy designed to ensure that all students are able to successfully participate in an activity, develop new skills, and experience a sense of belonging in the classroom. An inclusive school is a place where everyone belongs, and where students can support—and be supported by—their peers and the entire school community. This vision of inclusive education is a fitting model for delivering physical education (see Figure 2.1).

FIGURE **2.1**
All children should be able to experience the joys of movement and a sense of belonging in the classroom.

NONINCLUSION CAUSES FEELINGS OF SOCIAL ISOLATION

The chief benefit of inclusive physical education is to avoid isolating any children from the group. Unfortunately, many children do feel out of place in physical education. Some have been ridiculed for lack of skill, while others have been denied the chance for full participation because of their perceived physical, cultural, or psychological limitations. Regardless of the circumstances, children in noninclusive physical education settings feel socially isolated from their peers.

The following five scenarios introduce students who could be in your class one day. As you read, ask yourself how these children might perceive the importance of physical activity and physical education in their lives. What may cause each student to feel socially isolated?

> Naweeda's family is from Bangladesh. They live in a neighborhood that has a number of Muslim families. Her school requires students to wear shorts and a T-shirt in physical education class. Because of her cultural heritage, Naweeda usually wears a *shalwar* (loose, ankle-hugging trousers) under her shorts. But occasionally, to avoid the giggling of her classmates, she wears only the shorts. A family friend living near the school tells Naweeda's parents that she saw Naweeda wearing shorts in public.
>
> Henry is an obese boy who has difficulty with activities that require speed or agility. He is also not skillful at games, a trait exacerbated by his lack of

INQUIRING MINDS

Do you find problems with boys and girls not wanting to work together? How about children of different ethnicities? What strategies do you use to address this?

mobility and physical confidence. Fellow students seldom want Henry on their teams, and he is always left without a partner when students are asked to pair up. During recent softball lessons, Henry's teacher overheard some boys call Henry "the slug."

Foyzur and his family fled the continued political unrest in their native Ivory Coast, in western Africa. Although good at soccer, Foyzur has no experience with American-style football. Speaking only French and having no Francophone classmates, Foyzur is struggling with the rules and skills of this new activity.

Mandy is a chronic asthmatic who must always carry her inhaler. She enjoys some physical activities but struggles with any that require significant exertion. Her class is currently practicing relay races, and her teacher has designed a series of activities that all involve vigorous running.

Alex has used a wheelchair ever since a swimming pool accident in early childhood left her paralyzed below the waist. Alex enjoys being active and plays often with her brother and sister at home; but during physical education she is often asked to be the scorekeeper or umpire. Although Alex is sometimes given a chance to bat during individual practice sessions, she is never included in competitive situations.

Clearly, significant obstructions prevent each of the above students from full physical education achievement. However, are these "obstructions" (e.g., religious beliefs, lack of mobility) solely the children's problem? Examine your own notions of inclusivity, try to empathize with the children themselves, and respond accordingly to their needs.

THE FOUR S's: SAFE, SUCCESSFUL, SATISFYING, AND SKILL-APPROPRIATE

A positive way to plan an inclusive physical education setting, in which students can participate comfortably and confidently (Reeves & Stein, 1999) is by following the Four S's *safe, successful, satisfying,* and *skill-appropriate:*

1. *Safe:* During physical education, students should certainly feel protected from physical danger; but they should also feel safe from psychological or emotional danger, including any embarrassment or ridicule.

2. *Successful:* Students should have the opportunity to attain an appropriate level of proficiency. This will vary from student to student. For one,

TABLE 2.1 ■ Noninclusive and Inclusive Responses to a Child's Physical Performance

	Noninclusive Command	Inclusive Command
Dustin, a child with mental retardation, has difficulty skipping with peers during a game of tag.	"You need to skip like everyone else!" etc.	Because Dustin gallops very well, you go over to Dustin and quietly challenge him, "Show me how you gallop." Now Dustin successfully gallops while his peers skip.
Sarah spends more time chasing the 6-inch playground ball than bouncing it.	"Watch the ball!"	You quietly hand Sarah a 14-inch playground ball to bounce with both hands. Now Sarah beams with delight as she bounces the ball to the rhythm of music.
Nelda, a child with cerebral palsy, does a log roll on a diagonal.	"Log roll in a straight path!"	You encourage Nelda to log roll with her belly button on the mountain-climbing rope that is laid in a straight line down the center of the mat. Now Nelda log rolls right down the center of the mat.
Lance has the rhythm with his feet but has difficulty bringing the short jump rope over his head.	"Try harder!"	Because Lance has difficulty turning the rope, you instruct him to jump rope with the long jump rope.

Source: Adapted from "Developmentally Appropriate Pedagogy and Inclusion: 'Don't put the cart before the horse!'" by L. Reeves, and J. Stein, 1999, *Physical Educator, 56*(1), pp. 2–7.

success might mean dribbling two basketballs concurrently, while for another, it might mean repeatedly bouncing and catching a ball while standing or sitting in a stationary position.

3. *Satisfying:* Children's participation in physical activity should feel personally challenging and motivating, inspiring a real sense of accomplishment. Effective teachers adapt the curriculum, task, and teaching situation so that all students can experience this satisfaction.

4. *Skill-appropriate:* A skill-appropriate program is tailored to the physical and developmental capacities of the specific students being taught. Design the physical education program only after assessing each child's developmental status, fitness, skill levels, body size, and age.

Chapter 10 explains how to achieve the first S—a safe physical education environment; this chapter focuses on how the other three of the Four S's play out in an inclusive physical education setting. Table 2.1 compares a teacher's response to the performance of four children during a physical education session. The responses in the second column foster a sense of inclusion. Notice that each inclusive response is *satisfying* to the child, encourages the child's *success,* and is grounded in the teacher's choice of *skill-appropriate* activities.

Next, let's consider how these three S's—success, satisfaction, and skill appropriateness—apply to children who may feel unwelcome, excluded, and socially isolated in noninclusive physical education settings.

FIGURE **2.2**
Avoid the stereotype that African American children love only basketball.

INCLUDING CHILDREN'S RELIGIOUS AND CULTURAL VALUES

As a teacher you must be sensitive to the effect of cultural diversity on the planning and delivery of a physical education program. U.S. schools include children from a host of races, languages, religions, and cultures:

- Over 40 percent of all public school students are of non-Caucasian ancestry.

- More than 15 percent of school-age students speak a language other than English at home.

- Over 3 million children have limited English proficiency.

If you are a Latina teaching in the Bay Area of northern California, a large percentage of your students may be from the Pacific Rim. But the class of a white male teacher in Harlem, New York, is likely to include children who speak five different languages and only one or two children who are Caucasian.

First, acknowledge what you do and don't know about the beliefs and values of the children you teach, especially those whom *you* perceive to be different from you. Then, try to imagine how children perceive *your* cultural practices. Clearly, using your perceptions to make assumptions about children or to stereotype them can lead to prejudice and bias (Banks, 1994; see Figure 2.2).

BOX **2.1** ■ **Strategies for Building Positive Interactions, Tolerance, and Respect among Children**

Strategy	Example in Action
Encourage communication and socialization among peers in both native and dominant languages.	■ Encourage children whose native language is English to communicate with those from different backgrounds. ■ Make an effort to speak to bilingual students in both their native language and English. ■ Allow students to interact in a physical education setting using whatever language feels comfortable to them.
Structure situations where children from different backgrounds must work cooperatively—toward a goal.	■ Involve students from different ethnic backgrounds in peer teaching. ■ Ask students to partner up with someone they don't know very well.
Speak about "differences" rather than "deficiencies."	■ Explain that some children have a rich language other than English, and are not merely English-deficient. ■ Explain that while some children may not have practiced certain skills before, they may nevertheless be quite skillful at different activities that others in the class know nothing about.
Model positive attitudes.	■ Praise all children for their effort at mastering skills.

How can you get started with cultural assessment? First work with your school's principal, the school board, and neighborhood community social and religious organizations to learn about the cultural and ethnic groups in your school. According to Torrey and Ashy (1997), areas you might find helpful to investigate include:

■ Dress

■ Diet

■ Communication

■ Family structure, roles, and relationships

■ Values, beliefs, and ethics

Assessing your own culture, personal experiences, and personal history will also help you to develop positive attitudes toward cultural diversity.

But this is not enough. For a truly inclusive physical education setting, you must sincerely and specifically make an effort to counter your students' cultural ignorance or biases, especially any overt expressions of racism. Box 2.1 provides some instructional strategies for positive interactions and to build acceptance and trust among students (Torrey & Ashy, 1997).

BOX **2.2** ■ Strategies for Modifying Activities for Children Who Are Severely Overweight

- Avoid activities where the child must *lift* or *pull* his or her body. Instead, offer lots of opportunities to hang, climb, and crawl while providing physical support.
- Allow students to move at their own rate during aerobic work. For example, do not require that they keep up with the tempo of the music.
- Include some resistance training, starting at very low levels. The goal is to help the overweight child to *gain strength*.

INQUIRING MINDS

What types of strategies do you have in place that demonstrate to students the importance of appreciating and respecting all individuals?

INCLUDING CHILDREN WHO ARE SEVERELY OVERWEIGHT

In recent years, with concerns over the increasing incidence of obesity, the Centers for Disease Control and Prevention (CDC) have provided a simple field test to measure body composition—the *Body Mass Index*. A child's height and weight are needed in order to calculate his or her body composition using this formula:

$$\text{BMI} = \frac{\text{weight (lb)}}{[\text{height (inches)}]^2} \times 703$$

The CDC (2003) considers a child "at risk of overweight" if he or she exceeds the 85th percentile for his or her age and sex; a child is considered "overweight" if the score exceeds the 95th percentile.

Approximately 13 percent of children age 6–11 are estimated to be overweight. Children at the extreme end also may have low energy levels, poor flexibility, minimal strength, and limited physical stamina. Feeling discouraged about physical activities, they become more sedentary, only reinforcing a downward spiral of poor fitness.

Being severely overweight can significantly diminish children's social interactions with their more active peers. Failure to master skills further alienates them from activity, due to either feelings of inadequacy, or worse, to negative comments from more agile children. In the children's novel *Fat, Four-Eyed and Useless* (Hill, 1997), Ben tells how he avoids the rugby players; he also admits how frustrated he is at having nothing to do during school lunchtimes except for sports. Clearly, Ben does not find his physical activity settings to be inclusive.

Modified intensity is the key for physical activities for severely overweight children. Shorter distances and intermittent activity help these children experience success. More specific recommendations are included in Box 2.2. Always be aware

FIGURE **2.3**
There is no justification in elementary physical education for separate activities for boys and girls.

of the social climate in which overweight children engage in physical education and strongly discourage other students from further undermining their possibly fragile confidence. Focus rather on severely overweight children's successes as they attempt motor skills. By setting this example, you can indirectly draw the other students toward positive reinforcement rather than negative teasing.

INCLUDING GIRLS AND BOYS EQUALLY

Title IX, a federal law prohibiting gender discrimination in education, was enacted in 1972 to provide more equitable opportunities for boys and girls in academics, athletics, and physical education. While gender inequities continue to thrive in many middle and high school physical education programs, elementary school teachers must be aware of teaching behaviors, class management, and instructional strategies that might favor boys over girls. These may include expecting boys to perform skills better than girls referring to certain activities as "girls'" or "boys'" sports, expecting boys to be more disruptive than girls; or expecting girls to be more sensitive than boys. As shown in Figure 2.3, girls and boys can participate equally in all physical education activities. Box 2.3 provides strategies to promote gender fairness and equal participation by both boys and girls in your physical education class.

Attitudes

- Encourage and respect the interests and abilities of both genders.
- Create a class atmosphere that helps students develop consideration for, understanding of, and respect for each other.
- Use the same tone of voice and language when interacting with boys and girls.

Conduct and Activities

- Provide opportunities for both male and female students to assume leadership roles.
- Ensure that responsibilities are shared equally by male and female students, and expect all students to be equally active participants.
- Provide activities that require a cooperative focus in small mixed-gender groups.
- Purposefully acknowledge the contributions of women in physical education and sports and encourage children to do so as well. For example, mention Olympians and world champions like Mia Hamm when students are practicing soccer, the Williams sisters during tennis, or Jenny Finch during softball.

INCLUDING STUDENTS WITH DISABILITIES

Disabilities other than those associated with movement limitations can affect children's participation in physical education, including those related to cognitive development, physical limitations, and psychological disorders (see Box 2.4).

Although you may not be knowledgeable about each of these disabilities, ready help is at hand. The Internet Resources for Special Children web site provides information about the needs of children with disabilities. For a wealth of detail on specific disabilities, laws, adapted equipment and technologies, recreation and sports, and schooling, visit www.irsc.org.

Federal law (PL 94-142, PL 101-476, PL 105-17) mandates that physical education be provided to students with disabilities. It defines physical education as the development of: (1) physical and motor skills, (2) fundamental motor skills and patterns (throwing, catching, walking, running, and the like), and (3) skills in aquatics, dance, and individual and group games and sports (including intramural and lifetime sports).

BOX **2.4** ▪ Potential Childhood Disabilities or Special Needs

Autistic Spectrum Disorders

- Asperger's syndrome
- Pervasive development disorder
- Sensory integration dysfunction

Blind and Visually Impaired

- Requiring the use of guide dogs

Brain Injuries

- Acquired brain injury
- Concussion
- Traumatic brain injury

Cognitive Disabilities

- Down syndrome
- Fetal alcohol syndrome
- Fragile X syndrome
- Mental retardation

Communication Disorders

- Aphasia
- Semantic-pragmatic disorder
- Spasmodic dysphonia
- Stuttering

Deaf and Hearing Impaired

- Requiring the use of hearing dogs

Diseases and Conditions

- Asthma
- Cleft lip and palate
- Diabetes

Learning Disabilities

- Attention deficit disorder
- Central auditory processing disorder
- Dyscalculia–dyslexia–dysgraphia
- Dyspraxia–apraxia
- Hyperlexia

Mental Health

- Anxiety
- Attachment disorder
- Bipolar disorder
- Depression
- Eating disorders
- Obsessive-compulsive disorder
- Oppositional defiant disorder
- Personality disorder
- Schizophrenia

Musculoskeletal Disorders

- Amputees
- Arthritis
- Craniosynostosis
- Dwarfism
- Muscular dystrophy
- Scoliosis
- Spinal cord injury
- Spinal muscular atrophy

Neurological Disorders

- Cerebral palsy
- Chronic fatigue syndrome
- Epilepsy
- Hydrocephalus
- Myopathies
- Rett syndrome
- Spina bifida
- Tourette's syndrome
- Tuberous sclerosis

Consistent with these laws is the principle of instruction in a **least restrictive environment (LRE).** This means that children with special needs must be placed in the most inclusive environment they can handle. The Individualized Education Plan (IEP) outlines several possible physical education settings for a child with a disability:

- The general physical education class
- The general physical education class with a teaching assistant or peers (see Figure 2.4)
- A separate physical education class of peers with disabilities
- A separate class setting with assistants
- A one-to-one setting between a student and an instructor

least restrictive environment (LRE)
The concept of placing children with special needs in the most inclusive environment they can handle.

BOX **2.5** ■ The Benefits of Inclusion Programs for Physical Education

All students benefit from physical education inclusion programs.

Students with Disabilities
- Are placed in more stimulating environments.
- Acquire improved competence in IEP objectives.
- Have greater opportunities to make new friends and share new experiences.
- Tend to be better accepted by peers.
- Feel a stronger sense of membership in their class and school.

Students without Disabilities
- Become more accepting of individual differences.
- Become comfortable working with students with disabilities.
- Learn to be helpful in general (to all students).
- Can acquire leadership skills.

Include children with disabilities in regular physical education settings whenever possible. Studies show that this setting produces significant benefits for all children, whether disabled or not (see Box 2.5).

How can you give a child with a disability an experience of success and fulfillment in the movement setting? Accommodations may include modifying equipment, reducing the complexity of decision making, eliminating time restrictions, or providing alternate scoring options. Box 2.6 outlines more specific accommodations. Lieberman and Houston-Wilson's *Strategies for Inclusion: A Handbook for Physical Education* (2002) also provides useful strategies to integrate children with disabilities in physical education, with guidelines for appropriate inclusion in the least restrictive environment.

FIGURE **2.4**
Some children with disabilities attend physical education with a teacher's aide.

BOX **2.6** ■ **Modifications to Accommodate Students with Special Needs**

Provide adapted equipment that makes performance easier, such as:

- Larger bats
- Larger, lighter, and/or softer balls
- Larger bases, goals, baskets, and the like
- Larger rackets (face and shaft)

Decrease distances:

- Move bases closer together.
- Allow students to be closer to the target, goal, or net.
- In volleyball or badminton, allow them to serve from midcourt.

Modify activities:

- Allow a student to kick or hit a stationary ball that might otherwise be pitched.

- In volleying tasks, allow them either to catch the ball and throw it or simply to let the ball bounce.
- Allow students an amount of time to get to a base or goal that fits with their ability.
- Where indoor and outdoor venues are used concurrently, try to schedule the activity in the gymnasium or another spot with a smooth surface is (for example, avoid a grassy field).
- Let students with disabilities contribute to decisions about rule modifications.

Allow more time to perform the skill:

- Slow the pace of activity.
- Lengthen the time.
- Provide frequent rest periods.

FINAL WORDS

Strive to provide an environment where all children enjoy physical education, with a continuing motivation to be active. This requires quality instruction, developmentally appropriate content, and adequate resources so that all children are able to participate. Yet even if all these factors are in place, children who find themselves in settings where they feel unsafe—either emotionally or physically—will lose motivation; students who are subjected to classmates' racist, sexist, or derogatory comments or actions of any kind during physical education will soon conclude that physical education is not for them. Actively work to achieve a class climate that supports each child in his or her pursuit of skillful movement.

OVER TO YOU

1. What is your experience with exclusion and isolation in physical education? Is the problem of discrimination and alienation blown out of proportion?

2. Of which areas of inclusion discussed in this chapter do you have the most limited knowledge? Would you know where to find resources that would help you with a particular issue?

3. Discuss in class the following statement: "You may be accused of being *sexist* if you accept a cultural tradition of male domination that rejects policies of equal opportunity; you may be called *racist* if you reject cultural tradition and provide for equal opportunities."

PORTFOLIO TASKS

1. Rewrite the scenarios of the five children described early in this chapter so they reflect a physical education setting of support and inclusion.

2. Interview three classroom or specialist physical education teachers to determine (1) what diversity challenges they face and (2) what strategies they use to provide children with a positive experience.

3. You will have a severely hearing-impaired student in your physical education class next year. An interpreter will assist the student during class. List three strategies to use in your teaching that could benefit this student.

REFERENCES

Banks, J. A. (1994). Transforming the mainstream curriculum. *Educational Leadership, 51*(8), 4–8.

Centers for Disease Control. (2003). *Overweight children and adolescents: Recommendations to screen, assess and manage.* Atlanta, GA: CDC.

Hill, D. (1997). *Fat, four-eyed and useless.* Auckland, New Zealand: Scholastic.

Lieberman, L., & Houston-Wilson, C. (2002). *Strategies for inclusion: A handbook for physical education.* Champaign, IL: Human Kinetics.

Reeves, L., & Stein, J. (1999). Developmentally appropriate pedagogy and inclusion: "Don't put the cart before the horse!" *Physical Educator, 56*(1), 2–7.

Torrey, C. C., & Ashy, M. (1997). Culturally responsive teaching in physical education. *Physical Educator, 54*(3), 120–127.

CHAPTER 3

TEACHING MOTOR SKILLS TO CHILDREN

CHAPTER OUTLINE

1. What are some ways for children to acquire motor skills?

2. What progression do children typically follow in learning motor skills?

3. What does the phrase "motor development is age related but not age dependent" mean?

4. All movement activities are based on fundamental motor skills. What skills fall under this category?

The one-room schoolhouses of the early 1900s were filled with children of all ages and grade levels, taught by one teacher who assigned lessons according to each and every child's readiness to learn. Children in today's elementary classrooms are usually segregated by age, which is *not* a foolproof indicator of a child's "developmental readiness" to participate in physical education.

Courses in child growth and development have acquainted you with all dimensions of "developmental readiness." This chapter focuses on teaching **motor skill development,** the quantitative and qualitative changes in physical skills as children grow (Haywood & Getchell, 2001); it will help you select and design developmentally appropriate motor skill learning for elementary school children.

EXPECT WIDE VARIATIONS IN CHILDHOOD MOTOR SKILLS

---

motor skill development
The quantitative and qualitative changes in children as they move to more complex versions of physical skills throughout the lifespan.

interskill variability
The difference in students' performance among different skills.

intraskill variability
The difference in students' performance within the same skill.

Children develop at different rates and in different ways. You may observe that one first grader can skillfully kick a ball against a wall, while another has trouble simply making contact with the ball. When teaching physical education, you must design tasks to address children's differing motor skill abilities. Assigning the same task to all the children in a class will likely leave some feeling frustrated and discouraged.

Interskill variability refers to differences in children's performance of unrelated physical tasks or activities—such as jumping rope or kicking a ball—while **intraskill variability** refers to having different proficiencies in the skills needed for a single task or activity, such as jumping rope. You will see as much interskill and intraskill variability among children when teaching physical education as you do when teaching them to read, write, or do mathematics. For example, while one child may be just beginning to jump rope, another may excel at jumping rope rhythmically and continuously.

Ms. Davenport has designed a task for her second grade class. Each child has a tennis racket and must hit a ball back and forth over a net. The class's challenge is to have every group make ten hits in a row without losing control.

WHAT'S WRONG WITH THIS PICTURE?

CHILDREN DEVELOP MOTOR SKILLS PROGRESSIVELY

Motor skill development is age and experience *related* but not age and experience *dependent* (Barrett, Williams, & Whitall, 1992). Children tend to develop progressively more complex motor skills in the same order, but the rate of motor skill development varies from one child to another. For example, although children learn to sit before they learn to crawl (Figure 3.1), the age at which an individual child develops these motor skills varies. In teaching physical education do not assume that your students will be able to play the same games or perform the same activities with equal levels of skill simply because they are all the same age.

Think of motor skill development as occurring on a continuum. Each child will probably develop motor skills in a predictable and progressive sequence, but at a different pace from others. Children at different points along the continuum should have different difficulty levels of physical tasks and activities tailored to their current motor skills.

Because of the continuum of motor skill development, you should consider several factors when planning developmentally appropriate physical education experiences for children: a child's physical and psychological readiness, sequential development, cumulative development, and directional development.

Physical and Psychological Readiness

When a child is ready and motivated, he or she learns. You are ill-advised to force a child into new physical activities before he or she is prepared either physically (e.g., strength and endurance) or psychologically. The latter is important because a child's state of mind about a physical task affects motor skill acquisition as surely does his or her physical readiness. A child with the requisite strength and coordination to perform a task, such as crossing the horizontal bars, might be unable or unwilling to attempt this skill because of fear of falling.

If a child is not performing a skill correctly, then the task may be inappropriate for his or her current state of readiness. Plan a variety of easily modified physical tasks so students can work at their own level of readiness and motivation. For example, when teaching a lesson on balancing, let the child decide whether he or she wants to balance using a line on the floor or a low or high balance beam.

FIGURE **3.1**
Movement progression has a fixed order (that is, children must learn to sit before they learn to crawl), although timing may vary from individual to individual.

Sit   Crawl   Walk   Run

Likewise, when teaching a lesson on striking a ball with a bat, let the child decide whether to hit off a tee, hit a toss from the teacher, or hit as the child tosses to him- or herself. Each alternative addresses a different level of physical or psychological readiness.

Sequential Development

Children develop motor skills in a sequential and orderly fashion, learning simple skills before more complex ones (Haywood & Getchell, 2001). Researchers also notice two predictable sequences in children's motor skill development. First, they tend to develop motors skills starting at the head and moving toward the feet, a pattern called **cephalocaudal development.** You can see this pattern with infants who learn to control their upper bodies before their feet and learn to sit before they learn to walk. Second, children tend to develop motor skills from the trunk or midline out to their extremities, a pattern called **proximodistal development**; thus, children can throw before they can write.

Sequential development will affect children's range of activities during physical education; they run before they can skip, and they are likely to catch before they can climb. For this reason, you should introduce tasks in the appropriate order. For example, here is a sequence of locomotor skills matching children's sequential development:

walk > run > leap > jump > hop > gallop > slide > skip

The first five locomotor skills are singular or simple movements; the last three are more complex, combining at least two of the first five skills. For example, to skip a child must both walk and hop. Physical education tasks that reflect the pattern of sequential development will increase your students' success and overall sense of achievement.

Cumulative Development

A child's sequential development is, in effect, a naturally occurring sequence of *potentials* to learn new motor skills. Sequential development, however, doesn't describe *how* a child actually learns a new skill. Children acquire new motor skills by

cephalocaudal development
The sequence of growth occurs from the head to the feet.

proximodistal development
The sequence of growth occurs from the midline to the extremities.

FIGURE **3.2**
With cumulative development, children build on or incorporate previously learned motor skills when acquiring a new one. Devon is kicking a slow-moving object before he attempts to kick one that moves faster.

gradually building on or incorporating previously learned skills—a pattern called *cumulative development*. When a child is developmentally ready to acquire a new motor skill, the best pattern of instruction is progressive and sequential. For example, teach students to kick a stationary ball, then teach them to kick a slow-moving ball, and finally, a fast-moving one (see Figure 3.2). By gradually building skills, children can stand on a solid foundation as they try progressively more difficult versions of a physical skill.

Directional Development

Even after acquiring a motor skill, children—and most grownups—don't perform at the same level every time. Take golf as an example. Some days a golfer has no problem with driving the ball but can't putt for peanuts; other days, everything drops in the hole, but many balls are hit into the woods. Researchers call this skill *variability directional development*. Whether directional development represents an improvement or a decline, it's neither good nor bad, but simply to be expected.

Because of directional development, a child's decline in performance does not necessarily mean that an acquired skill is disappearing. Setbacks in motor skill performance can result from a growth spurt, a lack of practice, or an injury (NASPE, 1994). Children like to be recognized for what they can do at a given time, so keep your physical education plan flexible. Provide movement experiences so that students can advance their motor skills on a given day.

TEACHING MOTOR SKILLS IN PHYSICAL EDUCATION

There is usually something for everyone in the physical activity spectrum; one student may not be a very good softball or baseball player, but excels at calf roping. Both activities involve the same fundamental motor skill—throwing—but in a different context or manner. Elementary school physical education should help children acquire the fundamental motor skills they need for a variety of sports or physical activities, be it ball playing or even calf roping! Your goal is to select appropriate skill progressions so children develop mature patterns in a variety of motor skills. Children who have a repertoire of motor skills can use them to perform activities that they find interesting and rewarding.

Classifying Motor Skills

To design skill progressions, you must break a motor skill into its parts and then teach them in order of difficulty. How do you determine whether a motor skill is easy or difficult? Use these three motor skill classifications to help with this decision:

1. Environmental stability
2. Initiation of movement
3. Movement patterns

Environmental Stability: Closed Skills vs. Open Skills

One way to assess the difficulty of a motor skill is to observe the performance "environment," the object or person to be acted upon. Simpler, **closed skills** are performed in stable and predictable environments, whereas more difficult **open skills** are performed in changing or unpredictable environments (Table 3.1). A motor skill is determined to be open or closed in one of three ways:

1. *Mobility.* Is the student acting on a moving object? Hitting a pitched baseball is an open skill because the ball (the environment) is moving, whereas hitting a stationary ball off a tee is a closed skill. Consider this example from track and field: In the high hurdles, the hurdle (the environment) doesn't move when someone jumps over it, so hurdle jumping is considered a closed skill. See if you can identify open and closed motor skills for the activities listed in Application 3.1.

2. *The number of children involved.* A skill that requires working with a partner, such as kicking a ball back and forth while moving down the field, is open, because one child has to act on what the other is doing and respond to the moving ball. If both children are stationary, and the ball is the only moving object in the environment, the skill is considered more closed than open.

3. *Speed.* The speed at which an object moves affects the stability of the environment. It is easier to respond to slow-moving objects, reducing the instability of the environment. A ball tossed slowly is easier to catch than

INQUIRING MINDS

How do you handle the situation where students in your class differ significantly on the skills you are teaching?

closed skill
A skill whose environmental demands are predictable or stable.

open skill
A skill whose environmental demands are changing or unpredictable.

TABLE **3.1** ■ Closed vs. Open Skills

Classification of Skills	Environmental Conditions	Examples
Closed	No movement of objects	Striking a stationary object such as a ball off a tee
	No opponents or teammates	Throwing a ball at a target on the wall
	Slow speed or stationary	Shooting a free throw in basketball
		Jumping over a stationary rope
		Shooting an arrow at a still target
Open	Movement of objects	Striking a ball thrown from a pitcher
	Opponents and teammates	Throwing a ball to a moving partner
	Normal speed	Making a layup in basketball while defended
		Double Dutch jump roping
		Shooting a bullet at a moving clay target

APPLICATION **3.1** ■ Closed vs. Open Skills Reflection Sheet

DIRECTIONS: Identify skills that would be considered closed or open within a variety of sports.

Sport or Activity	Closed Skills	Open Skills
1. Basketball	1. 2.	1. 2.
2. Tennis	1. 2.	1. 2.
3. Track and Field	1. 2.	1. 2.
4. Gymnastics	1. 2.	1. 2.
5. Volleyball	1. 2.	1. 2.
6. Your Choice	1. 2.	1. 2.

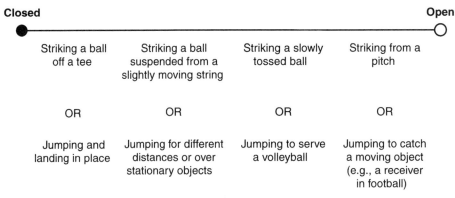

FIGURE 3.3
Examples of how skills might fall along the closed vs. open continuum.

Closed			Open
Striking a ball off a tee	Striking a ball suspended from a slightly moving string	Striking a slowly tossed ball	Striking from a pitch
OR	OR	OR	OR
Jumping and landing in place	Jumping for different distances or over stationary objects	Jumping to serve a volleyball	Jumping to catch a moving object (e.g., a receiver in football)

Nature of the environment

Source: Modified from *Teaching Physical Education for Learning* (4th ed.), by J. E. Rink, 2002, Boston: McGraw-Hill.

one thrown at full force. Catching a moving ball is an open skill; yet, if the ball is moving very slowly, the ball-catching environment can be considered stable enough to verge on being a closed skill. Confused? Just remember that motor skills exist on a continuum, with "open" and "closed" as extremes. Most skills fall somewhere in the middle (see Figure 3.3).

Judging the environmental variability of motor skills will help you decide where to start developing skill progressions. Motor skills performed in stable and predictable environments are the easiest to learn and should be taught first.

Initiation of Movement: Self-Paced vs. Externally Paced Skills

The difficulty of a motor skill also varies depending on whether the child initiates the movement. If a child initiates a motor skill when he or she is ready, the skill is **self-paced,** but if a motor skill is initiated in response to an outside circumstance, that skill is **externally paced.** These categories mark the opposite ends of a continuum with various motor skills in between (Figure 3.4). Because a person throwing a bowling ball can decide when to execute the movement, bowling is a self-paced skill, but because a dancer moves at a pace dictated by the music's tempo, dancing is an externally paced skill.

Notice that self-paced and closed motor skills tend to correlate with one another in terms of their difficulty, as do externally paced and open motor skills. Because putting is a self-paced activity and the golf course (hole) is a stable, non-moving environment, putting is a self-paced, closed motor skill. Tennis is at the other end of the skill continuum. During a rally (when tennis players hit the ball back and forth across the net), a player must hit a rapidly moving ball (an unstable environment), and the opponent determines its arrival time and position; so hitting the ball during a tennis rally is an open and externally paced motor skill.

To summarize: A motor skill is easier when you control *when* and *how* to execute the movement and more difficult when you have to respond before you are ready. So, when developing skill progressions, you should give children motor skills they can initiate at their own pace before asking them to attempt externally paced skills.

self-paced skill
A skill executed at a time decided upon by the performer.

externally paced skill
A skill initiated before the performer is ready, usually due to external stimuli.

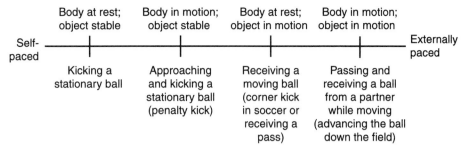

Pacing of Movement

Source: Modified from *Teaching Physical Education for Learning* (4th ed.), by J. E. Rink, 2002, Boston: McGraw-Hill.

FIGURE **3.4**
Example of self-paced and externally paced skills on a continuum.

Movement Patterns: Discrete and Serial Skills

Whether open or closed, self-paced or externally paced, a motor skill has a beginning and an end. Looking at whether a motor skill happens once, twice, or many times can also help you assess its relative difficulty. A **discrete skill**—one that happens once and that has a distinct beginning and end—is the easiest. Batting a ball or jumping over a box is an example of a discrete skill. A **serial skill**—two or more discrete motor skills performed in sequence—is more difficult. A softball fielder who catches the ball and then throws it to another player is performing a serial skill (catch-throw). You should plan skill progressions, teaching children to perform discrete skills as the foundation for serial skills. Table 3.2 provides numerous examples of skills that belong to each of these patterning categories.

Developing Logical Skill Progressions

Now that you've read about determining the difficulty of motor skill development, how can you design appropriate learning experiences when there are so many skills to be taught? This is a legitimate concern because teaching unfamiliar content is often intimidating.

Can you remember learning to ride a bicycle? Do you remember your progression in learning that skill? Did your parents attach training wheels to your bike before allowing you to ride on two wheels? Moving from the simple to the complex is a process with any skill. In fact, you may be smiling and shaking your head as you remember how the person who taught you to ride broke the skill down into simple parts. As your mastery of bike riding increased, so did the difficulty of the parts that were added.

In the initial stages of teaching children motor skills, the learning environment needs to be as stable (closed) as possible. Teach discrete foundation skills first. Children can practice these discrete skills at their own pace, making them easier than externally paced ones. Jumping and landing and throwing a ball or a Frisbee are discrete, closed skills that children can learn at their own pace.

As children acquire discrete motor skills, the next step is combining skills while practicing them in a closed environment. For instance, children can practice fielding a ball in a relatively closed environment by gathering a ball rolled slowly by a partner before they are asked to field a batted ball or to catch one that is bouncing.

discrete skill
A skill with definitive starting and ending points.

serial skill
A combination of two or more discrete skills used to perform a movement.

TABLE 3.2 ■ **Examples of Discrete and Serial Skills**

Discrete Skills (One Action)

Throwing an object

Catching an object

Jumping and landing

Standing long jump

Kicking an object (punting)

Volleying an object

Striking an object (golf)

Serial Skills (Combined Actions)

Fielding a softball (approach, gather, throw)

Layup in basketball (dribble, takeoff, release)

Serving in tennis (toss, swing, contact)

Shooting in team handball (run up, jump, deliver)

The final step in developing a logical skill progression is practicing in an open environment. When teaching a child to hit a ball with a paddle, first have the child hit a ball suspended from a string; when they have mastered this task, ask him or her to hit from a soft toss. Both these tasks lead up to the child eventually rallying with a partner (Figure 3.5).

Progression Trees as Logical Progressions

To help you develop skill progressions, we have designed "progression trees" to depict children's growth through three phases in acquiring motor skills:

1. Developing skills

2. Expanding skills

3. Mastering skills

The three parts of the tree take into account environmental demands, skill pacing, and progression of skills and should progress from simple to complex versions. An example of a progression tree for dribbling with the hand is shown in Figure 3.6.

In the *developing skills* phase, children should practice fundamental motor skills in a predictable and/or self-paced environment. For dribbling with the hand, these include bouncing the ball in self-space, dribbling around different parts of the body, and bouncing and catching a ball. As students master dribbling in these closed, simple situations, plan slightly less predictable tasks that are semi-self-paced. This is called the *expanding skill* phase. Examples from dribbling with the hand include dribbling while changing directions on a signal, dribbling in different directions, and dribbling around objects.

Introduce unpredictable and/or externally paced tasks when the students have enough control over the object to attend to outside factors such as other players. This phase is known as *mastering skills*. In the dribbling with the hand progression

FIGURE **3.5**
Thomas hits the suspended ball when he is ready. This is a self-paced task.

tree, activities include keep-away dribbling—the student with the ball attempts to control the dribble while evading a defender—and dribble tag—two students attempt to tag each other while maintaining control of their own balls.

As you examine Figure 3.6, realize that everything about a progression tree is related to its base. A living tree with a solid base grows to its full potential, but a tree with a weak foundation struggles to survive. The same is true with learning motor skills. A child with a solid foundation of motor skills can develop fully and enjoy being physically active over a lifetime.

The representation of the phases of motor skill development in Figure 3.6 may fail to reassure you about designing specific skill progressions for a range of activities. Fear not. Chapters 11 and 12 include examples of progression trees for many fundamental motor skills (skill themes) taught in a quality physical education program as well as sample learning experiences to use at each developmental phase.

Graham, Holt-Hale, and Parker (2004) use the phrase "generic levels of skill proficiency" (GLSP) to describe the four levels children pass though as they learn motor skills: precontrol, control, utilization, and proficiency. These GLSPs describe a child's performance at each level.

1. *Precontrol.* Initially, when acquiring a new motor skill, a child moves awkwardly or clumsily and has difficulty repeating movements. Success at this level is usually due to chance.

2. *Control.* During this level of the GLSP, children must concentrate intensely to replicate movements. Even so, the child performs the movement awkwardly.

3. *Utilization.* During this level, children repeat movements somewhat smoothly and automatically. This allows them to shift attention from controlling the object to other factors, such as eluding a defender.

4. *Proficiency.* Eventually, children learn movements automatically and with confidence. They are able to modify their learned movement skills to adjust for different situations. While dribbling a soccer ball, for example, a child uses all parts of his or her foot to get around a defender and make a shot to beat a goalkeeper.

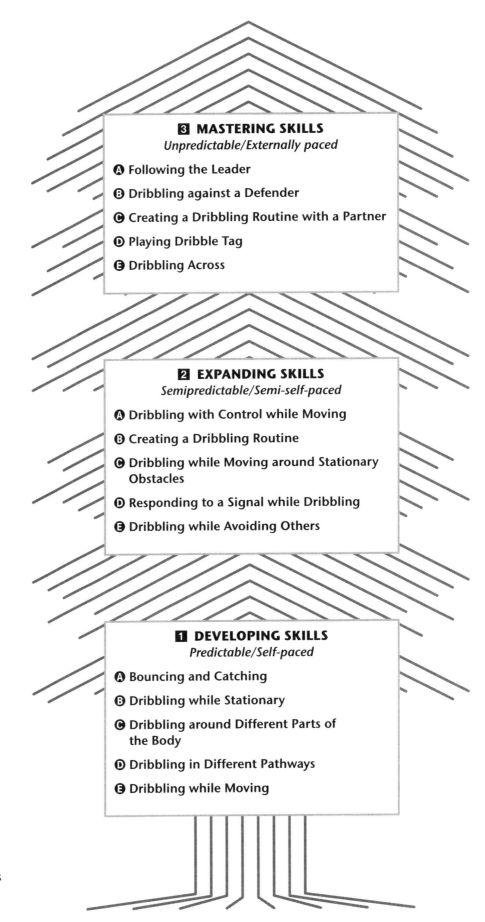

3 MASTERING SKILLS
Unpredictable/Externally paced

A Following the Leader

B Dribbling against a Defender

C Creating a Dribbling Routine with a Partner

D Playing Dribble Tag

E Dribbling Across

2 EXPANDING SKILLS
Semipredictable/Semi-self-paced

A Dribbling with Control while Moving

B Creating a Dribbling Routine

C Dribbling while Moving around Stationary Obstacles

D Responding to a Signal while Dribbling

E Dribbling while Avoiding Others

1 DEVELOPING SKILLS
Predictable/Self-paced

A Bouncing and Catching

B Dribbling while Stationary

C Dribbling around Different Parts of the Body

D Dribbling in Different Pathways

E Dribbling while Moving

FIGURE **3.6**
A progression tree illustrating the developmental process in learning to dribble with the hand.

> At the end of a series of dribbling lessons with his fifth grade class, Mr. Kenyon lets the students play a game as a reward for their efforts. He divides the class into two groups; half sit out and watch while the other half plays five-on-five adult regulation basketball on half of the gym court. The students on the floor show a wide range in skill level. The students seated talk quietly or cheer their friends on while waiting for the opportunity to participate.
>
> **WHAT'S WRONG WITH THIS PICTURE?**

The four levels of the GLSP correlate to the phases of the progression tree by highlighting that a person just learning a skill (developing phase) will look clumsy, awkward, or out of control. When dribbling, a child is controlled by the basketball instead of the child controlling the ball; or, when thrown, the ball fails to go in the targeted direction. Yet, children ready for the expanding phase activities are able to control the movement or skill, dribbling a basketball while moving or around obstacles. Children in the mastering skills phase perform the movement automatically and with fluidity.

The GLSP accounts for interskill and intraskill variability among children. A child can be at different GLSP levels for different motor skills, an example of interskill variability; a child may be at the precontrol level for kicking while at the utilization level for balancing. Or, one child in a group might be at the precontrol level for catching while another is at the utilization level, a reflection of intraskill variability. The GLSP helps qualify children's abilities as they acquire motor skills; specifically, it describes how well a child performs a skill. The utilization and proficiency levels also allow for variations in skill performance conditions.

The word *generic* in GLSP characterizes a child's performance at each level, regardless of the motor skill being learned; a child having trouble replicating a movement—whether dribbling a basketball or throwing a football—would be classified as performing at the precontrol level.

The following example demonstrates the various GLSP levels. Jack has been driving a car with an automatic transmission for several years. He has acquired proficiency with driving this type of vehicle. Therefore, he is able to listen to the radio, drink a cup of coffee, or talk to passengers while driving. Now, Jack wants to drive a car with a manual (stick shift) transmission. Suddenly he is back at the precontrol level for driving because new skills are needed for driving this type of vehicle. Once again, driving requires his careful thought and attention. He has to actively concentrate on the motor skills needed to shift the car through its gears, thinking about pushing in the clutch while letting off the gas. Jack finds himself attending less to the skill of shifting as he progresses through the control and utilization levels of the GLSP. Eventually he will regain the proficiency level he has acquired with the automatic transmission vehicle and he will be able to drive while drinking a cup of coffee or singing along to the radio.

In developing logical progressions, the progression tree includes activities to help students progress to the next phase. The GLSP helps you visualize students working in the different phases.

TABLE 3.3 ■ Movement Concepts Taught in Physical Education

Space Awareness: Where the Body Moves
- *Directions:* up/down; back/forward; right/left; or clockwise/counterclockwise
- *Levels:* low, medium, or high
- *Pathways:* straight, curved, or zigzag
- *Location:* self-space or general space

Effort: How the Body Moves
- *Time:* fast/slow
- *Force:* light/strong
- *Flow:* free/bounded

Relationships: Between the Mover and Others
- *Between parts of the body:* various positions
- *To other people:* passive support/active support; moving together/apart; or similar/dissimilar actions
- *To apparatus or the ground:* facing front, back, or side; above, below, or beside; or right way up/inverted

APPROPRIATE CONTENT FOR ELEMENTARY PHYSICAL EDUCATION

Elementary physical education programs should focus on teaching fundamental motor skills and movement concepts. Most physical activities and sports enjoyed by adults use specialized versions of skills and concepts learned in childhood. Thus, if children are given a solid foundation in the formative years, they are likely to feel comfortable participating in these activities well into adulthood.

Movement concepts tell the child how to perform a movement. When teaching a student to kick a ball, it's helpful to show the student what to do with the ball or how to position his or her body. You might say, "I want you to dribble the soccer ball using *light force,*" or "Balance your body at a *low* level on two body parts." The words *light force* and *low* tell the student how to perform a movement.

Movement Concepts

Movement concepts include space awareness, effort, and relationships (Table 3.3). In many physical education programs, the content in the early grades focuses on teaching children movement vocabulary. They are taught the difference between the terms *forward* and *backward* and *over* and *under,* and other movement-related concepts. Many of these concepts reflect content found in other areas of an early childhood curriculum—for example, teaching children about directions.

Fundamental Motor Skills (Skill Themes)

Whenever your body moves, you are performing a motor skill. Some motor skills move the body from one point to another while others, such as bending and stretching, are performed in one spot. Regardless of their difficulty or the extent

movement concept
A word that describes how to perform a movement.

TABLE 3.4 ■ **Different Skill Themes Taught in Physical Education**

Locomotor Skills	Nonlocomotor Skills	Manipulative Skills
Walking	Twisting	Throwing
Running	Turning	Catching
Leaping	Bending	Dribbling (hands/feet)
Jumping	Stretching	Kicking
Skipping	Balancing	Punting
Hopping	Rocking	Volleying
Sliding	Curling	Striking (long/short handles)
Galloping		

of movement, all fundamental motor skills can be grouped into the related "skill themes"—locomotor skills, manipulative skills, and nonlocomotor skills (see Table 3.4).

Locomotor Skills

Locomotor skills are skill themes in which a body moves from one place to another within a vertical plane. There are eight basic locomotor skills:

1. *Walking:* The transfer of weight from one foot to the other, with one foot always in contact with the ground

2. *Running:* The transfer of weight from one foot to the other, with a momentary loss of contact with the ground by both feet

3. *Leaping:* The transfer of weight from one foot to the ball of the other foot with a springing action

4. *Jumping:* The transfer of weight from one or both feet to both feet

5. *Hopping:* The transfer of weight from one foot to the same foot (Figure 3.7)

6. *Galloping:* A step forward with the other foot following quickly. The same foot always leads.

7. *Sliding:* A step sideward with the other foot following quickly. The same foot always leads.

8. *Skipping:* A combination of a long step and a short hop, alternating the lead foot

Manipulative Skills

The most recognizable skills are manipulative skills and are primarily associated with sport skills. They require the performer to manipulate an object with some part of the body. For example, striking is a manipulative skill using an object such as a bat, racket, or paddle. In volleying, the performer uses his or her head, arms, or feet to strike an object before it touches the ground. Manipulative skills are the most complex and often the most difficult for children to learn.

locomotor skill
A movement that moves the body from one place to another within a vertical plane.

FIGURE **3.7**
Hopping is a locomotor skill defined as a transfer of weight from one foot to the same foot.

Nonlocomotor Skills

Unlike manipulative skills, nonlocomotor skills do not involve objects; unlike locomotor skills, they do not require body movement from place to place. In fact, nonlocomotor skills are performed from a relatively stable position while either standing or sitting. Examples include bending, reaching, and twisting.

FINAL WORDS

Children learn motor skills when they are ready, although most children follow a general timeline. They progress developmentally through a certain sequence in learning motor skills, using previously learned skills to acquire more advanced skill patterns, but they often change patterns in skill performance.

To help children develop motor skills, move from simple to complex versions of the task. To develop skill progressions, consider the task's environmental demands, who initiates the task, and the complexity of the motor skill pattern. The first motor skills taught should be closed, self-paced, and discrete.

Elementary physical education programs should focus on children's acquisition of skill themes and movement concepts. The three categories of skill themes—locomotor, manipulative, and nonlocomotor skills—are used in a variety of sports and physical activities. Movement concepts describe performing a particular skill. By providing appropriate learning experiences, you will help children develop these skills and concepts.

Everyone has difficulty with a new concept or skill at some point. You need to teach motor skills so that children will be motivated to learn. Using a developmental perspective, you can increase children's motivation and success by having them work at the appropriate level.

1. After observing your third grade physical education lesson on throwing, your principal states that your lesson's skill progression was refreshingly appropriate. Describe what your principal might have observed.

2. Explain the progression tree and how it represents the developmental process. How could you improve the tree? Can you think of a more effective model?

3. Why might highly competitive tasks be unsuitable for children who are learning a new skill? Use the concepts discussed in this chapter to support your case.

4. List five ways to modify adult basketball so it is appropriate for children (*hint:* lower the basket).

1. Individually or with a group, put the following locomotor skills in the proper order of progression: skipping, galloping, walking, hopping, sliding, running, jumping, and leaping. Justify your order developmentally.

2. You have been asked to teach dribbling a soccer ball to children who have absolutely no experience with this skill. Using the information in this chapter and the different skill classification continuums, outline an appropriate teaching progression to help your students learn this new and exciting skill.

3. A friend has been ill for the past two weeks and missed the classes on the developmental perspective. You have time to highlight only two concepts for your friend. Write these two critical points with enough detail so your friend is crystal clear about the importance of the information.

REFERENCES

Barrett, K. R., Williams, K., & Whitall, J. (1992). What does it mean to have a developmentally appropriate physical education program? *Physical Educator, 49*(3), 114–118.

Graham, G., Holt/Hale, S. A., & Parker, M. (2004). *Children moving: A reflective approach to teaching physical education* (6th ed.). Boston: McGraw-Hill.

Haywood, K., & Getchell, N. (2001). *Life span motor development* (3rd ed.). Champaign, IL: Human Kinetics.

National Association for Sport and Physical Education (NASPE). (1994). *Looking at physical education from a developmental perspective: A guide for teaching.* A position statement of the National Association for Sport and Physical Education developed by the Motor Development Task Force. Reston, VA: American Alliance for Health, Physical Education, Recreation and Dance.

Rink, J. E. (2002). *Teaching physical education for learning* (4th ed.). Boston: McGraw-Hill.

What's the best way to teach physical education? Does teaching motor skills to children simply involve barking out some off-the-cuff advice? The chapters in this unit suggest that teaching physical education to children demands the same degree of forethought and creativity that you would apply to teaching any classroom topic. Quality physical education starts with a sound written lesson plan, as you will discover in Chapter 4. Chapter 5 will guide you in delivering the plan you have developed; you will learn how to select an instructional strategy that promotes learning the targeted motor skill and that takes into account your children's developmental readiness. In addition, you are responsible for documenting your children's progress in physical education just as you are for other topics. For this reason, Chapter 6 closes the unit with a look at physical education assessment methods.

INSTRUCTIONAL STRATEGIES FOR TEACHING PHYSICAL EDUCATION

UNIT II

THE DAILY PHYSICAL EDUCATION LESSON PLAN

1. Baseball legend Yogi Berra once said, "If you don't know where you're going, you might not get there." How does this statement capture the benefits of sound planning for teaching physical education?

2. What steps should you take in planning a physical education lesson, from identifying the content to delivering it to children?

3. What "critical elements" should be included in a daily physical education lesson plan?

4. What are extending, refining, and applying tasks? How are these used in developing activities for a physical education lesson?

There is an old adage that suggests, "Failure to plan is the same as planning to fail." The message is obvious: If you want to succeed, you have to plan. Without a plan, your success occurs simply by chance—if at all. Few people dispute this; sound planning practices are now seen from the boardroom to the classroom. An entire segment of business is now devoted to helping people and organizations plan effectively. This underscores two important points: planning is important, and planning is a methodical process.

Competent planning is the sixth of the National Association for Sport and Physical Education's (NASPE) nine standards for beginning physical education teachers (NASPE, 2003); it says that physical education teachers must understand the importance of planning "developmentally appropriate" lessons for children.

This chapter shows how to plan appropriate and effective lessons, suggests how to incorporate professional standards and state mandates into them, and comprehensively identifies the proper components of a daily lesson plan.

QUALITIES OF EFFECTIVE PLANNERS

Effective teachers are good planners with a firm understanding of the content and skill in organizing their teaching environment to help students learn. Planning is a skill that must be practiced over and over again. Before you begin learning to plan a physical education lesson, let's examine four traits or qualities of an effective planner.

Patience

Effective planning requires patience and effort. Effective lesson planners did not acquire this ability overnight. Like you, most struggled to learn about developing a lesson plan and its delivery. Elementary education teachers who plan effective physical education lessons understand their children's development and what activities will spark their interest. They understand when partnered or group activities might be valuable and when those same activities might end badly.

FIGURE **4.1**
With the teacher's guidance, these children discover that the ball goes in the desired direction if they keep the volleying surface flat.

Flexibility

Another piece of sage advice from Yogi Berra: "When you come to a fork in the road, take it." Planning requires flexibility. Classrooms are often in a state of organized chaos with many activities or events happening at once. An elementary education teacher might have groups of students working on various art, reading, or history projects in different areas of the classroom. Organizing and monitoring these involves careful planning. Unfortunately, even the most detailed plans can go awry due to circumstances beyond a teacher's control—such as a fire drill, a weather warning, or simply the students' mood.

Unforeseen difficulties pose problems for any teacher. However, inexperienced teachers find it more difficult to adjust their lesson plans than experienced teachers, who can adjust their plans fairly easily (Lee, 2003). Realize that you cannot always proceed as you intended; flexibility is an indispensable trait of seasoned lesson planners.

Persistence

Be persistent. Sometimes lesson plans go awry; sometimes results fall short of your expectations. For example, you might develop a lesson plan using the **guided discovery** teaching style (Figure 4.1). Guided discovery uses a predetermined set of questions or movement problems to lead students toward identifying one correct answer or solution. Despite your planning, students may consistently fail to choose the "right" movement answer or solution. Should you avoid this style in the future? Of course not! You should evaluate the lesson plan and then modify it to produce the intended **outcomes**—what students should know and be able to do. With persistence, you will master the planning and delivery of improved physical education content to your students.

guided discovery
A teaching style in which the teacher uses a predetermined set of questions or movement problems to help students identify one correct answer or response.

outcome
What students should know and be able to do.

Self-Knowledge

Above all, you must be true to yourself to plan effectively. A plan that works for another teacher may not work for you. The main problem with lesson plans found on the Internet or borrowed from other teachers is that they don't take advantage of your personal abilities or sidestep your areas of inexperience. A time-tested "canned" lesson plan may be useless if you can't deliver it as intended. Inventory your abilities and then plan lessons that you can teach with confidence and conviction.

PHYSICAL EDUCATION LESSON PLANS ARE VALUABLE DOCUMENTS

Sound documentation comes from effective planning. Inexperienced elementary education teachers sometimes forget that a physical education lesson plan also documents students' learning. The lesson plan shows parents, administrators, and state agencies what you are covering and how you are delivering it to your class. Sound documentation is especially important in physical education because of potential injury. If a child in your class were injured during a forward roll, your lesson plan could show that you taught how to tuck the head and curve the spine properly before you allowed students to perform the skill. That lesson plan would be evidence that you followed sound teaching principles with appropriate skill progressions. You can also file lesson plans for future reference. When you teach the same lesson again, you can easily retrieve, modify, and implement its existing plan.

ADDRESSING STATE REQUIREMENTS OR NATIONAL STANDARDS

The U.S. Constitution delegates much of the responsibility for overseeing the education of children to the individual states. Educational laws, required curriculum, and available educational resources consequently vary from one state to another. State requirements for physical education differ remarkably (Table 4.1), with recess counting toward meeting physical education mandates in some states.

TABLE **4.1** ■ Samples of Different State Requirements for Elementary Physical Education

State	Elementary Physical Education Requirement
Alabama	K–8: Daily physical education for 30 minutes
California	K–6: 200 minutes each ten days
Delaware	K–6: No mandatory physical education
Florida	K–8: No physical education requirement
Georgia	K–5: Required 90 hours per year
Illinois	K–12: Daily physical education but no time specified
New York	All levels: Required 120 minutes per week
Texas	K–8: Time decided by local school districts
Vermont	K–8: Required at least twice a week
Washington	K–8: Required at least 100 minutes per week

Source: From *Active Start: A Statement of Physical Activity Guidelines for Children Birth to Five Years,* by the National Association for Sport and Physical Education, 2002, Reston, VA: American Alliance for Health, Physical Education, Recreation and Dance.

BOX **4.1** ■ **National Content Standards for Physical Education**

1. Demonstrates competency in motor skills and movement patterns needed to perform a variety of physical activities.

2. Demonstrates understanding of movement concepts, principles, strategies, and tactics as they apply to the learning and performance of physical activities.

3. Participates regularly in physical activity.

4. Achieves and maintains a health-enhancing level of physical fitness.

5. Demonstrates responsible personal and social behavior that respects self and others in physical activity settings.

6. Values physical activity for health, enjoyment, challenge, self-expression, and/or social interaction.

Source: From *Moving into the Future: National Standards for Physical Education* (2nd ed.), by the National Association for Sport and Physical Education, 2004, Reston, VA: American Alliance for Health, Physical Education, Recreation and Dance.

The first step in planning a physical education curriculum is consulting state and district curriculum requirements to identify physical education goals and objectives. If state law requires physical education, then there is typically a corresponding curriculum guide closely aligned with the NASPE National Content Standards for Physical Education (see Box 4.1).

Some state and district-level physical education curriculum guides or courses of study are thoughtfully written and detailed, while others address content only cursorily. If you have insufficient state or district-level guidance, consult the NASPE Standards to help you identify appropriate core content for particular grade levels.

Although a curriculum guide (whether national, state, or local) is a good starting point, even the best of these guides address only what content should be taught and when; they do not include daily lesson plans. This is why you must learn to write your own. The following section shows the essential elements of quality plans.

THE DAILY PHYSICAL EDUCATION LESSON PLAN

In a static world you could devise one physical education lesson plan that worked for all students all the time. But because children are dynamic individuals, formulaic planning is both misguided and ineffective. Cookie-cutter approaches violate a fundamental principle of teaching: Teachers should address children's individuality when developing lesson plans.

The daily physical education lesson plan helps you create productive learning outcomes and details your actions in helping students meet them. Although your school may require a standardized physical education plan, if you are permitted to develop your own lesson plans, you can make the process easier and deliver more satisfying experiences by following guidelines developed by physical education professionals.

Physical education lesson plans are similar to those you would write for the classroom. Both will have an introduction, a learning progression, and a conclusion. The daily physical education lesson plan has 11 steps organized into four parts (Box 4.2). Let's walk through each of these essential steps.

The Lesson's Focus

Begin the daily physical education lesson plan with a list of the information you will need in order to focus on the lesson's purpose and desired outcomes. This information is outlined in the following steps.

BOX 4.2 ■ The 11 Parts of a Daily Physical Education Lesson Plan

The Lesson's Focus

1. Grade Level	Provides a general idea of where to focus the lesson
2. Skill Theme	Indicates the skill that will be the focus of the lesson
3. Learnable Piece	A physical act or behavior needed to perform a skill (or part of a skill) correctly

Preparations for the Lesson

4. Equipment and Materials	A list of all items that will be needed during the lesson
5. Protocols	Commands that your students need to follow before or during the physical education lesson instruction
6. Instant Activity	An activity that students engage in immediately before any instruction.

Content Progression

7. Set Induction	Informs the children what they will be learning and why it is important
8. Class Organization and Structure ■ grouping ■ performance space ■ equipment ■ formations	Managing the structure within a task and the classroom to ensure the best opportunity to learn
9. Developing the Content ■ extensions ■ applications ■ refinements	Presenting tasks to children to help them work at their own level and to take them from one performance level to another

Ending the Lesson

10. Closure	At the end of each lesson, sit down with the children for a short period (under two minutes) and discuss the lesson. Remind them of the learnable piece.
11. Assessment	How are you going to assess whether you met the lesson outcomes?

Step 1: Grade Level

Noting grade level is the first step toward making your lesson plans developmentally appropriate. Remember that development is age-related, not age-dependent (see Chapter 3). Students' abilities vary at different grade levels.

Step 2: Skill Theme

Specify the skill(s) you will teach during the lesson. Because elementary physical education develops skill themes, or fundamental motor skills, each lesson should focus on teaching a basic skill such as throwing, jumping, striking, or avoiding objects while traveling.

TABLE **4.2** ■ **Examples of Learnable Pieces**

Fundamental Motor Skills	Learnable Pieces
Throwing	Arm back
	Step with opposite foot
	Point, step, throw
Catching	Ready hands
	Reach
	Cushion ball into body
Jumping/Landing	Bend knees
	Reach arms way back
	Swing arms forward
Striking with a Paddle	Flat paddle
	Firm wrist
	Side to target
Volleying	Flat surface
	Eyes on the object
	Keep contact point firm
Galloping	Same foot always forward
	Belly button faces forward direction
	Hop-hop

Step 3: Learnable Piece

Identify your students' goals for this lesson. The lesson outcome is the **learnable piece,** a physical act or behavior needed to perform a skill (or part of a skill) correctly. Students should be able accomplish this learnable piece in the lesson's time frame. Although you might not be able to teach children to throw proficiently in one lesson, they could learn to step forward with the foot opposite the throwing arm as they throw a ball. Table 4.2 gives examples of learnable pieces associated with different basic motor skills. At the elementary school level, you should have no more than two learnable pieces in each lesson plan.

Preparations for the Lesson

Once you decide on your goals for the lesson, the next three steps involve assembling the lesson materials and planning how to manage students before the actual instruction begins.

Step 4: Equipment and Materials

Identify the equipment you need to teach the lesson, as well as the number of pieces needed (Figure 4.2). For your throwing lesson, for example, you might need

learnable piece
A physical act or behavior needed to perform a skill (or part of a skill) correctly.

FIGURE **4.2**
A list of how much and what type of equipment is needed will help you remember to bring everything for a successful lesson.

30 tennis balls, 20 cones, ten targets, two markers, stickers, and tape. A checklist can help ensure that you have everything in place before the lesson starts.

Step 5: Protocols

Next, record any special safety-related directions or commands your students need to follow before or during the physical education lesson. These directions, called **protocols,** are usually associated with the targeted skill theme. If you are teaching throwing, you will note on your lesson plan what you want students to do with the ball when you tell them to stop: "When you hear the stop signal, put the ball on the floor between your feet." Chapters 7 and 8 provide more strategies for using protocols.

Step 6: Instant Activity

An **instant activity** is one children start doing immediately upon entering the physical education setting. Used instead of traditional warm-ups or calisthenics, instant activities may include games, skill practice, or fitness tasks to prepare a child's body for physical activity. The instant activity should usually help prepare children for the lesson's designated skill theme. Chapter 5 gives more details about instant activities.

Content Progression

The next five steps of the daily physical education lesson plan show how to actually teach the lesson and manage its progress.

Step 7: Set Induction

During **set induction,** tell your students what they will be learning and why it's important. This should spark your students' interest and enthusiasm. Continuing the example of teaching throwing as a skill theme, your set induction might

protocols
Commands that your students need to follow before or during the lesson.

instant activity
A movement activity for children to engage in when first entering the classroom.

set induction
The beginning of the lesson that tells the students what they will be learning and why it is important.

involve saying, "Have you ever been to a carnival or a fair? Good! Remember all the games people were playing so they could win a prize? Well, in some of those games and activities, like the milk bottle throw, you have to be a really good thrower in order to win a prize. Today, let's pretend we are going to a carnival. One thing that will help you throw better is to take your arm way back and step forward with the foot opposite your throwing hand."

Step 8: Class Organization and Structure

Management and instruction occur simultaneously during a physical education lesson, so an effective daily lesson plan includes information on how to organize and structure the class. Recall from Chapter 1 that effective teachers minimize management and maximize instructional time. However, given children's energy and enthusiasm, managing your physical education class can be much more challenging than managing the very same group of children in a classroom.

What's the best strategy? Physical education management is similar to general classroom management in that you give students the activity and tell them how you want them organized while doing it. When you say to your children, "Come to the reading circle and listen to the story I am going to read about fire safety," you have introduced the instructional activity and said how it will be organized. You follow the same strategy in teaching and managing a physical education lesson.

Managing a physical education lesson involves (1) dividing students into groups, (2) telling them about the performance space, (3) explaining what equipment to use and how to use it, and (4) specifying the formations to follow during the activity. For example:

- *Grouping.* For any task, students will work independently, with a partner, or in a group.

- *Performance space.* Children will work either in **self-space,** the area around the body they can reach without moving, or in **general space,** the space within the activity area they can reach by moving.

- *Equipment.* The physical education teacher identifies what equipment to use and how the students will use it. You might say, "Choose a ball from the ones in the bins."

- *Formations.* In a lesson, the **formation** is the grouping or arrangement of children for practice. Different formations are appropriate for different practice activities (Figure 4.3). Children working individually in general space may use the *scattered formation,* spread out in the gym. The *circle formation* may be the best choice for children striking with a bat toward open space; while the *row formation* works better if they are hitting toward a wall. If they are tossing a ball back and forth to a partner, a *column formation* would be a good choice (see Figure 4.4), although the *scattered column formation* would work as well. Explain the formations to your students before explaining how to perform the skill or task; this keeps students concentrating on your instruction instead of wondering who their partner will be or where they are supposed to go.

Application 4.1 shows how to weave managerial tasks smoothly into the instructional tasks of physical education lessons for different skill themes.

INQUIRING MINDS

What are the steps you take in planning daily lessons for your students? How do you determine the student outcome?

self-space
The area around the body that the student can reach without moving.

general space
The space within the activity area that children can reach by moving.

formation
An arrangement or grouping of students for practice.

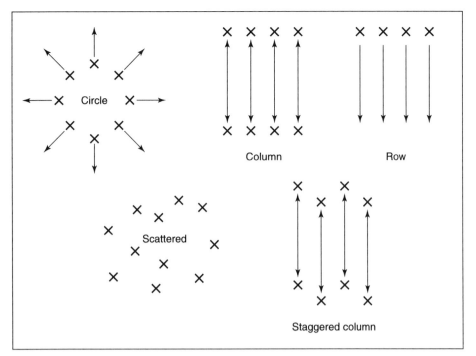

FIGURE **4.3**
Different formations are appropriate for different learning tasks in physical education classes.

FIGURE **4.4**
The column formation works well for practicing skills in partner work.

Step 9: Developing the Content

Developing the content is the process of presenting tasks to children, taking them from one performance level to another (Rink, 2002). In this process, you give children different tasks to aid their development. Three basic types of task in developing the content are extensions, applications, and refinements:

- **Extensions** are tasks that help children attain proficiency in the skill theme. Children might first throw at a large target on the wall to improve their throwing skills. You may then *extend* or *modify* the task. Changing it

extension
An adjustment that makes an existing task easier or more difficult.

- Get with a partner [*grouping*] and stand across from each other at the designated cones [*formation*]. There is one ball per set of cones [*equipment*]. When I say *go,* I want you to kick the ball back and forth with your partner using a light force until I say *stop* [*instructional aspect of task*].

- When I say *begin,* I want you to travel in general space [*space*] using your best airplane imitation [*instructional aspect of task*].

- Today we are going to be working on shooting with a hockey stick while keeping the blade low to the ground. Your first task is to shoot at the low target taped to the wall [*instructional aspect of task*]. When I say *go,* I want you to go get a stick and a puck [equipment] and go stand on one of the spots [*formation*] facing the wall. Begin practicing once you get to your spot. Ready? Go!

to make it more difficult is an extension; making the task easier (as by moving the target closer) is a modification. For simplicity's sake, however, we will use the term *extension* for changing the task to make it either easier or more difficult.

- **Applications** require children to perform a familiar task to a certain standard. They are measurable in some way, either quantitatively (performing a certain number in a row, increasing or decreasing time or distance) or qualitatively (showing a certain form). Applications motivate the child to continue practicing tasks in new, more challenging ways. See Table 4.3 for examples of quantitative and qualitative applications.

- **Refinements** are cues to help children perform the skill or task correctly. They are meant not to change the task but to remind children what they need to do to execute the skill properly. Refinements should be short and simple, as when you say, *"Look for an open space* when you are galloping." The cue "look for an open space" prompts students to remember to watch where they are going instead of bumping into their classmates.

Table 4.4, which lists and compares content development for specific skill themes, is designed to help you see the logical flow from task to application to refinement.

Ending the Lesson

Most good stories or movies have brief but meaningful endings. The last two steps of the daily physical education lesson plan follow the same idea to end a lesson.

application
A task that challenges children to perform to a certain standard.

refinement
A task that highlights the quality of student performance.

TABLE **4.3** ■ Quantitative and Qualitative Applications

Skill	Quantitative	Qualitative
Balance	See how long you can maintain your partner's balance.	See how still you can keep your body as you balance.
Dribbling with Hand	This time, see if you can decrease the time it takes you to dribble through the obstacle course.	See if you can maintain control of the ball as you dribble through the obstacle course.
Dance	See if you can perform at least three of the dance movements in the sequence we've practiced.	Try to perform the next three dance steps in time to the music.

TABLE **4.4** ■ Three Types of Tasks Used to Help Children Develop Various Skills

Skill	Extension [E]	Application [A]	Refinement [R]
Volleying	Volley the ball back and forth with your partner.	See how many times you and your partner can volley the ball back and forth without losing control.	I like the way you are keeping your volleying surface flat.
Catching	Toss the ball up into the air and catch it while remaining in your self-space.	See how high you can toss the ball and catch it without moving from your self-space.	Remember to keep your eye on the ball.
Punting	Stand behind the ball and kick it toward the target on the wall.	See how many times you can hit the target in your next five kicks.	Keep your chin tucked to your chest.
Striking with a Long-Handled Object (Golf Club)	There are several hoops placed on the ground at different distances. Pick one hoop and hit five shots toward it.	See if you can keep the same rhythm with your swing for all five shots.	Remember to swing your arms like a grandfather clock.

Step 10: Closure

During **closure** you use the time to review the lesson content because you want children to remember what was covered in the lesson. Closure also gives students time to settle down before returning to classroom studies. Refer to the learnable piece, and use closure to remind students about what they might need to think about or bring for the next lesson.

closure
The wrap-up of the lesson.

FIGURE **4.5**
Formal assessments can be placed in a student's folder to document student learning.

At lesson's end, children are typically tired, with waning attention spans; so limit closure to no more than two to three minutes. Tell students where to gather for closure. Your announcement signals that the content portion of the lesson is over.

Step 11: Assessment

The last step of the daily lesson plan is assessment, which can be completed formally or informally. Formal assessment is document-driven and informal assessment is observation-driven. Thus, an evaluation written on paper (or otherwise recorded) is a formal assessment. The advantage of formal assessments is that they can be collected and placed in students' folders to document their class progress (Figure 4.5). Strategies for formal lesson assessment are covered in Chapter 6.

Informal assessment relies on undocumented observation by the teacher. You can informally assess students with a quick scan of student responses to see what they know, what they can do, or how they feel. You can observe student performance, note what they did well, remark on areas they had trouble with, and observe student responses to questions. Quizzing students at the end of the lesson gives you information about how well they learned the material. Although remaining undocumented, such informal assessments can be used to decide whether the lesson outcome was met or needs to be revisited at a later time.

As you can now see, a daily physical education lesson plan is similar to a lesson plan you write for the classroom. There is an introduction, a learning progression, and conclusion in both types of plan. The principal difference is in content development. In a classroom lesson plan, the steps in a learning activity are few but more involved. A lesson on the importance and mechanics of brushing the teeth might involve: (1) reading a related story, (2) discussing the main points in the story, (3) giving a demonstration of brushing, (4) practicing brushing, and (5) writing a letter to parents telling them why brushing is important. But a physical education lesson plan typically lists many tasks, with quick transitions from one to the next when necessary.

LESSON PLAN FORMATS

Your plan format can range from very detailed to a mere outline. The most helpful formats for elementary education teachers are the **scripted format** and the **column format**. Each uses the same elements just discussed but arranges them differently.

Scripted Formats

The scripted format requires you to write down exactly what you plan to say to children throughout the lesson. From the *set induction* to the *closure*, you write the scripted part of the plan as if speaking to the children. Application 4.2 gives an example of a scripted lesson plan.

Although detailed and time-consuming to write, a scripted plan has conspicuous advantages. Beginning teachers benefit from this format because it forces them to think through all a lesson's transitions, such as from set induction to the first task, from one task to next, and from the last task to closure. Transition points often cause beginning teachers difficulty, either because teachers don't clearly say what to do next, leaving children to their own interpretations, or because they are unsure or forget what they want the children to do next. This leads to gaps in the lesson that may cause students to lose attention. Even though the scripted lesson takes more time to write, the detail helps you remember what to say and how and when to say it.

Column Lesson Plans

A column lesson plan is divided into sections that highlight the lesson's content development (see Application 4.3). Although the same information is included on the lesson plan, it takes less time to write and is less detailed than the scripted format.

The columns in this format remind the teacher where he or she plans to go next in the lesson. With less detail, teachers can rely on their knowledge and experience to know when and how to transition between tasks during the lesson. Think of the column lesson plan as a series of note cards to follow when giving a speech. Greater experience allows you to write a less explicit plan.

INQUIRING MINDS

When writing your daily lesson plan, how many extensions do you typically include? Applications? Refinements? Is this a different number if you are teaching younger or older age groups?

scripted format
A plan showing word-for-word what the teacher will say during the lesson.

column format
A lesson plan divided into sections of pertinent information.

Grade Level	1
Skill Theme	Dribbling with the hand
Lesson Outcome/ Learnable Piece	At the end of the lesson, children will have learned to dribble the ball while using the pads of their fingers for control.
Equipment/Materials	❏ 25 basketballs ❏ 50 cones, 25 hula hoops ❏ two red foam balls ❏ two green foam balls
Protocols	"Begin" to start an activity "Freeze" to stop an activity Home place—where class starts and ends Balls are to be placed under the arm each time an activity ends.
Instant Activity	*Title:* Germ tag[a] *Materials Needed:* Cones to define playing area, two red foam balls, and two green foam balls *Description:* Have students find a good self-space in the activity area. Give two students a green ball (make sure it is a ball they can hold in one hand) and give two students a red ball. The students with the red balls are the "germs" and the students with the green balls are the "doctors." On the teacher's signal ("Begin"), the students are to move throughout the area according to the teacher's locomotor movement choice (e.g., walking, sliding, skipping, etc.) trying to avoid being tagged by the students with the red "germ" balls. If the students without the balls get tagged (no throwing the ball) by a red "germ" ball, then they are to stop and pretend they are sick or hurt. To get unfrozen, they have to be tagged by students with the green "doctor" balls. Then they are free to move in the game again after being cured (i.e., tagged) by a "doctor" ball. Stop the game after a minute or so and have new students carry the doctor and germ balls.
Set Induction	Does anybody have a pet dog? Have you taught it any tricks like sit, roll over, or jump? When you teach dogs tricks, you must reward them for doing a good job. The best way to reward a dog is to pat him and tell him "good job." Well, this is my pet ball (holding up a basketball), and I am going to pretend it is a dog. I am going name my dog ball Bouncer. I am going to teach Bouncer how to dribble (demonstrate dribbling). I am going to give each of you a ball, and I want you to pretend it is a dog, too. First thing I want you to do is name your dogs. Then you are going to teach your dog ball a trick. You are going to teach it how to dribble. Remember, dogs work best if they are rewarded with pats. They love it when you use your finger pads to pat them. To get your dog balls to dribble, you must use your finger pads. a. Taken from PE Central, www.pecentral.org/lessonideas/ia/archive9798/ia199798.html

Extensions [E] Applications [A] Refinement [R]	1. **[E]** Stand in a hoop (home) and bounce the ball one time and catch it with two hands. Make sure to use your finger pads and say "good (insert name that you gave the ball)!" Continue practicinguntil I say, "Freeze."
	2. **[E]** Everybody is doing quite well practicing. Let's now try to teach our balls to dribble. Drop your ball as you did before, and instead of catching it, use your finger pads to push it back down with both hands. This motion is called dribbling. Let's try to dribble our balls once or twice and then catch them. Ready, begin!
	3. **[E]** I think you are ready to do it with one hand. Just as we did before, bounce your ball once and catch it while staying in your self-space, except this time put one hand behind your back.
	4. **[E]** Now try to dribble it with one hand and keep it going. Put your other hand behind your back. Ready, begin! **[R]** Don't forget to use your finger pads to pat your dog!
	5. **[A]** Good. If you think you are ready, let's see if you can get your dog to perform a trick. Let's see how many times you can dribble the ball before we need to catch it. **[R]** Dogs love for their owners to pet them, so don't forget to pat your dog with your finger pads while it is bouncing. Ready, begin!
	6. **[E]** Now change hands and try to bounce your dog once and catch it. Keep practicing until I say, "Freeze."
	7. **[E]** You are all still working nicely. This time, dribble with this hand and keep it going before catching it. **[R]** Remember to pat your dogs with your finger pads.
	8. **[E]** Everybody is training his or her dog well. Let's see if you can get your dog to bounce around your hoop using the hand you write with. Ready, begin!
	9. **[A]** Let's see if you can get your dog to perform another trick. Let's see if you can dribble the ball around your hoop without losing control. Ready, begin!
	10. **[E]** Good. Now I would like you to use your other hand and dribble it around the hoop.
	11. **[E]** I think our dogs are ready to go for a walk. When I say begin, dribble your ball in general space with one hand. As you dribble, try not to bump into your neighbor. **[R]** Don't forget to pat your dog with your finger pads.
	12. **[A]** Let's see if you can get your dog to perform another trick. Let's just see how well they are trained. See how long you can dribble your ball in general space without losing control.
Refinement	Finger pads
Closure	Today we focused on dribbling a ball better. We used a certain part of our hand in order to do this. What part of our hands do we use to dribble a ball? Show me the correct way to do this. The correct way to dribble a ball is to use the pads of your fingers. All right, let's pet our dog one last time as we put the balls up for the day.
Assessment	Individual observation

Grade Level:	2
Skill Theme:	Striking with paddle
Lesson Outcome/Learnable Piece:	Flat paddle; Firm wrist
Equipment/Materials:	One large balloon for each student
	One paddle for each student
	Tape
Protocols:	Start command: "Action"
	Stop command: "Cut"
	Equipment: Place balloons between feet on stop command
	Wrap-up: Home Base
Instant Activity:	Locomotor obstacle course
Set Induction:	Today we are going find out how to make a balloon go up in the air. We are going to do that by using a flat paddle.

Extensions [E]	Refinements [R]	Applications [A]	Organization
Hit balloons into air with paddles (stationary)	Flat like a pancake	See how many times you can hit it without moving from the spot.	Scatter Self-space
Hit balloon at different levels	Keep paddle flat		Scatter General space
Hit balloon back and forth with partner, keeping balloon off floor (close distance)	Firm wrist	See how long you can hit the balloon back and forth before it touches the ground. I'll time you . . . ready . . . go.	Staggered column
Continue the previous task, increasing the distance			
Stand sideways while hitting back and forth			Two cones, jump rope ▲ ▲
Stand across the net from your partner and strike back and forth without letting the balloon hit the floor	Flat paddle	Every time the balloon hits the paddles, say one letter of your name. See if you can keep it going long enough to spell both of your names.	Two cones, jump rope ▲ ▲
Hit the balloon to your partner (overhead)	Remember, the paddle should be flat on contact.		Two cones, jump rope ▲ ▲
Hit the balloon to your partner (underhand)	Firm wrist		

Refinement:	Flat paddle, firm wrist
Closure:	Review learnable piece/s: Flat paddle and firm wrist
Assessment:	Recognition check

FINAL WORDS

Planning a physical education lesson doesn't inspire enthusiasm in most teachers; it is hard work to plan creative lessons that motivate and engage children. But as you grow as a teacher, your planning ability will be aided by your classroom experience, and you will see the need for flexibility and persistence, since lessons very rarely go exactly as you plan them.

Teachers who fail to plan often revert to the three *R*'s of physical education: roll call, roll out the ball, and relax. This violates the fundamental tenet of teaching, which is to enhance student achievement. Your daily physical education lesson plans must have clearly identified outcomes and a sequence of tasks designed to meet them.

OVER TO YOU

1. Your classmate shares his concern with planning and implementing a lesson. What observations would you give him to alleviate some of his anxiety?

2. Your principal wants you to submit a yearly plan documenting what you will cover in physical education. What steps would you take and what resources would you use to gather this information?

3. What are three places on the daily lesson plan where you should see the student objective?

PORTFOLIO TASKS

1. Create a set of flash cards to be used as a study guide for the information covered in this chapter.

2. In developing the content of a daily lesson plan, there are three types of tasks: extending, refining, and applying. On a sheet of paper, distinguish among these and write an example of each that was not presented in the chapter.

3. In the following examples, underline the lesson objective in terms of the learnable piece:

   ■ By the end of the lesson, the student will have learned to keep step with the opposite foot when throwing.

   ■ By the end of the lesson, the student will have learned to keep head up while traveling in general space.

   ■ By the end of the lesson, the student will have learned when shooting in floor hockey to keep the blade low on the follow-through toward the target.

REFERENCES

Lee, A. (2003). How the field evolved. In S. J. Silverman & C. D. Ennis (eds.), *Student learning in physical education* (2nd ed.) (pp. 9–25). Champaign, IL: Human Kinetics.

National Association for Sport and Physical Education. (2002). *Shape of the nation report.* Reston, VA: American Alliance for Health, Physical Education, Recreation and Dance.

National Association for Sport and Physical Education. (2003). *National standards for beginning teachers* (2nd ed.). Reston, VA: American Alliance for Health, Physical Education, Recreation and Dance.

National Association for Sport and Physical Education. (2004). *Moving into the future: National standards for physical education* (2nd ed.). Reston, VA: Author.

Rink, J. E. (2002). *Teaching physical education for learning* (4th ed.). Boston: McGraw-Hill.

5

STRATEGIES FOR INSTRUCTION

CHAPTER OUTLINE

GETTING STARTED

1. How do teachers stimulate students' interest and engage them in a lesson?

2. What makes a good question? Give two examples of good questions for assessing student understanding.

3. What strategies can be used to individualize classroom instruction? Could these strategies be used in physical education?

M any teachers ask themselves, "How do I present content so that all my students benefit from my instruction?" Designing learning experiences to benefit each child is difficult, especially with children who have trouble sitting still, like to call out when others are talking, appear tired or bored by the material, or have different learning styles or ability levels.

Remember that teaching is a complex and continually evolving process, with no one best way to present content. Your delivery methods for instruction in physical education are as varied as your students. Many contextual variables will affect your teaching, including the number of children in the class and the available facilities. No two classes are the same, and neither are any two students. This chapter examines key instruction issues and presents strategies to create dynamic physical education lessons. The aim is to show you how to use these strategies from the beginning to the end to make instruction more meaningful and interactive.

THE IMPORTANCE OF EFFECTIVE COMMUNICATION

As discussed in Chapter 1, effective teachers are good communicators. Lessons succeed when the teacher communicates clearly and accurately with students. You can do this by breaking information down into manageable pieces to aid student understanding. For example, you can limit the number of learnable pieces in a lesson (Chapter 4) or limit the number of tasks students practice at one time.

You can enhance communication with rules and procedures (Chapters 7, 8, and 9) that speak directly to your expectations for student behavior, such as transitioning from the classroom to the gymnasium or giving the appropriate response when hearing stop and start signals. Not clearly communicating and reinforcing simple expectations can hinder instruction. Express satisfaction with how students meet expectations either verbally ("I like the way you stopped and put your equipment on the ground") or nonverbally (a frown or shake of the head). The research in physical education shows that students spend a lot of time listening to instructions, waiting, and transitioning between activities (Metzler, 1989), thus reducing practice time. However information is presented, it should be done quickly and efficiently so as not to detract from the learning process.

TABLE 5.1 ■ Anatomy of a Lesson

	Phase	Lesson Part	Teacher Strategy/Actions	
Lesson Start		Prelesson	Instant Activity	
	1	Beginning the Lesson	Set Induction (Scaffolding)	
	2	Body of the Lesson	Instructional Action • Demonstration • Questioning • Checking for Understanding • Monitoring	Associated Strategy • Direct Instruction • K-W-L • Problem Solving • Checking for Understanding • Feedback • Individualizing Instruction
Lesson End	3	Closure/Review	• Questioning • Checking for Understanding	

STRATEGIES FOR STRUCTURING A LESSON

Although there are numerous ways to present content to children, the lesson components are similar whether you are teaching in a classroom or a gymnasium. Most have three phases. The first phase, an introduction or introductory activity, stimulates interest in the lesson topic. The teacher might tell a story with a puppet, read a book related to the topic, review related material, or demonstrate the activity. The intent of these different beginning activities is to pique children's interest, getting them excited and ready to learn. During the second phase, the body of the lesson, teachers engage students in learning experiences or activities to promote understanding of the material. Finally, the teacher ends or closes the lesson by reviewing the lesson's outcome, assessing how well the children learned the material.

These three phases provide a foundation from which to build a lesson. Table 5.1 outlines our recommended anatomy of a lesson, showing teaching strategies for each phase from the beginning to the end of a lesson. This chapter explores some of these strategies in detail to see how they can be used within the context of a lesson.

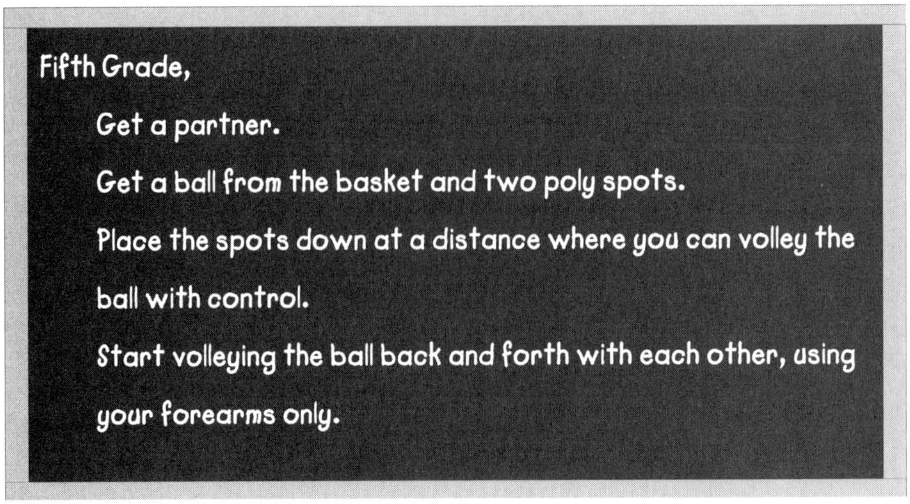

FIGURE **5.1**
This teacher has written instructions for an instant activity on the blackboard, making sure there is a minimum of reading for the students.

Fifth Grade,

  Get a partner.

  Get a ball from the basket and two poly spots.

  Place the spots down at a distance where you can volley the ball with control.

  Start volleying the ball back and forth with each other, using your forearms only.

BEGIN CLASS WITH AN INSTANT ACTIVITY

Most elementary school children love being active. Because they spend most of their day sitting, children can't wait to get up and move around. Unfortunately, many physical education teachers begin a lesson by sitting children down to explain the day's tasks.

Instead, provide children with an **instant activity**, a brief movement task that can begin immediately, with little or no instruction or explanation. Beginning class with an instant activity tells children you believe that being active is important. It also lets children burn off a little steam. But instant activities can also contribute to your lesson's content by reinforcing or reviewing a previous lesson's skill or developing a specific area of fitness, such as flexibility or muscular endurance.

Presenting the Instant Activity

As the name suggests, an instant activity's goal is to start children moving as soon as possible. These activities must be kept simple. Some physical education teachers defeat the purpose by creating an instant activity so complex that children have to wait and listen for two or more minutes of explanation before they begin.

There are two ways to present an instant activity. The first is simply to tell the students what you want them to do; and the second is to use a blackboard, posterboard, or whiteboard to present the activity. If you are introducing an instant activity on a board, you should minimize reading, and the activity should involve a task the students already know (see Figure 5.1). Application 5.1 gives instant activities that may be verbalized or read to students.

The Benefits of Instant Activities

instant activity
A brief movement task children will begin immediately upon arrival at the work area.

Instant activities have a number of benefits beyond providing children with the opportunity to move around. The instant activity also gives you a moment to gather your thoughts before the lesson begins; coming straight from the classroom, you need a brief time to switch into physical education teacher mode. As the physical education teacher, you have to allow students freedom to explore movement and must encourage them to be active, which requires a somewhat different frame of mind than the one you have in the classroom, where space and the freedom to engage in physical activity are limited.

The instant activity also makes it easier to present the next phase of the lesson. Children seem more attentive to instruction when they have been active at the beginning of the lesson. Brain research suggests that movement spurs cognition (Sylvester, 2000) and that young children have better focus and concentration after physical activity (Jensen, 2000).

The instant activity can also take you off center stage. As the students work independently, you have extra time to have a private chat with an individual student about his or her behavior in a previous lesson or to check on students who say they are not feeling well. You might also work exclusively on skill development with a child with a disability while monitoring the class.

Finally, instant activities can review material previously taught. If you already had taught a lesson on dribbling with the feet, you could allow students to work on that before the start of the new lesson. The instant activity could also be a lead-in to the day's lesson; students could check their heart rate after jumping rope for two minutes and then use that activity to start a lesson on cardiovascular endurance (see Chapter 15 for other examples of fitness tasks).

FIGURE **5.2**
It is important to communicate to students at the beginning of a lesson what they will be learning.

Creating Your Own Instant Activities

When creating an instant activity, keep it simple, short, and lively. Instant activities are fun and engaging and easy to create. An instant activity can be as simple as letting children practice a previously learned task for a short period of time when they first enter the gym. Or you can use the Internet to locate instant activities that other teachers have uploaded, which can be used as is or modified to suit your situation (by using whiffle balls instead of tennis balls, for example). An especially good website with numerous ideas for instant activities for all age groups and content areas is PE Central (www.pecentral.org).

BEGINNING A LESSON

Once the instant activity is over and children have released some pent-up energy from being in the classroom and are focused on moving, you can begin the lesson. This is the time to stimulate students' interest and describe what they will be learning. Children love to use their imaginations, and the beginning of a lesson is a good time to involve this part of their brains. You also want to communicate the lesson's goals to help children understand its importance. Teachers help children make these connections in different ways; books, videos, or playacting can tie the known to the unknown. The start of the lesson is critical in fostering children's interest and helping them understand the purpose of the material. The teacher in Figure 5.2 is using a balloon to begin a lesson on volleying.

Today we are going to pretend to be the person who walks the high wire at the circus. Because the wire is really high, we need to have good balance so we won't fall off when we "walk" across it. One thing you will need to do to be sure that you have good balance is to use airplane arms. Yoshiro, can you show me what you think I mean by airplane arms? That's right, arms out to the side as straight as they can be. Today, while we are pretending to walk the high wire, let's remember to use those airplane arms so we won't fall off the wire.

How to Introduce the Day's Lesson

At the beginning of any physical education lesson, you must tell children what they will be working on and why it is beneficial to them, letting them know what they will be accountable for learning during the lesson. This process of introducing a lesson is called the **set induction**, sometimes referred to as the *anticipatory set*. Knowing what they are going to be working on for the day and why it is important helps to alleviate some of the students' uncertainty and eliminates questions like "What are we going to be doing today?" See Application 5.2 for an example of a set induction for a balancing lesson.

The set induction tells students what they will be learning, motivates them, and sparks their interest. Whether you use a metaphor, riddle, story, picture, or question to bring the topic of the day to life, the set induction connects *what* is to be learned to *why* it is important. For example, the set induction or balancing should help students see how maintaining balance is critical to success in many physical activities in the gymnasium, on the playground, and in daily living. Children are more attentive and try harder when they can see how they will benefit from what they are learning.

Scaffolding: Building a Foundation for Present and Future Skills

When learning new material, we all benefit from relating to things we already know. The set induction makes this connection for children. Linking students' previous knowledge, work, or experiences with what will be covered in the present or future is called **scaffolding**. Physical education lessons, just like classroom lessons, are sequential in nature and build upon each other.

Consider a lesson on dribbling with the hand. Maybe your students have previous experience dribbling with control while stationary (past experience); now you want to teach them to use that control while moving around space and obstacles

set induction
A method for introducing the focus for the lesson.

scaffolding
Linking students' previous knowledge, work, or experience with what will be covered in the present or future.

in front of them (present and future skills). Dribbling while stationary is the piece of the scaffold that helps build up to dribbling while moving (see Application 5.3). The next level on the dribbling scaffold would involve helping children dribble with control while moving with someone guarding them, as in a modified game of basketball or team handball.

Scaffolding also makes clear to children that what is practiced today, such as balancing on various objects, can be used in related activities like riding a bike or skateboarding.

Designing a Set Induction

You have to excite children about learning, and set induction is your first opportunity to make this happen. Two key elements are needed to create an effective set induction. First, enter the world of the children you teach. Relate the content to things they know and like. For younger children you could use comic book superheroes, popular children's shows, zoo animals, or puppets. The following scenario uses a comic book superhero in a set induction to teach first graders about muscular strength:

> Today, we are going to learn how to make ourselves stronger. You know someone who is really strong? Superman! What are some of the things that Superman can lift? Right! Cars, buildings, and houses. In class today, we are going to participate in activities that help make our arms become stronger, like Superman's. For many of these activities (bear walk, crab walk, wall push-up), I want you to concentrate on keeping your arms straight to help keep your body upright.

For older children, use name games, popular movie characters, riddles, or athletes in various sports. Here is an example of using the name game in the set induction when teaching fifth graders about throwing a Frisbee:

> Let's play "What Am I?" I am thinking of an object, and I will give you three clues to figure out what it is. First, it is round and has a semiflat shape. What

FIGURE **5.3**
Body posture is an important way to demonstrate enthusiasm toward the content. This teacher shows a genuine interest in the student's response.

am I? Second, it can be thrown in the air in a number of ways. What am I? Third, it is sometimes referred to as a disc or a flying saucer. What am I? Right, it's a Frisbee! Today, we are going to learn how to throw the Frisbee while keeping the thumb on top, the index finger on the edge, and the other fingers underneath. Doing those things will help the Frisbee fly more naturally.

Relating the information to what students already know puts them in a receptive frame of mind. Second, you have to sell the lesson. You should set the tone by being enthusiastic about what you are going to teach. You often interest children by *how* you say things, not what you say. Your voice inflection and body gestures (moving hands or shaking the head) can change the tone of what you say and how it is perceived (see Figure 5.3). Salespeople, ringmasters, and emcees do this all the time to sell products or excite an audience. The set induction sets your tone, so use it to your advantage to get the lesson off to a good start.

THE BODY OF THE LESSON

As discussed in Chapter 4, the majority of the lesson should be spent developing content by providing learning tasks or practice activities for the students that help them meet the lesson outcomes. While presenting these tasks, use a variety of strategies to help students understand and get them involved. This section focuses on strategies to present, engage, interact with, and monitor students during the lesson.

VISUAL DEMONSTRATION

When teaching skills, children benefit from visual demonstrations of the skill the teacher wants them to perform. Visual demonstrations communicate specific information to students about performing a task or skill. They benefit students most in the beginning stages of skill practice and are most effective when they give children critical elements (cues) for performing the skill (Pollack & Lee, 1992). Giving such cues during the demonstration improves the form or quality of performance (Roach & Burwitz, 1986) and is particularly useful to young children who are acquiring a new movement pattern (McCullagh, Stiehl, & Weiss, 1990).

A four-pronged approach is recommended for presenting demonstrations to students:

INQUIRING MINDS

In what type of physical education activities do you most often use convergent and divergent problem solving? Why?

1. *Demonstrate the skill, but don't speak:* You can't possibly tell students everything they need to know about performing a skill in one lesson. Children suffering from information overload will have a hard time processing everything the teacher is saying. Talking during the demonstration is especially distracting to young children, so we suggest that you first demonstrate the skill without speaking. This helps the children to focus on only one thing—the skill itself.

2. *Repeat the demonstration, but slow it down:* After the initial demonstration, provide a second in slow speed while giving students verbal cues or critical elements of the skill you want them to practice. Keep the cues brief. The demonstration should show the cues you want to emphasize during the lesson. In a dribbling lesson, you might make sure students focus on using the "pads of the fingers" or keeping a "flexible wrist."

3. *Demonstrate the required task at full speed:* It is extremely important for children to see an accurate demonstration of the task you are asking them to perform, so be sure you demonstrate the skill again at full speed under the same conditions in which students will be required to practice it. If you are teaching dribbling around cones, use the cones in your demonstration. If you cannot demonstrate the skill accurately, find a talented student or a special guest who can.

4. *Provide different views:* When giving a demonstration, make sure you show students different views of it, such as front and side, while emphasizing the cues you want them to learn and practice. If a lesson is focused on dribbling using a flexible wrist, show this straight on as well as from the side.

QUESTIONING AND PROBLEM SOLVING

Throughout any lesson in physical education (or in the classroom), teachers use questioning or problem solving to keep students involved. Although these could be considered two different strategies, we believe that good questioning ties into

Mr. Curtis is concluding his lesson on putting with a series of questions. What are some inherent problems with these questions: "Who enjoyed using the golf clubs today?" "Do we focus on our wrists or on our entire arm when we are putting?" "Frankie, there are three critical cues we need to remember while putting. Can you name them?"

WHAT'S WRONG WITH THIS PICTURE?

problem-solving strategies, so in this book we refer to questioning and problem solving as the same strategy.

Both encourage children to be active participants in the learning process. Children must be involved learners, not just passive receivers of information. Good high-level questioning strategies engage students by fostering critical thinking skills, thereby encouraging interaction to create students' own sense of understanding.

Framing Questions

The first step in questioning students is deciding how to frame the question. This decision centers on the type of information you want the student to discover. Beginning teachers tend to ask closed or rhetorical questions. A *closed question* requires a simple "yes" or "no" answer or a brief response; it is best used simply to help students recall information. An example of a closed question would be, "Do we use our finger pads or our palms when we are dribbling?"

Rhetorical questions are bad because they solicit no response from students. Most often, they are asked merely for effect. Examples include:

- "We had fun today, didn't we?"

- "All right, let's get started. Can we get the balls out of the basket?"

- "We are going to use our finger pads, OK?"

Several ways of framing a question can encourage students to show what they know about the material. Students can also show differing levels of understanding depending on the type of question asked. Questions clarify what students understand, probe students' understanding of consequence, or seek justification or reasoning for a position or action.

Questions of clarification demonstrate whether students can recall or remember what has been said or taught. The teacher uses such a question to check quickly for basic knowledge or comprehension. Teachers also use questions that probe an action's consequences and urge students to use higher levels of thinking so they will apply what they know and determine what might happen next. For example, when you ask students what would happen if they used a firm wrist when dribbling a basketball, you would expect them to say it would make it more difficult to control the ball and keep it away from a defender. Finally, some questions examine whether students can justify the importance of certain actions or positions. To

TABLE 5.2 ■ Examples of Framing Questions

Type of Question	Example Questions
Clarification	What do I mean when I say to dribble your ball at a low level?
	Can you show me an example of a symmetrical shape?
	How can we be sure the ball is under control when we dribble?
Consequence	If I don't keep the ball close to my body while dribbling, what could a defender do more easily?
	What would happen if I didn't extend my arms out to the side while balancing?
	What would happen if I volleyed the ball on a tilted surface instead of a flat surface?
Justification or Reasoning	Why should I keep my head up when dribbling?
	What is the most critical element in balancing?
	Is there ever a time when using a flat surface is not desirable in volleying?

answer these, students must use previous knowledge to build or defend their position, making a relevant argument to support what they think is true. For example, a student who believes that having "tight muscles" is important in maintaining a good balanced position must be able to explain why. See Table 5.2 for a broader range of questions that require different levels of thinking.

A question that encourages students to make connections is a critical first step in engaging them in the course content and encouraging them to think for themselves. A good question enhances and extends learning while making the student want to know more. These higher-level questions are meant to take children beyond basic recall and challenge them to build on previous experience and prior knowledge so they can reach new levels of understanding.

Effective Strategies for Receiving Responses

A key issue tied closely with questioning is how to receive student responses. This can be a difficult area for new teachers, who often interpret silence as not knowing the answer to a question. Because some students process information quicker than others, the teacher needs a strategy that allows each student a chance to respond. This avoids situations in which one or two students consistently shout out the answer immediately after a question has been asked.

In the game show *Jeopardy,* contestants have to phrase their answer in the form of a question; failure to do so constitutes an incorrect response. Luckily, when you play *Jeopardy* at home, you can yell out the answer without consequence. Children also like to shout out when they think they know the answer. In a **callout,** children respond to a question simultaneously and immediately (Graham, 2001). Individual callouts are acceptable, but allowing the class to call out at one time can

callout
Responding to a question simultaneously and immediately.

FIGURE **5.4**
Having students raise their hands has a number of advantages; it allows you, the teacher, to select the student you wish to answer.

be problematic. Collective responding often leads students to become more excited and yell louder in order to be heard. This takes time away from instruction because it takes time for the children to calm down. The phrasing of a question often leads to spontaneous responding or calling out. Rhetorical questions and recall questions such as, "What sport does Michael Jordan play?" are especially prone to callouts.

One useful strategy that discourages calling out is to have students raise their hands (see Figure 5.4). When teachers encourage students to call out answers without raising their hands, children often continue to yell the answer at an ever-increasing volume to get the teacher's attention. While it is stimulating to see students this excited about answering, there are a number of reasons why students should raise their hands instead. For example, you may want to ask a specific student a question or find out from a show of hands how many students think they know the answer. Also, some students take longer to develop their answers, and a callout either distracts them or gives them the correct response without working it out for themselves.

We know a classroom teacher who uses this strategy for receiving responses, with points assigned for correctly given oral responses. This teacher then tallies the points to track student performance or responses to questions. Students are awarded a point each time they raise their hand and give the correct response in class. A student who accumulates a predetermined number of points is either given a particular grade or becomes eligible for a reward such as a library token (to help buy books) or some choice time at the end of the week.

You could also create a "Physical Education Response Club" where students earn membership when they have a certain number of points. Clearly, the teacher must establish a system that allows each child a chance to respond if this strategy is employed. A checklist can be used to record and track student points. Students can also keep track of the points themselves, keeping the information in a student portfolio (see Chapter 6 for more details on physical education portfolios).

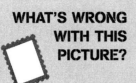

You may also want children to allow children to answer by giving a **movement response,** that is, to show you what they understand through a demonstration instead of verbally.

Wait Time

Some children need more time to think about questions and formulate answers before responding. Certain strategies can give these children the chance to engage in the class's question-and-answer session without feeling awkward or put on the spot. One teacher liked to drink bottled water while he taught. His students claimed he was notorious for saying, "You think while I drink," after asking a question. Students were to wait until after he had taken a sip of water before responding. He said he used that time to encourage children to think before responding and that students were more likely to respond when the pressure of answering quickly was off.

As discussed earlier in this chapter, the way a teacher asks a question can allow some students to excuse themselves from the question-and-answer process. If you frame the question with, "Who can tell me . . . ?" or "Can anyone name . . . ?" students may not bother to think of an answer because they realize the question was not addressed to anyone in particular. But if you use wait time and ask good questions, students won't have the comfort of dissociating themselves from the class like that. Wait time also allows students to think through possible answers to the question in case you do call on them. Some questions that allow for wait time might be:

- "Name three critical cues to remember while dribbling a ball with our hands . . . [wait] . . . Desiree?"

- "In a moment I'm going to call on someone to tell me how we can make our pelican stand more stable . . ."

- "I'm thinking of the name of a person who I want to answer the following question. Where does the ball go when we contact it with our arms held in front of us at shoulder level?"

Students must be encouraged to answer questions and participate. Providing wait time lets them reflect, formulate, ask, answer, and discuss questions.

movement response
Children provide answers to questions through movement rather than orally or by writing an answer. This could be prompted by asking them, "Show me a stable base that has only two body parts in contact with the floor."

TABLE **5.3** ■ K-W-L: Dribbling Example

K-W-L	Example Questions	Possible Student Responses
Know	Who can tell me everything they know about dribbling a basketball?	You have to bounce the ball. Use it in basketball. You can't walk with it. Try to keep it below the waist.
Want	In the game of basketball, people try to take the ball away from you as you dribble. Therefore, you need to make sure you can control the ball so it will be harder for them to take it away from you. So what part of your body do you think you should use to help you better control the ball?	Hand Fingers Palm You *want* them to learn to say: Finger pads Flexible wrist
Learn	Can you tell me one thing you learned today that will help you control the ball better when you dribble?	Use the pads of fingers. Keep the wrist loose.

TYPES OF QUESTIONS

Questioning is an important strategy if used appropriately. Most beginning teachers find that asking good questions to get children thinking is more difficult than it appears. Making sure you are asking questions of substance is part of the planning process for beginning teachers, so this section outlines different types of questions to probe children's higher-order thinking skills.

Know-Want-Learn (K-W-L)

One strategy to improve questioning quality comes from classroom literature on reading: *K-W-L* (Know, Want, and Learn). *K* or *know,* the first step in questioning, is used to establish what the student already knows. For example, ask students what they know about dribbling and note their responses. The next step, *W* or *want,* is used to help students understand the important concept or information; for example, that using one's finger pads helps control the ball while dribbling. Finally, the last step, *L* or *Learn,* establishes what the students learned about the topic. For example, at the end of the lesson on dribbling, ask children what part of their body helps them dribble with control. K-W-L questioning discovers what children already know, connects it to what you want them to learn, and then determines what was learned. Table 5.3 gives more examples on how to use K-W-L.

Convergent Problem Solving

Different types of problem-solving questions can be used to stimulate children to explore movement problems. **Convergent problem solving** uses a question or a linear progression of questions to guide the student in discovering one single

convergent problem solving
A type of inquiry that uses a linear progression of questions to guide the student in discovering one single answer.

answer (Mosston & Ashworth, 2003). In other words, your questions guide the student toward the right answer, so convergent problem solving is also known as *guided discovery.*

When you use this technique, give the child time to discover the answer. To make this process easier, you may need to give *guiding hints,* such as, "What part of the body do we use to contact the ball with while dribbling?" or "Should our arms look like an airplane or a pencil when we are trying to balance?" The key is to *help* students discover the answer, not to answer the question for them. Beginning teachers often struggle with this because they are so keen to move through a lesson quickly and feel awkward when students struggle. Here is an example of using convergent problem solving to help students discover the cue for balancing:

1. I want everyone to balance on one foot with your arms against your sides like a pencil and see how far you can lean forward without losing your balance.

2. Now, balance on one foot with your arms out forming a *V* on each side of the body. Again, see how far you can lean forward without losing your balance.

3. This time I want you to balance on one foot with your arms extended out from your sides like the wings of an airplane. See how far you can lean forward without losing your balance.

4. Raise your hand if you can tell me which one of the three ways of holding your arms allowed you to lean forward the most.

5. Right. It was the airplane wings.

Divergent Problem Solving

Open-ended or divergent questions have multiple correct answers. **Divergent problem solving** lets children independently generate their own correct responses (Mosston & Ashworth, 2003). This gives them the freedom to explore movement, experience new and creative solutions to movement challenges, and use higher-order thinking skills. For example, you might ask children to demonstrate the movement of an animal that travels quickly. Because there are numerous answers to this problem, such as traveling like a rabbit, tiger, or bird, the children can create their own unique response to meet the "movement problem" posed by the teacher.

Movement challenges or "problems" are thus explored. One key to fostering critical thinking skills and making children use higher order thinking is posing questions with multiple correct answers or solutions. Examples of divergent problem solving tasks or questions include:

- Show me all the different ways you can balance on two different body parts (see Figure 5.5 for one possible answer).

- What are some of the different ways you can hit the ball with the racket while remaining in self-space?

divergent problem solving
A type of inquiry in which the teacher presents the students with a problem and then challenges them to find multiple solutions.

FIGURE **5.5**
Divergent problem solving techniques use questions that typically require movement responses—sometimes many different correct responses. This student is demonstrating one correct answer to the problem of balancing on two different body parts.

- In your group, create a balancing routine on the beam with a mount, traveling sequence, and a dismount.
- Show me another way to protect your soccer ball from an opponent when dribbling.

CHECKING FOR UNDERSTANDING

Checking for understanding is an instructional strategy used to see how well students comprehend instructional content (Graham, 2001). "Does everybody understand?" is a typical question teachers pose to see whether students know what they are supposed to do. But this type of question seldom elicits enough responses to reveal anything. Teachers may also quickly scan the class to see whether students understand, relying on facial expressions, attentive looks, affirmative gestures, or appropriate movement responses. But these mannerisms may not match what students are actually doing or thinking. In fact, some students may look extremely interested in what you are saying while actually daydreaming about the next soccer game or newest Nintendo video game.

Strategies for Checking for Understanding

Siedentop and Tannehill (2000) suggest specifically checking to be sure the children accurately receive the information you've given. Use the following questioning techniques and demonstrations to make sure you are receiving an accurate picture of student understanding.

FIGURE **5.6**
The teacher of the students in this photo asked them to show how to trap a ball using the sole of the foot. This performance check quickly assessed student understanding of the task.

Performance Check

In a performance check, students are asked to physically demonstrate in unison the answer to the question. For example, you may ask students to demonstrate a balanced position or the correct body position to protect a ball from a defender while dribbling. You should develop a prompt word or words (e.g., "action," "show me") or another signal to alert children to demonstrate the skill. This doesn't guarantee student understanding, but it does encourage students to think through the task and then attempt to respond accordingly. Figure 5.6 shows a situation where the teacher has asked her students to demonstrate "use light force," a key cue for trapping a soccer ball.

Another performance check asks for student volunteers to demonstrate what they learned that day. In a warm and inviting environment, many students will willingly offer. For example, you might say, "Can someone show me the leg position for volleying a ball on the thigh?" Or, "In a second, I'm going to be looking for a volunteer to demonstrate a tripod balance."

Choral Responding

Students might respond to a question orally or with a physical action. The class responds orally if you have encouraged choral responding by saying, "I want you to respond 'yes' if this is a symmetrical balance position or 'no' if it is an asymmetrical balance position." Then do a quick check to see how many students responded. This method quickly assesses student understanding (Siedentop & Tannehill, 2000), but a drawback of choral responding is uncertainty about which children actually responded. A loud response may not truly indicate how many students know the answer.

Recognition Checks

A recognition check uses physical gestures, such as a thumbs-up or thumbs-down, to assess understanding. You might say, "Give me a thumbs-up if this is the correct way to volley a ball and a thumbs-down if it's wrong." After the demonstration, you need to wait for the hand signals to see whether students recognize the difference in performance techniques. Another example of a recognition check is for you to ask students to point to an area, boundary, or piece of equipment when prompted by a cue word or question:

- "Point to the picture on the wall that shows a person demonstrating a 'symmetrical' shape."
- "When I say 'hand,' place your finger pads on the ball in front of you."

These quick and unobtrusive ways to assess student understanding will help the learning process. Checking should be slow only when there is a conspicuous lack of understanding. Effective checks let you make ongoing assessments of student comprehension and lesson progress. The key to effective checking for understanding is to use strategies that accurately reflect what *all* students know, not just one or two. Questions like "Who can tell me what we worked on today?" or, "What is one thing I can do to be a better dribbler?" encourage a response from only *one* student, failing to give a true measure of what *most* students learned from the lesson. You want strategies that let you measure what the *whole* class learned.

Lack of Response to Checks for Understanding

Students may not respond to teachers' questions about comprehension for several reasons: they may fear being embarrassed; they may not understand what the teacher is asking; or they may be bored with the material. Some teachers may unknowingly foster an atmosphere where children fear reproach from the teacher or other children when asking questions. Such children's strategies for having their questions answered include silent observation, quietly asking classmates for clarification, or engaging in **competent bystander behavior** (Tousignant & Siedentop, 1983), which occurs when someone appears to be engaged in the lesson but avoids participating.

Our experience has shown that children who are comfortable with the material usually respond, while those not as confident remain silent. Children who lack confidence won't call attention to themselves by responding to questions. To avoid this problem, use performance checks, choral responding, and recognition checks to help relieve students' fear and concern about responding to your attempts to check for understanding.

MONITORING STUDENT WORK

Picture your class of 25 second-graders practicing their dribbling skills in a limited amount of space or a large outdoor space. You are expected to monitor their performance to be sure they are safe, stay on task, and are practicing the skills correctly. Actively monitoring students in your class involves moving around while children practice, providing them with appropriate feedback and adjusting tasks to make them individually challenging.

competent bystander behavior
Describes a child who appears to be engaged in the lesson but avoids participating.

Move around the Gymnasium

Teachers who constantly move around the gymnasium can better enhance student learning through observation. Constant monitoring by keeping children within your field of vision is called "Back to the Wall" (Graham, 2001). A stationary teacher's observations typically focus on the whole class and not on individuals, so instructional decisions such as changing tasks and providing feedback are given to the entire class regardless of individual student needs.

By walking and scanning, you can observe all individuals. The key to effective observation is to make quick judgments about performance and provide the necessary cues or information to remedy any error. With all the students in your classroom working at once, you cannot afford to spend much time with each student, so you have to check, assess, and remedy each student performance quickly. Moving around is the best way to do this.

Provide Students with Feedback

Providing students with immediate feedback is an important instructional strategy. As we discussed in Chapter 1, many physical education teachers find feedback to be critical to improving student performance. Feedback can focus the student's attention on critical aspects of a particular skill and motivate him or her to keep practicing. This is especially important in physical education, where students often see an error (e.g., landing behind or in front of the jumping line or forgetting to bend knees). Your responsibility is to help the student "see" how he or she can get better during practice. Usually, to determine an error in skill technique, you must watch the student perform the skill several times.

Of course, you can provide different types of feedback for students; each type serves a specific purpose. **General feedback** is the most common form given by teachers, meant to motivate and encourage children to keep trying without providing any information on skill performance. Statements like "good job" or "nice try" are examples of positive general feedback. Conversely, **specific feedback** is given to children to identify an error in skill technique without relating to the lesson's cue or task intent. **Congruent feedback** directly relates to the cues for the task, while **incongruent feedback** is information that may be helpful but does not relate to the cue or task focus. See Table 5.4 for a description and examples of the various types of feedback.

Due to large class sizes, specialist physical educators are not only challenged to give any type of feedback but often find it difficult to watch a student closely enough to give appropriate individual feedback. The good news for the classroom teacher is that because you will be teaching only students from your own class, your class will be much smaller than many physical education classes taught by specialist teachers. You can provide appropriate student feedback if you know the content (see Chapter 11 for extensive details about the content of physical education).

Most physical education teachers agree that specific congruent feedback, sometimes called **corrective feedback,** is the most useful because it provides the student with helpful information related to future performance. Children are believed to use this external information to make adjustments during their next

general feedback
Comments that do not provide children with information on how to improve.

specific feedback
Information about a consistent aspect or result of a performance.

congruent feedback
Information related to the learning cue or critical feature of the task focus.

incongruent feedback
Information not related to the cue or outcome of the lesson.

corrective feedback
Information related to the performance that tells the performer what to do in future attempts.

TABLE **5.4** ■ Student Feedback Examples

Types of Feedback	Description	Examples
General	Comments given that do not provide children with information on how to improve.	Good job! Nice balance. Looks good.
Specific	Information given to children identifying a consistent error in skill technique (i.e., does not have to relate to cue or outcome of lesson).	Be sure to bend your knees. This time make sure you keep your arms level as you try to volley the ball.
Congruent	Information related to the cue or outcome for the lesson.	You need to remember to reach your arm back (cue: "arm back"). Our focus today is arms extended (cue) while balancing. Keep your arms straight out from your side. Donny, remember to swing the racket from below your waist or low to high (cue: "low to high").
Incongruent	Information provided that is not related to the cue or outcome of the lesson.	Keep the ball in front of you while you dribble (the cue was finger pads). Don't swing at the ball when volleying (the cue was flat surface).
Corrective	Information related to the performance that tells the performer what to do in future attempts.	Remember to keep your head still. Next time, tuck your chin to your chest more.

Source: Modified from *Teaching Children Physical Education: Becoming a Master Teacher* (2nd ed.), by G. Graham, 2001, Champaign, IL: Human Kinetics.

attempts. Children need this information, and they often request it. For example, the child in Figure 5.7 was having difficulty striking the ball and asked "What am I doing wrong?" He wanted to know how to correct his performance.

But remember that it is better to provide no feedback than incorrect feedback; if you are unsure how to correct performance, then provide no feedback at all.

Individualizing Instruction

Children benefit from working on tasks appropriate for their skill level, which encourages them to continue mastering a skill even when the teacher is not watching. As you observe student performance, sometimes you will see the task needs to be changed or adjusted so students can have more success or work at a more appropriate difficulty level. Teaching by invitation and intratask variation are two strategies that give children opportunities to work at their own individual ability level.

FIGURE **5.7**
Corrective feedback is necessary for learning; students need more information than simply "well done" or "good job."

Teaching by Invitation

When you allow children a choice of tasks and let them decide which best suits their needs, you are **teaching by invitation.** Some examples of presenting a task with teaching by invitation include

- "When you work on traveling across the balance beam, you may use either the low beam or the high beam."

- "Choose a ball from the basket (e.g., volleyball, playground ball, foam ball) that you and your partner feel comfortable working with and start passing it back and forth."

- "As you travel while you dribble, choose a speed that lets you keep control of the ball."

- "Today you may work alone or with a partner."

Teaching by invitation allows students to adjust or modify the difficulty level of the task for themselves. There are two important points to remember when using this strategy: Make all options equally appealing, and be patient when some students seem to make poor decisions about task difficulty. Children will usually make a wiser decision after a short time.

Intratask Variation

teaching by invitation
A teaching strategy where the teacher invites students to change a task when they are ready.

intratask variation
A teaching strategy where the teacher changes or adjusts a task for a child or group of children.

If students continue to work at an unsuitable task for them, you may want to use **intratask variation.** In this strategy, the teacher is the decision-maker, not the student. Often, as you monitor students practicing the given task, you will notice that some have become disengaged because the task is either too hard or too easy for them. You need to change the task before this happens. Your adjustments are similar to the choices offered to students in teaching by invitation; the difference is that *you* decide who should do what and when. This strategy is critical during the lesson development to make sure individual student needs are met.

WRAPPING UP THE LESSON

Closure brings a lesson to its conclusion. It usually briefly wraps up what was covered in the lesson and lasts two to three minutes. This is the time to help children bring the content together in their own minds, making sense out of what went on during the lesson. Closure consolidates and reinforces the outcome of the lesson that you introduced in the set induction. In the example about Superman, the closure would focus on students telling what they needed to do to help make their arms stronger—to keep their arms straight.

closure
The strategy used to end or wrap up a lesson.

FINAL WORDS

Children love to learn. Good teachers use a variety of strategies to help them do it. Physical education teachers need to remember the importance of getting students active immediately upon entering the gym. An instant activity gets children moving, allows them time to release pent-up energy, and lets them adjust from being sedentary in a classroom to being in a movement environment.

Teachers also need to follow the phases identified in the "anatomy of a lesson" by providing children with a set induction, learning tasks, and closure. Set induction should set the stage and tell the students what they will be learning and why it is important. Your presentation of the learning tasks should always include providing students with a skill demonstration and checking their understanding through questioning. Increase students' learning by monitoring them as they practice the tasks while you move throughout the gymnasium. Provide appropriate feedback and change the learning task when necessary. Finally, end the lesson by reviewing what was covered. There are many ways to present a lesson, but the strategies discussed in this chapter will help you make lessons more relevant, meaningful, and dynamic for children.

OVER TO YOU

1. You want to help a child learn to walk across a balance beam, to volley a balloon, or jump rope. What elements of providing children with a demonstration do you need to remember?

2. A parent comes to you, concerned about how his child will do in physical education, because his child is not as "athletic" as the other children. What do you tell him to alleviate his concern?

3. Teachers use instructional strategies to present students with dynamic lessons. Explain the importance of each of the nine strategies presented in the chapter and the impact it could have on student need or interest.

PORTFOLIO TASKS

1. Develop a sequence of questions (convergent problem solving) that could help children gradually "discover" the solution to a problem that involves volleying or dribbling with the hand.

2. Write a set induction introducing the skill of striking with a golf club that does not refer to sports or well-known athletes. (*Hint:* Stay away from statements or questions such as, "Who can tell me who Tiger Woods is?")

3. Record yourself using one of the instructional strategies discussed in this chapter while you teach a physical education lesson to your peers or to children in a field-based experience.

4. Write three higher-order thinking (not just factual) multiple-choice test questions reflecting the content of this chapter on instructional strategies.

REFERENCES

Graham, G. (2001). *Teaching children physical education: Becoming a master teacher* (2nd ed.). Champaign, IL: Human Kinetics.

Jensen, E. (2000). *Learning with the body in mind.* San Diego: The Brain Store.

McCullagh, P., Stiehl, J., & Weiss, M. R. (1990). Developmental modeling effects on the quantitative and qualitative aspects of motor performance. *Research Quarterly for Exercise and Sport, 61*(4), 344–350.

Metzler, M. (1989). A review of the research on time in sport pedagogy. *Journal of Teaching in Physical Education, 64*(4), 271–285.

Mosston, M., & Ashworth, S. (2003). *Teaching physical education* (5th ed.). Columbus, OH: Merrill.

Pollack, B. J., & Lee, T. D. (1992). Effects of the models skill level on observational motor learning. *Research Quarterly for Exercise and Sport, 63*(1), 25–29.

Roach, N. K., & Burwitz, L. (1986). Observational learning in motor skill acquisition: The effect of verbal directing cues. *Trends and developments in physical education:* Proceedings of the VIII Commonwealth and International Conference on Sport, Physical Education, Dance, Recreation, and Health: Conference '86 Glasgow, 18–23 July. Publication Information: London, New York: E. & F. N. Spon, 1986.

Siedentop, D., & Tannehill, D. (2000). *Developing teaching skills in physical education* (4th ed.). Mountain View, CA: Mayfield.

Sylvester, R. (2000). *A biological brain in a cultural classroom.* Alexandria, VA: Skylight Publishers.

Tousignant, M., & Siedentop, D. (1983). A qualitative analysis of task structures in required secondary physical education classes. *Journal of Teaching in Physical Education, 3,* 47–56.

CHAPTER

6

STRATEGIES FOR ASSESSING STUDENT WORK

1. Should students be graded on effort or ability in physical education? Justify your answer.

2. As a parent, would you be concerned if your child received a poor grade in physical education?

3. How is assessment in physical education similar to and different from assessment in the regular classroom?

4. With your background as a classroom teacher, do you think you could effectively assess students in physical education? Why or why not?

Y ou are a full-time elementary classroom teacher. The first nine weeks of the new term just ended, and you are sending report cards home to let parents know how their child performed in language arts, math, and reading. You believe children will learn if they try hard in your class, so you don't worry about formal or informal assessments of your students. You just write "satisfactory" on the report card for each of your subject areas and seal it for the child to take home.

What do you think happens next? That's right—angry parents would call demanding an account of what you taught during this nine-week period.

Few parents would accept having their child complete a year of schooling while showing little progress toward mastering the content at that grade level. Parents demand that teachers provide evidence of what they have been teaching throughout the school year. In response, classroom teachers provide results from various assessment instruments such as written assignments, tests, quizzes, projects, and student logs to document student progress. The unique teaching environment and focus on physical activity in physical education do not preclude a physical education teacher from accountability. You should be able to support what your students are learning and their progress in your classes. Whether you are teaching in the classroom or in the gymnasium, determining and documenting what students are learning and how they are progressing toward meeting stated outcomes is your critical responsibility.

This chapter examines key issues related to assessment, giving you the necessary tools to assess student progress and work in physical education.

A CASE FOR ASSESSMENT IN PHYSICAL EDUCATION

assessment
The process of gathering information on students (documentation) and making a judgment about the results (achievement).

For every class you teach, you must ask, "What are students learning here?" It is not enough to list the material you have covered; you must provide documentation of how well students learned the material. **Assessment** involves gathering information on students (documentation) and making a judgment about the results (achievement). Just as in reading, math, and science, you must assess your students' progress in physical education. As we discussed in Chapter 1, you are responsible for helping students meet the goals and objectives of the physical education program. To determine your effectiveness in this role, you must assess.

Besides documenting progress, assessment can be used to diagnose where students are in terms of the class material being taught, thus enabling teachers to provide quality learning experiences for every child. Chapter 3 highlighted this by describing how to provide appropriate activities for children of differing skill levels. To do this effectively, you must know where the students are in terms of skill development.

Assessment can also help teachers group students of similar abilities. Sometimes children should work with a partner or group with similar skill levels for safety reasons. For example, throwing and catching can be dangerous if a child who throws well works with a partner who is not adept at catching; the child catching could easily get hurt due to a lack of skill. It also helps to group students by ability at activity stations designed for their specific skill level, such as one group hitting from a live pitch while another group hits off a batting tee.

Assessment can also help teachers create learning experiences that are relevant, meaningful, and motivating for children. Teachers can use it to evaluate students and provide practice tasks to engage students instead of excluding those who cannot complete a required task. As discussed in Chapter 1, student achievement is tied to children's success as they complete practice tasks, motivating children toward the lesson. A quick assessment of children while they work can tell you whether students are working at a level that is individually challenging for them.

Sometimes students have difficulty learning the material through no fault of their own; their teachers can use assessment as a tool to improve their instruction. Teachers can identify problem areas in instruction and modify content accordingly. After a lesson on the forward roll, if students cannot identify and/or perform the learnable piece (such as "tuck the chin") then the lesson needs to be modified and revisited. Table 6.1 shows many ways assessment items can help student learning. In physical education, assessment can be used just as in the classroom to diagnose areas of weakness, group students accordingly, document progress, motivate students to continue working, and improve instruction. The different uses of assessment promote student achievement.

TABLE **6.1** ■ Uses of Assessment in Student Learning

Use of Assessment	Meaning	Example
Diagnosis	Helps teachers determine where students are in terms of their understanding of the content	During a lesson on locomotor skills, the teacher asks all students to demonstrate straight, curved, and zigzag pathways. Because many children cannot correctly show a zigzag, the teacher decides to revisit this concept in the next lesson.
Grouping	Ensures that students are working with individuals of similar ability	Students have completed a throw-for-distance test. The teacher uses their scores to group stronger throwers together and weaker throwers together in the upcoming lesson that involves catching.
Improvement	Information used by teachers to address student needs and modify instruction accordingly	Early in the school year, many students had performed poorly on upper-body strength fitness tests. The teacher uses these results as a stimulus to include more activities requiring upper-body strength in subsequent units.
Achievement	Provides teachers with an indication of the degree of learning that occurred	Students are asked to create a gymnastics routine that includes rolling in two directions. The teacher uses a checklist to see if students are able to incorporate these rolls.
Motivation	Engages students in the learning process by providing realistic and meaningful information concerning what needs to be practiced	The teacher records students' time on a fun obstacle course. She then uses these times to help students plan a mini training program to improve their times in three weeks when they complete the course once again.

TYPES OF ASSESSMENT

Assessment is often classified as either formative or summative, differentiated by when the assessment is given and what purpose is served. When you use a collection of assessments over time or during a unit to provide feedback to the student, then you are using **formative assessment**. Advantages of this type of assessment include:

- Providing feedback to the teacher about student progress
- Helping the teacher modify instruction
- Empowering students by involving them in the assessment process
- Helping the teacher to identify areas of strength and weakness

formative assessment
Ongoing or continuous assessment used to show student progress toward meeting outcomes.

summative assessment
Evaluation at the end of a unit or lesson used to determine a level of achievement.

Assessment at the end of the unit or lesson that is used to denote student achievement or show how well students met the stated outcomes is termed **summative assessment**. This type of assessment usually:

- Occurs at the end of the unit or lesson
- Is formal in nature in documenting achievement
- Allows the teacher to grade and compare students
- Provides an indication of success
- Indicates whether learning occurred

No doubt you will use both types of assessment in your classroom. Formative assessment gives you valuable information on student progress, while summative assessment documents student achievement.

ALTERNATIVE ASSESSMENT

Now that you understand the many uses of assessment in learning, let's focus on creating assessments to generate meaningful and useful data you can actually use. Some physical education teachers evaluate student progress with assessment tools such as skill tests and written tests. Unfortunately, these forms of assessment provide only a limited amount of information as to what students know or are able to do. They are not always the best match for the content covered or the skills being assessed. For example, to assess a student's ability to make a forearm pass or bump to a partner in a volleyball-related activity, some teachers use the volleyball wall test. This is a form of skill test that requires students to see how many times they can bump the ball against the wall without missing. Although this assesses a student's ability to make a forearm pass to a wall, it cannot measure his or her ability to pass the ball back and forth with a partner, where the factors in skill execution are more variable. In another scenario, a written test will not show whether students can apply the rules while playing a game. Students who correctly identify the serving order used in four-square on a quiz or test may still rotate in the incorrect order or serve from the wrong square while playing the game.

Teachers constantly judge students' abilities and progress during instruction. Using these judgments to modify instruction or determine what students are learning daily is an important aspect of teaching. Because student learning is multifaceted, you need a variety of assessment tools to document how well and to what degree students are making progress toward identified outcomes. According to the National Association for Sport and Physical Education (NASPE), assessment should be ongoing and continuous, promoting growth and learning, not simply documenting it (2004). To make the collected information more meaningful, you should choose the assessment most appropriate to the particular lesson and you should do multiple assessments over time in a variety of settings.

Teachers use **alternative assessment** to gain a more detailed picture of individual student learning. These forms of assessment can include checklists, logs, journals, projects, papers, assignment sheets, and rating scales. Varying your assessment tools lets you evaluate a range of student abilities, for example how well a child reflects, poses questions, makes connections, performs skills during interactive play, and solves problems. Alternative assessment comes in many different forms and measures attributes or behaviors in any of the three learning domains—cognitive/know, psychomotor/skill, and affective/value—at any time.

INQUIRING MINDS

What types of assessments do you give to children in physical education? What would some of these assessments look like? Can you show me some examples?

alternative assessment
A type of evaluation instrument different from one-shot formalized tools such as written tests and skill tests.

The key to using alternative forms of assessment is that the tools used must have **validity** and **reliability**. A valid instrument measures what it is meant to measure. A teacher who wants to measure how far a student can jump would have to use a test that measures distance, not one that measures height, such as the vertical leap test. The basis for a valid assessment is that it actually reflects and measures what was taught. A reliable tool produces consistent scores. Following the same procedures for administering the test (such as using the same equipment, scoring method, or test conditions) promotes reliability. If the same test is given on separate days, the test scores should remain relatively stable or consistent. When you have accounted for these two measurement issues, then you can be confident that the tool appropriately measures the behavior, characteristic, or attribute of interest. If you violate either of these critical measurement issues, the judgment of student performance becomes meaningless.

THE ASSESSMENT ROAD MAP

Determining what students should know and be able to do (the desired outcome) is the first point on the "assessment road map" (see Figure 6.1). This road map highlights the instructional alignment necessary among outcomes, planning, instruction, and assessment to enhance, facilitate, and document student achievement. Think about the assessment road map in terms of going on a trip. What do you do first when you decide to travel? You pick a place to go—your desired outcome. Next, you consider whether you can actually take the trip. This preliminary assessment may influence choices about where to stay, the mode of travel, and/or how much money you'll need. In teaching, this process includes preassessing and using this information to make an initial plan. Once all necessary decisions have been made, you can plan for and implement your trip. Finally, after you return

validity
The degree to which a test measures the attribute or characteristic it intends to measure.

reliability
A measurement issue related to consistency of scores.

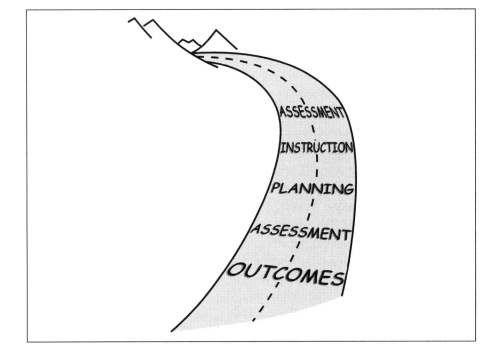

FIGURE **6.1**
The assessment road map represents the steps teachers take to ensure effective assessment.

home, you evaluate (i.e., assess) your trip. Perhaps it was good, but a few things could have made it better. Teachers go through this same process in assessing how well they meet their intended outcomes, using the assessment road map to identify, plan, instruct, and assess in order to modify planning and instruction to meet their desired outcomes.

STEP ONE:
DETERMINING STUDENT OUTCOMES

Chapter 1 discussed your important role in helping students develop the skills and attitudes necessary for physical activity to become part of their daily lives. A first step in this development is to determine the desired student outcomes. **Outcomes** are what students should know and be able to do as a result of instruction. Generally, individual states determine the outcomes for the different subject areas—math, science, reading, and physical education—for each grade level. School districts then modify these outcomes to meet students' individual needs. Although this process is similar from state to state, the terminology used by various state departments of education differs: core curriculum and standards, academic standards, course of study, quality core curriculum, and assessment standards.

Although the terminology varies, teachers are given information to let them know what skills and knowledge should be covered at the various grade levels. One method used by some states to guide their physical education curriculum outcomes is the National Content Standards for Physical Education (NASPE, 2004). These six national standards outline the knowledge and skills that children should exhibit upon completion of a physical education program (see Box 6.1). These standards are, essentially, the desired outcome: They define what students are expected to learn and are used to monitor student progress.

outcome
What students should know and be able to do as a result of instruction.

🖉 BOX **6.1** ■ **National Content Standards for Physical Education**

_____

A physically educated person:

1. Demonstrates competency in motor skills and movement patterns needed to perform a variety of physical activities.

2. Demonstrates understanding of movement concepts, principles, strategies, and tactics as they apply to the learning and performance of physical activities.

3. Participates regularly in physical activity.

4. Achieves and maintains a health-enhancing level of physical fitness.

5. Demonstrates responsible personal and social behavior that respects self and others in physical activity settings.

6. Values physical activity for health, enjoyment, challenge, self-expression, and/or social interaction.

_____

Source: From *Moving into the Future: National Standards for Physical Education* (2nd ed.), by NASPE, 2004, Reston, VA: American Alliance for Health, Physical Education, Recreation and Dance.

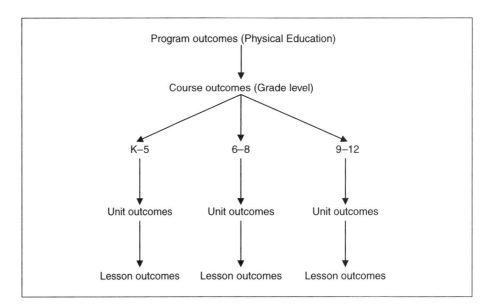

FIGURE **6.2**
The design down process of taking outcomes from the general to the specific.

As Figure 6.2 illustrates, the general physical education standards become more specific as planning moves from the grade level to the skill unit level to the individual lesson level. This process is referred to as *designing down outcomes* (Hopple, 1995). A practical example of taking outcomes from the broad (program) to the more specific is shown in Application 6.1.

To make the national standards for physical education (NASPE, 2004) into lesson outcomes is a simple process (Box 6.2). First, determine which standard you want to work toward and its appropriate learning domain. The links between the standards and the learning domains are

- NASPE Standards 1, 3, and 4:   Psychomotor
- NASPE Standard 2:   Cognitive
- NASPE Standards 5 and 6:   Affective

Second, identify related course outcomes by consulting state and local district curriculum guides for more grade-specific outcomes. Then, use physical education textbooks, lesson plan guides, and related professional websites for lesson activities and ideas.

There is a critical relationship between identifying expected student outcomes and assessment of student progress toward those outcomes. To make this relationship clearer, a sample assessment item for NASPE physical education standard 6 appears in Application 6.2. In the rest of this chapter, we will present samples for the remaining five standards. These practical examples show the direct link of assessment to student outcome and how student performance on an assessment item can be scored using a rubric. An accurate account of student progress requires several assessments throughout the grading period or school year.

Program Outcome

By the end of a K–12 physical education program, the students will have learned a variety of skills (NASPE Standard 1).

Course Outcome

By the end of elementary school, the students will have learned to competently perform a variety of locomotor, nonlocomotor, and manipulative skills.

Unit Outcome

By the end of the unit on throwing, the students will have learned to throw a variety of objects with speed, force, and accuracy.

Lesson Outcome

By the end of the lesson, the students will have learned to rotate the trunk when throwing.

BOX **6.2** ▪ **The Simple Steps in Turning Standards into Lesson Outcomes**

1. Identify the appropriate NASPE standard.

2. Consult the state and local district's curriculum guides.

3. Create unit and lesson outcomes from physical education textbooks and websites.

STANDARD 6: Understands that physical activity provides opportunities for enjoyment, challenge, self-expression, and social interaction.

Program Outcome: When leaving a K–12 physical education program, the student will value activity for health, enjoyment, challenge, self-expression, and/or social interaction.

Course: By the end of elementary school, the student will recognize some personally enjoyable activities and express his or her own creativity through personally designed routines, made up alone and with others.

Unit: By the end of the unit on Circus Arts, the student will select an activity from tumbling, juggling, and balance, and express him- or herself by working with a group of friends to create and perform a routine.

Lesson: Several lessons would build toward this learning experience. For example, the student will juggle two scarves in an up-and-down pattern, a crisscross applesauce pattern, and with one hand.

Assessment Task: Students choose a skill they most enjoy from tumbling, balancing, or juggling. Students will choose a group of two, three, or four people to create a routine together. The routine must have a starting position, five skills, an ending position, a name, and a costume. Students will memorize the routine and then perform for guests and parents.

RUBRIC

Choreographer: Students group together and plan a routine without any teacher assistance. The routine includes all requirements with some extra skills. Costumes are well designed. The routine is performed flawlessly and smoothly from memory.

Cast Member: Students group together and cooperatively plan and refine their routine with minimal teacher assistance. The routine includes a starting position, five skills, and an ending position. The group has a name, has costumes ready, and can perform the routine from memory.

Auditioned: Students need teacher assistance to define their group, write routine, and refine their performance. They are missing one part of the skill requirements. They have a costume, but little effort is put into it. They must have one or two prompts to perform the routine from memory.

Failed to Audition: The teacher must ask students to group together and cooperate. The teacher writes most of the performance, while routine requirements are incomplete with no costume. Students must be told the routine to perform.

continued

CIRCUS ARTS

Names of people in group:

1. _____

2. _____

3. _____

4. _____

Type of Act: Tumbling   Balancing   Juggling

Name of act: _____

Costume: _____

Starting position: _____

Skills: _____

                  _____

                  _____

                  _____

                  _____

                  _____

Ending position: _____

Practiced: 1   2   3

Memorized: yes   no

Dress rehearsal
(memorized):   yes   no

Costume ready: yes   no

Final Grade: ____ choreographer ____ cast member ____ auditioned ____ failed to audition

Source: Deana Schnuelle, Ogletree Elementary School, Auburn, Alabama.

STEP TWO: ASSESSMENT TOOLS

After determining student outcomes for your semester, unit, or lesson plan, you must be able to evaluate whether those outcomes have been met. Your students will have varying levels of success with the material; you must be able to measure what individual students have learned so far, how far they have come, and how far they have to go.

Children perform inconsistently in the initial stage of learning and student performance can fluctuate from day to day. A single assessment item or single administration of an assessment tool is therefore not enough to document student progress; assessment must be ongoing and continuous. The following section discusses several tools to assess student learning.

Observational Assessments

When teaching physical education, you spend a lot of your time observing students to make judgments about their performance. This can be used formally to document learning (see Figure 6.3) or informally to make a quick decision to adjust a given lesson.

A student's peers can also perform observational assessments. Peer assessment is important as part of a complete picture of a student's skills, grasp of information, and attitude toward the task at hand. But before assessing their peers accurately, students must be taught how to properly use the assessment. They need to learn how to focus their observations on the critical aspects of the assessment tool, such as learnable pieces, attitudes, or behaviors. To be effective, students should have already learned and practiced what to observe; then children will enjoy being the

FIGURE **6.3**
Teachers use observation to assess student performance. These observations can be used formally to document student progress.

SELF-ASSESSMENT: MY BASKETBALL SKILLS

DIRECTIONS: We have been practicing our basketball-related skills for the last two weeks. Using the rating scale below, indicate how you feel about your skill level. Place your sheet in your portfolio folder when you finish. Choose one of the tasks listed on the sheet and start practicing.

Name: _____

Task	You Bet	At Times	Not Really
1. Dribble the ball using a flexible wrist.	❑	❑	❑
2. Dribble the ball with control.	❑	❑	❑
3. Make a good chest pass to my teammate or partner.	❑	❑	❑
4. Make a good bounce pass to my teammate or partner.	❑	❑	❑
5. Play defense by sliding my feet.	❑	❑	❑

"teacher" and are usually honest in assessing others. Thus, peer assessment works only with students who have had initial instruction as to what is to be observed.

You can also learn where students are or how they feel about their own progress or experiences by allowing them to assess themselves. Self-assessment offers insight into students' perception of themselves or how they feel about their physical skills, content knowledge, attitudes, opinions, or thoughts on physical activity or sports (Application 6.3). This information lets you modify future learning experiences to meet individual student needs more appropriately. One word of caution: When having students rate themselves, young children (typically under the age of 7) often have an overly optimistic view of their abilities. As children get older, their self-ratings become more in line with those of the teacher.

Checklists

Teachers use checklists as observational tools to determine whether the criteria they want to assess are present or have occurred. A checklist can include statements, dimensions, characteristics, or behaviors that can be scored as yes/no or observed/not observed (Application 6.4).

Checklists are simple to create and easy to use; they provide quick information on student performance. You can administer a checklist to determine a child's skill level for throwing, for example. That checklist may alert you that some students have difficulty stating or performing your listed throwing cues. Knowing this helps you identify content to be revisited. See Application 6.5 for a checklist created to assess students' verbal and performance knowledge for different locomotor skills.

Checklists also lend themselves well to peer assessment by providing student observers with clear criteria to look for and then evaluate (see Application 6.6). Peer assessments can be easily built into your students' tasks; to assess students' landing skills, have one child perform the task while the assigned partner observes and completes a landing checklist. Checklists can also be used for self-assessment by having students check off whether or not they completed a task.

APPLICATION **6.4** ■ **An Example of a Performance Checklist for the Skill Theme of Striking with a Racket**

TENNIS FOREHAND CHECKLIST

DIRECTIONS: The student will hit the ball against the wall twice using the forehand stroke. Watch each forehand and check the "Yes" box if the student demonstrates the cue. Leave the box blank if the student does not demonstrate the cue.

Student	Forehand	Cue: Takes the racket back low below the waist	Cue: Nonracket side to the target	Cue: Swings low to high
1.	1.	❑ Yes	❑ Yes	❑ Yes
	2.	❑ Yes	❑ Yes	❑ Yes
2.	1.	❑ Yes	❑ Yes	❑ Yes
	2.	❑ Yes	❑ Yes	❑ Yes
3.	1.	❑ Yes	❑ Yes	❑ Yes
	2.	❑ Yes	❑ Yes	❑ Yes
4.	1.	❑ Yes	❑ Yes	❑ Yes
	2.	❑ Yes	❑ Yes	❑ Yes
5.	1.	❑ Yes	❑ Yes	❑ Yes
	2.	❑ Yes	❑ Yes	❑ Yes
6.	1.	❑ Yes	❑ Yes	❑ Yes
	2.	❑ Yes	❑ Yes	❑ Yes
7.	1.	❑ Yes	❑ Yes	❑ Yes
	2.	❑ Yes	❑ Yes	❑ Yes
8.	1.	❑ Yes	❑ Yes	❑ Yes
	2.	❑ Yes	❑ Yes	❑ Yes

COGNITIVE MEASURES CHECKLIST: LOCOMOTOR SKILLS

DIRECTIONS: Check the Stated box if the student says the critical element and the Performed box if the student demonstrates the critical element.

Jumping—Tell and show me some things I could do to jump better.

Student Name	Arms Way Back	Bend Knees	Reach Arms/Jump
1.	❑ Stated ❑ Performed	❑ Stated ❑ Performed	❑ Stated ❑ Performed
2.	❑ Stated ❑ Performed	❑ Stated ❑ Performed	❑ Stated ❑ Performed
3.	❑ Stated ❑ Performed	❑ Stated ❑ Performed	❑ Stated ❑ Performed

Hopping—Tell and show me some things I could do to hop better.

Student Name	One Foot Down	One Foot Back	Hop and Balance
1.	❑ Stated ❑ Performed	❑ Stated ❑ Performed	❑ Stated ❑ Performed
2.	❑ Stated ❑ Performed	❑ Stated ❑ Performed	❑ Stated ❑ Performed
3.	❑ Stated ❑ Performed	❑ Stated ❑ Performed	❑ Stated ❑ Performed

Leaping—Tell and show me some things I could do to leap better.

Student Name	Take Off— One Foot	Land on Opposite Foot	Reach
1.	❑ Stated ❑ Performed	❑ Stated ❑ Performed	❑ Stated ❑ Performed
2.	❑ Stated ❑ Performed	❑ Stated ❑ Performed	❑ Stated ❑ Performed
3.	❑ Stated ❑ Performed	❑ Stated ❑ Performed	❑ Stated ❑ Performed

PEER ASSESSMENT: LANDING CHECKLIST

PERFORMANCE TASK: Have students pair up. One partner goes through the jumping obstacle course, while the other partner peer-assesses his or her partner's landing skill. Have the assessing partner observe the landing at each of the five different jumping obstacles and complete the checklist below. After completing the obstacle course, have students change roles.

DIRECTIONS: Check the appropriate box to indicate whether your partner demonstrates the critical elements on each during the obstacle course.

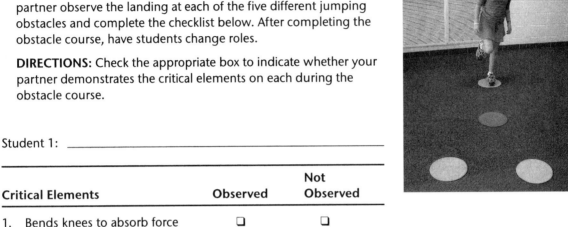

Student 1: _____

Critical Elements	Observed	Not Observed
1. Bends knees to absorb force	❏	❏
2. Lands of the balls of the feet	❏	❏
3. Lands with little to no sound	❏	❏

Student 2: _____

Critical Elements	Observed	Not Observed
1. Bends knees to absorb force	❏	❏
2. Lands of the balls of the feet	❏	❏
3. Lands with little to no sound	❏	❏

Rating Scales

While a checklist assesses the presence or absence of a characteristic, a rating scale assesses the degree or quality of a particular characteristic's occurrence (Application 6.7). In other words, a rating scale highlights the extent to which a characteristic was demonstrated by the student. There are various rating scales:

■ *Numerically (0–5):* Characteristics or behaviors can be measured on a numeric scale ranging from 0 to 5. Many teachers prefer this scale because the number can easily be converted into a grade. Although lending itself well to grading and providing a measure of performance, the numerical scale does not give an exact indication of student performance; there is always some subjectivity in such an assessment, and different observers may assign different numbers for the same performance. This scale is easily used for teacher, peer, or self-analysis. Application 6.8 highlights using a rating scale to assess NASPE standard 3.

JUMP ROPE ASSESSMENT

PERFORMANCE TASK: Get a jump rope from the box, find your personal space, and start jumping. I want you to work on fast jumps with buoyant landings. Keep jumping until you hear the whistle to stop.

DIRECTIONS: Rate the following by placing the corresponding number according to the rating scale in the appropriate number box.

3 = Always   2 = Sometimes   1 = Rarely   0 = Never

Student	Bends Knees When Pushing Off or Landing	Elbows Close to Body	Feet Barely Off the Ground with Soft Landing
1. Jose Vargas	3	2	1
2. Emile Patton	0	1	2
3. Gary Gibson	2	2	1
4. Willa Ford	2	3	2
5. Jacques Perry	0	0	1
6. Leslie Battle	2	3	1
7. LaDamion Smith	1	1	1
8. Tia Watts	3	3	3
9. Diana DeSoto	0	0	2
10. Uma Kratvitz	3	3	2

STANDARD 3: Exhibits a physically active lifestyle.

Program Outcome: When leaving a K–12 physical education program, the student will participate regularly in physical activity.

Course: By the end of elementary school, the student will recognize and participate in appropriate assessment of personal physical activity levels.

Unit: By the end of the unit on fitness, the student will recognize the physiological indicators that accompany moderate to vigorous physical activity.

Lesson: By the end of the lesson, the student will be able to distinguish among the different intensity levels of activity (i.e., light, moderate, and vigorous).

Portfolio Task: Set up six activity stations (dribble tag, jump rope, basketball shoot, scooters, hula hoops, and balance walk). Students, divided into six equal groups, will spend three minutes at each station. When the whistle blows, students will stop the activity, complete the activity sheet, then rotate to the next station.

RUBRIC

Olympian: The student completes the activity sheet for each station, recognizes that various activities cause the heart to beat at different rates, and correctly labels each activity for the proper intensity.

Amateur: The student completes the activity sheet for more than half of the stations, recognizes that some physical activities cause the heart to beat at different rates, and correctly labels three to five of the activity stations for the proper intensity.

Junior: The student completes the activity sheet for fewer than half of the stations, indicates that few activities cause the heart to beat at different rates, and correctly labels only one or two of the activity stations for the proper intensity.

Couch Potato: The student fails to complete the sheet at any station, fails to recognize that different physical activities cause the heart rate to change, and doesn't correctly label any station for proper activity intensity.

PHYSICAL ACTIVITY SHEET: HEART RATE AND INTENSITY

Activity	Intensity Level	Heart Rate				
		During these activities my heart beats:				
		Really fast			Not really fast	
Dribble tag	_____	5	4	3	2	1
Jump rope	_____	5	4	3	2	1
Basketball shoot	_____	5	4	3	2	1
Scooters	_____	5	4	3	2	1
Hula hoop	_____	5	4	3	2	1
Balance walk	_____	5	4	3	2	1
Hula hoop	_____	5	4	3	2	1

- *Descriptively (e.g., by saying always, often, sometimes, rarely, never):* Descriptive words differentiate among the characteristics or behaviors being measured. Although a descriptive scale isn't adaptable for grading, unlike the numerical scale, it gives a more detailed picture of student performance. Like the numerical scale, the descriptive scale is easily used for teacher, peer, or self-analysis.

- *Pictorially:* Pictures differentiate among the characteristics or behaviors being measured. This scale is usually used for self-analysis, with students self-rating their motor skill ability or their feelings on topics related to physical activity (see Application 6.9).

Some teachers find that a combination of the different scales can provide a clearer picture of student performance.

APPLICATION **6.9** ■ A Pictorial Rating Scale for Jumping Rope

SELF-RATING SCALE

DIRECTIONS: Think about yourself performing the activities in the pictures below. Circle the face that you wear when you think about yourself doing each activity.

Name: _____

| | I'm good at it! ☺ | I'm so-so, I guess! 😐 | I'm not good at it—yet! ☹ |

| | I'm good at it! ☺ | I'm so-so, I guess! 😐 | I'm not good at it—yet! ☹ |

| | I'm good at it! ☺ | I'm so-so, I guess! 😐 | I'm not good at it—yet! ☹ |

Standard 4: Achieves and maintains a health-enhancing level of fitness.

Program Outcome: By the time the student leaves a quality K–12 physical education program, the student will achieve and maintain a health-enhancing level of fitness.

Course: By the end of fifth to sixth grade, the student will understand the basic concepts of physical fitness and personal wellness and the relationship between the two.

Unit: By the end of the unit on fitness, the student will identify and demonstrate activities designed to improve the health-related components of physical fitness.

Lesson: By the end of the lesson, the student will identify activities to improve muscular strength and endurance, flexibility, and cardiorespiratory endurance.

Portfolio Task: After discussing specific muscle groups and participating in activities for each, use that knowledge and the information on the principles of weight training we have discussed in class to prepare a workout for your homeroom teacher to help improve his or her muscular strength. Use the diagram provided to complete this activity. Label the major muscle groups, and then identify two activities that develop each muscle group. Finally, decide on the number of sets, reps, and frequency for completing each exercise appropriate for your homeroom teacher.

RUBRIC

Personal Trainer (3 pts): The student correctly labels all the muscle groups, gives two appropriate activities for each, and identifies an appropriate number of sets, reps, and frequency for his or her teacher's current fitness level.

Personal Trainer Assistant (2 pts): The student correctly labels most of the muscle groups, provides at least one but sometimes two appropriate activities for each, and identifies an appropriate number of sets, reps, and frequency for his or her teacher's current fitness level.

Attending Trainer School (1 pt): The student correctly labels some of the muscle groups and provides only one appropriate activity for some of the muscle groups; the teacher's workout is somewhat appropriate for his or her current fitness level.

Trainer School Dropout (0 points): The student fails to label any of the muscle groups correctly or to provide an appropriate activity for each muscle group; the teacher's workout is not appropriate for his or her current fitness level.

continued

Other Forms of Assessment

Although you can judge students through observation skills, other types of assessment also generate meaningful data. These are just as valuable as observational assessment. They often provide unique insight into what students know and the skills they have learned, as well as their thoughts, feelings, and opinions about physical activity, which cannot be observed.

performance assessment Assessment requiring students to perform a movement or produce something.

Many forms of alternative physical education assessment don't involve observation but do involve **performance assessment**. In this type of assessment, students actually do, create, or make something—for example, by *performing* a dance routine, creating a new game, or *making* a sport collage. Application 6.10 is a

HOMEROOM TEACHER'S CURRENT ACTIVITY LEVEL

1. Place the correct name of the major muscle group on the line below.

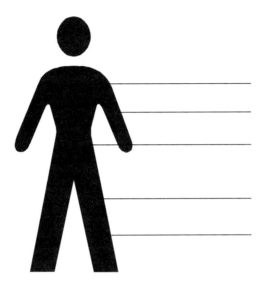

2. Teacher Workout:

Muscle Group	Activity 1	Activity 2	Sets and Reps	Per Week
Biceps				
Abdominals				
Quadriceps				
Deltoids				
Gastrocnemius				

performance assessment that assesses NASPE standard 4. Demonstrating and assessing a behavior or attribute in a real-world setting, such as dribbling a ball while being guarded by another student (in contrast to dribbling in isolation) is considered an **authentic performance assessment.** If a student is evaluated on the ability to physically perform a skill in isolation, such as throwing a ball or striking an object, then the assessment is a **performance task** (psychomotor). In contrast, a **portfolio task** is when a student does not have to perform a physical task but rather one that is cognitive or affective, such as completing an assignment sheet or keeping a log or journal.

authentic performance assessment
An assessment requiring students to demonstrate the behaviors the teacher wants to assess in a real-world context.

performance task
A performance assessment in which students physically perform a given task.

portfolio task
A performance assessment requiring students to perform a task that is cognitive or affective in nature.

MOVE IT

DIRECTIONS: Review the dance steps we have practiced for three minutes. In your group, choose from the steps listed to create your own routine. You must have at least four different patterns in your routine, which will last for a total of 24 counts. You will be assessed on how well you perform the steps in your routine and how well you stay on beat.

Steps: Grapevine, Walk, Heel-Toe, Shuffle, Collapse, Rock Step, Boogie Turn, Cha-Cha-Cha

Group Members _____

Dance Steps	Yes	Fluid	On Beat
1. _____			
2. _____			
3. _____			
4. _____			
5. _____			
6. _____			

Source: Courtney Cooper, Meadowlane Elementary School, Phenix City, Alabama.

Assignment Sheets

Assignment sheets are assessment items that can be completed by students during a lesson or at the end of one. With a little work on your end, these are easy to design and implement. Like most assessments, they can be used in a variety of ways to assess a wide range of information in the psychomotor, cognitive, and affective learning domains, helping to show the whole child's physical, mental, and emotional progress. Application 6.11 is an assignment sheet to use in the psychomotor domain, requiring students to create and perform a dance routine. You can create an assignment sheet asking children to show what they know (cognitive domain) about different locomotor skills by circling or identifying a picture of correct versus incorrect performance (see Figure 6.4).

An assignment from the affective domain (assessing student values, attitudes or opinions) might involve a teacher who has just taught a lesson on the importance of sportsmanship and how to encourage others. She then decides to assess whether the student understood the lesson outcome. Figure 6.5 shows an assignment sheet that students would complete to assess their understanding of how to display sportsmanship.

One note of caution is that assignment sheets can easily become "busywork" worksheets rather than being educationally relevant. An assignment sheet should have a related educational purpose. Before creating an assignment sheet, ask yourself, "What is the purpose and use of this assessment?"

LOCOMOTOR SKILLS

Name: _____

DIRECTIONS: Circle the picture that shows an individual leaping.

FIGURE **6.4**
Assignment sheets can be used to assess what students know (cognitive domain).

WAYS TO ENCOURAGE SOMEONE

Name: _____

DIRECTIONS: Circle the pictures that shows good manners and sportsmanship by encouraging someone.

FIGURE **6.5**
This assignment sheet, used to assess in the affective domain, asks students to recognize good manners and sportsmanship.

Source: Reprinted with permission from PE Central.

An assignment sheet might have different looks and requirements depending on how it is designed and created. It might have students:

- Design a gymnastic routine, dance, or game.
- Make a drawing or rendering of specific physical education concepts.
- Give a report or presentation.
- Evaluate an activity for specific fitness components.
- Create a fitness plan for their teacher, parent, or friend.

Student Logs and Journals

Students can maintain logs to document their progress over time and to assess fitness information, motor skill development, or physical activity time. Logs can present a daily, weekly, or monthly record (see Application 6.12).

Some teachers use logs to help students set short- and long-range goals throughout the year. Students record their starting and subsequent performances on several fitness measures, such as cardiovascular endurance, flexibility, and muscular endurance. The log helps them see and track their progress over time. Such a log is quantitative in nature.

Journals are written records in which students can reflect, analyze, pose questions, and express feelings privately without peer pressure. Journals let students express their feelings about their experiences participating in physical education activities and are qualitative in nature. By having students share feelings or

---

APPLICATION **6.12** ■ **A Partially Completed Daily Activity Log Sheet**

MY JUMPING ACTIVITY LOG

Name: _____

Date	Activity	Where	Comments	How I Felt about My Progress		
January 16	Jumping on and off boxes	PE class	I tried hard but didn't seem to improve much.	Good	OK	**Not Good**
January 17	Jump rope	Outside with friends	It was fun. I like working with my friends.	**Good**	OK	Not Good
January 18	Jumping to touch the balloons at different heights	PE class	I really wanted to touch the yellow balloon, so I really thought about bending my knees so I could jump higher—and I did it.	**Good**	OK	Not Good
January 19	Jump and head the ball in soccer	Soccer practice	It was practice—not very fun!	Good	**OK**	Not Good

---

> *September 10: I didn't like class today because we had to hit the ball back and forth across the net with a partner. The ball was heavy, and it hurt when it hit my arm. I wanted to try, but I was scared of getting hurt. I saw some groups using a different ball, and it seemed better than the one we had to use.*

opinions, you can assess in the affective domain. For example, asking students to reflect on an in-class competitive game might reveal why certain children did not seem to try very hard during the game. You may discover that a student was trying but wasn't feeling successful, felt unwell, or was concentrating on or thinking about something else. The game itself was not the reason for a student's lack of effort; it was something entirely unrelated (see Application 6.13).

The valuable information from student journals can be obtained only if students feel safe in reacting honestly. That is, students have to know that the teacher won't hold their response against them either academically or emotionally. A grade would be inappropriate, encouraging students to write dishonest responses for a high grade or to ensure their psychological safety.

INQUIRING MINDS

How do you grade your students in physical education? What was the basis for this decision?

STEP THREE:
EVALUATING STUDENT PROGRESS

Let us revisit the scenario from the beginning of this chapter, in which you were completing grades without any evidence of students' progress because you didn't assess them. Now you have created and administered various forms of assessment throughout the grading period to authenticate your students' progress. Yet you cannot put those assessments on the report card—so what do you do?

Rubrics

To document students' achievement properly, a system must be in place to score their performance. A **rubric** is a fixed rating scale used to judge student performance on a particular assessment item. It includes criteria for a task you want the student to perform and has different degrees or levels of achievement for evaluation purposes (see Application 6.14).

Writing quality rubrics takes time, but they are critical in documenting student progress. Developing quality rubrics somewhat addresses the measurement issues of validity (i.e., does it measure what is intended?) and reliability (i.e., do we get consistent results?) when using alternative forms of assessment. Before writing a

rubric
A rating scale used to judge student performance on a particular assessment item.

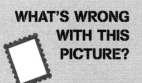

APPLICATION **6.14** ■ A Sample Rubric for Assessing a Checklist

JUMPING FOR DISTANCE

At the jump for distance station, the student displays the critical elements on the jump checklist.

Critical Element	Observed (Record Date Observed)
Feet shoulder-width apart	_____
Bend hips and knees	_____
Push off balls of feet	_____
Arms swing back to front	_____

LEVEL OF PERFORMANCE

3	Kangaroo	Demonstrates all of the critical elements
2	Rabbit	Demonstrates only three of the critical elements
1	Frog	Demonstrates one or two of the critical elements
0	Turtle	Demonstrates none of the critical elements

---

rubric, you should first picture what you would like student performance on a particular task to look like. Then create a rubric (see Figure 6.6).

Rubrics generally have at least three descriptive levels and include

1. The key points, criteria, or characteristics describing the necessary elements being measured. For example, a jumping rubric would include bent knees, arms back, and reach arms forward.

2. Definitions or descriptors for interpreting the levels of performance of student responses, such as beginner, intermediate, advanced.

3. A rating scale or scoring strategy that is a measure of the student response for the task.

The rubrics at the bottom of Figure 6.6 and in Application 6.15 provide examples of these three components and how they can be displayed in different formats.

HOW TO HOP

Name: _____

DIRECTIONS: Which picture shows a person who is hopping? Circle it.

_____   _____

Place the letter for the cue we worked on in class today in the blank under the correct picture.

D = one foot Down   **B** = Bend knee

S = Swing knee forward   **F** = top of up leg is Flat and level

RUBRIC

Professional: Correctly identifies the picture and cue showing one foot down

Semi-professional: Correctly identifies the picture and cue but places in the wrong blank

Amateur: Correctly identifies the picture but does not recognize the proper cue or vice versa

Novice: Incorrectly identifies the picture and cue

FIGURE **6.6**
The rubric on this assignment sheet shows how student performance on the sheet would be assessed. Rubrics generally have at *least* three descriptive levels.

STUDENT RESPONSIBILITY LEVEL

DIRECTIONS: At the end of the lesson, indicate the level of student responsibility that each student displayed by writing the appropriate color by their name.

Student's Name	Color

RUBRIC

Super Green

■ Always follows directions

■ Always on task

■ Never interrupts the teacher

■ Asks the teacher if he or she needs help setting up and cleaning up

■ Tries to help peers in skill work in games

Green

■ Always follows directions

■ Usually on task

■ Never interrupts teacher

■ Never bothers other students

Yellow

■ Follows most directions

■ Usually on task

■ Usually does not interrupt teacher

■ Usually does not bother other students

Red

■ Does not follow most directions

■ Often off task

■ Often interrupts teacher

■ Often bothers other students

Student Portfolios

Student portfolios have recently been seen as a more comprehensive means for assessing student learning (Hebert, 1998; Herman & Winters, 1994; Melograno, 1994; O'Neil, 1992). **Portfolios** are purposeful collections of student work (various alternative assessment tools) and can be used to document students' comprehension of content, motor skill ability, understanding of concepts, and thoughts or feelings about physical activity.

portfolio
A collection of student work gathered over time and used to document progress.

STANDARD 2: Applies movement concepts and principles to the learning and development of motor skills.

Program Outcome: By leaving K–12 physical education program, the student will understand movement concepts, principles, strategies, and tactics as they apply to the learning and performance of physical activities.

Course: By the end of elementary school, the student will identify cues and principles relative to specific locomotor, nonlocomotor, and manipulative skills to improve skill performance.

Unit: By the end of the unit on throwing, the student will demonstrate knowledge of movement concepts and performance cues for all types of throws.

Lesson: By the end of the lesson, the student will identify the common performance cues for the underhand and overhand throw.

Portfolio Task: At the end of class, students will complete the diagram comparing and contrasting the parts of the underhand and overhand throw.

RUBRIC

Excellent: The student correctly identifies all the common cues of the overhand and underhand throw.

Good: The student correctly identifies some of the common cues of the overhand and underhand throw.

Needs work: The student fails to correctly identify any of the common cues of the overhand and underhand throw.

THROWING CUES COMPARE/CONTRAST SHEET

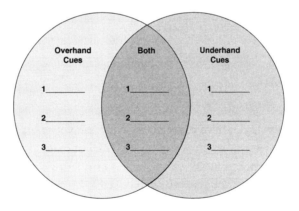

Portfolios document student progress because they include the various alternative assessment tools administered over time. The results of these assessments give a more realistic picture of what students know and are able to perform. Portfolios are assembled throughout the year with thought and purpose to document the knowledge and skills the student has mastered toward the established learning outcomes. Applications 6.16 and 6.17 are examples of performance tasks that assess NASPE standards 2 and 5 and could be placed in the student's portfolio to demonstrate knowledge of throwing cues and how they feel about differences in people.

STANDARD 5: Demonstrate an understanding and respect for differences among people in physical activity settings.

Program Outcome: By K-12 physical education program, the student will show responsible personal and social behavior that respects self and others in physical activity settings.

Course: By the end of elementary school, the student will begin to recognize and respect some differences among people in physical activity.

Unit: By the end of fifth grade, the student will be able to recognize that some physical activity is stereotyped a "girl" activity and some is stereotyped a "boy" activity. They will respect the right of each individual to pursue physical activity because of enjoyment and challenge and not because of how the sport is labeled.

Lesson: By the end of the lesson on baton twirling, students will recognize that people enjoy different types of activities.

Assessment Task: Students will complete a questionnaire about the activity of baton twirling. Students will say who they believe should participate in this activity and why.

RUBRIC

Respectful: The student recognizes that many physical activities are stereotyped according to gender. The student expresses respect for the right of others to choose a physical activity based on personal enjoyment.

Trying to Understand: The student recognizes that some sports may be stereotyped by gender. The student does not feel that it is OK for students to choose stereotyped sports.

Disrespectful: The student does not recognize that there is stereotyping of sports. The student feels that it is unacceptable to choose stereotyped sports. The student expresses rejection toward a person choosing such an activity.

continued

Once you have selected the outcomes you want to assess, keeping track of all the assessment items can be difficult, but managing the physical education portfolio is not unlike keeping track of a student's classroom portfolio. You can manage student portfolios by using manila folders, milk crates, three-ring binders, boxes, or accordion folders. To save critical time when using portfolios, teach students (1) where to find the physical education portfolio in the classroom; (2) how and where to file the results of assessment items; and (3) how to document progress versus showing evidence of their best work.

STEP FOUR: GRADING

Most elementary schools require only an *S* (satisfactory) or *U* (unsatisfactory), *P* (pass) or *F* (fail) grade in physical education. Those who teach physical education should still be held accountable for what students are learning. You still want to be able to determine how well children are meeting physical education outcomes. See

RESPECTING DIFFERENCES

Name _____

1. Did you enjoy learning how to twirl a baton? Why or why not?

   _____

   _____

2. In your opinion, which gender group most often does baton twirling, boys or girls?

   _____

   _____

3. John is a third grade boy. He wants to play a sport after school. What should be John's main reason for choosing his activity? Check your answer.

   ❏ Because it is a boy activity   ❏ Because he enjoys doing the activity

4. What do you think a boy should do if he really likes to twirl batons? Do you think he should be told he cannot do baton twirling because it is a "girl" activity?

   _____

   _____

   a. Do you think other people would make fun of a boy who chose to twirl a baton?

      _____

      _____

   b. Do you think this would be right or wrong? Explain your answer.

      _____

      _____

5. Look at the activities listed below. Tell if you think they are "boy" activities, "girl" activities, or can be both boy and girl. Write boy, girl, or both on the line following the activity.

   Gymnastics _____   Football _____

   Hockey _____   Ballet _____

   Horsback riding _____   Ping-Pong _____

   Tennis _____   Wrestling _____

6. Pick one activity from above. Explain why you chose the answer you did.

   _____

   _____

Source: Deana Schnuelle, Ogletree Elementary School, Auburn, Alabama.

STANDARD 1: Demonstrate competency in many movement forms and proficiency in a few movement forms.

Program Outcome: By K–12 physical education program, the student will be able to demonstrate competency in motor skills and movement patterns needed to perform a variety of physical activities.

Course Outcome: By the end of elementary school, the student will competently use individual locomotor, nonlocomotor, and manipulative skills in a variety of appropriate practice situations.

Unit: By the end of the unit on dribbling with the feet, the student will dribble in various directions and with different speeds while demonstrating mature form.

Lesson: By the end of the lesson, the student will dribble while looking forward, using the inside of the feet, and keeping the ball close.

Performance Task: Have students work with a partner. One partner dribbles through the obstacle course twice. The grading partner observes each trial and completes the checklist. After two trials through the course, have students change roles.

RUBRIC

Excellent: The student demonstrates all three critical elements on each trial.

Good: The student demonstrates all of the critical elements on two trials.

Improving: The student demonstrates all of the critical elements on one throw or demonstrates two or fewer critical elements on any trial.

Needs Work: The student fails to demonstrate any of the critical elements on any trial.

DRIBBLING WITH THE FEET

As you are observing, check the "observed" box if your partner demonstrates the critical element. Leave the box blank if your partner does not demonstrate the critical element.

Name	Looks Forward	Uses Inside of Feet	Keeps the Ball Close
1.	❑ Observed	❑ Observed	❑ Observed
2.	❑ Observed	❑ Observed	❑ Observed
3.	❑ Observed	❑ Observed	❑ Observed
4.	❑ Observed	❑ Observed	❑ Observed
5.	❑ Observed	❑ Observed	❑ Observed

Application 6.18 for an assessment to meet a physical education program outcome (NASPE Standard 1). To do this accurately, you must first decide what to assess and the rubrics to determine student achievement. Then use a variety of assessment tools to document student achievement. These tools inform parents and administrators what children are learning.

To overcome the broad generalities in current grading, teachers should base physical education grades on student achievement, not behavior. For example, for a *P* or *S* grade, students need to perform adequately on several assessment items during the grading period. A portfolio can keep the results of student performance

PLAINSMAN ELEMENTARY SCHOOL PHYSICAL EDUCATION PROGRESS REPORT

First and Second Grade: First nine weeks (August 16–October 20, 20__)

Name _____ PE Grade _____ Conduct Grade _____

Dear Parents:

Listed below are the skills and concepts your child has been working on for the first nine weeks. Please look at the specific skills to see where your child might need additional practice. We enjoy working with your child in physical education class. Please call if you have questions.

Thank you,

Plainsman PE Teachers

Skills	Skill Is Consistent	Needs Practice
RUN—trunk leans forward, arms bent, knees bend and extend	❑	❑
SKIP—forward, alternate feet	❑	❑
GALLOP—forward, one foot leads, smooth	❑	❑
SLIDE—sideways movement, in air	❑	❑
JUMP—two feet together, bends knees, swings arms	❑	❑
HOP—one foot, on toes, lands lightly	❑	❑
Personal Space—can find a good space without touching anyone else	❑	❑
General Space—travels in the shared space without touching others	❑	❑
General Space—travels and changes directions	❑	❑
Volleys a beach ball upward continuously with control	❑	❑
Identifies and moves parts of the body	❑	❑
Combines locomotor skills with pathways, speeds, and force	❑	❑
Levels—identifies and works in high, middle, and low levels	❑	❑
Throws and catches a ball alone	❑	❑

Source: Deana Schnuelle, Ogletree Elementary School, Auburn, Alabama.

on a variety of alternative assessments like rating scales, assignment sheets, and journals specifically relating to program outcomes. Once you have determined how grades will be decided, communicate this clearly to parents and students. You can do this through class discussions at the start of the school year as well as by creating a newsletter or pamphlet that goes home to parents detailing the grading process.

Sometimes children's progress is hard to explain to parents in one grading period, so progress reports may help document where children are in developing fundamental motor skills, basic knowledge of physical activity concepts, and interactive behavior. Progress reports can be sent at the end of the grading term or periodically after various assessments have been given (see Application 6.19).

Besides telling parents about their child's progress, you should provide some suggestions for how they can help their child improve in specific motor skill areas. For example, if a child has difficulty catching a tossed ball, suggest that the parent help the child practice by tossing a large soft foam ball to him or her from a short distance. This would help the child work on tracking skills and alleviate his or her fear of getting hurt by the thrown object.

THE RIGHT TIME TO ASSESS

Now that you know *how* to assess, here are some general guidelines for *when* to assess. As discussed in Chapter 4, the last step in the daily lesson plan is assessment—you should assess every lesson you teach. This can be done informally with a quick observational strategy such as checking for understanding or a recognition check. A quick assessment doesn't give you a formal documented account of student progress, but it does provide some idea of how well the child learned the material. More formal or documented assessments should be completed for each of your state's curriculum standards. For example, Georgia has ten standards that fifth graders should meet in physical education. By the end of the year, you should have at least two separate assessments for each standard identified, spread equally over the course of the grading periods. This general rule is not true for all situations, because physical education time allocations vary from state to state; so sometimes completing even one assessment per standard may present a challenge in itself.

FINAL WORDS

It is part of your job as a teacher to document and evaluate student learning. This is one of your most critical roles. Assessment determines and documents students' progress in learning the intended content.

As pictured in the road map in Figure 6.1, assessment starts with the teacher identifying the course's desired outcomes—what students need to know and should be able to do as a result of instruction. These outcomes subsequently inform the planning and instruction process. Giving students learning activities without identifying outcomes effectively nullifies the teacher's ability to document learning.

This chapter was designed to help you understand the importance of assessment in diagnosing, grouping, motivating, improving, and documenting student achievement. To do this effectively, administer alternative forms of assessment to measure characteristics, attributes, and behaviors in the three learning domains. This helps paint a more realistic picture of student progress. After gathering various assessment data, your evaluation in rubrics or student portfolios connects assessment to achievement. You can then report this information to parents and administrators to document what students are *learning* in physical education.

OVER TO YOU

1. You are interviewing for a job in a local elementary school. The principal asks how you see the role of assessment relating to student learning. What would you answer?

2. What are the advantages and disadvantages of the different assessment tools presented in this chapter, such as checklists, rating scales, and student journals?

3. Respond to the statement, "Children should be graded on improvement and participation in physical education." Use the information in this chapter to justify your answer.

4. Differentiate between formative and summative assessment.

PORTFOLIO TASKS

1. You have just completed a lesson on jumping and landing. Create a checklist or rating scale to assess the students in your physical education classroom.

2. In this chapter, the "assessment road map" was used to tie assessment to outcomes. Create a new graphic that better shows the relationship among outcomes, instruction, and assessment. Explain how your picture reflects this relationship.

3. Review at least six websites with information about assessment. Write a short critique of each website's usefulness to teachers.

4. Create a crossword puzzle for the assessment terms covered in this chapter.

REFERENCES

Hebert, E. A. (1998). Lessons learned about student portfolios. *Phi Delta Kappan, 79*(8), 583–585.

Herman, J., & Winters, L. (1994). Portfolio research: A slim collection. *Educational Leadership, 52*(3), 80–84.

Hopple, C. J. (1995). *Teaching outcomes in elementary physical education: A guide for curriculum and assessment.* Champaign, IL: Human Kinetics.

Melograno, V. J. (1994). Portfolio assessment: Documenting authentic student learning. *Journal of Physical Education, Recreation & Dance, 65*(8), 50–61.

National Association for Sport and Physical Education (NASPE). (2004). *Moving into the future: National standards for physical education* (2nd ed.). Reston, VA: American Alliance for Health, Physical Education, Recreation and Dance.

O'Neil, J. (1992). Putting performance assessment to the test. *Educational Leadership, 49*(5), 14–19.

Physical activity is important to children! Think about the spontaneity with which children run and play. Consider too the friendships that are forged during play. From a child's point of view, physical activity is a meaningful and joyous part of life. But the joy inherent in movement and play can be clouded by the distractions of discipline problems, equipment failures, and safety concerns. This unit invites you to mirror your students' natural enthusiasm for physical activity by managing your physical education lessons with care. Chapter 7 discusses how to promote rules of conduct; Chapter 8 covers how to manage equipment and space; and Chapter 9 offers valuable information on how to manage students' behavior during the lesson. The unit closes with Chapter 10, which takes an important look at promoting physical safety.

MANAGING THE DELIVERY OF THE PHYSICAL EDUCATION LESSON

UNIT III

"We've done a lot of important playing here today."

MANAGING A PHYSICAL EDUCATION CLASS: PROTOCOLS, RULES, AND ACCOUNTABILITY SYSTEMS

CHAPTER

7

1. What are your expectations for the quality of student work in physical education class?

2. Other than by verbal praise, how can you recognize your students' good work during physical education lessons?

3. Explain the statement: "What you reinforce is what you get."

4. Why is it important to move about your class during a physical education lesson?

INQUIRING MINDS

Children need to be held accountable for their behavior. How do you do this in your classroom?

Perhaps you can recall from your own elementary school days teachers who had different approaches to managing a classroom full of students. Some were probably very strict and businesslike, while others made learning fun, so that time seemed to fly during class. Still other teachers were probably so lax that you could get away with nearly anything. This chapter introduces broad concepts and practices for managing your classroom efficiently while teaching physical education. Subsequent chapters in this unit focus on more specific topics: managing space, equipment, and time (Chapter 8); managing student behavior (Chapter 9); and safety management (Chapter 10).

TASKS AS OBJECTS OF MANAGEMENT

What all levels of schooling, all subject areas, and all classrooms have in common is that they require students to engage in "tasks." But tasks aren't only centered on study; they also involve specifics of student behavior and conduct. During a physical education lesson, a simple behavioral task might involve holding a ball still while the teacher is talking, while a more complex one might be for a small group to work cooperatively to create a kicking game using specific equipment.

Thus, any class includes an **instructional task system** that teaches subject matter and a **managerial task system** that establishes and maintains appropriate behavior. The managerial task system in a classroom tends to focus on tasks that students need to perform to be "in good standing," such as those related to appropriate behavior and dress.

As we discussed in Chapter 1, effective teachers are good managers who present managerial tasks so precisely that children are never confused about expectations. Precisely delivered tasks leave students little room to stretch parameters without risking correction. Physical education teachers present tasks precisely with a system of protocols and rules.

instructional task system
Those tasks relating to the subject matter.

managerial task system
Those tasks relating to the establishment and maintenance of appropriate behavior.

FIGURE **7.1**
Practicing a protocol for stopping. When the teacher raises her arm, the students stop in place and raise their hands to signal that they understand the protocol. The teacher practices the protocol until she is confident that all her students are responding correctly.

BOX 7.1 ■ **Management Protocols Used in Physical Education**

1. Starting and stopping work

2. Listening to instructions

3. Getting with a partner or into groups

4. Getting and returning equipment

5. Transitions between tasks

6. Lining up at the end of class

Source: Adapted from *Developing Teaching Skills in Physical Education,* by D. Siedentop and D. Tannehill, 2000, Mountain View, CA: Mayfield Publishing.

PROTOCOLS AS MANAGEMENT TOOLS

Protocols are simply customary routines for handling a particular situation (Rink, 2002). In physical education, protocols promote efficient management of movement and classroom events. Paradoxically, protocols are useful management tools exactly because they *minimize* the time spent on classroom management, thus allowing you to *maximize* your sudents' time for practicing movement skills.

For protocols to be useful, students have to understand what you expect them to do and how to go about doing it. You should formally present each new protocol to students and then have them *practice it until they learn it* (see Figure 7.1). Later in this chapter, you will read how time-tested strategies can help students learn the expected behaviors associated with a protocol. It's important to understand immediately that you must hold students accountable for their responses to protocols. If you teach a new protocol and then do nothing when students stop behaving as expected, that protocol will do little to help you manage them. Box 7.1 lists

protocol
Customary way of handling a situation.

WHAT'S WRONG WITH THIS PICTURE?

Ms. Brown notices that Terry and Samantha are using the wrong technique in kicking their soccer ball. She stops the class and tells all the children to watch how Terry is "not getting his shoelaces anywhere close to the ball" while Samantha "has no clue about stepping next to the ball with her nonkicking foot." Ms. Brown then demonstrates the correct technique.

management goals that apply to nearly every physical education class taught to elementary school children. Chapters 8 and 9 present protocols to help you address each of these classroom management goals when delivering a physical education lesson.

APPLYING RULES

While a protocol is an often-repeated routine, a **rule** is a stated expectation. A protocol applies to a specific situation (such as what to do when asked to line up), whereas a rule may apply to many different situations. A rule about working safely could be applied to a chasing, fleeing, and dodging game as well as a gymnastics lesson. In both activities, you would expect students to behave so as to avoid harm to themselves or their classmates.

Many of your classroom rules also apply to the physical education setting. These all-encompassing rules are most likely to relate to student–teacher interactions (such as not talking when the teacher is giving directions) and student–student interactions (such as treating classmates with respect). You will find a detailed discussion of specific rules for managing children's behavior during physical education in Chapter 9.

ACCOUNTABILITY IN PHYSICAL EDUCATION

rule
A stated expectation with regard to personal conduct.

Your managerial task system cannot be divorced from your instructional task system. Classrooms are not managed in a vacuum; management goals typically come out of the learning goals you set for your class, and children must be held equally accountable to the managerial and instructional task systems. Physical education is meant to teach students to move purposefully by developing basic motor skills. This is why you give students ample practice time to master the motor skills that are the object of your lesson plan (i.e., your instructional task system). In turn, you hold your students accountable for completing the lesson plan according to your expectations (e.g., for a specific number of repetitions or successful tries). Figure 7.2 explains the relationship between a lesson plan and its accountability system.

FIGURE **7.2**
The relationship between the physical education lesson plan and an accountability system. The plan lets students practice new motor skills, while the accountability system tracks their performance.

Since the basic physical education lesson plan was already covered in Chapter 4, the rest of this chapter turns to accountability. As with every facet of teaching physical education, your aim in developing accountability is to create a supportive and inclusive experience for all your children.

Accountability Systems

During a lesson, you are likely to tell your students how well they are doing. You might refer to instructional tasks ("You used your shoelaces really well that time with your kick") or managerial tasks ("You need to stay within the boundaries"). Evaluation connects task performance to your accountability system. **Accountability systems** are routines or procedures that you follow to hold your students accountable for their performance and conduct. Accountability is the link between the teacher and the behavior of the teacher's students.

Levels of Accountability

There are three levels of accountability in physical education, distinguished by feedback from the teacher about children's participation, effort, and performance quality (see Figure 7.3). The third and highest level of accountability is reflected in the teacher's feedback (both positive and negative) about students' performance quality.

Indeed, the reason why the teacher's reactions to effort and performance quality (the second and third levels of this model) are so important is that what *really* matters in accountability is the degree to which the teacher *responds to student work*. In fact, a student's success at practicing a task depends more on what happens *after* the initial period of instruction. Let's look at the following scenario to understand this very important idea:

> Ms. Brown's fourth grade class is learning about trapping a soccer ball. She has focused on trapping with the sole of the foot (i.e., putting the sole of the foot on the rolling ball and holding it to the ground).
>
> Ms. Brown demonstrates the skill and provides the following instruction: "With a partner, I want you to tap the ball back and forth using light force and stop the ball with the sole of your foot." She now observes while her students practice.
>
> After two or three passes, Billy and Jermel decide that passing the ball back and forth without stopping it is a lot more fun. They keep moving farther apart, kicking the ball harder and harder. Meanwhile, Kobe and

accountability system
The routines and procedures used by teachers for establishing and maintaining student responsibility for their work in the classroom.

Participation	Effort	Performance Quality
"You boys over there need to quit worrying about throwing stones and start passing that soccer ball."	"Nice try, Henry. You and Jessica are really working today."	"Chantel, keep that toe pointed down on your punts." "Eric, what did we say about where to hold the ball before you punt it?"

Lower level ⟶ Higher level

FIGURE **7.3**
Three levels of accountability in physical education

Source: Adapted from "A Qualitative Analysis of Task Structure in Required Secondary Physical Education Classes," by M. Tousignant and D. Siedentop, 1983, *Journal of Teaching in Physical Education.*

INQUIRING MINDS

Do you find some active supervision strategies more effective in your classroom? Why?

Jessica are using a foot trap to stop the ball. (In a foot trap, the ball is stopped using the inside or outside of the foot, as it "gives" with the motion of the ball.) Angela and Amy, out of view of the teacher, start talking about the school skate night scheduled for this Friday.

Ms. Brown's response to her students has important implications for the actual work that gets done in the allocated time, which we call the "actual task," as opposed to the original assignment or "stated task." The following list of response options shows the difference between the "stated task" and the "actual task" that emerges on the basis of the teacher's feedback:

1. Ms. Brown provides no feedback to any of her students.

   Actual task: "Do what you like, as long as it doesn't break any managerial rules, such as not fighting or disrupting other students."

2. Ms. Brown ignores Billy and Jermel but tells Amy and Angela to get working.

   Actual task: "Make sure you at least kick the ball to each other, but don't worry about how well."

3. Ms. Brown tells Amy and Angela to get to work and asks Billy and Jermel if they need a time-out because they were told to trap the ball.

   Actual task: "Make sure you kick the ball to each other and stop it in some fashion."

4. Ms. Brown stops the class and asks them to watch Kobe and Jessica. She points out that while they are using light force to pass the ball, they are not using their soles, but their insteps. She again shows her sole to remind them to use this part of the foot to trap the ball and then asks Billy and Jermel to demonstrate how well they can do this task.

   Actual task: Same as the stated task.

When the level of instructional accountability is insufficiently demanding, even students who originally were on task (i.e., doing the stated task) may drift off task and invent their own challenges if they conclude that accountability applies only to the managerial system. You must be disciplined enough to keep everyone on the stated task.

148   Unit III ■ Managing the Delivery of the Physical Education Lesson

TABLE **7.1** ■ Informal Accountability Strategies

Form of Feedback	Accountability
Public recognition	John and Li, good job! I like the way you stopped when I gave the signal.
	Eric, give yourself a point on the chart. You were the first to get your equipment all put away.
Hustles and prompts	Hey, you guys over there—get with it!
	Charlton, keep that rope turning quickly! That's the way!
Monitoring	Intently watching students perform a task so they are aware of your presence.
Task-related feedback	That's the way to use light force, Dante. See how the ball stays right close to you?
	Everyone in this group over here is really making contact with their shoelaces.
	Sam, get behind the ball before it gets to you. Don't wait 'til it's almost there.
Skill challenges	Let's see if we can make five good serves in a row. Your partner will keep score and return the ball.
	The challenge is to go for 30 seconds without stopping.

Source: Adapted from "Assessment and Accountability in Secondary Physical Education," by J. Lund, 1992, *Quest 44*, pp. 352–360.

Formal and Informal Accountability

Accountability can be formal or informal. **Formal accountability** involves giving students grades (see Chapter 6). **Informal accountability** is real-time feedback to students about how well each student is doing, with no grading involved. Table 7.1 shows some informal accountability strategies a teacher might use in a physical education lesson. The types of feedback can include public recognition, hustles, monitoring, task-related feedback, and skill challenges.

Active Supervision

To make the informal accountability strategies in Table 7.1 effective, you must use supervision strategies. In **active supervision,** a teacher moves about, interacting with students and providing a constant stream of high-level feedback. A teacher using **passive supervision** has little interaction with students.

Researchers (van der Mars et al., 1994, 1998) have concluded that three supervision patterns correlate with children's activity levels and success during a physical education lesson:

1. The teacher's location
2. The teacher's rate of movement
3. The provision of verbal feedback

formal accountability
System in which mechanisms such as tests or assignments are used to give students grades.

informal accountability
System where the performance does not directly contribute toward a grade; examples include practice exams, active supervision, sitting out, public recognition, and teacher feedback.

active supervision
A pattern of teaching that includes higher rates of interaction between students and movement.

passive supervision
A pattern of teaching with little interaction between the teacher and students.

FIGURE **7.4**
Back to the wall. This active supervision strategy of keeping outside the group while watching inwards lets you observe your students while not intruding on their practice space.

When teachers spent more time along the sides of the activity area, actively moved from place to place, and provided enthusiastic verbal feedback, their students tended to be more engaged in activity and more likely to stay on task. Four particularly useful strategies for engaging in active supervision are

1. Movement
2. Back to the wall
3. Proximity reinforcement
4. Pinpointing

Movement

As an active-supervision strategy, **movement** involves constantly changing position around the physical education work area. Teachers standing in one place become predictable, and students soon discover places in the work area to which they can retreat without the teacher noticing. Your constant movement makes children less able to predict your presence, so they are less likely to work off task. Constantly changing position also lets you work individually with more students.

Back to the Wall

Although moving about is good, you don't want to intrude into your students' work area and disrupt their skill practice. In the strategy called **back to the wall,** the teacher stands on the periphery where he or she can see what all students are doing without impinging on their space, as if leaning back against an imaginary wall to watch, rather than trying to direct things from the group's center (Graham, Holt/Hale, & Parker, 2004).

Using a back-to-the-wall strategy lets you watch your students to be sure they remain on task (see Figure 7.4). When you notice students working off task, you should immediately redirect their behavior to stop it from escalating. You also want to prevent a "ripple effect" whereby one student's off-task behavior influences another student and then another (Kounin, 1970).

movement
The teacher's constant changing of position around the physical education work area.

back to the wall
The strategy of standing on the periphery of the classroom or instructional session to better see what all students are doing.

FIGURE **7.5**
Cross-group feedback. The teacher is working with one student while providing feedback or management comments to a group at a distance. This lets all students know they are being monitored.

A back-to-the-wall strategy also lets you watch *all* students as they practice skill tasks. By scanning the class, you can identify students who deserve praise, as well as alert students to specific refinements (modifications in performance) they may need while practicing. Researchers have found that **cross-group feedback,** or feedback directed to students from the periphery of the work area, consistently reduces off-task behavior (Ryan and Berg, 2001). But cross-group feedback is possible only when all of your students remain in full view (see Figure 7.5).

However you mix these strategies, you should always avoid becoming "grounded," or stuck in one spot on the work area. As we said before, students are quick to realize where they can move out of your line of sight and engage in off-task behavior.

Proximity Reinforcement

While verbal and gestural feedback (like a thumbs-up) are useful for holding students accountable, even your mere proximity can positively affect students' behavior. When an individual or group of students are off task, you don't always need to tell them to desist. Simply moving toward the students makes it known that you are aware of their behavior and is often enough to bring them back on task.

Pinpointing

Pinpointing directs the class to the work of *two or more students* to highlight a specific cue or outcome. (Note: We ask students to watch more than one classmate to avoid the stress of making a single student the center of attention.) Here is

cross-group feedback
Feedback for students who are across the gym or work area from the teacher.

pinpointing
The act of directing the class to the work of *two or more students* to highlight a specific cue or outcome.

a specific example in which students are practicing kicking a ball long distances with their insteps:

> Girls and boys, watch Sam and Tony, Lee and Quang, and Enrique and Will. I want you to watch how each of them places their nonkicking foot alongside the ball. Some of us are putting that foot behind the ball instead of alongside it.

Pinpointing serves as an accountability strategy for reinforcing your expectations for students' success. It is important to note, however, that pinpointing should only be used to highlight good work. It should not be used to shame students who are not on task. Pinpointing shows all students how to do the task well. It also lets students know that you have "eyes in the back of your head" and can see everyone who is working.

FINAL WORDS

Any lesson in any subject area is made up of a series of tasks which serve to direct students' actions during both management and instruction. To reiterate, efficient physical education teachers address managerial tasks by teaching protocols that *minimize* management and thus *maximize* time for practicing skills and achieving fitness. But protocols are effective only insofar as you hold students accountable for following them accurately. Furthermore, accountability is not for management issues alone. Children should also be held accountable for the quality of their performance. Only then will they achieve their maximum potential.

OVER TO YOU

1. Which management protocol will be the most difficult for you during physical education lessons?

2. How well do the protocols presented in this chapter match those in your own non-physical education classroom? Will many be directly transferable from one setting to the other?

1. Write a philosophy statement describing your attitude toward classroom management in physical education.

2. Explain to a classmate how instruction and management are *interdependent;* that is, how events related to management have a direct effect on instruction.

3. Write a script for a short videotape (one that includes your students) demonstrating the six protocols in Box 7.1.

REFERENCES

Graham, G., Holt/Hale, S. A., & Parker, M. (2004). *Children moving: A reflective approach to teaching physical education* (6th ed.). Boston: McGraw-Hill.

Kounin, J. S. (1970). *Discipline and group management in classrooms.* Huntington, NY: R. E. Krieger.

Lund, J. (1992). Assessment and accountability in secondary physical education. *Quest 44,* 352–360.

Rink, J. E. (2002). *Teaching physical education for learning* (4th ed.). Dubuque, IA: McGraw-Hill.

Ryan, S., & Yerg, B. (2001). The effects of crossgroup feedback on off-task behavior in a physical education setting. *Journal of Teaching in Physical Education, 20,* 172–188.

Siedentop, D., & Tannehill, D. (2000). *Developing teaching skills in physical education.* Mountain View, CA: Mayfield Publishing.

Tousignant, M., & Siedentop, D. (1983). A qualitative analysis of task structure in required secondary physical education classes. *Journal of Teaching in Physical Education, 33,* 47–57.

van der Mars, H., Darst, P., Vogler, B., & Cusimano, B. (1994). Active supervision patterns of physical education teachers and their relationship with student behaviors. *Journal of Teaching in Physical Education, 14,* 99–112.

van der Mars, H., Vogler, B., Darst, P., & Cusimano, B. (1998). Students' physical activity levels and teachers' active supervision during fitness instruction. *Journal of Teaching in Physical Education, 18,* 57–75.

CHAPTER

8

MANAGING EQUIPMENT, SPACE, AND TIME

1. Why does teaching physical education involve different strategies from those you use to manage other classes?

2. How do children use equipment differently during physical education from the way they use equipment while studying other classroom topics?

3. Which features of physical education have significant potential for wasting time?

4. How might you use the concept of learning centers in physical education?

Teaching pysical education differs in a very important respect from teaching other topics: The object of a physical education lesson is deliberate physical movement. Although students may move about during other lessons, your aim is to make them move purposefully during physical education. Because *moving is the point of learning,* it is necessary to employ special techniques and skills to manage your children during a physical education lesson.

Teaching physical education also differs from teaching in the classroom in the use of equipment. Students may be manipulating bats, rackets, and a variety of balls. Sometimes these implements are projected over large distances—throwing, punting, or striking. So a physical education class needs protocols (routines) to move equipment to and from work areas and to control how it's used during the lesson (see Figure 8.1).

Finally, the size of the work area requires special management protocols. Physical education work areas are either outdoors or in relatively large indoor spaces. This extra space allows children to work safely but also makes communicating more difficult. Students may need extra time to gather when you need to give

FIGURE **8.1**
Students' use of hoops, balls, and other equipment poses management challenges that differ from the teaching of other classroom subjects.

instructions, and noise and other environmental distractions may disrupt teacher-to-student communication. Some physical education teachers tell how a fire truck, ambulance, or helicopter totally captured their students' attention, leaving the teachers talking to themselves.

This chapter teaches you how to manage equipment, work space, and time during a physical education lesson. The aim is to use strategies that *minimize* management time and *maximize* instruction time. Introducing the physical education management protocols in this chapter during the first few weeks of the school term can help make them a routine part of every physical education experience.

MANAGING EQUIPMENT

Bats and balls are significantly bigger than pencils and books. Taking equipment out of storage, distributing it to students, and then putting it away can consume a great deal of time that would better be spent actually teaching the physical education lesson. You can minimize your equipment management time with some simple strategies for transporting physical education equipment, distributing it, and returning it to storage.

Transporting Equipment

Planning which equipment to use during a physical education lesson typically requires far less time than collecting and moving it to the work area. Fortunately, some everyday tools and "human resources" can help you simplify this task. For example, a supermarket-style shopping cart can transport equipment from storage to the work area. Although shopping carts are almost impossible to purchase, you might ask a local store for one of their old stock. The alternative is to purchase a

FIGURE **8.2**
Shopping carts are handy for moving physical education equipment to a play area. You may be able to ask a supermarket to donate an old cart.

FIGURE **8.3**
Students can serve as "equipment managers" to transport equipment to and from the work area.

folding laundry or shopping cart. These typically sell for between $15 and $30, and seem to be a better investment than the ball carts sold by the sports equipment supply chains, which often retail at over $250. This type of cart can carry a lot of equipment, is relatively easy to maneuver, and provides a central point where students can retrieve and return equipment (see Figure 8.2). Placing large plastic tubs or trash cans in the cart can help to keep equipment properly sorted during the course of the lesson.

When an activity requires transport of a lot of equipment to the work area, or when areas need to be set up before game play, assign some students to be **equipment managers** (see Figure 8.3). Used often in games units (see Chapter 12), equipment managers are students responsible for collecting equipment (e.g., hockey sticks, balls, or team flags) and taking it to the work area. An advantage is that only a few students will gather around the equipment area at one time.

All students should be capable of being equipment managers. Learning this responsibility fits comfortably within national physical education standard 5—exhibiting "responsible personal and social behavior that respects self and others in physical activity settings."

Equipment managers are especially helpful when you organize older students into teams. At the beginning of the lesson, each equipment manager collects the equipment his or her team needs. Meanwhile, an appointed warm-up leader leads the team through a series of exercises in preparation for play. A variation on this strategy is for all the students to share in equipment management tasks by being assigned to a particular equipment team. Before and after a lacrosse lesson, for example, the blue team collects the lacrosse sticks, while the gold team collects the balls and the red team collects the goals.

Of course, for an equipment manager strategy to run smoothly, you must train students in advance, teaching designated equipment managers what their responsibilities are and how to carry them out. Your equipment managers should know where to put equipment on arrival at the work area and how to return it to storage after the lesson.

equipment managers
Students who have responsibilities for collecting and returning specific pieces of equipment to and from the work area in which the lesson will be completed.

FIGURE **8.4**
Spreading rackets and balls across the work area minimizes distribution time and maximizes practice time.

Distributing Equipment to Children

When the equipment for a physical education lesson is in the work area, your next goal is to distribute it to your students quickly. Handing out equipment student by student usually is both time wasting and impractical. Choose from a couple of strategies to be sure that students receive equipment quickly and spend most of the lesson time practicing skills.

One strategy involves distributing the equipment across the work area, rather than keeping it in one central place (see Figure 8.4). For example, if students will be working with beanbags, place the beanbags in separate piles around the room, instructing the children:

> Girls and boys, as you look around the room you will see a number of hoops with beanbags in them. When I say "go," I want you to walk to the closest hoop, get a beanbag, and begin tossing and catching it with one hand.

If students are working in pairs, you can ask each member of a pair to collect a different piece of equipment. To implement this strategy, first ask the students to select one of two paired names, then use these names as directives for distributing equipment:

> If you're an orange, I want you to take a scoop from the bin. But if you're an apple, come to me and get a ball. When you are both back at your work area, you may begin rolling ground balls to your partner. Remember that our cue is to have the scoop all the way on the ground, so you are going to have to bend your knees.

Using name pairs such as "apples" and "oranges," you can allocate equipment distribution tasks among your students. This strategy also helps during the instructional phase of the physical education lesson; an apple might complete one task, while an orange completes another.

Mr. Todd is about to begin a lesson on juggling with his second grade class. He has decided to use scarves to make the task more appropriate for this age group. Mr. Todd's class is seated along the edge of the playing area, and he is walking along the row handing out three scarves to each student, one student at a time.

WHAT'S WRONG WITH THIS PICTURE?

Returning Equipment

A protocol helps when asking students to return equipment after a lesson, but phrase your expectations carefully. Consider the outcome, for example, if you simply tell students to toss their balls into a bucket at the end of a lesson. Few things are more fun to a fourth grader than trying to toss a ball into a bucket, so you shouldn't be surprised to see some students charging toward the container, treating it like a target or a basketball hoop. Use the word *place* instead, communicating that you expect students to set the balls carefully in the container. You will spend time wisely at the beginning of a school term when you make sure students understand the difference between *place* and *toss!*

You can adopt the same apples and oranges strategy in reverse for returning equipment. Even if every child has the same piece of equipment, such as a Frisbee, ask different groups to return the equipment at different times. Your related instructions might be:

> I'd like those of you wearing blue T-shirts to bring your Frisbees to the basket and place them in carefully. . . . Now those wearing red T-shirts. . . . Anyone else can now bring his or her Frisbee.

INQUIRING MINDS

What protocol do you have to deal with students giving out and putting away equipment? What do you ask the students to do with equipment while you are giving instructions?

MANAGING SPACE

Because physical education is about purposeful movement, you should teach students how to move about in a designated space. This skill lets them work independently during a physical education lesson, and it also fosters their safety. Children need to know the difference between *personal space* and *general space*. You especially must teach and reinforce these distinctions at the kindergarten and first grade levels.

Personal Space

All the space you can reach without moving from a particular spot is your **personal space** (see Figure 8.5). Try the following exercise to teach this idea to students. Ask each child to stand in place inside a hoop and then say:

> I want you to imagine that the area inside your hoop is your "house." Only you are allowed in your house. Now I want you to "explore" your house by

personal space
All the space you can take up without moving from a particular point.

FIGURE **8.5**
All the space each child can reach without moving from a particular spot is personal space.

bending, stretching, twisting, and turning without moving off the spot you're standing on. All the space around you that you can touch is your personal space.

General Space

The other spatial distinction, **general space,** is the area in which all the members of the class are working. General space usually has boundaries, either the natural ones of walls or fences or artificial ones defined by marker cones. Students need to learn to move in general space without bumping into each other, and they also need to be able to move from general space into personal space when directed. The following exercise can help students grasp the relationship between personal space and general space:

> I want each of you to surround yourself with an imaginary invisible bubble. The area inside your bubble is your personal space. When I say "Go," start walking very slowly around the room. If your bubble touches anybody else's bubble, it will pop! So you might have to stop and wait for somebody near you to move away before you can walk.

Throughout a physical education lesson, you will need to provide cues to help students manage their personal space or to direct them about moving about in general space. Application 8.1 demonstrates how personal space and general space can be factors when teaching throwing and catching skills to students in different elementary school grade levels.

general space
The area in which the entire class is working.

These examples show how the concepts of personal space and general space can be taught in physical education to children in different elementary grade level settings.

KINDERGARTEN

When I say "go," I want you to sit in your personal space facing a partner. As you face your partner, make sure that you are not in anybody else's personal space. You are going to roll the ball to your partner in a straight line and reach out to catch it.

SECOND GRADE

I want you to throw your beanbag in the air and catch it at various places around your body. Try to catch it above your head, out to the side, or at a low level below your knees. The challenge is to toss the beanbag so that you don't have to move out of your personal space to catch it. So don't throw it so high that it goes too far away from you, but toss it high enough so that it gives you a good challenge.

FOURTH GRADE

I want you to experiment with different ways to throw a Frisbee to a moving partner. The challenge is for the thrower to lead the receiver so that the Frisbee arrives at the same time and place as your partner does. Be aware that you are moving in general space, and so are other pairs. Be careful when you throw so that you don't move into the space of another group's throws. It is the responsibility of the thrower to toss to an open spot and not run your partner into another group.

MANAGING TIME

Once more, your goal is to maximize your students' practice time for movement skills by minimizing your time managing the class, following proven time management protocols for (1) stopping work and gaining students' attention, (2) beginning or resuming work, and (3) gathering students together. You can further increase activity time by providing an instant activity before the start of the lesson.

Stopping Work, Gaining Attention, and Dealing with Equipment

One of the most important protocols in teaching physical education is delivering the signal for students to stop work and give you their full attention. A whistle is the classic physical education tool for delivering a stop-and-attend signal. While a whistle can be effective outdoors, its sound may be jarring indoors, especially in a small space.

FIGURE **8.6**
The protocol for dealing with equipment after stopping work for these children is to hold the ball beneath one foot as they listen to instructions.

Fortunately, there are other effective stop-and-attend signals. The most commonly used verbal command is "Freeze!" You might clap your hands, use a drumbeat, or stop the music. You may also simply raise your hand and then wait until all your students raise theirs to indicate that they have understood your command.

Students also need to know what you expect them to do with their equipment when you signal them to stop. With their abundant energy, children can unthinkingly start tossing beanbags or dribbling balls when they should be paying full attention to you. Hence, *before* beginning a lesson, you should explain what students are to do with equipment when they hear or see the "stop" signal. Your choices can include directing students to:

- Place the equipment on the space in front of them

- Hold the equipment with a body part (for example, "put your foot on the ball" (see Figure 8.6) or "hold the balloon on your belly and the paddle on your hip")

- Put the equipment down and take two steps back

Some teachers use a countdown sequence to get attention, stop work, and deal with equipment. The practice of "Give Me 5"[a] is one such sequence:

1. Stop.

2. Have your eyes on the teacher.

3. Be quiet and still.

4. Have your hands free (not touching anybody or anything).

5. Be ready to listen.

---

a. With permission, PE Central: pecentral.com/lessonideas/ViewLesson.asp?ID=871

When every student understands each step of the sequence, you can collapse this protocol into a single simple command: "Give me 5!"

Protocols for Resuming Work

Students often begin an activity while you are still teaching. If you want pairs of students to throw and catch a ball, some of them will begin this task before you have finished your explanation. To prevent this, preface any instruction with "when I say go." It also helps to (1) present the task, (2) ask students to organize themselves, and then (3) prior to the "go" signal, ask them to show you that they are ready. Box 8.1 gives a specific verbal example. "Go" can produce a frenzied response from very young, enthusiastic children. Other phrases might be "start practicing" or "begin." Both of these commands are simple and clearly understood and help preface the task.

Signal for Gathering

During a physical education lesson, your students may be spread out over a large general space. You will sometimes want them to come and gather around you after they see or hear the "stop" signal. One strategy for telling students to gather is to use a clearly distinguishable hand signal or particular body motion. You might use a lasso motion to indicate to students to move in quickly to wherever you are, circling the imaginary lasso to mimic "gathering in" all your students for the next set of instructions or a new demonstration.

USING STATIONS AS A WAY OF MANAGING SPACE, EQUIPMENT, AND TIME

The physical education work area available to you may be an outdoor playing field, a gymnasium, or your everyday classroom. Regardless of the work area's size, managing that space, equipment, and time well will maximize your students' opportunity to benefit from and enjoy the lesson. Dividing the physical education work area into stations is one way to achieve this goal.

INQUIRING MINDS

When do you use stations for instructional purposes?

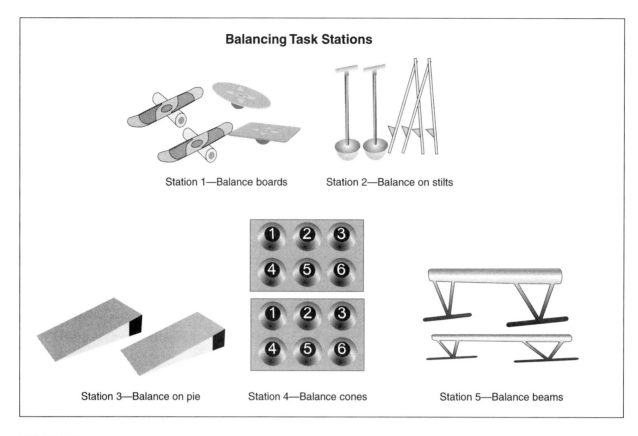

Balancing Task Stations

Station 1—Balance boards Station 2—Balance on stilts

Station 3—Balance on pie Station 4—Balance cones Station 5—Balance beams

FIGURE **8.7**
Stations allow efficient use of scarce equipment. In this example, the teacher has set up five stations, each focused on developing balancing skills. Students rotate from station to station so that everyone can try out each piece of equipment before the lesson is over.

A **station** is a learning center at which students concentrate on developing a set of skills. Usually stations are set up as a series so students rotate from one to another independently or in small groups. In physical education, stations allow students to develop specific motor skills around a common theme such as catching. Stations can also offer students practice in a variety of unrelated skills such as dribbling, volleying, striking, and throwing.

Advantages of Stations

There are a number of advantages to using stations during a physical education lesson. First, they provide an efficient use of space, with students distributed throughout the work area but still engaged in productive activity, even if not under your direct supervision. Second, stations are particularly useful when you have limited equipment. You may have a bucket of softballs but only a few pieces of specialized equipment like batting tees. Distributing scarce equipment among stations allows maximum participation by each student. During a lesson on balancing, for example, one group of students can practice on balance boards at Station 1 while another group practices with stilts at Station 2 (see Figure 8.7). By rotating from station to station, every student is able to try out each piece of equipment. Third, stations provide an efficient way of using lesson time, with students maximally engaged in practicing skills and minimally engaged in listening to instructions and waiting for turns. Of course, this depends on your making sure that the

stations
An instructional strategy in which children rotate from one learning task to another systematically throughout a lesson.

- **Addressing children's attention spans.** Stations let students rotate from one learning task to another throughout a physical education lesson. A rapid progression through a series of stations works particularly well with children, whose short attention spans may lead them to lose interest in certain activities fairly quickly.

- **Fostering heterogeneous grouping.** Stations let students work with other children whom they might not have partnered with or who are outside their usual cohort of friends.

- **Tailoring lessons to accommodate individual abilities.** You can offer multiple levels of a task at each station to accommodate different skill levels among students in your class. Stations can also give safe and inclusive learning experiences for differently abled students or those with special needs (see Chapter 2).

number of students in a group corresponds to the available equipment (i.e., four balls for four students). Other advantages to using stations are given in Box 8.2.

Designing Stations

The key to the successful use of stations lies in planning. To help you design stations for a physical education lesson, we have listed the four key questions:

1. How many stations should I have?
2. What is the best way to identify the different stations?
3. How should I group the children at stations?
4. What is the best way of communicating the task at each station?

How Many Stations Should I Have?

The number of stations you will include in a lesson will depend first on your class size and the amount of equipment and space available. With a small class and lots of equipment and space, you may have enough stations so that only two students are practicing at each, while a large class with limited resources might require you to set up stations where five students are either practicing or waiting for a turn. The station format can help when you don't have a sufficient quantity of equipment for every child in class. For example, in a striking lesson, you can avoid the problem of children waiting for turns by using paddles and foam balls at one station, badminton rackets and birdies at a second, and golf clubs and softball bats at a third. The general goal is to distribute equipment among stations so all students are practicing skills throughout the lesson.

Class size and equipment availability are not the only factors to consider when determining the number of stations. Safety issues and the need for close

WHAT'S WRONG WITH THIS PICTURE?

Ms. Thomas is teaching striking with hockey sticks to her third grade class of 24 children. She has borrowed four large sticks from the high school coach. The students have been placed in groups of six and have been asked to hit a puck to each other in turn.

supervision also play a big part. During a gymnastics lesson, you may want fewer stations than in a lesson where the focus is on dribbling with the hands and feet.

The amount of time students need to practice a skill also affects the number of stations to include. When the tasks at each station take longer to complete, you will need fewer stations. In a lesson on throwing for distance, time will be needed for the retrieval of balls and other objects that are thrown. In a lesson on underarm throwing for accuracy, you will need time to re-set targets that get knocked over, like cans, pins, or cones. Lessons like these won't need many stations.

Finally, children's developmental level will influence the number of stations. Younger students with less experience need fewer stations to work through, while older students with more experience can rotate through more.

What Is the Best Way to Identify the Different Stations?

After you determine the number of stations you need, you must next identify the location and mark the boundaries of each station so students understand where they will be working. "Landmarks" in the work area can designate station locations. A pair of basketball goals might serve as the sites of two different stations. Hoops strung on a fence or taped to a wall might indicate other station locations.

Once you have located each station, mark out its boundaries. If your class is working indoors, you can identify station boundaries with cones or tape lines on the floor. Cones work for most outdoor work areas, too. On an outdoor work area with a hard surface, you can use playground chalk to make station boundaries and draw arrows showing the rotation pattern among stations.

Finally, give each station a distinct identity. With very young children, color is the most effective way to differentiate stations. You can tie colored balloons or tape blocks of colored paper next to each station. If you have them, different colored cones can also help children distinguish each station. For older students, you could mark each station with numbers or letters.

How Should I Group Children at Stations?

The number of students who can participate at a station primarily depends on the equipment, which in turn determines the number of stations you need. You should try to limit each station to a small number of students. What is small? Two or three students is an ideal number, although as many as five or six students could work concurrently at some fitness stations. What is important, though, is to distribute students evenly among the stations. It is desirable, although not always possible, to have the same number of students working at each station.

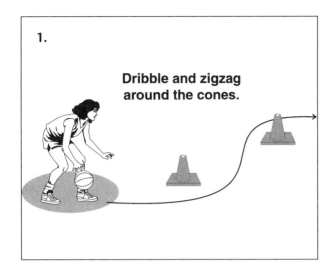

1.

Dribble and zigzag around the cones.

2.

See how many times you can dribble the basketball around your hoop

FIGURE **8.8**
Sample task cards when using stations.

Communicating the Tasks at Each Station

The tasks students practice at each station should be communicated clearly. Consider using task cards, posters, or class handouts to describe a station's tasks and give necessary directions. Whichever communication method you select, make your directions simple, brief, and clear. For example: "Volley the ball to the wall continuously. Count how many times you can volley in a row."

Most lessons involving stations use tasks cards with a picture or drawing of the organization of that station (see Figure 8.8). The learning progression for children at each new station will follow a consistent pattern:

1. Read the card.

2. Look at the picture or diagram.

3. Begin to practice the task.

Rotating Students among Stations

Have students rotate among stations on your command according to a schedule that you devise. That schedule will usually be set so each child has a turn at each station during a lesson. The simplest way to calculate this time is to divide the number of stations by the length of the lesson (with time allocated for transitions between stations). You will also need a protocol for the transitions between stations. One efficient protocol involves four steps:

1. Stop work on the signal.

2. Replace any equipment in its correct place.

3. Identify the next station.

4. Move in an orderly manner to the next station.

When delivering a physical education lesson to younger children, have them point to their next station to be sure they know where they are going next (see Figure 8.9).

FIGURE **8.9**
Students pointing to the next station. It is helpful to have younger children identify the next station each time they rotate.

The Teacher's Role during Station Work

While lessons incorporating stations free you from being the primary *organizer* of a lesson, they are not designed so you can take time off from instruction. Using stations simply shifts your role from primary lesson director to facilitator of learning (see Figure 8.10). Some possible roles you can fulfill during station work are:

- Rotate among stations offering individual assistance.
- Rotate among stations completing assessments.
- Alternate between stations where students have the most difficulty.
- Remain at one station teaching a new skill.
- Remain at one station completing assessment of students.
- Remain at a station where safety could be a concern.

Whichever role you choose, you must do three things each time students rotate among stations:

1. Monitor the whole class to check that all students have progressed to the correct station.
2. Check that students are performing the correct task at each station.
3. Check for safety or behavioral concerns.

When to Avoid Using Stations

Stations work best with familiar tasks that students can practice without your constant intervention. Stations are not the most effective way to introduce new skills; reserve them for reviewing skills or revisiting particular themes. Stations also work

FIGURE **8.10**
During station work, the teacher is freed up to provide more individual attention to students.

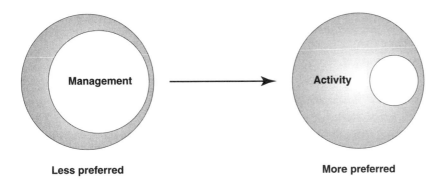

Management

Less preferred

Activity

More preferred

FIGURE **8.11**
The model of preferred time allocation in physical education. You should try to maximize the time allocated to activity rather than to management.

best when the set of tasks at each station requires about the same completion time. If Station 1 requires about 10 minutes of students' time, while Station 2 requires 15 minutes to complete, students at Station 1 may start off-task behavior while they wait to rotate to the next station.

FINAL WORDS

With limited time devoted to physical education in most elementary schools, you want to make the best use of every moment you have. As we have said before, your challenge is to maximize activity time and minimize the management time needed for transitions, organizing equipment, and moving students into personal or general space (see Figure 8.11). This gives students more opportunities to practice motor skills, develop their fitness, and learn to solve movement problems.

OVER TO YOU

1. What are the advantages and disadvantages of having a piece of equipment for each student?

2. Some teachers paint large spots on their playground as personal space markers for the beginning of lessons. How might you use such a system in a work space that you cannot paint, like a grassy field or a carpeted indoor area?

3. Describe in your own words the importance of having well-practiced protocols.

PORTFOLIO TASKS

1. You are planning a task that focuses on catching a softball using a glove. One student will be tossing soft throws to a partner. Draw a plan of how you would place equipment around the work area and where you would place students. Also plan the specific verbal directions to have the children collect the equipment and begin working.

2. You are completing a lesson on throwing and catching for fourth grade students. You have available four Frisbees, four tennis balls, four softballs, four softball gloves, one large wall, and six hoops. Design a series of stations for a class of 24 students, including the following details:

   - Number of stations
   - A task for each station
   - Number of children per station
   - Time spent at each station
   - Rotation system
   - Directions for placing students at the initial station

3. Browse through the catalogues of one or two sports equipment suppliers, selecting three items for equipment storage or transport. Your spending limit is $250. Justify your choices.

STRATEGIES FOR MANAGING BEHAVIOR DURING THE PHYSICAL EDUCATION LESSON

1. When you were in elementary school, how did your *best* teachers manage student behavior in their classes?

2. Give your reaction to the following statement: "The teacher's role in discipline is helping pupils to impose limits on themselves."

3. Should you threaten not to go outside for physical education as a strategy for behavior management in the classroom?

4. Did you ever have to run laps or do push-ups for misbehaving? Is it ever justifiable to use exercise as a form of punishment?

---

ncouraging appropriate student behavior is as important a management responsibility during physical education as in other classroom settings. But exactly what is "appropriate" student behavior? Some observers have noted that it is *not* merely the absence of inappropriate behavior (Graham, Holt/Hale, & Parker, 2004). If you glance at the National Association for Sport and Physical Education (NASPE) national content standards, you will discover that a physically educated student "demonstrates responsible personal and social behavior that reflects self and others in physical activity settings" (NASPE, Standard 5). In expanding on this general NASPE standard, most teachers would agree that a child is behaving appropriately in class when he or she:

- Works well individually
- Works well with a partner or in a group
- Works with *any* partner or group
- Supports and encourages others
- Follows the ethic of "try hard—try everything"

These five sets of appropriate behaviors promote successful learning in every elementary school classroom setting as well as in physical education.

This chapter contributes to the discussion about management in physical education. It offers you specific behavioral rules and protocols that are useful at key moments throughout a physical education class or those moments when inappropriate behaviors are most likely to occur.

GENERAL RULES
FOR PHYSICAL EDUCATION SETTINGS

As discussed in Chapter 7, many rules for the elementary school classroom apply equally well to the physical education setting. These universal rules typically relate to teacher–student interactions—such as not talking when the teacher is giving directions—and student–student interactions—such as treating classmates with respect. However, these rules sometimes require modification to apply better during physical education.

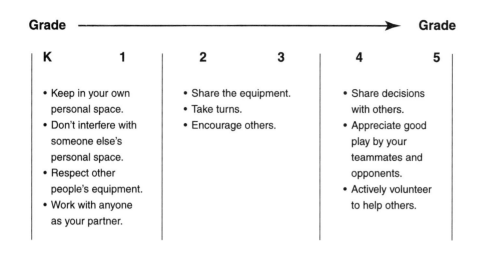

FIGURE **9.1**
This chart shows a progression of personal responsibility. As the chart implies, it isn't reasonable for teachers to expect kindergarten and first grade students to exhibit more sophisticated forms of cooperation and collaboration that will emerge only later in their emotional and social development.

It's useful to remember that rules cannot be developed arbitrarily or without considering your students' developmental level. For example, passing a ball accurately to a moving partner or playing a game of three-on-three keep-away Frisbee requires that students work cooperatively. Ideally, the process of teaching students to work cooperatively begins at the earliest stages of education. As shown by Figure 9.1, the ability to engage in more sophisticated forms of cooperation generally doesn't emerge until the later grades, so you must tailor rules about cooperation to accommodate your students' social and emotional developmental level.

This section discusses four cardinal rules that are the backbone for managing students' behavior during any physical education lesson:

1. Listen and follow directions.
2. Be respectful of others.
3. Take care of equipment.
4. Work safely in your environment.

Rule 1: Listen and Follow Directions

Most teachers across all grade levels have a rule that when the teacher talks, students stay quiet and listen (Figure 9.2). Not only is this a matter of common courtesy but in physical education it is a matter of safety as well. Particularly when you are teaching kindergarten and first grade, students may be so eager to please that they find it hard not to call out as you give instructions. Be patient as you help them remember that to listen, they need to use their ears, not their mouths.

Remember that consistency is the key in establishing this rule. As with most rules and protocols, if you want students to behave in a certain way, then you must respond only to those who follow the established rule. Although this may seem easy, it is difficult with students who are excited about interacting with you. However, recognizing a student who calls out while you or another student is talking inadvertently sends the message that the listen-and-follow-directions rule is not important.

FIGURE **9.2**
It is important for many reasons to have all children listening while the teacher is talking.

Rule 2: Be Respectful of Others

From their very first physical education lesson teach your students to respect their classmates. Showing respect to other students during a physical education lesson means:

- Working with any student as a partner
- Sharing and taking turns
- Encouraging others
- Sharing decisions
- Appreciating good play by a teammate or an opponent

Partnership

From the outset, develop the rule that each student may be partnered with anyone. This rule is not important merely for management. To promote inclusivity and tolerance, students should learn alongside *all* children of various abilities, genders, and ethnicities. Because you must foster a climate of caring and sensitivity in your class to pave the way for your students to abide by this rule, it is worthwhile to spend time explaining why working in pairs is beneficial. It teaches the value of working with somebody besides a best friend.

Once you establish the rule of "we work with anyone as a partner," simply announce, "You have three seconds to find a partner," or, "Partner with the person next to you." When a child is left out, you might say: "Please put up your hand if you do not have a partner. Thank you. Jessica, would you be Rebekka's partner, please?" This same process works reasonably well when asking students to form groups of three. When forming groups of four, ask one pair to join with another pair.

FIGURE **9.3**
One strategy for matching partners is for students to join named body parts with the person closest when the music stops. Here, two boys are touching hips.

You can use a number of other methods to help students form pairs in quick and nonnegotiable ways. The first, more suited to children in the earliest grades, also reinforces awareness of body parts (see Figure 9.3):

> Boys and girls, you are going to move about slowly in general space, and when the music stops, I will call out a body part. I want to see who can find a partner the quickest by touching your partner only with the body part I call out. Go . . . Hips!

A numbers game also can help students form quickly into groups. Have them start by finding a space around the work area where they practice throwing a yarn ball at a target on the wall. When you call out a number students quickly form groups of that number. The game continues as you call out a succession of random numbers. From time to time, you repeat that the objective is to form groups quickly and not to worry about the group's composition.

Some teachers find the "partner card" strategy useful for organizing students into pairs. Every student is given a laminated card at the beginning of a lesson or activity (see Figure 9.4). The cards show particular shapes (e.g., rectangle or circle) in different colors and in quantities of one to four. For the first task, you might ask students to partner with someone whose card bears the same shape. Next time, the partner's card may have the same color or number of shapes. In this way, students have no idea who their partner is until you announce the selected trait on the card.

Share Equipment and Take Turns

Children also show respect to one another by taking turns. Students will sometimes be required to share equipment during certain tasks due to space or safety concerns. There are also tasks where students perform in a line (such as on a

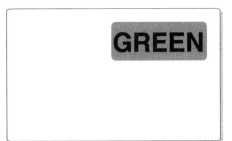

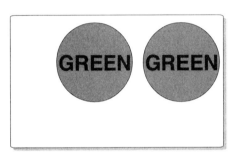

FIGURE **9.4**
Students randomly pick cards and then find a partner whose card has the same color, shape, or number.

balance obstacle course), and they must learn not to jump in front of someone in line, or to push someone from behind even if he or she is going too slowly (Figure 9.5).

Encourage Others

Another way students show respect for one another is by encouraging each other. Such positive social behavior does not automatically spring up when students partner together. The opposite may even occur, with students displaying body language that suggests frustration or intolerance toward a partner. This is most likely to occur when the skill levels of students do not match. A more highly skilled student gets upset when the task breaks down (e.g., in a catching task where one partner continually drops the ball). You must watch for any words or actions by one student that might discourage another. Without positive role models in out-of-school contexts, some students may not recognize an opportunity for offering encouragement. Ask students to give examples of encouraging phrases and words and to identify words or actions that are hurtful and unhelpful (Application 9.1).

Share in Decisions

Explain to children that being respectful also means valuing others' contributions and sharing in decisions. Students should understand that within any pair or group, one student should not dominate, but actively seek the input of others.

FIGURE **9.5**
Being respectful means taking turns, sharing, and not pushing.

APPLICATION **9.1** ■ **Helpful vs. Hurtful Comments**

Helpful Comments	Hurtful Comments
You're doing well!	How come you can't do this?
Good catch!	You're pathetic!
Nice try!	How come she makes me work with you?
We can do this together.	I'll do it myself.
Here's how you can do it.	Throw it properly!

Many tasks in physical education require students to make decisions. The scenario that follows provides an example:

> Boys and girls, your challenge is to hit the puck to each other through a target. Set up the cones so that they form the target through which you will pass the puck. Decide first how far apart you are going to put the cones, and then decide how far each of you will stand on either side of the goal. Your challenge is to make five consecutive passes through the goal. Try to make it so that it's not too easy, but that you have a realistic chance of making five. If, after your first series, you find that you were easily successful, you may make the goal narrower, or you might chose to move back further to create a harder challenge.

In this explicit task, one student may dominate. Without consultation or discussion, he or she simply places the markers in a set position, moves back from the goal, and expects the partner to do the same. Your responsibility as a teacher is to

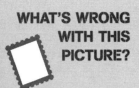

WHAT'S WRONG WITH THIS PICTURE?

Ms. Thomason's class is being quite unruly today, having just returned from a field trip to the circus. Some of the children are still acting out the hilarious clown stunts as Ms. Thomason is trying to explain the first activity. Billy and Sarah are being particularly bothersome. Ms. Thomason tells Billy and Sarah that because they have so much energy, they will go and run three laps around the gym to get their focus on the lesson. Mary and Greg are quite amused at this and pass comment. Ms. Thomason, who is not amused, tells Mary and Greg to go do push-ups while their classmates are running laps.

INQUIRING MINDS

What general rules are in place in your physical education class? How closely do these rules resemble the four listed in this chapter?

interact with your students as they set about these tasks. You might question the members of each pair as to how they reached decisions and verify that both partners had input.

A less explicit task is to design a game. The challenge may be to devise a three-on-three keep-away Frisbee game in which decisions about boundaries, turnovers, and scoring are left up to the students. In a group of six, one or two students can easily be silent or silenced, with no input into the rules. Consistently encourage students to value and appreciate the suggestions of others. Cohen's (1994) book on designing group work offers specific strategies to promote all students' involvement in decision-making.

While Cohen's model calls for giving students specific roles in group work, she lists the following specific behaviors as requirements for a successful group:

- Listening
- Asking for others' opinions
- Giving reasons for ideas
- Allowing everyone to contribute
- Finding out what others think

Appreciate Good Play by a Teammate or an Opponent

Students must learn to appreciate the role of other participants when playing games. Foster this appreciation by asking students to discuss why a game can't work if the teams don't collaborate. The logical extension of this is for participants in a game to thank each other for the opportunity of actually playing. Whichever team won or lost, both had an opportunity to play that would have been impossible without the opponent. The same case applies to cooperative activities. Challenges involving the cooperation of two groups require that they work together, and students should be encouraged to recognize and appreciate that contribution.

Rule 3: Take Care of Equipment

Physical education equipment can be expensive. Students should be taught to treat equipment appropriately, using it only for the purpose for which it was intended. In particular, they should learn to transport equipment in ways that prolong its useful life, such as carrying it rather than dragging it. Balls take frequent abuse, especially by being sat on while the teacher is giving instructions.

Rule 4: Work Safely in Your Environment

Physical education always involves movement, and it frequently involves using equipment. Students collide with one another or get hit by equipment other students are using. State all rules about working safely in the environment clearly and explicitly and reinforce them repeatedly.

In the earliest grades, teaching students to work safely often means teaching them to maintain their personal space and respect that of others. Young children tend to lose control of equipment when practicing new motor skills, and rules can help them retrieve errant equipment without disrupting others. Application 9.2 lists two such rules. Notice how the teacher phrases the rules to contrast unacceptable and acceptable behaviors so that young children can appreciate why the rule-based behavior is both a safer and more respectful response.

When teaching older students what constitutes "safe," your goal is to help them understand that safety "is a personal decision about what you do." The following scenario from a tag game shows how students sometimes need to forgo certain movement options in favor of others that make safety a priority:

> Girls and boys, when you are moving around with each other, you have to make a safe choice for your movement. You can run fast to get away from someone, but if that means you are going to hurt someone else, then you can't pick that. You have to pick a safe way to move versus the best way to move sometimes—because we have to be safe before we can move.

INQUIRING MINDS

How do you handle situations where one student refuses to work with another?

PROTOCOLS FOR ENDING PHYSICAL EDUCATION LESSONS

You and your students need to complete a number of organizational tasks at the end of a physical education lesson. First, students need to leave the work area and gather at a point where they can return to class. Second, equipment must be

FIGURE **9.6**
Here are children lining up in A-B-C, or alphabetical, order.

returned to its collection point or storage location. Lastly, students must return to the classroom without disrupting the rest of the school. Protocols for the first two of these management tasks were discussed in the previous chapter. Here, we will focus solely on the behaviorally oriented protocols for lining up and returning to class.

Lining Up

There are many strategies you can use to have students line up in an orderly fashion. One is simply called *A-B-C order* (Figure 9.6). At the beginning of the school year, teach students to learn the alphabetical order of their surnames. Then teach them to move quickly and efficiently in that order. Some kindergarten and first grade teachers use a daily "line leader," a student (or pair of students) who has done a particularly good job during the lesson. Once the line leader is in place, other students form one or two lines behind.

Returning to Class

Physical education lessons usually take place in settings where students can be boisterous. The school hallway is not such a place, however—something students may easily forget after strenuous physical activity. Student noise and the difficulty many students have in maintaining their personal space in a line are two challenges you face when accompanying your students back to a classroom. Use a number of creative protocols to help students remain quiet as they travel back to class. Application 9.3 presents two sample strategies.

Many teachers also use a reward system for successful transitions back to class. Based on specific criteria (no noise, no one cutting in line, and no physical contact with other students), you might award a token such as a star or a checkmark on a notice board for a satisfactory move from the work area to the classroom. At the end of each week or month, if your students have earned enough stars or checks, give them a reward.

Ryan Either, a teacher at Laura Donovan School in Freehold, New Jersey, gives an example of such a reward system for returning to class after a physical education lesson. Called *keep your caboose,* this activity requires children to know the rules for walking in the hallway (see Application 9.4).

CONSEQUENCES OF BREAKING BEHAVIORAL RULES AND PROTOCOLS

If you are like most elementary education teachers, you work hard to keep minor behavioral infractions from escalating into serious ones. As this chapter has demonstrated, one of the surest ways to promote appropriate behaviors during physical education is the adoption of managerial protocols that encourage cooperation rather than those demanding blind obedience. Adopt a proactive strategy to encourage appropriate student behavior by communicating your expectations

Brookside Elementary School
1301 Sansome Street
San Francisco, CA 94111

Dear Parents,
To have the best possible physical education class, it is important for both the student and parent to know what is expected. The class goal is to enhance physical and social well-being through motor skills, sports skills, and fitness activities. For each child to have the best opportunity to learn, the students in this class have established the following rules. Please review this plan with your child so you will both be aware of the rules. We are looking forward to teaching your child that physical activity is both fun and health enhancing. Thank you for being a vital part of the physical education program. We encourage you to also become active with your child as much as possible. If you have any questions or comments, please send us a note. Thank you again.

Sincerely,

Sandra John
Brookside Physical Education

FIGURE 9.7
Expectations letters to parents can not only explain the expectations for student behavior in physical education but can serve as advocacy tools for the subject.

APPLICATION **9.5** ■ **System of Progressive Behavioral Consequences for Kindergarteners: Three Strikes and You're Out**

Strike 1: *Give a warning:* Tell the child what he or she did wrong.

Strike 2: *Announce consequences:* "Next time you will go to time-out."

Strike 3: *Deliver consequences:* Send the child to time-out; the child sits and watches. After a third strike, the teacher talks with the child. When the child can describe the rule that was broken, the teacher allows the child to return to the activity.

---

directly to parents. Figure 9.7 shows an example of a simple form letter that you can mail at the start of the school term. The letter encourages parental participation in the student's physical education.

When your students do misbehave, you will need a system of behavioral consequences. Communicate consequences for behavioral infractions clearly and apply them fairly. As an elementary education student, you probably have already studied and debated dozens of theories and methods about student discipline, so here we discuss only the most commonly used discipline strategy for physical education lessons.

To keep minor behavioral infractions from escalating, most teachers develop progressive scales of consequences, with the most punitive consequences called into play only after repeated infractions. Applications 9.5 (kindergarten and first

APPLICATION **9.6** ■ Sequence of Behavioral Consequences for Upper Grades

1. Verbal warning

2. Sent to time-out until the student chooses to correct the behavior

3. Time-out for the remainder of the lesson and loss of other privileges

4. Removal from physical education, ISS or office notification, parent notification

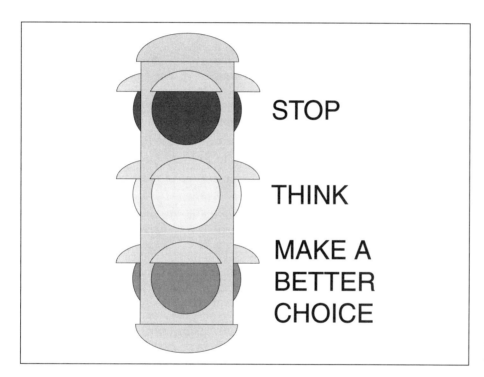

STOP

THINK

MAKE A BETTER CHOICE

FIGURE **9.8**
Students are asked to go to the designated time-out station and read the card. When they can return and explain to the teacher how they could have made a better choice, they are free to re-enter the activity.

grade) and 9.6 (higher grade levels) show two simple systems of progressive consequences for behavioral infractions. Both strategies incorporate a temporary removal from activity, or time-out.

Time-out is the most common and effective strategy for dealing with students who break rules or fail to follow protocols during a physical education lesson. A time-out is particularly effective for physical education because most children enjoy participating and are eager to get back into the action. For time-out to be most effective, however, the child must reflect during the lost activity time to understand why he or she was sent to time-out in the first place. Many teachers allow students to re-enter the class once they have had time to understand what they did inappropriately and can express this and their subsequent behavior plan to the teacher. Figure 9.8 shows a time-out station used by one successful physical educator. Notice that the main purpose of this task card is to get the child to stop and think.

WHAT'S WRONG WITH THIS PICTURE? Mr. Brown's class has been to the zoo. On the bus back to school, some of the students had become a little unruly. Given that the students missed a social studies lesson, as well as behaving inappropriately, Mr. Brown announces that his class will not be having physical education today.

A CARDINAL RULE OF BEHAVIOR FOR *TEACHERS:* NEVER USE EXERCISE AS PUNISHMENT

A system of behavioral consequences is meant to teach students to avoid inappropriate behaviors while reinforcing appropriate ones. Nowhere in the preceding discussion has the word *punishment* been used. Punishment discourages inappropriate behaviors because the offender wants to avoid the undesirable effects of punishment itself. It does nothing to teach and encourage appropriate behavior.

With this point in mind, *it is never correct to use exercise as a form of punishment for inappropriate behavior!* The overriding theme of this entire book is to show you how to encourage your students to embrace physical activity as something they love. Whatever your position on punishment in education is, we cannot foresee any situation that would ever justify the use of exercise as a form of punishment.

FINAL WORDS

From our experience in watching hundreds of physical education lessons, from those taught by veteran educators to those taught by complete novices, situations where students are extremely disruptive are rare. The most common managerial challenge for teachers lies in harnessing students' energy and directing it to serious engagement with the content. The strategies we have outlined in this chapter, and in earlier chapters in this unit, should give enough avenues for you to provide clear expectations for students' behavior and work without suppressing their natural enthusiasm for activity. We do encourage you, however, to set high standards for managerial tasks, remembering that good class management maximizes the time spent practicing skills and participating in health-enhancing physical activity.

OVER TO YOU

1. How can students demonstrate "being respectful" in physical education? Include in your answer both interpersonal actions and those dealing with other class rules.

2. What teacher behaviors are critical for preventing small management issues from becoming major management issues?

3. What area of management in physical education needs specific attention beyond the general class rules?

1. Design a good behavior contract you might use with a student who struggles with certain aspects of the managerial system. In this contract, include (1) what the student will do, (2) what the teacher will do, and (3) the precise contingencies of the contract (i.e., how much and for how long).

2. Develop a "help others" chart you could post in your classroom or the physical education area. Provide examples of both helping and nonhelping behaviors.

3. Sander (1989) gives four categories of rules relevant to the elementary classroom: traffic rules (listening to the teacher); friendship rules (cooperating and working with anyone); golden rules (personal behavior control); and safety rules (dealing with equipment and working in space). Using these categories, develop formally stated rules you would include for use in your physical education classes.

REFERENCES

Cohen, E. G. (1994). *Designing group work*. New York: Teachers College Press.

Graham, G., Holt/Hale, S. A., & Parker, M. (2004). *Children moving: A reflective approach to teaching physical education* (6th ed.). Boston: McGraw-Hill.

Sander, A. (1989). Classroom management skills. *Strategies, 2*(3), 14–18.

CHAPTER

10

CREATING
A PHYSICALLY SAFE
LEARNING ENVIRONMENT

CHAPTER OUTLINE

1. What major safety issues do you face teaching physical education?

2. Did you or a friend ever have an accident at school? What circumstances led up to the incident?

3. As a society, are we *too* safety conscious, thus stifling our children's sense of adventure and exploration?

In Chapters 8 and 9 we discussed protocols and rules as being essential to an effective learning environment for physical education. A number of those protocols and rules related to safety issues. Physical education places students in high-risk settings where they may be injured. By creating a safe and supportive physical education setting, you will both protect students from injury and encourage their lifelong participation in regular activity.

INQUIRING MINDS

What procedure does your school follow for reporting accidents or injuries?

GUIDING PRINCIPLES OF PHYSICAL EDUCATION SAFETY

Five domains of safety practices apply to physical education:

1. Facility safety
2. Equipment safety
3. Instruction
4. Supervision
5. Footwear

Facility Safety

Regularly inspect facilities for damage or hazards and deal with all problems as soon as you identify them. You should also make sure the perimeter of the working area is free of obstacles and indoor activity areas are clear of stored equipment and furniture. When a gym or activity room has immovable obstacles such as doors or protruding drinking fountains, modify the rules of play so these do not become obstructions. You will also need to modify the rules of play for maximum safety when a gym or activity room is a nonstandard size (see Figure 10.1). Never use walls or stages in gyms as turning or ending points for activities. Designate a line before the wall instead. In outdoor settings as well, you need to keep students clear of obstructions. When using a basketball court for hockey lessons, for example, students should practice clear of the basketball standards.

Also consider the playing area itself. The playing surface should be clean and free of all obstacles and provide good traction. In outdoor settings, make every effort to avoid using areas with uneven surfaces or holes. If this is unavoidable, first

FIGURE **10.1**
When working in a small area, modify the activity so children can safely work on skills without endangering others.

INQUIRING MINDS

What problems or safety issues have you had while supervising your class at recess?

clearly mark these areas and secondly make students aware of them, perhaps by doing a walk-through of the area with them to point out the rough areas.

Equipment Safety

The key phrase for equipment safety is: "Inspect, maintain, repair, replace." Regularly inspect equipment for structural faults or breakage, *record your results, and keep these on file*. The most common faults include cracks, splinters, and loosened parts on equipment—like handles. When equipment is found to be defective, you have two options. First, if the defect can be fixed, note the fault in writing and then repair it. Immediately remove from use equipment that is beyond repair. In some cases, as shown in Figure 10.2, you will need to repair equipment during the activity itself.

Access to and Storage of Equipment

Students should have access to and use of equipment only under supervision and/or with your permission. All equipment should be safely stored after each lesson. Teach students appropriate ways to carry and move equipment. They should not drag mats, swing sticks wildly, or kick balls instead of carrying them.

Selecting Appropriate Equipment

The equipment you select for various activities should be appropriate for the students and used for its intended purpose. Organize the equipment to prevent unsafe situations. For example, place batting stations so balls from one station are not directed to an area where other students are fielding. Of course, give specific instructions about using and handling equipment appropriately. Specific details regarding equipment use are discussed in Chapters 11 through 15.

FIGURE **10.2**
In some cases, when equipment becomes faulty during activity, repairs can be made on the run. If this is not possible, you should remove the item from use immediately.

All personal safety equipment must fit a child properly and should be appropriate for the individual student's skill level. Tell your students to report all equipment problems to you promptly.

Instructional Practices That Promote Safety

The ways you select, plan, and conduct activities all help to promote a safe learning environment. Assess all activities for potential risk, determining what is foreseeable whenever possible. Indeed, the first question you should ask when planning a lesson is whether the activity is suitable to the students' physical and mental condition.

You should also establish safety rules about the correct use of equipment. Before beginning a lesson, check to be sure that your students understand the safety factors and the potential risk. To avoid a dangerous situation, word your instructions clearly. Be sure that students with special needs (e.g., those with hearing impairments or English as a second language) understand the instructions as well. Instruct your students that pieces of equipment need to be used in ways appropriate to the task. For example, in teaching hockey, your three safety rules could be expressed as simply as:

- Two hands on the stick at all times
- Stick on the ground
- Swing no higher than the knees (see Figure 10.3)

FIGURE **10.3**
Children should clearly understand the safety rules about using equipment. These children have both hands on the hockey sticks and are keeping the sticks on the ground.

The safest approach is to teach skills for specific activities *in appropriate progression.* Base new activities on skills that children have already mastered (see the discussion on "scaffolding" in Chapter 5), so a student is never required to perform a skill beyond his or her capabilities. If a student displays hesitation either verbally or nonverbally, find out why. If you believe hesitancy concerning a skill could put the student at risk, direct him or her toward a more basic skill. Chapters 11 and 12 give considerable detail on designing appropriate skill progressions.

Promote Safety by Modifying the Rules

Modifying the rules of the activities to suit the age, strength, experience, and abilities of your students is key to promoting safety. Allow children with insufficient upper body strength to use a modified push-up position; other students may need to use slower and softer balls in catching tasks. Because students may already be familiar with the usual rules of a game or activity, it's especially important to make it clear (1) when you are modifying the rules, (2) why you are modifying the rules, and (3) what the new rules are. Be sure to enforce the new rules consistently during play.

Behavior Protocols That Enhance Safety

As mentioned in Chapter 9, besides planning safe activities, at the beginning of each year, you should establish safety routines, rules of acceptable behavior, and students' safety duties and then reinforce these year-round. For example, establish daily routines for appropriate dress (if applicable), movement patterns to activity areas, class meeting locations, and entry and exit procedures. In particular, early each year reinforce whatever "stop" signal you use to tell students they must stop play immediately, freeze where they are, and pay attention. In addition to developing class rules, reprimand students for unsafe play or unacceptable behavior whenever it occurs. Chapters 7 and 8 discuss in detail of the use of signals and routines.

FIGURE **10.4**
This girl is wearing shoes unsuitable for physical education; they are not fastened at the back and could easily slip off.

Students should also be taught appropriate behavior when an accident occurs. A good rule is: "Stand back, do not move the injured person, and alert a teacher immediately." Also teach students the location of the fire alarms, fire exits, and alternate routes from the gymnasium or activity area.

Supervision

Most court cases concerning injuries during physical activity deal with some aspect of supervision. While appropriate supervision depends on the activity's risk level, the participants' skill level, and the participants' age and maturity, it is nevertheless essential that you be *present at all times* and that you *actively monitor students*. You should never leave your class or send students to work where you cannot see them. If a serious accident occurs, send a responsible student to the office to seek assistance.

Footwear

All students should wear clothing and footwear appropriate for the activity, the weather, their age, and their skill level. Although many elementary school programs do not require students to change clothes, appropriate footwear is essential. **Appropriate footwear** has a rubber sole and can be securely fastened to the child's feet. Backless shoes that can slip off are inappropriate, while sandals with a rubber sole that remain secure are suitable. The young girl jumping rope in Figure 10.4 is not wearing appropriate footwear for physical education. Students should also remove all jewelry before participating in physical education activities.

INQUIRING MINDS

What injury do you deal with most frequently in your classroom? Why do you think this is so?

appropriate footwear
Footwear with rubber soles that will not come off during activity.

BOX **10.1** ■ **Emergency Action Plan**

Know the following information:

1. Your school's policy for reporting an accident: Can you call 911 directly or must you call the office first for them to do this?

2. The location and means of access to a first aid kit

3. The location of a telephone

4. Telephone numbers of ambulance and hospital

When an injury occurs:

1. Take control and assess the situation.

2. Remember the basic first aid rule: Do not move the injured student. If a student cannot start a movement by himself or herself, do not move any part of the body.

3. Tell your students to leave the injured student alone.

4. Leave the student's equipment in place.

5. Evaluate the injury. Once you have assessed the severity of the injury, decide whether further assistance is required.

6. If an ambulance is not needed, decide how to remove the injured student from the playing surface.

7. If an ambulance is required:

   a. Request assistance from another adult (teacher/administrator/parent)

   b. Have the second person call an ambulance and give the following information:

      (1) State that it is a medical emergency.

      (2) State what the emergency is.

      (3) Give the exact location and the name of the closest cross streets.

   c. Give the telephone number from which you are calling.

   d. After the other person has called the ambulance, he or she should report back to the person in charge, confirm the call, and give the estimated time until the ambulance will arrive.

   e. Have someone go to the entrance and wait for the ambulance.

8. Once the ambulance has been called, observe the injured person carefully for any change in condition and try to reassure the injured student until professional help arrives.

9. Do not move the injured person unnecessarily.

10. Do not give the injured person food or drink.

11. Stay calm. Keep an even tone in your voice.

12. Have another adult supervise the class.

13. When ambulance attendants arrive, tell them what happened, how it happened, and what you have done. If possible, inform the ambulance attendants about any medical problems or past injuries that the injured person may have experienced.

14. Contact the student's parents or guardians as soon as possible after the injury.

15. Complete an accident report and file it with appropriate school board official and school administrator.

Source: Adapted with permission from: http://www.sasked.gov.sk.ca/docs/physed/safe/

WHAT'S WRONG WITH THIS PICTURE?

Mrs. Felton's first grade class is completing a lesson on jumping and landing, and Mrs. Felton has designed a circuit involving a lot of obstacles for her children to climb on and jump off, to jump over, and to jump through. It's raining outside today, so Mrs. Felton's class is completing the circuit indoors on a carpeted area in the hallway near her classroom.

BOX **10.2** ■ Contents of a Portable First Aid Kit

32 adhesive strips, 1″ × 3″	10 adhesive pads, 2″ × 3″	1 roll of adhesive tape, 1/2″ × 5 yd.
3 ammonia inhalants	1 antiseptic and burn ointment, 1/8 oz.	6 antiseptic wipes
1 bandage roll, 1″ × 4.1 yd.	1 bandage roll, 2″ × 4.1 yd.	1 pair of tweezers
1 triangular bandage	1 small cold pack	1 sterile combine pad, 5″ × 9″
2 eye pads	1 first aid handbook	10 gauze pads, 8-ply, 3″ × 3″
1 pair latex gloves	1 pair scissors	

RESPONDING TO ACCIDENTS AND INJURIES

It is important to have an emergency action plan in case a student is injured. Get professional care to the student as quickly as possible. All schools should have an accident response plan that describes what to do when an injury or accident occurs. Such a plan, practiced regularly, will reduce confusion if there is an injury or accident and ensure that the injured student gets help quickly. Box 10.1 lists the key elements in such an emergency action plan.

In spite of all your preparation and supervision, accidents may occur during lessons. Most of these will be minor scrapes and bumps. Carry a portable first aid kit to outdoor lessons. An appropriate list of contents for such a kit is given in Box 10.2. Some schools do not allow teachers to directly treat students for injuries. Where there is a resident school nurse, some policies require *all* students to be treated by that professional. Be sure you know the appropriate policy for your setting.

Name of Student: _____

1. Please indicate if your child has been subject to any of the following and provide pertinent details: epilepsy, diabetes, orthopedic problems, heart disorders, asthma, allergies:

_____

_____

Head or back conditions or injuries (in the past two years):

_____

Arthritis or rheumatism; chronic nosebleeds; dizziness; fainting; headaches; dislocated shoulder; hernia; swollen, hypermobility or painful joints; trick or lock knee:

_____

2. What medication(s) should your child have on hand during physical education activities?

_____

Please note that medicine is dispensed in accordance with board of education policy. Contact the school principal for more information.

3. Does your child wear a medic alert neck chain or bracelet, or carry a medic alert card?

Yes _____   No _____

If yes, please specify what is written on it:

_____

4. Please describe any other relevant medical conditions that will limit your child's full participation in physical activities.

_____

LEARNING A CHILD'S MEDICAL HISTORY

All schools have a medical register, a list of students with medical problems. Keep current medical information on file for each student and carry these forms (or at least the essential information for at-risk students) with you to physical activity settings. Of special concern in physical education are heart disorders, asthma, epilepsy, diabetes, and severe allergies (e.g., to bee stings). Application 10.1 is a sample medical information form you could use to collect this important information.

RESPONSIBLE PLAYGROUND SUPERVISION

In many schools, you may be asked to supervise children at recess on the playground. The National Program for Playground Safety has an excellent website with safety tips, frequently asked questions, and numerous checklists (http://www.uni.

✓ Supervision is present, but strings and ropes aren't.
Adult presence is needed to watch for potential hazards, observe, intercede, and facilitate play when necessary. Strings on clothing or ropes used for play can cause accidental strangulation if caught on equipment.

✓ All children play on age-appropriate equipment.
Preschoolers, ages 2–5, and children, ages 5–12, are developmentally different and need different equipment located in separate areas to keep the playground safe and fun for all.

✓ Falls to the surface are cushioned.
Nearly 70 percent of all playground injuries are related to falls to the surface. Acceptable surfaces include hardwood fiber/mulch, pea gravel, sand, and synthetic materials such as poured-in-place rubber mats or tiles (see Figure 10.5). Playground surfaces should not be concrete, asphalt, grass, blacktop, packed dirt, or rock.

✓ Equipment is safe.
Check to be sure that all equipment is anchored safely in the ground and in good working order; that S-hooks are entirely closed, bolts are not protruding, and no footings are exposed.

FIGURE **10.5**
Note the cushioned surface of this playground.

WHAT'S WRONG WITH THIS PICTURE? Mr. Jones has just been given an old trampoline donated by a family that is moving to another city. Mr. Jones decides he will use the trampoline as a good behavior incentive. During lessons, he allows children who have been well behaved to spend two minutes bouncing on the trampoline, which is in a spare room around the corner from the gym.

edu/playground/home.html). You can use the checklist in Application 10.2 to examine the key features of playground safety. The checklist includes Supervision, Age-appropriate, Falls, and Equipment (SAFE).

FINAL WORDS

Your legal duty is to instruct students without injuring them and to have your students behave so that they don't harm others. As a teacher, you are acting in loco parentis—in place of a parent. You have a legal duty to care for a child just as his or her parents would do. The activities you teach in physical education require a standard of care that a reasonable professional would offer in a similar situation. You are expected to anticipate safety issues and take appropriate precautions to prevent foreseeable problems. We provide the following Ten Golden Rules of Safety as an appropriate checklist:

1. Know your material.
2. Have a written lesson plan that demonstrates safe activities.
3. Inspect the activity area.
4. Use appropriate space.
5. Make regular inspections of equipment.
6. Use protective equipment (mats and the like).
7. Require proper clothing.
8. Be present and aware at all times.
9. Organize your class according to class size, activity, and fitness level.
10. Instruct students on appropriate use of equipment.

OVER TO YOU

1. How can poor supervision lead to accidents and injury during physical education?
2. What constitutes a reasonable standard of care when supervising students? What would you do if a student turned his ankle during a lesson?
3. Implementing a physical education safety policy is the first step in accident prevention. What are the subsequent steps in this process?

1. Design a safety poster you could use in your physical education classes. Include your class rules relating to the safe use of equipment, space, and footwear.

2. Write a safety scenario in which everything is *faulty,* considering those areas listed in promoting safety to help develop your story. Try not to be ridiculous, but don't hold back either. Then trade with a partner and rewrite each other's scenarios so the situations are made safe.

Are sports and motor skills the same thing? Ask somebody to state the first thing that comes to mind when you say "physical education," and they will probably name a sport—basketball, soccer, or the like. But most people don't realize that adult sports are *not* a helpful model for the physical education of elementary school children. Sports typically have specific performance expectations and are freighted with social values that can leave some children, like poor little Jason in the cartoon, feeling left out of the fun. On the other hand, a motor skills–based approach to teaching physical education promotes active participation among all the students in your class. In this unit, Chapters 11 and 12 will show you how to select content to teach locomotor and nonlocomotor skills and manipulative skills. These skills provide the foundation for teaching the *appropriate* games you will learn about in Chapter 13 and the rhythmic movement skills in Chapter 14.

SELECTING PHYSICAL EDUCATION CONTENT

UNIT IV

"Jason, I'd like to let you play, but soccer is a girls' game."

LOCOMOTOR AND NONLOCOMOTOR SKILLS

1. What are some of the fundamental motor skills included in a variety of sports or physical activities?

2. Which locomotor skills do you think would be the most difficult to learn?

3. How does gymnastics contribute to the development of a physically educated person?

4. What might we mean by "educational" gymnastics?

In Chapter 3, we noted that physical education specialists divide motor skills into three sets of "skill themes": (1) locomotor skills, (2) nonlocomotor skills, and (3) manipulative skills. This chapter focuses on the first two categories, which are fundamental for successful performance of manipulative skills, the most difficult for a child to learn. The chapter is not meant to include all the skills and tasks you might give students to help them develop their locomotor and non-locomotor skills, but it does highlight the progression that should be taken in skill development. This chapter demonstrates and provides step-by-step guidance on teaching various skill themes to students.

WHAT ARE LOCOMOTOR SKILLS?

Locomotor skills involve a body moving from one place to another within a vertical plane. Our objective in teaching these skills is to let children develop control of their bodies when traveling in various directions, at various speeds, and on various pathways. The eight basic locomotor skills introduced in Chapter 3 were walking, running, leaping, jumping, hopping, galloping, sliding, and skipping. Students can explore these different locomotor skills in three ways. Lessons with kindergarten and first grade students should include

1. Travel using a locomotor skill in general space
2. Travel using a locomotor skill on different pathways (e.g., straight, curved, and zigzag), directions (e.g., forwards, backwards and sideways), and at different speeds (e.g., slow, medium, and fast)
3. Travel in response to a signal (e.g., stop and start; change from one locomotor movement to another; change from one pathway, direction, or speed to another)

locomotor skills
Those skills with a body moving from one place to another within a vertical plane.

Once students have explored these foundational locomotor skills, they can then use them in applied tasks such as chasing, fleeing, and dodging. These skills can also be combined with nonlocomotor skills to create gymnastics routines.

WHAT ARE NONLOCOMOTOR SKILLS?

Two features characterize nonlocomotor skills. First, they do not require the body to move from place to place; second, they do not incorporate objects into the movement. Most nonlocomotor skills are performed from a relatively stable position while either standing or sitting. Again, from Chapter 3, nonlocomotor skills include twisting, turning, bending, stretching, rocking, and curling.

This chapter focuses on the nonlocomotor skill of balancing. Like many locomotor skills, balance is important in performing many manipulative skills used in games. How to teach the other nonlocomotor skills is discussed later in this chapter.

MOTOR SKILL PROGRESSION TREES

You may recall from Chapter 3 that children typically acquire and develop motor skills in three phases:

1. The developing skill phase

2. The expanding skill phase

3. The mastering skill phase

A *progression tree* helps chart students' progress in acquiring motor skills. Figure 11.1 demonstrates a generic progression tree. Typically, students spend a considerable amount of time working in predictable self-paced environments at the developing stage to acquire new motor skills. Notice that the developing skills are at the base of the tree. Students must develop motor skills before expanding on them. Then, just as a tree grows, students pass through an expanding skill stage in which they learn to use acquired motor skills in semipredictable and semi-self-paced conditions. Finally, in the last stage of motor skill development, the branching of the tree's crown reflects children's ability to use motor skills in an array of physical activities that are individually challenging, uniquely different, or constantly changing.

In this chapter, progression trees are provided for a variety of fundamental skills that children must master. Every progression tree lists a series of tasks students are to perform that will help them achieve proficiency with a particular skill. A series of task cards is also included for each progression tree. Each task card gives specific instructions and examples of activities for students to do. The task cards are identified by phase—**1** Developing Skills (DS), **2** Expanding Skills (ES), and **3** Mastering Skills (MS)—and task: **A**, **B**, **C**, etc. Note that Developing Skills are listed at the base of the tree, while the Mastering Skills appear at the top of the tree.

To highlight this learning process for you, this chapter introduces the locomotor skill themes of chasing, fleeing, and dodging, as well as jumping and landing, together with the nonlocomotor skill theme of balancing. The chapter includes the skill progressions as well as *sample learning tasks* you could use in each phase to aid skill development. Chapter 3 also discussed children's progress at

INQUIRING MINDS

Which locomotor skills do you find the most difficult to teach? How can you help your students learn these skills?

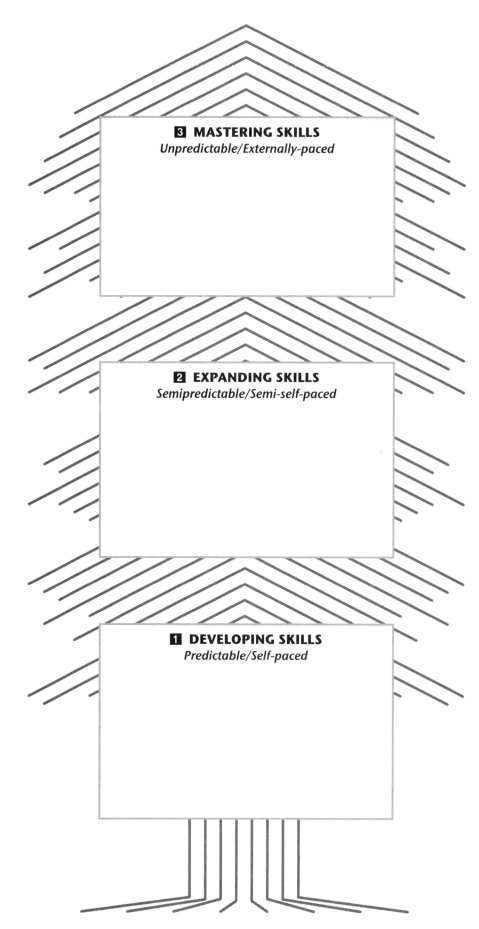

3 MASTERING SKILLS
Unpredictable/Externally-paced

2 EXPANDING SKILLS
Semipredictable/Semi-self-paced

1 DEVELOPING SKILLS
Predictable/Self-paced

FIGURE **11.1**
A skills progression tree

different rates in their development. In our sample activities, the grade level on each card is meant as a guideline only—a starting point for your preparation if you don't have any prior knowledge about the students you will teach or their skill level. You may have to modify your starting point once you know your students. We do not mean to suggest that children can do only those activities that fall into the level associated with their age/grade level. For some children, the tasks at the designated phase for their age group will be too simple, while for others they will be too difficult; and some of the tasks presented do not lend themselves specifically to any one phase. In fact, as children progress, some tasks will serve as transitional tasks because they cross the various phases.

CHASING, FLEEING, AND DODGING

Chasing, fleeing, and dodging use locomotor skills that involve **traveling**, or moving the entire body from one place to another. Specifically:

- **Chasing** is traveling quickly to overtake or tag a fleeing person.
- **Fleeing** is traveling quickly away from a pursuing person or object.
- **Dodging** is abruptly shifting the body from one line of movement to another. (Graham, Holt/Hale, & Parker, 2004)

Teaching Chasing, Fleeing, and Dodging

Chasing, fleeing, and dodging are used both in games where the player must change direction or speed and in those involving faking an opponent to make them go one way while the player goes another. The same skills may be used in games or sports that require a child to remain in control of an object such as a stick

traveling
Changing location from one place to another.

chasing
Traveling quickly to overtake or tag a fleeing person.

fleeing
Traveling quickly away from a pursuing person or object.

dodging
Abruptly shifting the body from one line of movement to another.

BOX **11.1** ■ Progression for Teaching the Skills of Chasing, Fleeing, and Dodging

1. Practice chasing, fleeing, and dodging as separate skills.
2. Avoid an invisible opponent while stationary.
3. Avoid stationary objects or obstacles.
4. Combine at least two of the skills while working with a partner.
5. Chase, flee, and dodge in simple tag games.
6. Chase, flee, and dodge in more complex game situations.

or a ball (and sometimes both). Box 11.1 outlines motor skill progression for children learning to chase, flee, and dodge. This progression takes into account the environmental demands, the pacing of skills, and the way skills progress from simple to complex as a student develops mature skill patterns.

Sample Learning Tasks for Chasing, Fleeing, and Dodging

Introduce students to chasing, fleeing, and dodging skills after they develop a working understanding of these space awareness concepts:

- General space and self-space
- Pathways (curved, zigzag, straight)
- Directions (forward, backward, right, left, up, down)
- Levels (low, medium, high)
- Extensions (near and far)

Students who have learned these space awareness concepts and mastered their locomotor skills can then develop chasing, fleeing, and dodging skills. Figure 11.2 highlights tasks that can be used to acquire these skills.

Developing Skills (Typically Kindergarten through Grade 2)

At the developing phase, students should practice chasing, fleeing, and dodging without the distractions of working in an unpredictable environment, against an actual opponent, or in adherence to game rules such as tag. The learning tasks that cultivate these skills include ducking, turning, spinning, and faking an *invisible* or *imaginary* opponent. These tasks can advance to changing direction and speed in order to dodge stationary obstacles and then to activities where the chasing, fleeing, and dodging will occur simultaneously. Although students have to respond to an external signal for some tasks, they can still determine the speed at which to perform these actions, making them more self-paced and easier to perform.

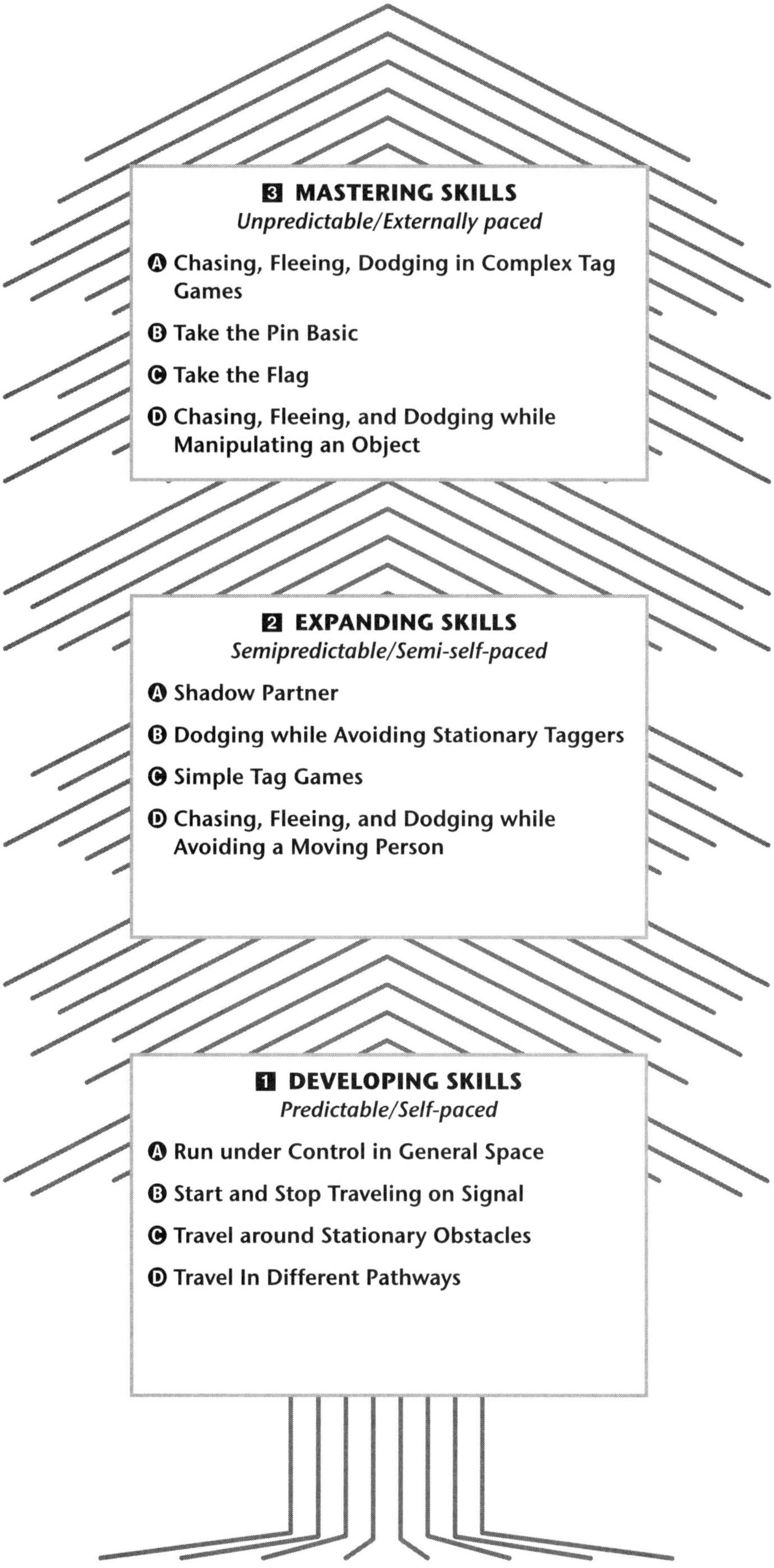

3 MASTERING SKILLS
Unpredictable/Externally paced

Ⓐ Chasing, Fleeing, Dodging in Complex Tag Games

Ⓑ Take the Pin Basic

Ⓒ Take the Flag

Ⓓ Chasing, Fleeing, and Dodging while Manipulating an Object

2 EXPANDING SKILLS
Semipredictable/Semi-self-paced

Ⓐ Shadow Partner

Ⓑ Dodging while Avoiding Stationary Taggers

Ⓒ Simple Tag Games

Ⓓ Chasing, Fleeing, and Dodging while Avoiding a Moving Person

1 DEVELOPING SKILLS
Predictable/Self-paced

Ⓐ Run under Control in General Space

Ⓑ Start and Stop Traveling on Signal

Ⓒ Travel around Stationary Obstacles

Ⓓ Travel In Different Pathways

FIGURE **11.2**
Progression tree for chasing, fleeing, and dodging

DS Ⓐ   **Run under Control in General Space**

Pacing:	*Self-paced*
Grade Level:	Typically lower elementary (K–2)
Content Focus:	*Exploration of traveling in general space*
Setup:	Children are standing behind one line and running to another. Lines are set between 20 to 30 ft. apart.
Task:	On my signal, run as quickly as you can from the red line to the blue line. Be sure to run so that you don't touch your neighbor as you move. Ready, begin! (Chasing, fleeing)
	I want you to pretend that you are taking your dog for a walk. We are going to travel slowly while we walk the dog. Suddenly, your dog has gotten off the leash. Run as quickly as you can to try and catch your dog. Ready, begin! (Chasing)
Cues:	Keep your head up.
	Use your arms for speed.
Variation:	Vary the amount of space or distance.

DS Ⓑ   **Start and Stop Traveling on Signal**

Pacing:	*Self-paced*
Grade Level:	Lower elementary (K–2)
Content Focus:	*Exploration of travel and responding to a signal*
Setup:	Children are scattered in general space.
Task:	On the "Go" signal, start traveling in general space. When you hear the drumbeat one time, stop as quickly as you can. Ready, action! (Dodging)
	This time, when you are traveling and hear the drumbeat, I want you to stop without having to take another step. Ready, action! (Dodging)
	Travel slowly in general space. When you hear the drumbeat, I want you to pretend you are crossing a street and that you must change directions quickly to avoid an approaching car. Remember to change direction quickly on the drumbeat. Ready, begin! (Dodging, fleeing)
Cues:	Use quick steps.
	Stay low by bending your knees on stop.
Variations:	Use different stop signals, vary time for stop.

DS Ⓒ   **Travel around Stationary Obstacles**

Pacing:	*Self-paced*
Grade Level:	Typically lower elementary (K–2)
Content Focus:	*Exploration of traveling in general space while avoiding obstacles*
Setup:	Children are scattered in general space with cones and jump ropes spread throughout the space.
Task:	On the signal, travel slowly around the cones on the floor. Every time you hear the drumbeat, I want you to travel faster. Our travel pattern will be slow, medium, and fast. Ready, begin! (Chasing, fleeing)
	I have placed many obstacles on the floor. Your task is to travel as quickly as you can through general space while avoiding the objects and your fellow classmates. Keep traveling until you hear the signal to stop. Ready, begin! (Dodging)
	This time I have reduced the amount of traveling space that you have to avoid the obstacles. Remember to keep your head up so that you don't bump into your neighbor. Keep traveling until you hear the signal to stop. Ready, begin! (Dodging)
Cues:	Keep your head up.
	Plant the foot and quickly change directions.
Variation:	Vary the amount of obstacles, mode of travel.

DS Ⓓ	**Travel in Different Pathways**
Pacing:	*Self-paced*
Grade Level:	Typically lower elementary (K–2)
Content Focus:	*Exploration of traveling in various pathways*
Setup:	Children are scattered in general space. Two lines (one blue and one red) are set about 20 yd. apart.
Task:	This time, as you travel quickly from the red line to the blue line, I want you to run in a zigzag pattern. Ready, begin! (Fleeing)
	As you are traveling around in general space, I want you to move only in a curved or straight pathway. Ready, action! (Chasing, fleeing)
	This time, when you hear the drumbeat, move in a different pathway. Ready, action! (Chasing, fleeing)
Cues:	Keep your head up.
	Use your arms for speed.
Variation:	Vary pathway and speed.

Expanding Skills (Typically Grades 1 through 3)

As children develop their ability to chase, flee, and dodge in relatively stable environments, the next step is for them to use these skills in less stable and less self-paced environments. A task is more difficult when children have to follow another person or use their skills to avoid potential "taggers." During the expanding phase, children should begin to use their chasing, fleeing, and dodging skills in simple tag games.

ES Ⓐ	**Shadow Partner**
Pacing:	*Semi-self-paced*
Grade Level:	Typically elementary (1–3)
Content Focus:	*Expanding traveling in general space*
Setup:	Children are scattered in a large indoor or outdoor space with a number of poly spots spread throughout the space to serve as bases.
Task:	On the signal, you and your partner will begin traveling in general space. One partner will be the leader, and one will be the shadow. The shadow follows and imitates all the different movements the leader makes. Follower, don't let the leader lose you. Leader, challenge the follower to keep up. Leaders, give yourselves a point if you are able to lose your shadow. Ready, begin! (Dodging, chasing)
	On the signal, you and your partner will begin traveling in general space. One partner will be the leader, and one will be the shadow. The shadow (chaser) is to follow the fleer until you hear the drumbeat. On the drumbeat, leaders (fleers) should get to one of the home bases before the shadow can tag them. Then change roles on the next signal to go. Ready, begin! (Chasing, fleeing)
	This time, we are going to take away a few of the home bases and move the rest of them farther apart. Remember, on the signal, the leader/fleer is trying to avoid being tagged by the shadow. We will change roles after each drumbeat. Ready, begin! (Chasing, fleeing)
Cues:	Chaser—watch the leader's waist (hips).
	Leader—use quick change of direction steps (plant and go).
Variation:	Vary the amount of space or distance, number of bases.

ES Ⓑ　　　　　　　　Dodging while Avoiding Stationary Taggers

Pacing:	*Semi self-paced*
Grade Level:	Typically elementary (1–3)
Content Focus:	*Expanding dodging skills to elude a stationary tagger*
Setup:	One half of the class is scattered in general space, with each student standing on an orange spot. The other half of the class is standing behind a start line.
Task:	Children standing on an orange spot are "immovable objects," while those on the line are the "movers." The immovable objects can reach out and try to touch the movers as they cross from one side of the work area to the other. Movers, each time you are touched, you receive a point. The goal is for the mover to cross the room three times while getting the *fewest* number of points. Then you will switch roles. Everybody ready, OK, begin! (Dodging)
	Let's try that again. But every time a mover is touched, pretend you are stung and lose the ability to use that body part. So, if a mover is touched on the leg, he or she still tries to cross the work area by hopping. Again movers will cross three times before switching roles. Ready, begin! (Dodging)
Cues:	Stay low and plant your foot on dodge.
	Look ahead.
Variation:	Vary the amount of space, number of taggers.

ES Ⓒ　　　　　　　　Simple Tag Games

Pacing:	*Semi-self-paced*
Grade Level:	Typically elementary (1–3)
Content Focus:	*Expanding chasing, fleeing, and dodging while playing a simple tag game*
Setup:	Children are scattered in general space.
Task:	On the signal, you will travel in general space trying to avoid being tagged. If you are wearing a blue shirt today, you will be "It"—one of the chasers. If you are not wearing a blue shirt, you will be running from the taggers. If you get tagged, you must stand still and wait for someone who is free to come and give you a "high five." Nobody may tag you when you are giving someone a high five. Spread out in general space and wait for the go signal. Ready, begin! (Chasing, fleeing)
Cues:	Fleer—use quick steps and movements.
	Dodger—plant and go.
	Chaser—watch the waist.
Variation:	Vary the way children are frozen or unfrozen.

ES Ⓓ　　　　　　　　Chasing, Fleeing, and Dodging while Avoiding a Moving Person

Pacing:	*Semi-self-paced*
Grade Level:	Typically elementary (1–3)
Content Focus:	*Expanding chasing, fleeing, and dodging while moving against one person*
Setup:	Children are working in partners, with one box per group. Three lines (baseline, centerline, endline) are marked on the basketball court or a large field about 10 yd. apart. The centerline is the midcourt line. The box is placed behind the endline.
Task:	Quickly stand by a partner. One person will be the running back and the other the defense. The running back's job is to put the football in the box on the other side of the line without being tagged by the defense. Runners start on the baseline; defenders start on the midcourt line. Remember, runners, you are trying to put the football in the box without being tagged. You will switch roles after each attempt. Ready, begin!
Cues:	Use quick movements (running back).
	Keep your eye on the waist (defense).
Variation:	Vary the object used and the distance.

Mastering Skills (Typically Grades 3 through 5)

In mastering these skills, students chase, flee, and dodge using different speeds and directions in a controlled manner to tag or avoid being tagged. They should be able to attend to other dynamics within the activity, such as catching a ball, avoiding a defender or developing tactics to avoid being tagged in more complex tag games. The environment in this phase is dynamic and changing. Because chasing, fleeing, and dodging skills are combined, students must be able to perform them instinctively so they can pay attention to what is happening around them.

MS Ⓐ	**Chasing, Fleeing, and Dodging in Complex Tag Games**
Pacing:	*Externally paced*
Grade Level:	Typically upper elementary (3–5)
Content Focus:	*Mastering chasing, fleeing, and dodging while playing a complex tag game*
Setup:	Groups of three are scattered in general space. Each group has two bases and one ball. Children decide the distance between the two bases. Refer to the diagram below.
Task:	Two people will be the throwers (taggers), and one will be the runner. The taggers can throw the ball to each other but must be holding the ball in their hands to tag the runner out.
	1st set: On the signal, the runner who starts in the middle of the lane will attempt to make it to one of the two bases before being tagged by either tagger. The taggers must tag the runner with the ball. Ready, begin. (Chasing, fleeing, dodging)
	2nd set: This time, we will increase the distance between the bases. Once again, try to get to the base without being tagged. Ready, begin! (Chasing, fleeing, dodging)
Diagram:	

Cues:	Use quick movements.
	Look for an open space.
Variation:	Vary the way children are frozen or unfrozen.

MS Ⓑ	**Take the Pin Basic**
Pacing:	*Externally paced*
Grade Level:	Typically upper elementary (3–5)
Content Focus:	*Mastering chasing, fleeing, and dodging while playing a simple tag game*
Setup:	Partners are scattered in general space, with two spots and one bowling pin per group. Children can decide the distance of bases from pin. Refer to the diagram on the next page.
Task:	Stand by a partner. For this game, stand on the spots (bases) directly across from each other. A bowling pin is midway between you. On the signal, your task is to snatch the pin and try to return to your base without getting tagged. The person who gets to the pin first is the "snatcher" and the other becomes the "tagger." Go to the areas that have been set up for this game. Ready, begin! (Chasing, fleeing, dodging)
	This time, let's change the person you're working with. On the signal, you have three seconds to find a new person. Ready, go! Now we will continue to play take the pin but with a new opponent. Ready, begin! (Chasing, fleeing, dodging)

continued

MS ⓑ   *Take the Pin Basic, continued*

Diagram:

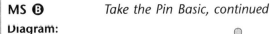

Base   Bowling   Base
player 1   pin   player 2

Cues: Use quick movements.

                Look for an open space.

Variation: Vary the distance, change opponents.

MS ⓒ   **Take the Flag**

Pacing: *Externally paced*

Grade Level: Typically upper elementary (3–5)

Content Focus: *Mastering chasing, fleeing, and dodging while playing a complex tag game*

Setup: Children are scattered in general space. Each student has two flags attached to his or her waist.

Task: Everyone should be wearing two flags on his or her waist. On the signal, you are to try to take as many flags from others as you can while protecting your own. Once a flag is taken, you must attach it to your body. You receive a point for every flag you take and are able to keep before time is called. These flags can still be taken from you by another person, so you have to protect all your flags. So, if you have three flags at the end, you will receive 3 points. Spread out in general space and wait for the signal to start. Ready, action!

Cues: Use quick movements.

                     Look for an open space.

Variation: Vary the object (clothespin).

MS ⓓ   **Chasing, Fleeing, and Dodging while Manipulating an Object**

Pacing: *Externally paced*

Grade Level: Typically upper elementary (3–5)

Content Focus: *Mastering chasing, fleeing, and dodging while manipulating an object*

Setup: Groups of three are scattered in general space with one ball per group. Children decide the playing area. Refer to the diagram below.

Task: Today we are going to play a game of three-on-three basketball. Remember, we must use our good faking moves in order to get open to receive the pass from our teammates. Your team must pass the ball over the goal line to score. There must be at least three passes before a team can score. Dribbling is not allowed. The only way you can move the ball is by passing. Go to your designated areas and begin play on my signal.

Diagram:

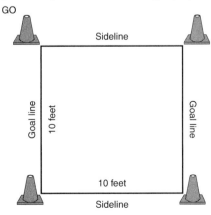

continued

MS **Ⓓ**	*Chasing, Fleeing, and Dodging while Manipulating an Object, continued*
Cues:	Use quick movements.
	Look for an open space.
Variation:	Vary the object used and playing area.

JUMPING AND LANDING

Learning to jump and land successfully is essential to many team sports such as basketball, volleyball, and even soccer. However, in gymnastics, dance, and skating it is the *quality* of jumps and landings that demonstrates mastery.

Teaching Jumping and Landing

Children can jump starting around the age of 2. The progression that most children follow as they acquire jumping and landing skills is learning to land on two feet and then to land on one foot. This is related to the child's strength and ability to balance his or her body when landing.

A jump is a spring off the ground by a muscular effort of the legs and feet. However, a jump can be divided into three parts—**takeoff, flight,** and **landing**— and jumping and landing lessons therefore focus on each of these elements. Students can explore jumping for distance or height and can investigate different ways to take off and land. The five basic jumps represent the five different ways to take off and land on your feet. For jumping *far* the best ones are the "hop" (jump from one foot to the same foot), the "leap" (jump from one foot to the opposite foot), and the "one-foot takeoff" (jump from one foot to land on two feet). Best for

takeoff
The act of getting the body off the ground.

flight
The act of traveling in the air.

landing
The act of coming down to the ground or other surface (e.g., a mat).

BOX 11.2 ■ Progression for Teaching the Skill of Jumping and Landing

1. Jump and land in self-space.

2. Jump and land over stationary objects.

3. Jump and land while moving in general space over stationary objects.

4. Jump a rope turned by an experienced turner.

5. Jump a self-turned rope (related to predictability not pacing).

6. Jump and land while moving to rhythm or to catch a moving object.

jumping *high* is the "two-foot takeoff" (jump from two feet to two feet). The fifth jump involves jumping from two feet and landing on one foot.

Sample Learning Tasks for Jumping and Landing

After students master the fundamentals of jumping and landing on a horizontal surface, they can progress to jumping on and off apparatus. Box 11.2 highlights the skill progression for students learning to jump and land. See Figure 11.3 for a graphic representation of sample learning tasks that follow this progression.

Developing Skills (Typically Kindergarten through Grade 2)

In the developing phase of jumping and landing, children need to practice all five variations of jumping patterns individually. These variations should be practiced from a stationary position while trying to attain height or distance. As students gain control over their ability to jump and land, you can add some complexity by having them jump over stationary objects or obstacles.

DS ❹	Jump and Land over Stationary Objects
Pacing:	*Self-paced*
Grade Level:	Typically lower elementary (K–2)
Content Focus:	*Exploration of jumping and landing over stationary objects*
Setup:	Children and poly spots are scattered in general space. A jump rope is placed on the floor next to each spot.
Task:	When I say, "Ready, begin," go stand on one of the spots that have been placed throughout general space. When you get to a spot, show me how many different ways you can jump over the rope placed on the floor. Ready, begin! (Jumping)
	This time, on the signal, take your jump rope and make a shape with it on the floor. Your shape can be narrow or wide. Jump over the shape you made with your rope. Continue to jump back and forth over the rope until you hear the signal to stop (two claps). Try to get higher over the rope each time. Be sure to bend your knees when you land. Ready, begin! (Jumping, landing)
Cues:	Bend knees.
	Push from toes. (Jumping)
Variation:	Vary the shape of the rope and type of object to jump.

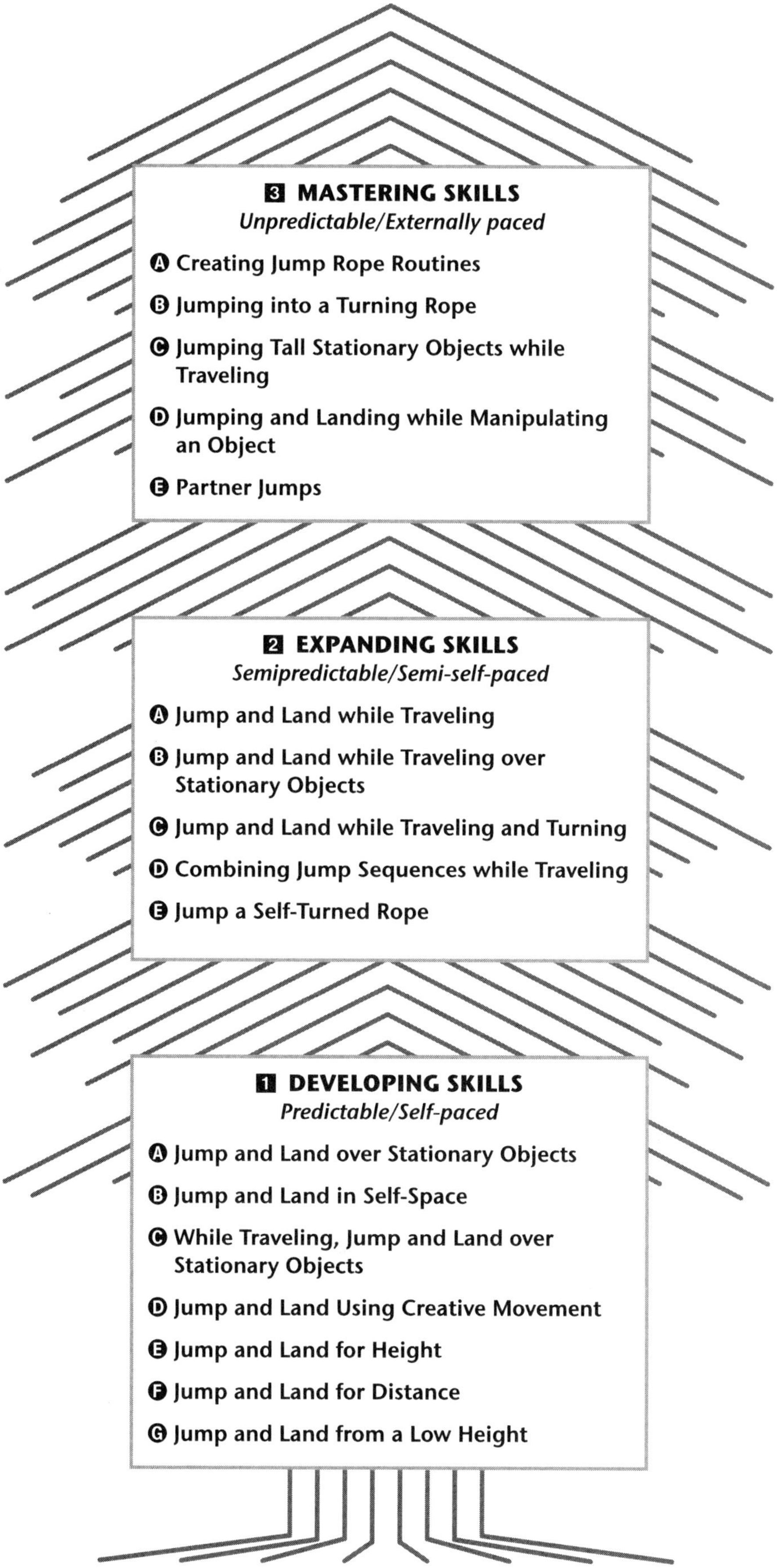

❸ MASTERING SKILLS
Unpredictable/Externally paced

Ⓐ Creating Jump Rope Routines

Ⓑ Jumping into a Turning Rope

Ⓒ Jumping Tall Stationary Objects while Traveling

Ⓓ Jumping and Landing while Manipulating an Object

Ⓔ Partner Jumps

❷ EXPANDING SKILLS
Semipredictable/Semi-self-paced

Ⓐ Jump and Land while Traveling

Ⓑ Jump and Land while Traveling over Stationary Objects

Ⓒ Jump and Land while Traveling and Turning

Ⓓ Combining Jump Sequences while Traveling

Ⓔ Jump a Self-Turned Rope

❶ DEVELOPING SKILLS
Predictable/Self-paced

Ⓐ Jump and Land over Stationary Objects

Ⓑ Jump and Land in Self-Space

Ⓒ While Traveling, Jump and Land over Stationary Objects

Ⓓ Jump and Land Using Creative Movement

Ⓔ Jump and Land for Height

Ⓕ Jump and Land for Distance

Ⓖ Jump and Land from a Low Height

FIGURE **11.3**
Progression tree for jumping and landing

DS Ⓑ   **Jump and Land in Self-Space**

Pacing:	*Self paced*
Grade Level:	Lower elementary (K–2)
Content Focus:	*Exploration of different actions while jumping and landing*
Setup:	Children and poly spots are scattered in general space.
Task:	Stand on your spot, and on the signal ("Ready, begin") try to jump and click your heels together before you land. Jump high so that you have enough time to click your heels. See how many heel clicks you can do before landing. Ready, begin! (Jumping)
	This time, how many times can you clap your hands together before you land? Try to land quietly. (Jumping, landing)
Cues:	Reach arms back (jump).
	Bend knees.
Variation:	Vary number of clicks and action to perform.

DS Ⓒ   **While Traveling, Jump and Land over Stationary Objects**

Pacing:	*Self-paced*
Grade Level:	Typically lower elementary (K–2)
Content Focus:	*Exploration of jumping and landing while moving*
Setup:	Children, poly spots, hoops, and ropes are scattered in general space.
Task:	Stand on one of the spots that are placed in general space. See the hoops (turtles) and ropes (snakes) placed throughout our space. On the signal, travel in general space. Jump over the snakes and leap over the turtles when you come to them. Be sure to keep your head up so that you don't run into any of your classmates. Ready, begin! (Jumping, leaping)
	On my signal, hop (one foot to the same foot) over the snakes and jump (one or two feet to two feet) the turtles. Try to land as quietly as you can by landing on the rounded part of your foot. Keep moving until you hear the signal to stop. Remember to land quietly as a mouse. Ready, begin! (Landing)
Cues:	Try this going in a backward direction. Ready, begin!
	Land quietly as a mouse.
	Bend knees.
Variation:	Vary the objects (bean bags, hoops) and direction.

DS Ⓓ   **Jump and Land Using Creative Movement**

Pacing:	*Self-paced*
Grade Level:	Typically lower elementary (K–2)
Content Focus:	*Exploration of jumping and landing using creative movement*
Setup:	Children are scattered in general space.
Task:	**1st set:** As we use all our space, I want you to jump like a kangaroo. Ready, begin! (Jumping)
	2nd set: You are using your space well. This time, jump like a frog. Ready, begin! (Jumping)
	3rd set: Can you name another animal that jumps? That's right—a rabbit. This time, jump like a rabbit. Ready, begin! (Jumping)
Cues:	Push from toes.
	Keep your head up—look forward.
Variation:	Vary the imagery, pathway, and speed.

DS ⓔ   **Jump and Land for Height**

Pacing:	*Self-paced*
Grade Level:	Typically lower elementary (K–2)
Content Focus:	*Exploration of jumping and landing for height*
Setup:	Balloons are attached to a rope strung between two poles. Each child stands in front of one of the balloons.
Task:	On the rope that I have strung from one pole to another, you will see balloons dangling from various heights. On the signal I want you to go to one of the balloons, then jump with a two-foot takeoff to try to touch the balloon. Just try to touch the balloon, don't try to grab it. Find all the different balloons you can touch. Watch out for your neighbor. Go to a different balloon if someone is already at the one you want to try. Remember to bend your knees and swing your arms in order to get higher. Ready, begin! (Jumping, landing)
Cues:	Gather feet for explosion. (Jumping)
	Reach arms back. (Jumping)
	Absorb body weight—sink. (Landing)
Variation:	Vary the height, the objects, and the type of jump.

DS ⓕ   **Jump and Land for Distance**

Pacing:	*Self-paced*
Grade Level:	Typically lower elementary (K–2)
Content Focus:	*Exploration of jumping and landing for distance*
Setup:	Children are scattered in general space standing on a poly spot.
Task:	Stand on your spot with your dot. Jump (two feet to two feet) three times, then mark the distance with your dot. Try to jump a little farther on each attempt. You need to maintain your balance on the landing. Next, challenge yourself to see if you can jump farther on your next three attempts. Move your dot if you jump farther. Remember to swing your arms back and forward to help you gain more distance. Ready, begin! (Jumping, landing)
Cues:	Swing arms back and forward. (Jumping)
	Land on balls of feet. (Landing)
Variation:	Vary distance and the type of jump, use an approach.

DS ⓖ   **Jump and Land from a Low Height**

Pacing:	*Self-paced*
Grade Level:	Typically lower elementary (K–2)
Content Focus:	*Exploration of landing from a low height*
Setup:	Children are scattered in general space, each with a low bench (aerobic bench step).
Task:	Stand on your step bench. On signal, jump off the bench and land very quietly in front of your bench. Remember to bend your knees when you land. Ready, begin! (Landing)
	You are doing a good job landing with your knees bent. This time let's see if you can make a shape in the air before you land. Ready, begin! I'm seeing some nice shapes and good quiet landings! (Landing)
Cues:	Bend knees.
	Land quietly as a mouse.
Variation:	Vary height and shapes.

Expanding Skills (Typically Grades 1 through 3)

In the expanding phase of jumping and landing, students can jump and land in controlled environments, performing tasks that are less controlled and self-paced. In this phase, students start to attain height on jumps so that other movements can be performed while in the air. They consistently land balanced after various jump patterns. They begin to use jumping and landing tasks that require the body to be in motion prior to takeoff.

ES Ⓐ **Jump and Land while Traveling**

Pacing:	*Semi-self-paced*
Grade Level:	Typically elementary (1–3)
Content Focus:	*Expanding jumping skills while traveling in general space*
Setup:	Children are scattered in general space.
Task:	When I say, "Ready, begin," travel around in general space. On the drumbeat, jump and then continue traveling until you hear the next drumbeat. Every time you hear the drumbeat, remember to jump. Ready, begin! (Jumping)
	This time, when you hear the drumbeat, jump and make a shape in the air before landing. See how many different shapes you can make before you land. (Jumping)
Cues:	Keep your eyes forward.
	Maintain good posture (shoulders up).
Variation:	Vary the type of jump and speed of travel.

ES Ⓑ **Jump and Land while Traveling over Stationary Objects**

Pacing:	*Semi-self-paced*
Grade Level:	Typically elementary (1–3)
Content Focus:	*Expanding jumping and landing while traveling and jumping stationary objects*
Setup:	Children and boxes are scattered in general space. Two cones and a jump rope or yardstick are used to make hurdles.
Task:	**1st set:** I have placed various low hurdles and boxes throughout general space. On the signal, begin traveling in general space. I want you to leap over the hurdles or the boxes. Be sure you use a leaping pattern (take off from one foot and land on the ball of the other foot). Watch out for your neighbor. Ready, begin! (Leaping)
	2nd set: This time I have placed two hurdles, one right after the other. As you leap the first hurdle, make sure you land balanced so that you can leap the second hurdle without having to stop. Ready, begin! (Leaping)
Cues:	Use quick feet.
	Land from one foot to the other foot. (Leaping)
	Gather your feet.
Variation:	Vary the distance between objects and the jump sequence (hop/leap, leap/jump, jump/jump).

ES Ⓒ **Jump and Land while Traveling and Turning**

Pacing:	*Semi-self-paced*
Grade Level:	Typically elementary (1–3)
Content Focus:	*Expanding jumping and landing while traveling and turning*
Setup:	Children are scattered in general space.
Task:	**1st set:** When I say, "Begin," travel around in general space. At the sound of the drum, jump and make a quarter turn to your left. Remember, you may use any locomotor pattern you want as you travel. Ready, begin! (Jumping, landing)

continued

ES **C**	Jump and Land while Traveling and Turning, *continued*
	2nd set: This time, let's try a half turn when you hear the drumbeat. Try to land softly on the balls of your feet. Ready, begin! (Jumping, landing)
Cues:	Bend knees.
	Land with soft feet.
Variation:	Vary the direction of turn.

ES **D**	**Combining Jump Sequences while Traveling**
Pacing:	*Semi-self-paced*
Grade Level:	Typically elementary (1–3)
Content Focus:	*Expanding jumping and landing by combining sequences while traveling*
Setup:	Children are scattered in general space.
Task:	**1st set:** On the signal, travel in general space (you may use any locomotor pattern to travel) and, when you hear the drumbeat, I want you to step, hop, then jump. Ready, begin! Good! (Step, hop, jump)
	2nd set: This time I want you to really concentrate on the second skill in the pattern, the hop. When you get to the hop, I want you to cover some distance, so concentrate on moving forward when you hop and not straight up and down. Ready, begin! (Step, hop, jump)
Cues:	Step, same (hop), both (jump).
	Land on balls of feet.
Variation:	Vary pattern and distance.

ES **E**	**Jumping a Self-Turned Rope**
Pacing:	*Semi-self-paced*
Grade Level:	Typically elementary (1–3)
Content Focus:	*Expanding jumping over a self-turned rope*
Setup:	Children are scattered in general space standing on an X.
Task:	On my signal, stand on one of the Xs that you see around the gym. At each X you will find a jump rope. As you get to your X, pick up the jump rope and start jumping. If you are having trouble jumping the turned rope, think horseshoe (rope behind back), toss, and step. That is the pattern I want you to focus on. Say the pattern to yourself as you practice jumping. Ready, begin! (Jumping, landing)
Cues:	Take rope behind back like a horseshoe, then toss and step.
	Practice quiet landings.
Variation:	Vary the way children jump rope (forward, backward, crisscross), jump with a partner.

Mastering Skills (Typically Grades 3 through 5)

In mastering jumping and landing skills, students perform the movements automatically and can attend to a changing and uncertain environment, such as working with a partner or jumping and executing another skill while in the air, such as throwing or catching. They can also respond to external stimuli like jumping two ropes turned at once (double Dutch).

MS Ⓐ   **Creating Jump Rope Routines**

Pacing:	*Externally paced*
Grade Level:	Typically upper elementary (3–5)
Content Focus:	*Mastering jumping a rope by combining various jumping sequences into a routine*
Setup:	Children and jump ropes are scattered in general space.
Task:	Go stand by one of the jump ropes that have been placed throughout the gym. On my signal, you are going to work on creating a jump rope routine. Your routine will include: Hop on one foot, jump on two feet, crisscross arms, and jump and turn. You may turn the rope as fast as you want, but make sure all the elements are included in your routine. You have five minutes to create your routine. Ready, begin! (Jumping, landing)
Cues:	Use quick feet. (Jumping)
	Have soft feet. (Landing)
Variation:	Vary the sequence, add more complex moves.

MS Ⓑ   **Jumping into a Turning Rope**

Pacing:	*Externally paced*
Grade Level:	Typically upper elementary (3–5)
Content Focus:	*Mastering jumping and landing while jumping a rope turned by others*
Setup:	Groups of three are standing in an assigned space with one long rope per group.
Task:	Let's get in the groups of three that you have been assigned and work on jumping into a turning rope. Two of you will turn the rope while the other student will be the jumper.
	Remember the technique for jumping in the front door (i.e., rope turns toward jumper and the jumper waits for the rope to move away before running in) and jumping in the back door (i.e., rope turns away from the jumper and the jumper waits until the rope has passed its highest point before jumping in). When I say, "Ready, begin," I want the jumper to practice the following skills: Run under the rope and through; run in and jump once and run out; run in, jump on alternating feet, and run out. Keep practicing until you hear me say, "Freeze." Ready, begin!
	Now, let's change positions. You are to rotate positions (holder 1 to holder 2, holder 2 to jumper, and jumper to holder 1). Ready, begin!
Cues:	Front door—let the rope hit the floor and then go.
	Back door—wait until rope reaches highest point and then go.
Variation:	Vary the number of jumps, the number of children jumping at one time, or the number of ropes (double Dutch).

MS Ⓒ   **Jumping Tall Stationary Objects while Traveling**

Pacing:	*Externally paced*
Grade Level:	Typically upper elementary (3–5)
Content Focus:	*Mastering jumping and landing over objects while traveling*
Setup:	Groups of three are scattered in general space. There are three hurdles for each group. Hurdles consist of two cones and a jump rope. Hurdles are set about 7 ft. apart and in a row.
Task:	**1st set:** We are going to work on our hurdling technique today. On my signal, your group of three will go to one of the hurdling tracks I have set up. This first time we are going to practice by running to the side of the hurdles instead of going over them. One person will go at a time. Ready, begin!
	This time, let's work on our stride pattern. Remember to leap off your dominant foot and land on the other foot. If you are right dominant, your pattern should be right, leap, land on left, right, left, right, and leap. If you are left dominant, your pattern should be left, leap, land on right, left, right, left, leap. Try to make sure you get to the second hurdle in good position. Wait until the first hurdler has finished the course before the second hurdler starts. Ready begin!

continued

MS ⓒ	*Jumping Tall Stationary Objects while Traveling, continued*
	2nd set: Now that we've all had a chance to learn the course, this time I want you to leap the various low hurdles I have placed on the course. Ready, begin!
	3rd set: Replace low hurdles with higher ones for the next task.
Cues:	Maintain good posture.
	Keep eyes forward.
Variation:	Vary the height, type of jump, or distance between objects.

MS ⓓ	**Jumping and Landing while Manipulating an Object**
Pacing:	*Externally paced*
Grade Level:	Typically upper elementary (3–5)
Content Focus:	*Mastering jumping and landing while performing other skills while moving*
Setup:	Partners are scattered in general space with one ball per pair.
Task:	Your partner is going to throw you a ball while you are traveling so that you have to jump to catch it. The tosser needs to throw the ball high enough so that it requires the receiver to jump to catch it. On the signal, change roles. Remember to bend your knees so that you can get high to catch the ball. Ready, begin! (Jumping, landing)
Cues:	Keep your head up.
	Bend knees.
Variation:	Vary the distance of throw, height of throw, or type of ball.

MS ⓔ	**Partner Jumps**
Pacing:	*Externally paced*
Grade Level:	Typically upper elementary (3–5)
Content Focus:	*Mastering jumping and landing while moving with a partner*
Setup:	Children are scattered in general space. See Table 11.1 for descriptions of the various jumps performed in this task.
Task:	We are going to practice our different jump patterns with our partner: the tuck, or C shape; the pike, or L shape; and the straddle, or V shape. Each of you will do the same jump at the same time. Really work hard on coordinating the jump height and movement with your partner. You and your partner should land at the same time. (Jumping, landing)
	Now let's work on moving in time with our partner using a running approach to help us attain height. Remember to land in a balanced position at the same time as your partner. Ready, begin!
Diagram:	See Table 11.1.
Cues:	Bend knees.
	Swing arms.
Variation:	Vary types of jump or number of students working together.

HOW TO TEACH NONLOCOMOTOR SKILLS

While locomotor skills move the body through space, nonlocomotor skills are movements occurring in the same place. Essentially, most nonlocomotor skills are used in gymnastics sequences or as cue words when learning other skills. For example, we use the word *stretch* to teach volleying skills, and being "tucked" is important in moving quickly to change direction.

Table 11.1 ▪ Possible Shapes when Jumping

Skill	Description	Image
Tuck	Bent at the hips and the knees	
Pike	Bent only at the hips (legs are straight)	
Straddle	Legs are separated with neither leg being in front of or behind the other	

Typically, nonlocomotor skills do not have one best, correct form. While technique is involved in good running and skipping, there is no one best way to bend, stretch, or curl. The words are more conceptual than definitive. As a result, we have two goals in teaching nonlocomotor skills. The first is to explain the meaning of the skill so students understand the concept. The second is to give students opportunities to demonstrate their understanding of the skill by producing several examples of it. Table 11.2 shows the nonlocomotor vocabulary that we think all students should learn. The table provides the term, its definition, and a sample photograph.

Table 11.2 ■ **Essential Nonlocomotor Movement Vocabulary**

Skill	Description	Image
Twist	Turn one part of the body while keeping another part still	
Turn	Move around a central point	
Bend	Move body parts closer together	

continued

Table 11.2 ▪ Essential Nonlocomotor Movement Vocabulary, *continued*

Skill	Description	Image
Stretch	Move body parts away from each other	
Curl	Form a curved shape	

BALANCING

As noted in the chapter introduction, the one nonlocomotor skill that deserves particular attention is balancing. **Balancing** involves keeping the body's center of gravity above its base of support. Balance is controlled through posture, by managing muscular contractions and relaxation. Tensing muscles helps position the body over its center of gravity while relaxing them shifts the body with respect to its center of gravity.

The ability to balance while either stationary or moving is a key to success in any sport or physical activity. In fact, keeping the body stable helps produce force and smoothly transition from one movement to another. The feet are the primary mode of balance, but there are numerous other ways to balance the body.

Teaching Balancing

When you teach balancing, children need to understand two key concepts. The first is the base of support, that part of the body in contact with the ground. In most locomotor skills, our base of support is our feet, but when we sit on the floor,

balancing
The skill of safely supporting one's body weight.

our base of support would be our bottom and legs. When kneeling, the base of support is the knees, shins, and feet.

The second key point is the concept of stable and unstable balances. A stable balance resists gravity or force and cannot be pushed over easily, while an unstable balance is easily disrupted. A balance where the base is only one hand and one foot is easy to disrupt. Children should learn that a stable balance has a low and wide base, while an unstable balance has a base that is high and narrow.

To teach the concepts of base of support and stability, your strategies can be demonstration followed by exploration, as we noted in Chapter 5. After you first explain a base of support and how it helps make a balance stable or unstable, use a series of "show me" tasks to help students explore the effects of different bases of support and how these relate to stable and unstable bases. Box 11.3 lists a series of sample questions you can use to help this process.

Sample Learning Tasks for Balancing

There are three main balancing skills:

1. Balancing your own body

2. Balancing an object

3. Balancing another person

Initially, lessons should explore balancing safely on different bases of support as well as show postural exercises to help children understand how to control their muscular contractions. You can select balancing tasks that can easily be individualized to the developmental level, strength, and flexibility levels of your students.

BOX **11.3** ■ Sample Tasks for Teaching Base of Support

The part of you in contact with the ground or our apparatus is called your *base of support*. See if you can find three body parts that provide a *large* area in touch with the ground.

Find a position on your mat that's so stable that no one could push you off your spot. Which body part are you resting on? Is it low or high? Are you all tucked up or spread over a wide area?

Try a balance that is hard to hold for more than two seconds.

How about just using your hands as a base? Is this difficult? Notice that when you have a small base it's much harder to control.

BOX **11.4** ■ Progression for Teaching the Skill of Balancing

1. Stationary balance on different bases of support
2. Stationary balance while balancing different objects on body
3. Balance after jumping and making shapes in the air
4. Balance on low stationary objects (e.g., balance beam)
5. Balance while moving on stationary objects
6. Partner balances (on floor)
7. Balance on less stable objects, such as balance boards and stilts
8. Weight-bearing inverted balances

As students learn to gain, lose, and regain balance, they can progress to activities that combine traveling and balancing. Finally, children can work in pairs or groups to create balances involving more than one person. Box 11.4 highlights the skill progression for children learning the skill theme of balancing. See Figure 11.4 for a graphic representation of sample learning tasks that follow this progression.

Developing Skills (Typically Kindergarten through Grade 2)

In the developing phase of balance, students learn to balance the body while stationary (static balance). In this environment, students practice balancing tasks for which they can control the outcome by learning to use different bases of support, balancing on stationary objects, and balancing different objects on various body parts. The student can easily control these tasks.

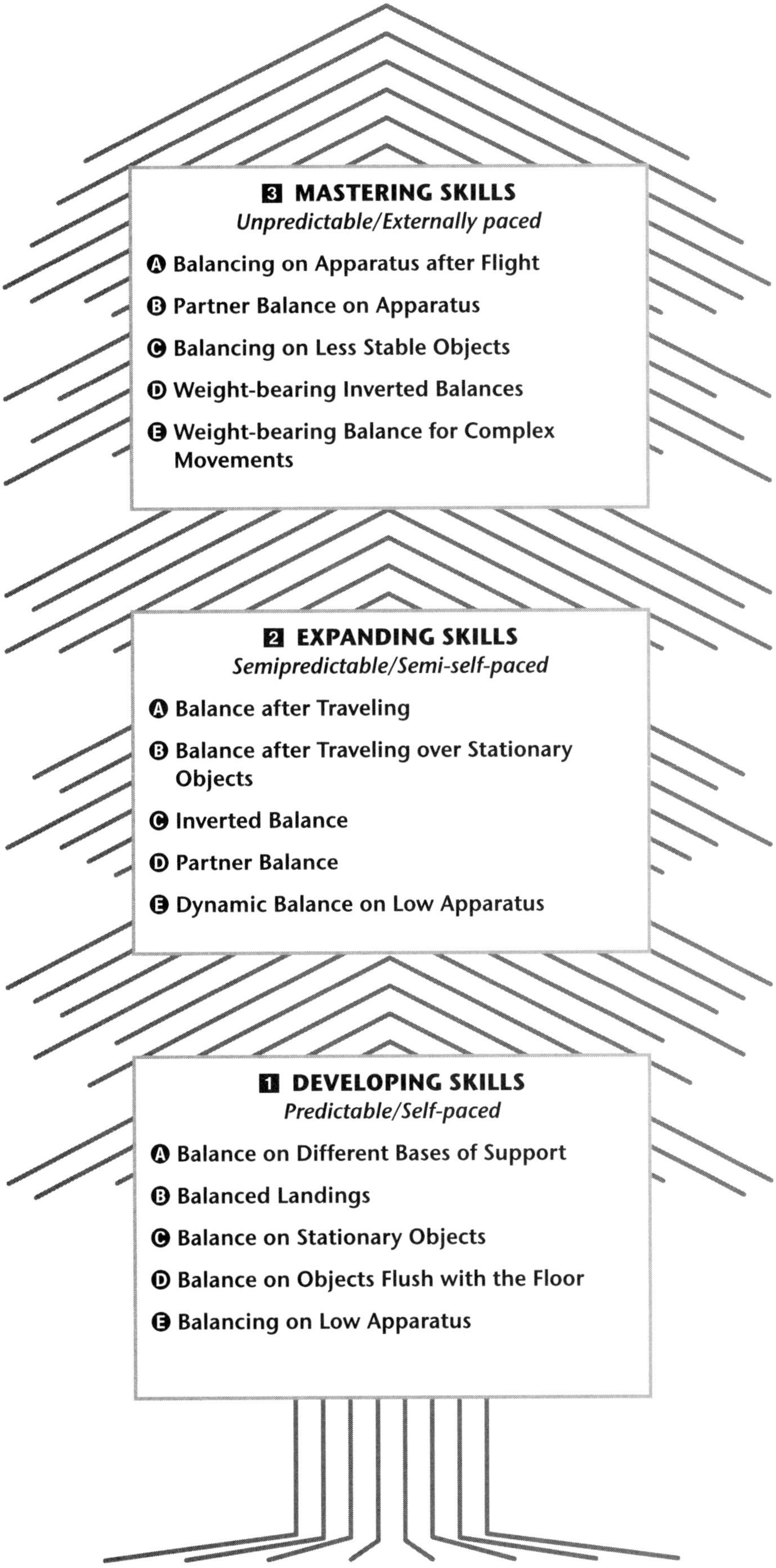

3 MASTERING SKILLS
Unpredictable/Externally paced

Ⓐ Balancing on Apparatus after Flight

Ⓑ Partner Balance on Apparatus

Ⓒ Balancing on Less Stable Objects

Ⓓ Weight-bearing Inverted Balances

Ⓔ Weight-bearing Balance for Complex Movements

2 EXPANDING SKILLS
Semipredictable/Semi-self-paced

Ⓐ Balance after Traveling

Ⓑ Balance after Traveling over Stationary Objects

Ⓒ Inverted Balance

Ⓓ Partner Balance

Ⓔ Dynamic Balance on Low Apparatus

1 DEVELOPING SKILLS
Predictable/Self-paced

Ⓐ Balance on Different Bases of Support

Ⓑ Balanced Landings

Ⓒ Balance on Stationary Objects

Ⓓ Balance on Objects Flush with the Floor

Ⓔ Balancing on Low Apparatus

FIGURE **11.4**
Progression tree for balancing

DS Ⓐ   **Balance on Different Bases of Support**

Pacing:	*Self-paced*
Grade Level:	Typically lower elementary (K–2)
Content Focus:	*Exploration of balancing on various bases of support*
Setup:	Children are scattered in general space while standing on an *X* made from floor tape.
Task:	On my signal, go stand on one of the *X*s that have been placed throughout general space. When you get to your *X*, I want you to try to balance on one foot until you hear me say, "Freeze." Ready, begin!
	This time, I want you to balance using three body parts. For example, you may use a foot and two hands or two feet and an elbow. See how many different ways you can balance on three body parts.
Cues:	Keep your base flat.
	Be still like a statue.
Variation:	Vary the base of support or the width (narrow, wide).

DS Ⓑ   **Balanced Landings**

Pacing:	*Self-paced*
Grade Level:	Typically lower elementary (K–2)
Content Focus:	*Exploration of balancing while landing from jumps*
Setup:	Children are scattered in general space.
Task:	On my signal in your personal space, jump in the air as high as you can while landing in a balanced position on two feet. Let's explore various shapes we can make with our bodies as we are in the air. Keep exploring until I say, "Freeze." Ready, begin!
Cues:	Land with your feet flat.
	Stay low.
Variation:	Vary time to balance, height of jump, or shapes.

DS Ⓒ   **Balance on Stationary Objects**

Pacing:	*Self-paced*
Grade Level:	Typically lower elementary (K–2)
Content Focus:	*Exploration of static balance using small objects*
Setup:	Children are scattered in general space while standing on a poly spot. At each spot are three items (beanbag, ball, foam Frisbees) to be used during balancing activities.
Task:	**1st set:** On the signal, go to one of the spots, choose one of the items, and try to balance that item on any body part while standing on your poly spot. Ready, begin!
	2nd set: This time, balance one of the objects on your head while standing on one foot. Keep trying, until I say, "Freeze." Ready, begin!
	3rd set: This time, you are going to be sitting, but only on your hips. Try to balance the ball between your feet while keeping your feet off the ground. Don't let them touch the floor! Ready, begin!
Cues:	Be as still as possible.
	Keep your balancing surface flat.
Variation:	Vary the objects or body parts.

DS **Ⓓ**	Balance on Objects Flush with the Floor
Pacing:	*Self-paced*
Grade Level:	Typically lower elementary (K–2)
Content Focus:	*Exploration of static balance on objects flush with floor*
Setup:	Children are scattered in general space standing on a carpet strip.
Task:	When I say, "Ready, begin," stand on your carpet strip and make a narrow shape with your body—like a pencil. Hold this position. Freeze! Now balance on your carpet square using a wide shape—really stretched. Ready, begin!
	Go stand on one of the *X*s at one end of the carpet strips you see spread throughout general space. Now, when I say, "Begin," I want you to walk to the center of the carpet strip and try to balance on one leg.
	Try to hold this balance for five seconds. Try this again using the opposite leg as the base of support. Ready, begin!
Cues:	Look forward.
	Tight muscles.
Variation:	Vary the time, shapes, and the base of support.

DS **Ⓔ**	Balance on Low Apparatus
Pacing:	*Self-paced*
Grade Level:	Typically lower elementary (K–2)
Content Focus:	*Exploration of balance on a low and level apparatus (balance beam)*
Setup:	Children are scattered in general space standing three to a low balance beam (1 ft. high).
Task:	**1st set:** On the signal, go stand on the *X* beside one of the balance beams. Good! When I say, "Ready, begin," the first person waiting will step on the balance beam and will balance for three seconds, or until they say "alligator" three times. Ready, begin! Nice balance. Go to the end of the line and the next person step on the beam. Ready, begin! (Proceed until all children have done the task.)
	2nd set: On the signal, this time balance on the beam like Superman (with your arms up showing your muscles). Hold for three alligators. Ready, begin! (Proceed until all children have done the task.)
Cues:	Use airplane arms (arms extended out to side).
	Keep the muscles tight.
Variation:	Vary the base of support.

Figure 11.5 shows a circuit children can carry out after they have completed a series of tasks in this developing phase. Verbal instructions are given for each station in the circuit.

Expanding Skills (Typically Grades 1 through 3)

The expanding phase of balancing can be made more difficult by adding locomotor movement, flight, or partners to the task demands. These variables make the tasks less predictable or self-paced, because students have to execute a task after moving or while still moving. Balance while moving is "dynamic balance."

As students transition out of this phase, they begin to work with partner balances on the floor or with balances that require sustaining only a *portion* of their body weight. These are expanding tasks, because working with a partner or lacking requisite strength to sustain body weight gives the students less control of the movement.

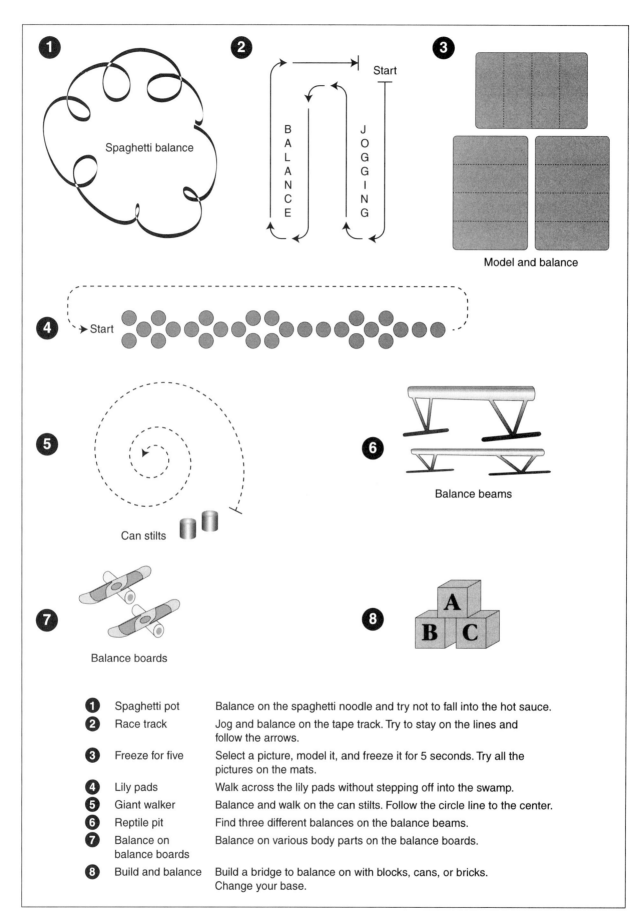

1	Spaghetti pot	Balance on the spaghetti noodle and try not to fall into the hot sauce.
2	Race track	Jog and balance on the tape track. Try to stay on the lines and follow the arrows.
3	Freeze for five	Select a picture, model it, and freeze it for 5 seconds. Try all the pictures on the mats.
4	Lily pads	Walk across the lily pads without stepping off into the swamp.
5	Giant walker	Balance and walk on the can stilts. Follow the circle line to the center.
6	Reptile pit	Find three different balances on the balance beams.
7	Balance on balance boards	Balance on various body parts on the balance boards.
8	Build and balance	Build a bridge to balance on with blocks, cans, or bricks. Change your base.

FIGURE **11.5**
Balance circuit for kindergarten and first grades

ES Ⓐ   **Balance after Traveling**

Pacing:	*Semi-self-paced*
Grade Level:	Typically elementary (1–3)
Content Focus:	*Expanding balancing skills after traveling*
Setup:	Children are scattered in general space.
Task:	**1st set:** When I say, "Ready, begin," travel around in general space. On the signal, stop and balance for a count of two alligators on two body parts that are not the same. Ready, begin!
	2nd set: On the signal, travel in general space; when you hear the drumbeat, leap and land in a balanced position. Hold that position for the count of two alligators. Ready, begin!
Cues:	Keep your head up.
	Look for an open space.
Variation:	Vary the type of jump or speed of travel.

ES Ⓑ   **Balance after Traveling over Stationary Objects**

Pacing:	*Semi-self-paced*
Grade Level:	Typically elementary (1–3)
Content Focus:	*Expanding balancing while traveling over stationary objects*
Setup:	Children are scattered in general space along with ropes and cones.
Task:	**1st set:** Various objects are placed around the gym. On the signal, begin traveling in general space. (You may use any locomotor pattern to travel.) When you hear the drumbeat, leap over one of the objects and land in a balanced position on two feet. Ready, begin!
	2nd set: Now, when you hear the signal, jump over the object, making a twisted shape while you're in the air, and then land in a balanced position on one foot. Ready, begin!
Cues:	Keep stomach in and tight.
	Glue your feet to the floor on the finish.
Variation:	Vary the height of objects or type of balanced landing.

ES Ⓒ   **Inverted Balance**

Pacing:	*Semi-self-paced*
Grade Level:	Typically elementary (1–3)
Content Focus:	*Expanding balancing while exploring inverted balances*
Setup:	Children work on trifold mats spread throughout the gym, two students per mat.
Task:	On the signal, go stand by one of the spots in front of the mats spread throughout the gym. We are going to be working on taking body weight on our shoulders (shoulder stand). The first thing I want you to do is start in a crouched position with your fingers touching the mat. Rock back so that your bottom, then back, then shoulders touch the floor. Support your weight by bending your arms at the elbows and supporting your hips with your hands. Hold that balance for three seconds and then slowly roll back into a crouched position.
	[*Note:* Remind children not to roll onto the neck and head or into a piked position.]
Cues:	Tighten your bottom and tummy.
	Keep your toes pointed.
Variation:	Vary shape of legs when balanced.

┌──┐
│ **WHAT'S WRONG**   Ms. Mitchell's third grade class has just completed a series of lessons
│ **WITH THIS**   on jumping, landing, and balancing. As the assessment for this work,
│ **PICTURE?**   Ms. Mitchell is requiring all students to perform the following routine:
│ (1) jump onto a beam, (2) perform a straight-legged toe touch, (3) skip
│ along the beam for five steps, (4) jump up and land again on the beam,
│ (5) twist to face the opposite direction, and (6) perform a tuck jump off
│ the beam and land quietly without a bobble.
└──┘

ES Ⓓ   **Partner Balance**

Pacing:	*Semi-self-paced*
Grade Level:	Typically elementary (1–3)
Content Focus:	*Expanding balance while working with a partner without apparatus*
Setup:	Partners are scattered in general space.
Task:	**1st set:** You have three seconds to find a partner. Ready, go! Spread out in general space. With your partner, I want you to show me a partner balance using only one base of support for each partner. For example, while facing your partner, use your hands and one foot from each partner to make a partner balance. This is just one example. There are many different ways you and your partner can balance with each person using only one base of support. Ready, begin!
	2nd set: Still using only one base of support each, show me a different partner balance than the one you did before. This time you may not use the foot as a base of support. Ready, begin!
Cues:	Keep the base of support flat.
	Be still—no teeter-tottering.
Variation:	Vary the balance or base of support.

ES Ⓔ   **Dynamic Balance on Low Apparatus**

Pacing:	*Semi-self-paced*
Grade Level:	Typically elementary (1–3)
Content Focus:	*Expanding balancing by mounting or dismounting a stationary object*
Setup:	Children are grouped three per balance beam, with mats under the beam for safety. Some beams are low 1-ft. beams, and some are higher at 3 ft.
Task:	We have our balance beams set at different heights. On my signal, choose the beam height you feel comfortable working at by standing on one of the spots you see in front of each beam. There are three spots for each beam.
	Today we are working on using different locomotor patterns (walk, slide, glide, gallop) to travel across the beam. Remember one person on the beam at a time. Ready, begin!
Cues:	Keep stomach in and tight.
	Use airplane arms.
Variation:	Vary the beam or locomotor pattern.

During the expanding phase, you may also wish to introduce balances in **inverted positions**, any position where the hips are above the head. It is important that when your students work in any kind of inverted position, they should be positioned on a mat and not work on the bare floor. The following section shows two skills in which students can be inverted: the shoulder balance and the hand balance with the body curled. Both are safe and easy for students to learn.

inverted position
Any body position that finds the hips higher than the head.

FIGURE **11.6**
**Action sketch for
shoulder balance**

Shoulder Balance

The shoulder balance allows children to assume an inverted-but-stable and extended position. The child's weight is carried on a large body surface, but his or her legs are free to move and assume a stretched, tucked, or curled position, so the child can mimic a number of different shapes.

The progression for the shoulder balance begins by rocking from a seated position onto the shoulders and then returning to the seated position—all while keeping the body curled. The child progresses by rocking to a point where weight is evenly distributed on the shoulders and the body. Eventually, the child reaches a stopping point at which weight is fully on the shoulders. From this point, the child slowly extends his or her legs upward. In the early stages of learning, the child can support his or her hips using the forearms and elbows. Later, the goal is to have the hips off the ground as well as the legs. Figure 11.6 shows a stop-action sketch supporting this sequence.

Children typically have difficulty extending their hips as they try a shoulder stand, so have your students focus mainly on what it feels like to bear weight on their shoulders. As they grow accustomed to this, hip extensions tend to follow naturally.

Hand Balance, Body Curled

A hand balance with the body curled helps children get used to (1) taking their weight on their hands and (2) having their body in an inverted position (see Figure 11.7). Students begin a hand balance by tipping from a standing position and putting their hands on the floor. In one continuous movement, they try to kick just one foot off the floor. Less confident children might begin this task by placing their hands on a bench or a box, so they do not have to reach so far down.

A child who has grown used to bearing weight on his or her hands can progress to kicking both feet off the floor, one after the other. With repeated practice, the aim is to elevate the hips over the shoulders. It is important, however, to repeatedly remind your children to keep their body curled with the head up. This helps

FIGURE **11.7**
The hand balance helps students experience an inverted position.

FIGURE **11.8**
Action sketch for hand balance

keep the body from tipping over. The aim here is *not* for children to complete a handstand but to have a safer and easier option. Figure 11.8 shows the stop-action sketch for the skill.

Mastering Skills (Typically Grades 3 through 5)

In mastering balancing, children can incorporate their ability to balance their body while both stationary and moving (dynamic) into a more challenging environment. Tasks in this phase require students to respond to changing conditions with the body as well as the environment. Traveling while balancing on a balance beam or walking on stilts (see Figure 11.9) are two examples. Safety is a primary issue for many tasks in this phase. When working with high apparatus, place mats around and under the apparatus to create a landing area with no open spaces. These landing mats should be 12 to 24 inches thick. Sufficient space between apparatus will also allow free movement on the apparatus and space to dismount.

FIGURE **11.9**
Walking on stilts is an example of dynamic balance.

MS **A**	**Balancing on Apparatus after Flight**
Pacing:	*Externally paced*
Grade Level:	Typically upper elementary (3–5)
Content Focus:	*Mastering balancing on apparatus after flight*
Setup:	There are four children per balance beam, with beams scattered in general space and thick mats under the beams for safety.
Task:	We have a variety of balance beams at different levels (1 ft. and 3 ft.—two of each height). On my signal, choose the beam height you feel comfortable working at by standing on one of the spots you see in front of each beam. There are three spots for each beam.
	When I say, "Begin," the first person in each line is to walk to the center of the beam. Once in the center of the beam, I want you to try leaping, jumping, or hopping once on the beam the way we practiced on the floor. Remember, only one person on the beam at a time. When you are done, go to the end of the line, and the next person in line can go. Ready, begin!
Cues:	Finish still and tall.
	Think "nice even rhythm" as you move on the beam.
Variation:	Vary the type of jump and height of beam.

MS **B**	**Partner Balance on Apparatus**
Pacing:	*Externally paced*
Grade Level:	Typically upper elementary (3–5)
Content Focus:	*Mastering balance with a partner on apparatus*
Setup:	Two partner groups are assigned to each beam, with mats under the beam for safety.

continued

MS B	*Partner Balance on Apparatus, continued*
Task:	With a partner, I want you to create a balance beam routine that includes a mount, travel sequence on beam where partners end on the other side they started from, and a dismount. One thing to remember, partners will start on opposite ends of the beam, so you have to figure out a way to go around your partner on the beam in order to transition to the other side. Ready, begin!
Cues:	Finish tall.
	Keep a nice easy rhythm as you move on the beam.
Variation:	Vary the height of beam.

MS C	**Balancing on Less Stable Objects**
Pacing:	*Externally paced*
Grade Level:	Typically upper elementary (3–5)
Content Focus:	*Mastering balancing on less stable objects*
Setup:	Children are scattered in general space with one balance ball per student. (Balance balls are the large inflatable balls used by many during abdominal workouts.)
Task:	On the signal, using your balance balls, find a balanced position on the ball using two body parts touching the ball. The rest of your base can be touching the floor. Ready, begin!
	This time, on the signal, find a balanced position on the ball using only one body part touching the ball. The body part has to be above the waist. Keep your feet on the floor. Ready, begin!
Cues:	Keep the muscles tight.
	Try to be very still.
Variation:	Vary the object, such as balance boards or stilts.

MS D	**Weight-Bearing Inverted Balances**
Pacing:	*Externally paced*
Grade Level:	Typically upper elementary (3–5)
Content Focus:	*Mastering balancing while bearing the body weight using inverted balances*
Setup:	Children are scattered in general space standing by a carpet strip.
Task:	On the signal, go stand by one of the carpet strips that have been placed throughout the gym. We are going to be working on taking our *full* body weight on our hands. The first thing I want you to do is try to take as much weight on your hands as you can, using your hand balance with body curled balance. (See Figure 11.8.)
	[*Note:* The progression is (1) dominant leg steps forward, (2) nondominant leg is kicked into the air, (3) dominant leg is kicked into the air.]
	Keep your knees bent, but try to get your legs together at the same height. Ready, begin!
Cues:	Keep your arms strong.
	Keep your body curled.
Variation:	Allow children who are tentative to begin by placing their hands on a box or other elevated surface.

MS E	**Weight-Bearing Balance for Complex Movements**
Pacing:	*Externally paced*
Grade Level:	Typically upper elementary (3–5)
Content Focus:	*Mastering balancing to perform complex movements*
Setup:	Children work on trifold mats spread throughout the gym, two per mat.

continued

MS **ⓔ**	*Weight-Bearing Balance for Complex Movements, continued*
Task:	As we continue working on taking our body weight on our hands, try, once your legs are parallel, to twist your body and legs so that your legs land to the left or right of where you placed your hands (round off). Focus on trying to sustain your weight before the body twist. Try to make the transition as smooth as possible. Ready, begin!
Cues:	Keep your arms strong.
	Hold and slowly land.
Variation:	Vary tempo.

COMBINING LOCOMOTOR AND NONLOCOMOTOR SKILLS—GYMNASTICS

Locomotor and nonlocomotor skills can be taught individually, but they can also be combined to form the aesthetic sequences that we call gymnastics. In essence, gymnastics is the performance of sequences of locomotor and nonlocomotor movements that require strength, flexibility, and kinesthetic awareness.

Can you imagine what it must be like to be an elite gymnast? Watching this sport during the Olympics, you may marvel at the abilities of young women and men as they rely on their own strength, balance, and coordination to perform such intricate physical maneuvers. From your spectator's chair, you may also notice that Olympic gymnastic success appears to be correlated with a single specific body type. Tall and rotund people, you might infer, shouldn't be encouraged to hope for a career as an elite gymnast.

Given the typical assortment of body types in elementary school classrooms, not to mention children's divergent motor abilities, many teachers hesitate to make gymnastics instruction a part of their physical education program. That attitude is both unfortunate and misguided, for these teachers are overlooking a simple fact: *You don't have to teach gymnastics the way it's performed competitively!*

Educational gymnastics, the form taught in elementary schools, focuses on helping children learn to use their bodies in safe, efficient, and creative ways. This form of gymnastics is beneficial for *all* elementary school children because:

- Children decide how to solve movement problems according their own abilities.

- Success is measured on the basis of what a child can actually achieve, rather than against his or her ability to complete a specific routine that all students must master.

educational gymnastics
A form of gymnastics that develops skill within the ability and understanding of the individual student.

There is a distinct difference in focus between elite gymnastics and educational gymnastics. Elite gymnastics focuses on skills and sequences performed on traditional equipment such as the balance beam, parallel bars, and vault, with all competitors judged to a single standard. Educational gymnastics, on the other hand, focuses on challenges and problem solving. Students are given tasks that explore a movement category to encourage individual and developmentally appropriate engagement. These tasks are frequently presented as "show me" or "find different ways" statements. Students also work individually, in pairs, or in groups to design movement sequences using newly learned skills.

Furthermore, educational gymnastics doesn't require expensive or sophisticated equipment. Educational gymnastics simply involves modified, open-ended tasks that are appropriate to a child's developmental readiness. Instead of teaching all your students a forward roll, for example, your gymnastic lesson might ask students to discover ways to perform a roll comfortable for each one's body style.

INQUIRING MINDS

How do you address the need for teaching gymnastics activities in your classroom? How do you justify including or excluding this content?

IS EQUIPMENT NECESSARY TO TEACH GYMNASTICS?

Olympic gymnastics equipment is bulky, expensive, and difficult to move. To effectively teach educational gymnastics, however, you need only a few mats and a little imagination. If you add in a low balance beam or some benches, you can develop a challenging and fulfilling gymnastics unit.

Gymnastics equipment is useful in allowing you to set up a horizontal task progression. For example, tasks generally become more difficult as students progress from floor-level work to using small equipment. Small equipment includes hula hoops, jump ropes, carpet squares, stacked mats, benches, and low beams (see Figure 11.10). Small equipment can enhance a child's control and coordination, regardless of experience level, by providing smaller, lower surfaces to balance on or travel over, under, or through.

Equipment Safety Issues during Gymnastics Lessons

First, you need to be sure the equipment is in good condition. Bases (of benches and low beams, for example) must be stable, and mats must be in good enough condition to actually provide cushioning. There must be appropriate and adequate matting under and around all equipment, extending as far as a child is likely to travel when performing a movement. Ensure that mats do not move. Matting must not overlap but be joined without ridges. Velcro edges help join matting seamlessly.

Second, place gymnastics equipment in the workspace so that students do not collide with each other or with walls or other obstacles. Remember too that students may design movement routines that take them beyond the boundary of a piece of equipment. For gymnastic routines involving locomotor skills, be particularly sure to allow sufficient space between equipment so that there is ample room for rolling and recovery.

FIGURE **11.10**
Task difficulty generally increases as students progress from floor-level work to using small equipment.

As you might suspect, you need to develop specific safety protocols for teaching gymnastics when mats or benches are used. First, limit the number of children using a piece of equipment. Never allow inappropriate behavior such as pushing and shoving. Students should also be taught to remove equipment that's in the workspace but not being used. Finally, students need to learn to carry and move equipment appropriately. Benches and mats will last longer when they are carried and not dragged and when they are placed carefully on the floor and not dropped.

HOW TO TEACH EDUCATIONAL GYMNASTICS

The fundamental teaching style of gymnastics for elementary school children is one of problem solving. The teacher sets a **movement problem,** usually in the form of "show me" or "find different ways" statements, and the students produce a movement answer. Note that this style often requires no one *best* answer—just an answer that fulfills the criteria set in the problem. For example:

> Girls and boys, show me how you can work with your partner to create a partner balance that you could not do by yourself.

Figure 11.11 shows girls on a beam with one solution to this task. There are other possible solutions such as facing toward or away from each other and kneeling or sitting on the beam rather than standing. However, in all cases there must be a partner balance, with the individual balances impossible without the partner.

Designing Movement Problems

One skill key to providing quality movement experiences for children is formulating challenging and imaginative movement problems. Table 11.3 is a useful tool for doing just that, with all movement problems stated using the following pattern:

1. The body performs some *action* . . .

2. in a position in *space* . . .

3. in some form of *relationship.*

movement problems
Tasks given to students asking them to explore a movement category in a way that encourages individual and developmentally appropriate engagement. These are frequently presented as "show me" or "find different ways" statements.

FIGURE **11.11**
Educational gymnastics involves students solving movement problems. Here two girls are solving the challenge of making a partner balance.

Table 11.3 ■ A Tool for Expressing Creative Movement Problems

Action	Space	Relationship
■ *Traveling:* Walk, run, leap, skip, roll, step, spring, jump, slide ■ *Nontraveling:* Bend, stretch, balance	■ *Direction:* Forward, backward, sideways ■ *Level:* High, medium, low ■ *Pathway:* Straight, curved, zigzag	■ *To the floor:* Right way up, inverted ■ *To a mat or a bench:* Facing front, back, or side; above; below ■ *To other people:* No contact, in contact, moving together, moving apart, supporting

Use the table by simply reading from left to right, selecting action, space, and relationship content from two or more columns. For example, "Spring backward away from your partner" involves action (spring), space (backward) and relationship (from your partner). Remember that you don't have to use material from all three columns. For example, "Make a balance that is really steady (column 1) at a low level (column 2)" and "Slide (column 1) across your mat (column 3)" are examples of two-column tasks. You also don't necessarily have to select content from adjacent columns. For example, a movement problem may involve balancing on different body parts (column 1) while facing a partner (column 3).

WHAT'S WRONG WITH THIS PICTURE?

Mr. Kostas's fourth grade class has been developing gymnastics routines and has just completed a series of lessons in which they learned three routines. To earn a grade for this unit, each student must perform one of these routines (picked out of a hat) and do it solo while the remainder of the class sits and watches. These routines are the sole basis for each student's grade.

The Necessity of Spotting

Educational gymnastics encourages children to develop competent body management skills. Accordingly, children should not depend on **spotters** (assistants who stand by a performer to prevent injury) to help them perform skills. Incompetent spotting (e.g., getting in the way of the child) is in fact potentially dangerous, and spotting should never be used:

- To substitute for inadequate strength and flexibility
- To augment defective or inappropriate equipment
- To let a child try an advanced skill before mastering foundational skills

If students feel they need spotting, this indicates that they lack the necessary developmental or motor skills to successfully and safely perform a skill. Rather than attempting the skill with a spotter, students should select a different strategy to solve a gymnastics movement problem. This approach will both reduce students' tendency to become dependent on a spotter and reflect the reality that the teacher cannot spot all the students in a large group.

In learning gymnastics, students should never have to perform skills beyond their perceived level of ability. When a student hesitates, either verbally or nonverbally, discuss the reason(s) for doubt with the student. If this discussion leads you to believe that hesitancy could put the child at risk during the performance of the skill, direct that student toward a simpler skill.

Sequences as Advanced Movement Problems

In educational gymnastics, a **sequence** is a logical and skillfully executed series of movements in which the individual movements flow seamlessly from one to the next (Allison & Barrett, 2000). A sequence typically has a clear beginning shape, a middle portion that incorporates required elements, and an ending shape.

Although you might want to give your children a great deal of autonomy in developing gymnastic movement sequences, such as asking them to put together a series of movements to create a "pleasant-looking" sequence, it's easier to evaluate student performance and promote safety if you keep control of the script. For example, you can develop a task card (see Application 11.1) that outlines the **working rules** and lets each child select from the same set of movement skills to create a sequence. A task card like the one shown makes your expectations very clear, while giving students sufficient latitude to be creative.

spotters
Assistants who stand by a performer during gymnastics skills to prevent injury.

sequence
A series of actions so skillfully aligned that all movements within the sequence fit together logically.

working rules
Rules giving children details about the number and type of actions that need to be involved, the equipment that may or must be used, and the number of people involved when solving a movement problem.

WHAT'S WRONG WITH THIS PICTURE?

Mr. Franklin's brother teaches at a nearby high school that has just fired its gymnastics coach. As a result, the school has a number of pieces of gymnastics equipment available. Mr. Franklin makes a successful bid for two full-sized balance beams as well as two vaulting horses. Wanting to take full advantage of these new resources, Mr. Franklin designs a series of lessons in which all his fifth grade students will be learning to do a standard routine on the beam, as well as two different vaults over the horse.

APPLICATION 11.1 ■ Gymnastics Routine Task Card for Sequences

1. Put together a sequence that combines two jumps, one inverted balance, one twist, and one case of weight on the hands, so they flow together without having jerky stops and starts. Begin your sequence with an asymmetrical shape and end your sequence with a symmetrical shape.

2. Write the skills you are going to use in the spaces below and turn this in.

Start: Opening shape _____

1st skill   _____

2nd skill   _____

3rd skill   _____

4th skill   _____

5th skill   _____

Ending shape   _____

3. Check to see if you have:

Two jumps	Yes	No
One inverted balance	Yes	No
One twist	Yes	No
One weight on hands	Yes	No

Peer Evaluation

When your students are proficient enough in gymnastics to begin developing their own complex sequences, you can also introduce peer evaluation. Students will be responsible for watching other students perform and making qualitative judgments about the performances. Peer evaluations help children appreciate the skills and aesthetic dimensions of gymnastics as well as refining their analytical abilities. A sample peer evaluation form is provided in Application 11.2.

APPLICATION **11.2** ■ **Gymnastics Routine Score Sheet**

Name of student performing the routine _____

Your name _____

Did they:	Yes	No
1. Salute at the beginning?	_____	_____
2. Hold their balances for 3 seconds?	_____	_____
3. Jump and land quietly?	_____	_____
4. Salute at the end of the routine?	_____	_____
5. Know the routine from memory?	_____	_____

Take off half a point for each No. _____

How many falls? _____

Take off half a point for each fall. _____

Choose one of the following:

1. The routine was mostly done neatly.   _____
2. The routine was partly done neatly.   _____
3. The routine was quite sloppy.   _____

Take off half a point if the routine was partly neat.

Take off 1 point if the routine was sloppy.

Circle the final score:

10.0   9.5   9.0   8.5   8.0   7.5   7.0   6.5   6.0

PROGRESSION THROUGH THE GRADE LEVELS

The first objective in selecting suitable gymnastic content for a particular grade level is to assess the skills and knowledge of the students as they enter your class. Some children may not have had any school gymnastics experience, even in the upper elementary grades. Others may be experienced in exploring their bodies in space and can skillfully complete jumping, landing, and balancing skills at the expanding stage. Your challenge is to determine a starting point for your students in terms of (1) their skill and (2) their understanding of the terminology.

When you come to decide what to include in gymnastics at different grade levels, we have the following suggestions. In the early grades, focus on exploration

Table 11.4 ■ Areas for Exploration and Discovery in Locomotion and Nonlocomotion

Content Related to Locomotion and Nonlocomotion	Sample Instructional Tasks
1. Travel on different parts of the body ■ Hands and feet ■ Other body parts	Let's see everyone move about the room using their hands and feet. Can you go in different directions? Can you do this with your tummy facing the sky? What other body parts can you use to travel with?
2. Travel by ■ Walking ■ Running ■ Rolling ■ Sliding (cue is "step—together") ■ Jumping ■ Skipping (cue is "step—hop") ■ Galloping (cue is "same foot forward")	Show me how you can travel across your space by *sliding.* I want you to try to slide really low. We are going to travel around the room as animals. If I say kangaroo, what would that be? [Jumping.] Or horse? [Galloping.] Let's see if everyone can move in the same way to the call.
3. Travel in various directions ■ Forward ■ Backward ■ Sideways	Boys and girls, I want you to hop three steps forward, jump two steps backward, and then slide four steps sideways. Point to where you think you will end up when you are finished.
4. Travel on various pathways ■ Straight ■ Zigzag ■ Curved	You have in front of you a drawing with some lines on it. See if you can walk the pathway shown. Can you name the pathways? Can you create a sequence that travels only those pathways? You have to travel on at least two different body parts.
5. Travel with a change of speed ■ Slow ■ Fast ■ Accelerate ■ Decelerate	I want you to combine two different jumps. The first will be really fast, the second will be really slow. See if you can sideways roll, but gradually slow down until you are completely still.

and body control. Tables 11.4 and 11.5 list some sample activities and content foci for nonlocomotor, locomotor, and balancing activities. In the middle grades, more time should be spent in more dynamic contexts, with activities at the expanding stages of jumping and landing as well as balancing. In the upper grades, the focus should be on designing routines and peer evaluation.

Table 11.5 ■ **Areas for Exploration and Discovery in Balancing**

Content Related to Balancing	Sample Instructional Tasks
1. Large bases of support ■ Back ■ Hips ■ Shoulders ■ Stomach	The part of us that is in contact with the ground or our apparatus is called the base of support. See if you can find three body parts that provide a *large* area in touch with the ground.
2. Stable and unstable bases ■ Stable = wide, low, and strong ■ Unstable = small, narrow, and high	Find a position on your mat where no one could push you off that spot. Which body part are you resting on? Is it low or high? Are you all tucked up or spread over a wide area? What about trying a balance that is hard to hold for more than 2 seconds? How about just using your hands as a base? Is this difficult? Notice that when you have a small base it's much harder to control.

Through locomotor and nonlocomotor skills, students can develop control of their bodies when traveling in various directions, at various speeds, and on various pathways. Balancing keeps the body's center of gravity within the limits of the body's base of support. Losing one's balance or falling means the center of gravity is no longer above but rather *outside* the limits of the body's base of support. Learning to balance prevents you from falling; learning to land prevents you from getting injured if you do fall. Together with balancing, locomotor and nonlocomotor skills are generic in not being limited to any single sport or activity. Indeed, most motor skills have a strong foundation on balance, locomotor, and nonlocomotor skills.

Educational gymnastics (a means of combining locomotor, nonlocomotor, and balance skills in nonmanipulative settings) presents an enjoyable, noncompetitive movement education program to elementary school children. Educational gymnastics gives *all* children the opportunity to experience and develop confidence with a wide range of movement skills focusing on body control. Not only do students develop skills; they also learn to understand movement in a variety of practical situations. Focusing on challenge and problem solving, educational gymnastics allows students to work at their own level and make progressions appropriate for each child, so each child is free to discover and select his or her own answer to a given movement task.

FINAL WORDS

OVER TO YOU

1. How does learning locomotor and nonlocomotor skills contribute to children learning "in," "through," and "about" movement?

2. What would be your major instructional challenge in incorporating educational gymnastics into your program? Compare your feelings with those of other members of your class to determine some solutions.

3. Why should we spend considerable time working on balancing tasks?

PORTFOLIO TASKS

1. Write a lesson plan for a first grade class that focuses on sliding and galloping. Include a layout of the gym and a list of equipment you might use.

2. Design four gymnastics routine task cards that children could use as a blueprint for creating a sequence.

3. Design a gymnastics rules poster to post in your gym or classroom.

4. Find a reading book about the circus. What activities in this book could you use as examples for students when they design a circus program?

REFERENCES

Allison, P. C. & Barrett, K. R. (2000). *Constructing children's physical education experiences: Understanding the content for teaching.* Boston: Allyn and Bacon.

Graham, G., Holt/Hale, S. A., & Parker, M. (2004). *Children moving: A reflective approach to teaching physical education* (6th ed.). Boston: McGraw-Hill.

12

MANIPULATIVE SKILLS

1. Name some manipulative skills that are part of different games or physical activities.

2. Which manipulative skills do you think would be the most difficult to learn?

3. Why is a tree a good model of how children learn motor skills?

4. Can you remember cue words or phrases your elementary school teachers used to help you develop motor skills?

C hapter 11 highlighted locomotor and nonlocomotor skills, the first two skill theme categories. This chapter highlights the third and last category, the so-called manipulative skills. These are the skills most associated with games and sports. Often they are also the most difficult skills for students to learn, because they require students to control both the body itself and an object beyond it. When a student performs the manipulative skill of *striking,* for example, she uses her hands to manipulate a bat, racket, or paddle. *Volleying* is a manipulative skill that uses any part of the body—head, arms, or feet—to contact an object in the air.

This chapter is not meant to include all the skills and tasks you might give students to help them develop their manipulative skills. However, it does highlight the progression that should be taken in skill development. This chapter demonstrates and provides step-by-step guidance on teaching various manipulative skills

to students. Each skill can be used in sports, games, rhythmic dances, and other fitness-related activities, all vital to any elementary school physical education curriculum. We next explore each of these skills individually.

THROWING AND CATCHING

Throwing and catching skills are important to many student games and activities in elementary school and beyond. These include softball, baseball, team handball, soccer, lacrosse, and football. While throwing and catching seem particularly complementary, they meet different objectives. Throwing is a target skill, while catching is an object-reception skill. Yet it is sometimes difficult to practice one without the other. This is especially true with catching, because you have to be able to catch an object thrown to you or one that you toss to yourself. Thus, many teachers use the same tasks when teaching students to throw and catch. We believe, however, that you should distinguish between the two in a lesson. The cue or learnable piece you choose for the lesson determines whether the focus is on throwing or catching and then sets the learning tasks based on that cue.

Let's take a lesson on throwing, where the cue is "Step with the opposite foot." Having students toss the ball over their heads while staying in self-space would be an inappropriate activity, because that task is geared toward catching and does not require students to use the cue. To avoid this confusion we have created two separate progression trees, one for throwing and one for catching. Remember, some students will be good throwers but not very adept at catching and vice versa. Therefore, specific tasks are needed to help develop each skill separately.

INQUIRING MINDS

Which manipulative skill is the most difficult for you to teach? How do you help your students learn this skill?

Sample Learning Tasks for Throwing

The aim in **throwing** is to accurately propel the object away from the body toward a target. As seen in Figure 12.1, different throwing patterns (underhand, sidearm, overarm) can be used to meet the objective. Throwing skills can involve the large round balls used in soccer and basketball or small balls like tennis balls or the whiffle balls used in tennis or baseball. Box 12.1 highlights the skill progression for students learning to throw. The throwing progression tree is shown in Figure 12.2.

Developing Skills (Typically Grades K through 2)

When first learning to throw a ball, students need to throw from a stationary position as hard as they can against a wall or backstop. Throwing for force first gives children a more fluid throwing motion because the body is not restricted by trying to hit a target. After throwing as hard as they can to develop the throwing motion, students can then progress to throwing at stationary targets, throwing for distance, or throwing different objects while standing still (self-paced and closed). As students move from developing the skill to expanding the skill, they begin to throw at a stationary target while on the move.

throwing
Accurately propelling an object away from the body.

FIGURE **12.1**
Throwing can be underhand, sidearm, or overhand. Here you see the skill patterns for each of these.

Source: Reprinted with permission from Queensland Studies Authority.

BOX **12.1** ■ **Progression for Children Developing Throwing Skills**

Throwing

1. Throw as hard as you can against a wall (no target).

2. Throw while stationary at stationary targets.

3. Throw while on the move to a stationary target.

4. Throw back and forth to a partner (stationary).

5. Throw while stationary to a moving target.

6. Throw back and forth with a partner while moving.

7. Throw against a defender.

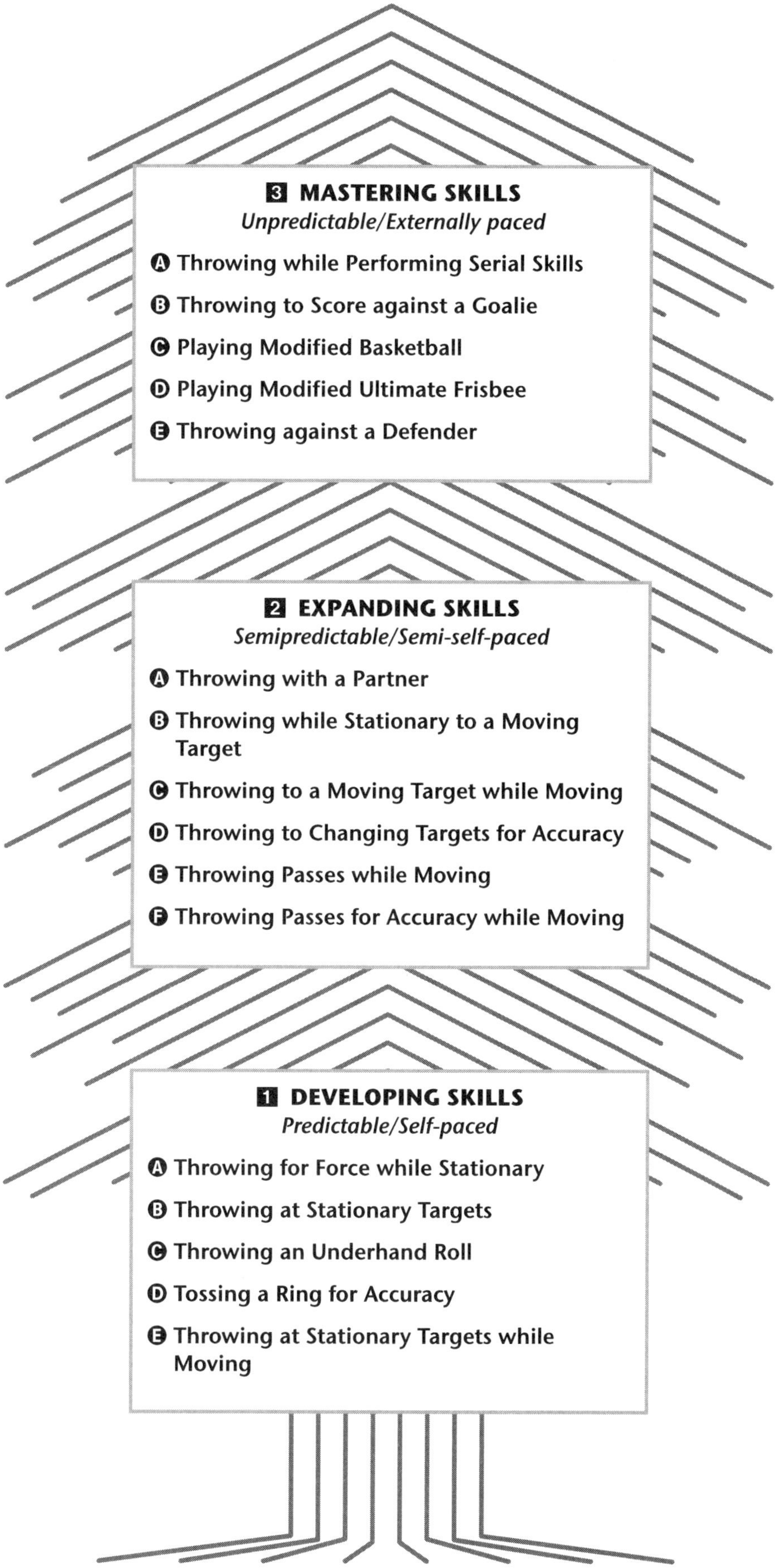

3 MASTERING SKILLS
Unpredictable/Externally paced

A Throwing while Performing Serial Skills

B Throwing to Score against a Goalie

C Playing Modified Basketball

D Playing Modified Ultimate Frisbee

E Throwing against a Defender

2 EXPANDING SKILLS
Semipredictable/Semi-self-paced

A Throwing with a Partner

B Throwing while Stationary to a Moving Target

C Throwing to a Moving Target while Moving

D Throwing to Changing Targets for Accuracy

E Throwing Passes while Moving

F Throwing Passes for Accuracy while Moving

1 DEVELOPING SKILLS
Predictable/Self-paced

A Throwing for Force while Stationary

B Throwing at Stationary Targets

C Throwing an Underhand Roll

D Tossing a Ring for Accuracy

E Throwing at Stationary Targets while Moving

FIGURE **12.2**
Progression tree for throwing

DS Ⓐ   **Throwing for Force while Stationary**

Pacing:	*Self-paced*
Grade Level:	Typically lower elementary (K–2)
Content Focus:	*Exploration of throwing for force while standing still*
Setup:	Children are scattered in general space, standing on a spot facing a wall. Children choose from a number of different types of balls.
Task:	Scattered around the room are different types and sizes of balls. When I say, "begin," I want you to select a ball and go to one of the spots in front of the wall and begin throwing overhand to the wall as hard as you can. Wait for the ball to come back to you before picking it up and throwing it again. Keep practicing until you hear the signal to stop. Ready, begin!
Cues:	Stand with your side to the target.
	Swing down, around, and back.
Variation:	Vary the distance or object.

DS Ⓑ   **Throwing at Stationary Targets**

Pacing:	*Self-paced*
Grade Level:	Lower elementary (K–2)
Content Focus:	*Exploration of throwing at different stationary targets*
Setup:	Children, each with a ball, are scattered in general space facing a wall. Targets are placed on the wall at low, medium, and high levels.
Task:	On my signal, throw the ball so that it hits the target that has been placed at a low level. Continue throwing overhand at the target at a low level until you hear the signal to stop. Ready, action!
	This time, throw to hit the target that has been placed at a middle level. Continue throwing overhand at the target at a middle level until you hear the signal to stop. Ready, action!
Cues:	Step with the opposite foot.
	Keep your side to the target.
	Bow and follow through.
Variations:	Vary levels, distance, targets, or objects thrown.

DS Ⓒ   **Throwing an Underhand Roll**

Pacing:	*Self-paced*
Grade Level:	Typically lower elementary (K–2)
Content Focus:	*Exploration of throwing the ball underhand*
Setup:	Children are scattered in general space facing a wall, each holding a ball of his or her choice. For each child, two bowling pins are placed side-by-side, flush with the wall.
Task:	On my signal, go stand on one of the *X*s marked on the floor in front of the wall, where you will find a ball. Today we are going to pretend we are at the bowling alley, and we are going to roll the ball and try to knock down as many pins as we can with our roll. After each roll, retrieve the ball and reset the pins you knocked down. Remember, we are not taking any steps at this time. Ready, begin!
	This time we are going to take five rolls toward the pins, remembering to bend our knees to lower our body. Keep track of how many pins you knock down on your five rolls. Ready, begin!
	I now want us to work on the approach. On my signal, practice taking two steps before you roll the ball. The first step you take is with the hand you write with. So, the process is step, step, and roll. Continue practicing taking your steps and rolling the ball until you hear me say, "Freeze."

continued

DS ⓒ	*Throwing an Underhand Roll, continued*
Cues:	Take the arm back.
	Bend your knees.
	Step, step, and roll.
Variation:	Vary the objects thrown, distance, and targets.

DS ⓓ	**Tossing a Ring for Accuracy**
Pacing:	*Self-paced*
Grade Level:	Typically lower elementary (K–2)
Content Focus:	*Exploration of tossing a ring for accuracy*
Setup:	Children are standing outside a large circle. Each child has two rings. Inside the circle are some 2-liter bottles, small beanbags, 20-oz. plastic bottles, and spools of thread.
Task:	There are a large number of items placed in the circle in front of you. On my signal, underhand toss the two rings you have, one at a time, trying to ring one of the objects. If you ring an item, you can take it back to your spot. Go stand on one of the spots surrounding the circle and begin tossing. Wait until I say, "Retrieve," before you try to retrieve your rings. Action! Freeze! Retrieve!
	Do you feel that you are at a carnival? Let's try this again, ringing only the large items like the 2-liter bottles. Action!
Cues:	Keep your arms back.
	Swing through (smooth).
Variation:	Vary the number of targets and distance.

DS ⓔ	**Throwing at Stationary Targets while Moving**
Pacing:	*Self-paced*
Grade Level:	Typically lower elementary (K–2)
Content Focus:	*Exploration of throwing while on the move to stationary targets*
Setup:	Children, each with a ball, are scattered in general space facing a wall, standing on a poly spot. Hoops and balloons affixed to the wall with tape serve as targets.
Task:	I have placed several targets on the wall, some large (hoops) and some small (balloons). In many sports, you have to throw accurately while on the move. Today, we are going to practice throwing while in the air. So, when I say, "Action," I want you to go to one of the poly spots you see in front of the wall. When you get there, start practicing taking at least two steps, jumping in the air, and trying to hit one of the targets. Action!
	This time try to hit the balloon with your throw. Keep practicing until you hear the signal to stop.
Cues:	Step with the opposite foot.
	Turn your shoulders.
Variation:	Vary the size of targets, the distance, object thrown and type of throw (sidearm, overhand).

Expanding Skills (Typically Grades 1 through 3)

In the expanding phase of throwing, students can throw while adapting to changing conditions in the environment, such as standing still while throwing to a moving target. Keeping the environment somewhat predictable helps students as they learn to throw back and forth with a partner. In these tasks, either both people are stationary, or one person is moving while the other is stationary. This controls the environment to some degree and allows students to throw when they are ready.

ES Ⓐ   **Throwing with a Partner**

Pacing: *Semi-self-paced*

Grade Level: Typically elementary (1–3)

Content Focus: *Expanding throwing to include working with a partner*

Setup: Partners are standing on poly spots scattered in general space on the floor. Children determine initial distance to stand from their partner.

Task: On my signal, I want you to quickly go stand on one of the poly spots that are scattered around the gym. Ready, go! If you are standing on a red poly spot where the balls are, stay where you are. If you are standing on a blue spot, partner with someone on a red spot. Now, with your partner, I want you to throw the ball *back and forth* so that your throw hits your partner around chest high. Continue throwing until I say, "Freeze."

                       This time, on my signal, throw the ball so that your partner has to catch it on the right side of his or her body (five throws). Now throw it so that your partner has to catch it on the left side of his or her body. Continue throwing until you hear the signal to stop. Ready, begin!

Cues: Bow and follow through.

                       Make an *L* with the throwing arm.

Variation: Vary the target and distance.

ES Ⓑ   **Throwing while Stationary to a Moving Target**

Pacing: *Semi-self-paced*

Grade Level: Typically elementary (1–3)

Content Focus: *Expanding throwing while stationary to a moving target*

Setup: Groups of four are scattered in general space. Each group has one ball and one hula hoop. Refer to the diagram below.

Task: Now that you are in a group of four, we are going to practice throwing at a moving target. Each group will have one ball and one hula hoop. One person will be the thrower, two will roll the hula hoop back and forth to each other, and one will retrieve the ball after the throw. While the hula hoop is rolling, the thrower will attempt to throw the ball through the hoop. Take five throws and then rotate positions. Ready, begin.

Diagram:

R
Retriever

R   ⟳- - - - - - - - - - - - - - →R
Roller   Hula   Roller
         Hoop

T
Thrower

Cues: Throw ahead of the target.

                       Take your arm back.

                       Step with the opposite foot.

Variation: Vary the object thrown, distance from the hoop, and speed of rolling the hoop.

ES Ⓒ | **Throwing to a Moving Target while Moving**

Pacing:	*Semi-self-paced*
Grade Level:	Typically elementary (1–3)
Content Focus:	*Expanding throwing while moving to a moving target*
Setup:	Partners are scattered in general space with one ball per pair.
Task:	On my signal, you and your partner will throw and catch while traveling from one end of the field to the other. While you are traveling, you may take three steps with the ball before you have to throw it to your partner. When you throw the ball, try to make sure that you lead (throw the ball ahead of your partner so he or she has to run and catch it) your partner with the throw. Ready, begin.
Cues:	Throw ahead of your partner.
	Snap your wrist.
Variation:	Vary the speed, distance, and object thrown.

ES Ⓓ | **Throwing to Changing Targets for Accuracy**

Pacing:	*Semi-self-paced*
Grade Level:	Typically elementary (1–3)
Content Focus:	*Expanding throwing for accuracy by changing the distance to targets and number of throws to reach target*
Setup:	In a large outdoor space, nine hula hoops serve as the golf holes, nine cones represent the start of each hole, and the course is set up to maximize the space available. There is one Frisbee per student and three students per hole, with each group starting at a different hole. Groups go through the holes in ascending order.
Task:	As you can see, we have a Frisbee golf course set up outside today. There are nine holes. Your task is to go through the course with the fewest number of throws. Get into the playing groups that I have already assigned and start at the hole indicated on your scorecard. You may begin when you are ready.
Cues:	Place your index finger on the edge of the Frisbee.
	Hug the Frisbee and release.
Variation:	Vary the course and the number of throws per hole.

ES Ⓔ | **Throwing Passes while Moving**

Pacing:	*Semi-self-paced*
Grade Level:	Typically elementary (1–3)
Content Focus:	*Expanding throwing to practice passing while moving with a partner*
Setup:	There will be two lines (start and finish) 30 ft. apart. Each pair of children has a ball. Partners will begin on the start line and move to the finish. You may use an indoor or outdoor space.
Task:	Using the chest pass, you are to work with your partner in moving the ball down the court. Once you get to the line in front of your goal, take a shot at the basket (no shot if working outside). Once you rebound the ball, continue chest passing with your partner as you move along the sideline of the court back to the starting position. You may begin when the pair in front of you reaches the free throw line.
Cues:	Extend both arms at the same time.
	Turn thumbs down on finish.
Variation:	Vary speed and the ball passed.

ES 🅕   **Throwing Passes for Accuracy while Moving**

Pacing:	*Semi-self-paced*
Grade Level:	Typically elementary (1–3)
Content Focus:	*Expanding throwing to gain accuracy while moving*
Setup:	Children are standing side-by-side behind the throwing line (line *A*) in a large outdoor space. There are a variety of balls (footballs, softballs, baseballs) for children to choose from. Hoops, boxes, and cones serve as the targets and are scattered in the target area (refer to the diagram below).
Task:	Down the field, you see several large and small targets. Your task is to throw the object of your choice so that it hits or lands in the target of your choice. This task will require you to be able to throw a ball accurately from a distance. The key is for you to run and throw the ball while you are moving from line *A* to line *B*. Remember to get your feet set before you throw. After your throw, wait for the signal before retrieving your ball. Ready, begin! Retrieve!
Diagram:	

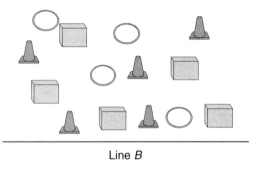

Line *B*

Line *A*

Cues:	Extend both arms at same time.
	Turn thumbs down on finishing.
Variation:	Vary the speed and the ball passed.

Mastering Skills (Typically Grades 3 through 5)

In the mastering phase of throwing, the motion of the throw is automatic, allowing children to think about what is happening in a changing environment. This dynamic environment could include throwing while being defended or throwing on the move to a moving receiver. In this phase, children can perform serial skills (two or more discrete skills in a row) with ease.

MS 🅐   **Throwing while Performing Serial Skills**

Pacing:	*Externally paced*
Grade Level:	Typically upper elementary (3–5)
Content Focus:	*Mastering throwing while performing serial skills*
Setup:	Partners are scattered in general space at a distance determined by the students. Each pair has a ball.
Task:	On my signal, catch the *ground* ball thrown by your partner and quickly throw it back to your partner in the air so he or she doesn't have to move to catch the ball. Field five balls and then change roles. Ready, begin!
	This time, back up a few steps and try it again. Remember, the goal is to field the ball and accurately throw it to your partner. Ready, begin!

continued

MS Ⓐ	*Throwing while Performing Serial Skills, continued*
	This time I want your partner to toss you a ball high in the air so that you have to move to catch it. When you catch it, set your feet, and throw it toward the target set by your partner's glove. Ready, begin.
Cues:	Start with your elbow leading the throw.
	Snap your wrist on release of ball.
Variation:	Vary the distance and ball.

MS Ⓑ	**Throwing to Score against a Goalie**
Pacing:	*Externally paced*
Grade Level:	Typically upper elementary (3–5)
Content Focus:	*Mastering throwing while attempting to score against a goalie*
Setup:	Partners are scattered in general space in one of the set-up play areas (refer to diagram below). Each pair has a ball. Goals are 4 or 6 ft. wide and placed flush against a wall.
Task:	For this task one person will be the shooter and the other the goaltender. The shooter should be sure to stay outside the goal area when attempting a throw at the goal (4 or 6 ft. wide). On my signal, the shooter is to take three steps (i.e., R-L-R for a right-handed player) and jump forward while trying to score on the goalie. Take five shots apiece and then change roles. Action!
Diagram:	Goal **G** Goalie 10 feet —————————————— Shooting line **S** Shooter
Cues:	Keep your shooting arm in the shape of an L.
	Rotate your shoulders.
Variation:	Vary the size (4 inches to 6 inches) and type of object thrown (Nerf ball, soft rubber).

MS Ⓒ	**Playing Modified Basketball**
Pacing:	*Externally paced*
Grade Level:	Typically upper elementary (3–5)
Content Focus:	*Mastering throwing while playing a modified basketball game*
Setup:	Groups of four stand in a 10-ft. × 10-ft. playing area, with two trash cans to use as baskets. Each group has a ball.
Task:	This game is called minibasketball. Basketball rules apply, except that the only way you can advance the ball is by passing it—dribbling is not allowed. If you travel (walk) with the ball, the other team gains possession. Change possession after every basket is scored (shooting into a trash can). Get with your group of four, go to the area I indicated, and you may start.
Cues:	Lead the receiver.
	Move to get open.
Variation:	Vary the height of the basket and size of the playing area.

MS Ⓓ	Playing Modified Ultimate Frisbee
Pacing:	*Externally paced*
Grade Level:	Typically upper elementary (3–5)
Content Focus:	*Mastering throwing while playing modified ultimate Frisbee*
Setup:	Groups of three are scattered in general space. The groups set playing boundaries with four cones. Each pair of teams has a Frisbee.
Task:	In your team of three, you are going to play a small-sided game of ultimate Frisbee. Your team's goal is to pass the Frisbee down the field so that your team catches across the other team's endline. If your team drops the Frisbee or the other team intercepts it, then possession changes. Each team is attempting to score. The different colored cones mark the boundaries of each playing area. When I say, "Begin," you may start play.
Cues:	Hug and release.
	Hold the Frisbee with your thumb on top and index finger on the edge.
Variation:	Vary the distance of throw, height of throw, and type of ball.

MS Ⓔ	Throwing against a Defender
Pacing:	*Externally paced*
Grade Level:	Typically upper elementary (3–5)
Content Focus:	*Mastering throwing while eluding a defender*
Setup:	Groups of four are scattered in general space. Refer to the diagram below. Each group has a ball.
Task:	For this task you will have one quarterback or passer, one receiver, and one defender. On the quarterback's signal, the receiver will run to get open while being defended. The defender is trying to keep the receiver from catching the ball. However, the receiver and defender are not allowed to run into or touch the other player. Change roles, with the quarterback becoming the receiver, the receiver becoming the defender, and the defender becoming the quarterback. Continue this rotation until you hear the signal to stop.
Diagram:	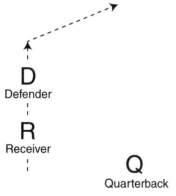
Cues:	Throw ahead of the receiver.
Variation:	Release the ball quickly.
	Vary the distance and ball thrown.

Sample Learning Tasks for Catching

catching
Receiving and controlling a propelled object.

The intent in **catching** is to receive and control a propelled object. Catching requires the child to visually track the object and move his or her body to the necessary position to successfully receive the object (see Figure 12.3). Children can catch with one hand, two hands, or an implement such as a glove or scoop. When

FIGURE **12.3**
Catching involves both visual tracking and movement to receive the ball. Here you see the skill progression for catching a large ball.

Source: Reprinted with permission from Queensland Studies Authority.

discussing catching, we include fielding balls that are either rolling along the ground or bouncing (sometimes unevenly) toward us. Box 12.2 highlights the progression for students learning the skill theme of catching, while Figure 12.4 shows the progression tree.

Developing Skills (Typically K through 2)

Children in the developing phase of catching are just learning to catch an object using their hands instead of their body. They need to practice catching with lightweight, slow-moving objects that are easy to see and track. Catching is difficult to

BOX **12.2** ■ Progression for Children Developing Catching Skills

Catching

1. Throw the ball in the air and catch it with two hands.

2. Throw the ball into the air, let it bounce and then catch it.

3. Throw the ball at the wall and catch it after it bounces.

4. Throw the ball at the wall and catch it before it bounces.

5. Catch from an experienced tosser.

6. Toss and catch with a partner (stationary).

7. Toss and catch while moving.

learn because it is almost impossible to keep the environment stable and predictable. At some point, the object has to be in the air to catch it. The simplest tasks are ones where the child initiates the movement or catches from an experienced tosser.

DS Ⓐ	Catching a Rolling Ball
Pacing:	*Self-paced*
Grade Level:	Typically lower elementary (K–2)
Content Focus:	*Exploration of catching by learning how to hold the hands when catching a rolling ball*
Setup:	Partners are scattered in general space with one ball per group.
Task:	Sit on the floor with your legs spread in a *V*. Gently roll the ball so your partner catches it. Continue rolling the ball to each other until you hear the stop signal.
Cues:	Reach for the ball with your hands.
	Keep your hands open with pinkies together to stop.
Variation:	Vary the size of ball and speed of roll.

DS Ⓑ	Catching a Ball while Sitting
Pacing:	*Self-paced*
Grade Level:	Lower elementary (K–2)
Content Focus:	*Exploration of catching while sitting in self-space*
Setup:	Children are scattered sitting on the floor in general space with a yarn ball per child.
Task:	On my signal, start tossing and catching the yarn ball to yourself. Toss it just above your head. The key to success is being able to stay in your self-space. Ready, begin!
	This time, toss the yarn ball over your head and try to catch it behind your back. Remember to stay in your self-space. Ready, begin!
Cues:	Keep your hands out.
	Make a basket with your hands.
Variation:	Vary the number of hands catching ball, type of object, and levels.

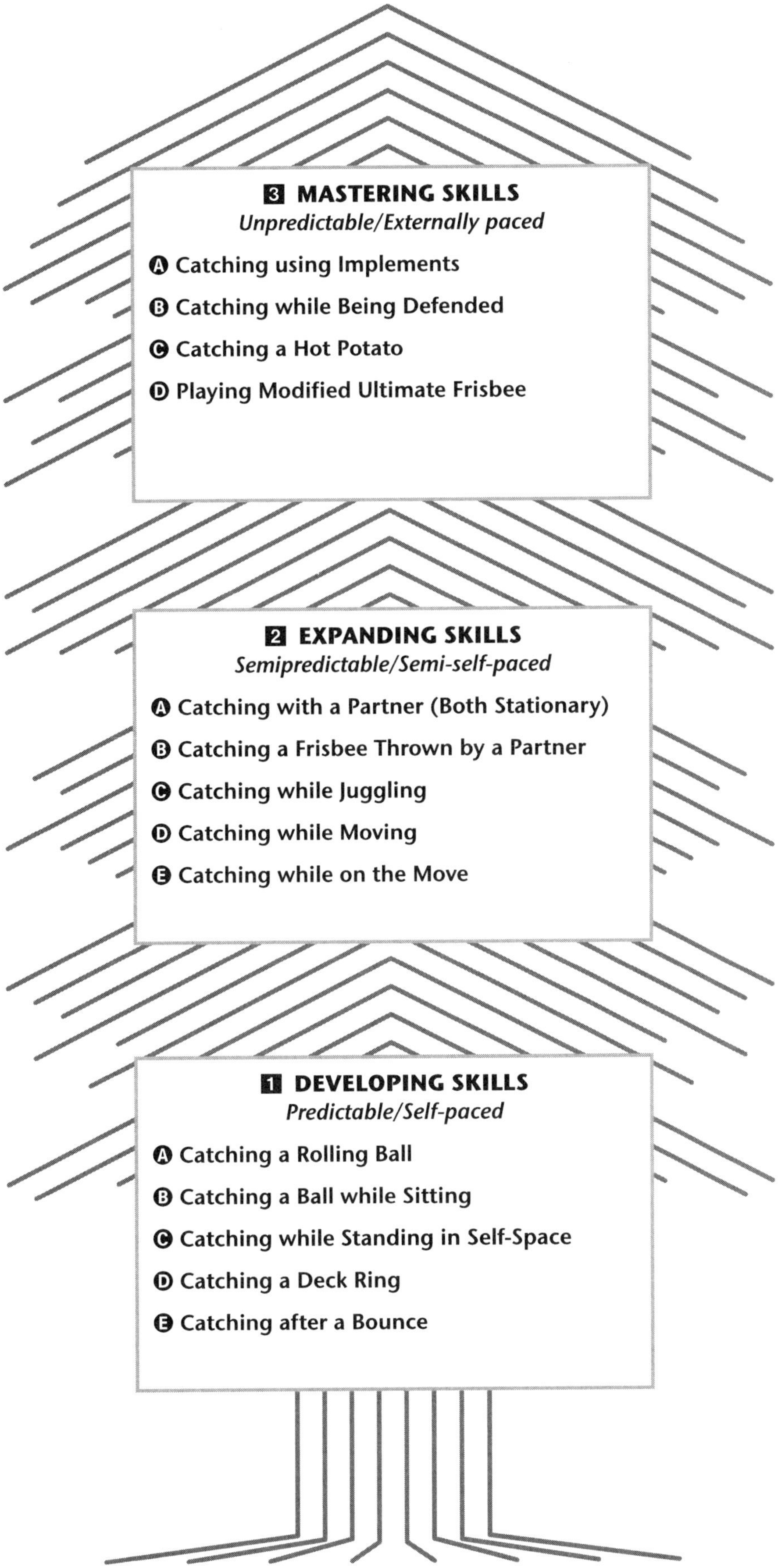

3 MASTERING SKILLS
Unpredictable/Externally paced

- Ⓐ Catching using Implements
- Ⓑ Catching while Being Defended
- Ⓒ Catching a Hot Potato
- Ⓓ Playing Modified Ultimate Frisbee

2 EXPANDING SKILLS
Semipredictable/Semi-self-paced

- Ⓐ Catching with a Partner (Both Stationary)
- Ⓑ Catching a Frisbee Thrown by a Partner
- Ⓒ Catching while Juggling
- Ⓓ Catching while Moving
- Ⓔ Catching while on the Move

1 DEVELOPING SKILLS
Predictable/Self-paced

- Ⓐ Catching a Rolling Ball
- Ⓑ Catching a Ball while Sitting
- Ⓒ Catching while Standing in Self-Space
- Ⓓ Catching a Deck Ring
- Ⓔ Catching after a Bounce

FIGURE **12.4**
Progression tree for catching

DS ⊙ **Catching while Standing in Self-Space**

Pacing:	*Self-paced*
Grade Level:	Typically lower elementary (K–2)
Content Focus:	*Exploration of catching while standing in self-space*
Setup:	Children are scattered standing in general space, each with a beanbag.
Task:	When I say, "Action," I want you to toss your beanbag into the air so that it goes above your head and you do not have to move out of your self-space. Use two hands to catch the beanbag. Keep tossing and catching until you hear me say, "Cut." Action!
	On my signal, toss your beanbag into the air high enough so that you can make a complete turn (360°) before you catch it. You can choose to catch it with one or two hands. Again, keep tossing and catching until you hear me say, "Cut." Action!
Cues:	Reach for the beanbag.
	Pull the beanbag in.
Variation:	Vary the objects, height, and level of the catch.

DS ⊙ **Catching a Deck Ring**

Pacing:	*Self-paced*
Grade Level:	Typically lower elementary (K–2)
Content Focus:	*Exploration of catching a deck ring*
Setup:	Children are scattered in general space, each with a deck ring.
Task:	Each of you should have a deck ring (looks like a doughnut). On my signal, toss the ring up with one hand and catch it with the other while remaining in your self-space. Remember the ring must be thrown and caught so that it looks like a pancake turned on its side. Ready, begin!
	This time, toss the deck ring into the air and see if you can catch it at a low level. Ready, action!
Cues:	Keep your eye on the ring.
	Catch with the hand in the shape of a *U*.
Variation:	Vary the height of toss and hand to catch.

DS ⊙ **Catching after a Bounce**

Pacing:	*Self-paced*
Grade Level:	Typically lower elementary (K–2)
Content Focus:	*Exploration of catching after the object bounces*
Setup:	Children, each with a ball, are scattered in general space. A poly spot for each child has been placed in front of the wall.
Task:	On my signal, toss your ball above your head and let it bounce once before trying to catch it, while staying in your self-space. Remember to keep your hands ready. Ready, action!
	This time, I want you to catch the ball after it has bounced twice. Remember to keep your eye on the ball. Keep practicing until you hear the signal to stop. Ready, action!
	On my signal, take your ball and stand on your poly spot, which has been placed in front of the wall. Throw your ball against the wall; I want you to catch it after it bounces once. Remember to keep your hands ready and your knees bent. Keep practicing until I say, "Freeze." Ready, begin!
	This time, catch the ball before it bounces after it rebounds off the wall. You will need to move to the first spot and throw your ball above the blue line so that you will have time to catch it. Ready, begin!
Cues:	Start with ready hands.
	Keep your eye on the ball.
	Bend your knees.
Variation:	Vary the number of bounces, object caught, and surface of rebound.

Mr. Allen is teaching his second grade class to throw and catch. He distributes one tennis ball to every second student. Mr. Allen asks his class to form two straight lines, with each student opposite a partner. He asks them to throw the ball overhand to their partner. Mr. Allen sets up a challenge for the class: All pairs will have made five throws in 30 seconds.

WHAT'S WRONG WITH THIS PICTURE?

Expanding Skills (Typically Grades 1 through 3)

In the expanding phase of catching, children begin learning to catch a lightweight and slow moving object thrown by a partner. They are becoming more adept at catching objects cleanly (no bumbling) with one hand. The challenge in this phase is that catching moving objects varies the task. Children are starting to more consistently catch heavier and faster-moving balls thrown by another person.

ES Ⓐ	**Catching with a Partner (Both Stationary)**
Pacing:	*Semi-self-paced*
Grade Level:	Typically elementary (1–3)
Content Focus:	*Expanding catching to include working with a partner while standing still*
Setup:	Partners are scattered in general space; each pair has a ball.
Task:	On my signal, stand across from your partner and keep yours arms out and ready to catch the ball. Tosser, remember to toss the ball slowly with an underhand motion and with a small arch. Ready, action!
	This time, toss the ball so that your partner has to take one step to catch the ball at a low level. Ready, action!
Cues:	Reach to the ball.
	Pull the ball in.
Variation:	Vary the object, distance, and levels of catch.

ES Ⓑ	**Catching a Frisbee Thrown by a Partner**
Pacing:	*Semi-self-paced*
Grade Level:	Typically elementary (1–3)
Content Focus:	*Expanding catching a Frisbee thrown by a partner*
Setup:	Partners are scattered in general space, standing on a poly spot at a distance of their choosing. Each pair has a Frisbee.
Task:	We are going to practice catching the Frisbee with two hands using the "sandwich" (one hand on top and one on bottom) or "clam" (base of palms together with fingers of one hand pointing up and the fingers of the other hand pointing down) catch. On the signal, with your assigned partner, go to one of the pairs of poly spots you see and begin tossing and catching the Frisbee. Focus on catching the Frisbee with two hands. Keep practicing until you hear me say, "Freeze." Ready, begin!
Cues:	Use the sandwich or clam catch.
	Watch the Frisbee.
Variation:	Vary the distance and type of catch.

ES C	**Catching while Juggling**
Pacing:	*Semi-self-paced*
Grade Level:	Typically elementary (1–3)
Content Focus:	*Expanding catching while attempting to juggle*
Setup:	Children are scattered in general space with two scarves each.
Task:	Everyone should be holding their two scarves with the fingertips, one in each hand. On my signal, you will use the crisscross pattern (toss the scarves across the body, right-hand scarf to left side of body and left-hand scarf to right side of body) to "juggle" your two scarves. Remember to claw the scarf when you try to catch it. Keep practicing until you hear the signal to stop. Ready, begin!
	This time, we are going to hold both scarves in one hand. Toss the first scarf and then toss the second. Catch the scarves with the other hand. The pattern will be toss, toss, and catch, catch. Ready, begin!
Cues:	Claw the scarf.
	Keep your eye on the scarf.
Variation:	Vary the number of scarves or type of object to juggle.

ES D	**Catching while Moving**
Pacing:	*Semi-self-paced*
Grade Level:	Typically elementary (1–3)
Content Focus:	*Expanding throwing for accuracy by changing the distance to targets and number of throws to reach target.*
Setup:	Partners are scattered in general space at a distance of their choosing. Each pair has a Frisbee.
Task:	Your partner is going to throw the Frisbee to you while you are moving. Try to catch the Frisbee using the C catch (the catching hand forms the letter C). Throw the Frisbee back to your partner, who will try to catch it in the same manner. Keep moving, throwing, and catching, until you hear the signal to stop.
Cues:	Use the C catch (one hand).
	Keep your eye on the Frisbee.
Variation:	Vary the speed and distance of the throw and catch.

ES E	**Catching while on the Move**
Pacing:	*Semi-self-paced*
Grade Level:	Typically elementary (1–3)
Content Focus:	*Expanding catching while both people are on the move*
Setup:	Partners are scattered in general space. Partners decide the task distance. Each pair has a ball.
Task:	On my signal, start tossing back and forth with your partner as you move in general space. Focus on making a good catch by keeping your hands ready. Ready, begin!
Cues:	Start with ready hands.
	Watch the ball.
Variation:	Vary the speed and the type of ball passed.

Mastering Skills (Typically Grades 3 through 5)

In the mastering phase of catching, children can catch different objects at various levels, thrown at various speeds, and while moving. They are ready to challenge themselves by using these skills in more dynamic environments, such as catching while eluding a defender or catching using gloves or scoops.

MS Ⓐ	Catching Using Implements
Pacing:	*Externally paced*
Grade Level:	Typically upper elementary (3–5)
Content Focus:	*Mastering catching using implements*
Setup:	Partners are scattered in general space. Each pair has two scoops (one each) and one whiffle ball.
Task:	On the signal, start tossing and catching the ball back and forth with a partner using the scoops you have been given. This type of implement is used in a game called jai alai. Try to catch the ball at all different levels and angles. Ready, begin!
Cues:	Watch the ball.
	Scoop it in.
Variation:	Vary the type of implement and ball.

MS Ⓑ	Catching while Being Defended
Pacing:	*Externally paced*
Grade Level:	Typically upper elementary (3–5)
Content Focus:	*Mastering catching while being defended*
Setup:	Groups of three are scattered in general space. Refer to the diagram below.
Task:	In a group of three, one person will be the passer, one the receiver, and one the defender. On the signal, the receiver will run straight ahead while being defended (a person trying to keep the receiver from catching the ball). Contact between the receiver and defender is not permitted. The passer will throw the ball once the receiver has taken five steps. Receivers are to catch the ball while being defended. Change roles after each pass. For every pass you catch, you earn a point. You may begin when you are ready.

Diagram:

```
        ▲
        ¦
        ¦
        ¦
        D
     Defender
        ¦
        R
     Receiver
        ¦              P
        ¦           Passer
```

Cues:	Reach and pull it.
	Watch the ball in.
Variation:	Vary the distance and ball.

MS **C**	Catching a Hot Potato
Pacing:	*Externally paced*
Grade Level:	Typically upper elementary (3–5)
Content Focus:	*Mastering catching a ball thrown quickly*
Setup:	Partners are scattered in general space at a distance of about 5 ft. Each pair has a ball.
Task:	With your partner, you are going to play hot potato. Each person has a ball. Stand about 5 ft. from your partner. On my signal, see how quickly you can throw and catch the balls with your partner without dropping them. Both balls should be moving at the same time. Keep practicing until you hear the signal to stop. Ready, begin.
Cues:	Start with your hands ready.
	Watch, catch, release.
Variation:	Vary the height and distance between objects.

MS **D**	Modified Ultimate Frisbee
Pacing:	*Externally paced*
Grade Level:	Typically upper elementary (3–5)
Content Focus:	*Mastering throwing while playing modified ultimate Frisbee*
Setup:	There are three children per team with two teams playing against each other. The two teams will decide the playing area and outline area with four cones of the same color. Each pair of teams has a Frisbee.
Task:	In your team of three, you are going to play a small-sided game of ultimate Frisbee. Your team's goal is to pass the Frisbee down the field so that your team catches the Frisbee across the other team's end line. The key for your team's success is to catch the Frisbee. Use the clam catch and the one-handed C catch to help your team be successful. If your team drops the Frisbee or the other team intercepts it, then possession changes. Each team is attempting to score. The different colored cones mark the boundaries of each playing area. When I say, "Begin," you may start play.
Cues:	Use the clam catch.
	Use the C catch.
Variation:	Vary the number of players and the size of the playing area.

KICKING AND PUNTING

Kicking and **punting** are whole-body motor skills that rely on foot–eye coordination. Both skills are found in games such as soccer and football and are used to send a ball into the air or along the ground. While kicking and punting both use the foot to apply force to an object, the difference is in the origin of that object. In kicking, the object begins on the ground (see Figure 12.5), while in punting, the ball starts in the hands.

Children must be able to balance their body well to successfully punt and kick. If you remember the developmental progression discussed in Chapter 3, children learn to control the upper half of the body before the lower half, so punting and kicking will naturally be more difficult to learn than throwing and catching.

kicking
Using the foot to apply force to an object on the ground.

punting
Use the foot to apply force to an object that begins in the hands.

FIGURE **12.5**
Kicking involves striking a ball with the foot while it is on the ground. Here you see the progression for kicking a stationary ball.

Source: Reprinted with permission from Queensland Studies Authority.

Students will need to practice kicking and punting for both distance and accuracy, both in the air and along the ground. With practice and experience, the targets of accurate kicking will progress from stationary to moving, eventually leading to kicking and punting to open spaces and ahead of a moving target. Finally, children will practice these skills in contexts involving pressure from an opponent.

Sample Learning Tasks for Kicking

Kicking is a manipulative skill using the foot to apply force to an object on the ground. The ball on the ground can be rolling or stationary, but to successful kick it the child needs good eye–foot coordination. When beginning to learn kicking,

BOX **12.3** ■ **Progression for Children Developing Kicking Skills**

Kicking

1. Kick a stationary ball against a wall.

2. Approach a stationary ball and kick it.

3. Kick a stationary ball for distance, then accuracy.

4. Kick a rolling ball from a stationary position for distance, then accuracy.

5. Kick a ball back and forth with a partner (stationary).

6. Kick a ball back and forth with a partner while moving.

children often swing the kicking leg toward the ball and miss it completely. Box 12.3 highlights the progression for students learning the skill theme of kicking; Figure 12.6 shows a graphic representation of sample learning tasks that follow this progression.

Developing Skills (Typically Grades K through 2)

In the developing phase of learning to kick (with the ball on the ground), students need to practice kicking a stationary ball from a stationary position. Practicing tasks in a stable, self-paced environment allows them to work on making contact with the ball and sending it in the desired direction. Tasks that encourage students to explore kicking different types of balls from different distances to a variety of targets would be appropriate. As students make the transition out of this phase, they begin to approach a stationary ball to kick it on the ground or in the air.

DS Ⓐ	**Kicking a Stationary Ball While Stationary**
Pacing:	*Self-paced*
Grade Level:	Typically lower elementary (K–2)
Content Focus:	*Exploration of kicking a stationary ball*
Setup:	Children scattered in general space standing next to a poly spot while facing a wall. Each child has a ball.
Task:	Place your ball on the spot in front of you. On my signal, use the inside part of your foot to kick the ball to the wall. Kick it hard enough so that it comes back to you. Keep practicing kicking against the wall until I clap twice. Action!
Cues:	Kick using the inside part of the foot.
	Follow through to the target.
Variation:	Vary the distance or ball.

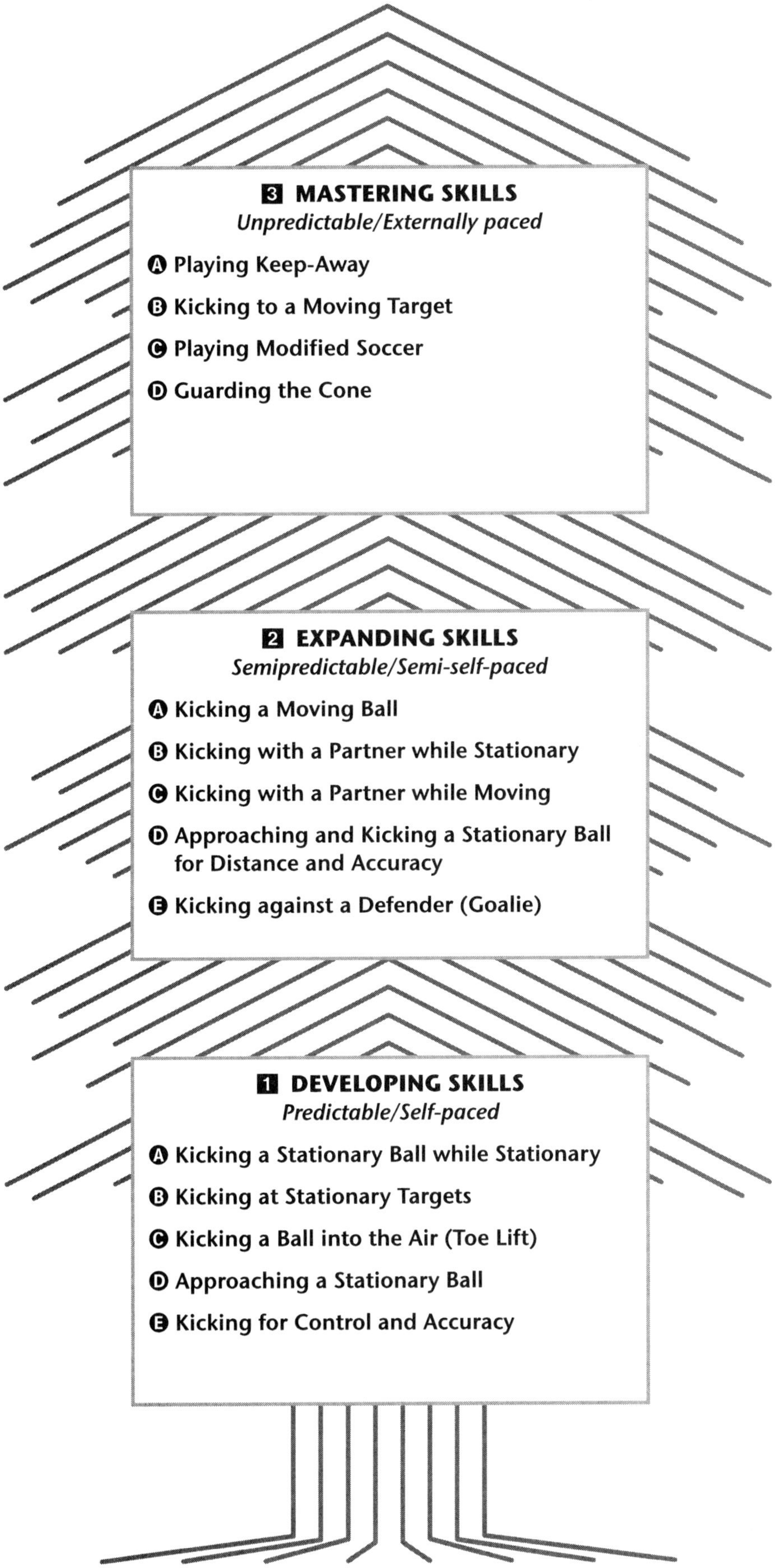

3 MASTERING SKILLS
Unpredictable/Externally paced

Ⓐ Playing Keep-Away

Ⓑ Kicking to a Moving Target

Ⓒ Playing Modified Soccer

Ⓓ Guarding the Cone

2 EXPANDING SKILLS
Semipredictable/Semi-self-paced

Ⓐ Kicking a Moving Ball

Ⓑ Kicking with a Partner while Stationary

Ⓒ Kicking with a Partner while Moving

Ⓓ Approaching and Kicking a Stationary Ball for Distance and Accuracy

Ⓔ Kicking against a Defender (Goalie)

1 DEVELOPING SKILLS
Predictable/Self-paced

Ⓐ Kicking a Stationary Ball while Stationary

Ⓑ Kicking at Stationary Targets

Ⓒ Kicking a Ball into the Air (Toe Lift)

Ⓓ Approaching a Stationary Ball

Ⓔ Kicking for Control and Accuracy

FIGURE **12.6**
Progression tree for kicking

DS Ⓑ

Kicking at Stationary Targets

Pacing:	*Self-paced*
Grade Level:	Lower elementary (K–2)
Content Focus:	*Exploration of kicking at stationary targets*
Setup:	Children are scattered in general space while standing on one of three spots (5, 8, and 10 ft. from a wall). Targets are hanging at three levels (low, medium, and high).
Task:	There are three spots in front of the wall. On my signal, choose one of the three spots to kick from. Also, there are three targets hanging on the wall (high, middle, and low). Choose one of the targets to aim for as you kick the ball against the wall. Remember to kick with enough force so that the ball comes directly back to you. Keep practicing until you hear the signal to stop. Ready, begin!
	This time, use the sole trap to stop the ball before you kick it again. So, you are going to kick, trap, kick, trap, until you hear me say, "Freeze."
Cues:	Place the nonkicking leg beside the ball.
	Use your shoelaces.
	Place the sole of your foot slightly behind ball—sole trap.
Variation:	Vary the levels, distance, targets, or balls.

DS Ⓒ

Kicking a Ball into the Air (Toe Lift)

Pacing:	*Self-paced*
Grade Level:	Typically lower elementary (K–2)
Content Focus:	*Exploration of kicking to gain height on the ball*
Setup:	Children are scattered in general space standing on a spot in front of wall. On each spot is a playground ball.
Task:	Today, we are going to work on getting the ball up into the air from the ground by using the "toe lift" or flick. On my signal, stand on your spot in front of the wall, where you will see a ball. Place your toe slightly under the ball and flick your toe forward to lift the ball so that it hits the wall. Keep practicing until I say, "Freeze." Ready, begin! Freeze!
	Nice job of getting your toe under the ball. This time, pick out one of the targets you see on the wall and, using the toe lift, try to hit the target of you choice. Keep practicing until you hear the signal to stop. Ready, begin!
Cues:	Place your toe under the ball.
	Lean back slightly.
Variation:	Vary ball, distance, and target.

DS Ⓓ

Approaching a Stationary Ball

Pacing:	*Self-paced*
Grade Level:	Typically lower elementary (K–2)
Content Focus:	*Exploration of approaching a stationary ball to kick*
Setup:	Children find a space behind the kicking line to stand, side by side, in a large outdoor area. Balls are placed on ground as children approach to kick them.
Task:	On my signal, get your ball and stand behind the line. Take three running steps to approach the ball to generate more force on your kick. Remember to use your shoelaces, not your toes, when kicking. Kick the ball as far as you can. Retrieve your ball when you hear the signal. Ready, begin! Retrieve!
Cues:	Contact the ball using the shoelaces.
	Plant nonkicking foot next to ball.
Variation:	Vary the number of approach steps, and distance; add targets.

DS ⓔ	**Kicking for Control and Accuracy**
Pacing:	*Self-paced*
Grade Level:	Typically lower elementary (K–2)
Content Focus:	*Exploration of throwing while on the move to stationary targets*
Setup:	Children are standing side by side behind the kicking line in a large outdoor space. Targets (hula hoops) are randomly spread throughout the target area. Refer to the diagram below.
Task:	This game is called pinpoint accuracy. I have placed numerous target areas in the field outside. Your job is to kick your ball so that it goes over the line and lands in the target area. The ball must go in the air before it lands in the target area for it to count. You must use the correct amount of force to be successful in this game. Let's see as a class how many we can get to land in the target area. Ready, begin!
Diagram:	

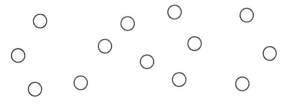

Kicking line

K K K K K K

Cues:	Bend the kicking leg before you kick.
	Look at the lower part of the ball.
Variation:	Vary the size of targets and the distance.

Expanding Skills (Typically Grades 1 through 3)

As children move into the expanding phase of kicking, they begin to kick a variety of balls on the ground or into the air with consistency. To help them expand their ability to kick, they need to be challenged to perform the skill in a less-predictable environment. This would involve kicking a moving ball, kicking with a partner, or kicking and passing while moving.

ES ⓐ	**Kicking a Moving Ball**
Pacing:	*Semi-self-paced*
Grade Level:	Typically elementary (1–3)
Content Focus:	*Expanding throwing to include working with a partner*
Setup:	Partners are scattered in general space with one ball per pair. Each pair decides the space in which they are going to work.
Task:	On my signal, get with a partner and get two cones and a ball out of the cart. Stand across from your partner. Your partner will roll the ball to you, and you are going to use the toe lift to kick the ball back to your partner. Take five turns each before you change roles. If you finish before the stop signal, start over. Ready, begin!
	This time, as we practice the toe lift from a rolling ball, I want the person rolling the ball to start moving after the ball is rolled. The kicker has to be accurate with the kick, so that the

continued

ES Ⓐ	*Kicking a Moving Ball, continued*
	roller is able to catch the ball while it is moving. Remember, you will have to kick the ball slightly in front of your partner so that they can catch the ball without having to stop. Again, change roles after five kicks. Ready, begin!
Cues:	Place your toe under the ball.
	Get your body behind the ball.
Variation:	Vary the target and distance.

ES Ⓑ	**Kicking with a Partner while Stationary**
Pacing:	*Semi-self-paced*
Grade Level:	Typically elementary (1–3)
Content Focus:	*Expanding kicking with a partner*
Setup:	Partners are scattered in general space, with one ball per pair. They are working at a distance of their choice.
Task:	Choose a distance that you are able to work in responsibly (not interfering with other groups) with your partner. Stand across from your partner. On my signal, I want you to begin kicking the ball back and forth with your partner using the inside of your foot. When you receive the ball, use the inside of the foot trap (inside of foot angled toward ground) to stop the ball. Remember to give with the ball to absorb the force. Once you have the ball under control, kick it back to your partner. Keep practicing kicking until you hear me say, "Cut." Ready, begin!
	This time, kick the ball back and forth with your partner using the outside of your foot. When you receive the ball, use the inside of the foot trap. Remember to give with the ball to absorb the force. Once you have the ball under control, kick it back to your partner. Keep practicing kicking until you hear me say, "Cut." Ready, begin!
Cues:	Use the inside of the foot.
	Use the outside of the foot.
	Follow through to target.
Variation:	Vary parts of the foot used, the distance, and the ball.

ES Ⓒ	**Kicking with a Partner while Moving**
Pacing:	*Semi-self-paced*
Grade Level:	Typically elementary (1–3)
Content Focus:	*Expanding kicking with a partner while moving*
Setup:	Partners are scattered and moving in general space with one ball per pair.
Task:	On my signal, kick back and forth with your partner as you move in general space. Start out at a slow speed until you get the feel of moving and kicking with your partner. For this task, be sure to use all of your general space. I don't want to see any empty space in the activity area. Keep kicking with your partner until you hear the signal to stop. Ready, action!
	This time, move at a speed where you can control the ball. If you can move fast, then do so; if you are having trouble controlling the ball then move at a slower speed. Ready, begin.
Cues:	Use both the inside and outside of your foot.
	Use quick feet.
Variation:	Vary the speed, direction, and pathway.

ES **D**	Approaching and Kicking a Stationary Ball for Distance and Accuracy
Pacing:	*Semi-self-paced*
Grade Level:	Typically elementary (1–3)
Content Focus:	*Expanding throwing for accuracy by changing the distance to targets and the number of kicks to reach the target*
Setup:	Children, each with a ball, stand side by side in a large outdoor space behind a kicking line. Four zones are outlined in the playing area. Refer to the diagram below.
Task:	There are four distance zones in our playing area today. In each zone you see targets that you will try to hit with your kick. I know the distance is pretty far, but I want us to be able to kick the ball for distance and with accuracy. On signal, approach with your hop (same foot to same foot), step to the ball, kick it, and see if you can hit one of the targets in the zone closest to you. Wait for the signal to retrieve your ball. Ready, action! Retrieve!

Diagram:

Zone 4   △ △ △ △ △   10 ft.
Zone 3   △ △ △ △ △   10 ft.
Zone 2   △ △ △ △ △   10 ft.
Zone 1   △ △ △ △ △   10 ft.

20 ft.

○ ○ ○ ○ ○ ○
Kicking line
K K K K K K

Cues:	Hop, step, and kick.
	Make contact below the center of the ball.
Variation:	Vary approach and distance.

ES **E**	Kicking against a Defender (Goalie)
Pacing:	*Semi-self-paced*
Grade Level:	Typically elementary (1–3)
Content Focus:	*Expanding kicking while trying to score*
Setup:	Partners are standing in one of the 12 sets of goal areas (two cones, five ft. apart) in front of the wall. There is one ball per pair. Index cards with letters of the alphabet on them are used for the letter cards. There must be two of each letter of the alphabet. Refer to the diagram below.
Task:	On signal, you have three seconds to find the person with the same letter card as you. This is your partner for the day. Go! Now, on signal, go to one of the goal areas that I have set up in the gym. One person will be the kicker and must kick from a stationary position. The other person is the goalie. To score a goal, the ball must be kicked on the ground. The goalies can use any part of their body to keep the kickers from scoring a goal. Let's start with the medium foam ball. The kicker will continue kicking until I say, "Cut." Then we will change roles. Ready, action!
	For this round, the kicker may approach the ball to kick for the goal. Ready, action!

Diagram:

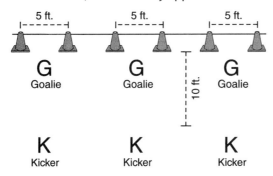

continued

ES ❺	*Kicking against a Defender (Goalie), continued*
Cues:	Place your nonkicking foot beside the ball.
	Follow through after your kick.
Variation:	Vary the ball, distance, and size of goal area.

Mastering Skills (Typically Grades 3 through 5)

In the mastering phase of kicking, students can kick for distance and accuracy while working alone or with a partner. They are now challenged by using their kicking skills in unpredictable environments, with the pacing outside their control. Students must now be able to combine dodging and kicking skills to elude defenders in more gamelike situations.

MS ❶	**Playing Keep-Away**
Pacing:	*Externally paced*
Grade Level:	Typically upper elementary (3–5)
Content Focus:	*Mastering kicking to keep a ball away from a defender*
Setup:	Groups of three are scattered in general space. Each group has two cones, used to denote the distance between the two kickers, and one ball. Refer to the diagram below.
Task:	In each group of three, there will be two kickers and one defender. The kickers' job is to keep the ball away from the defender in the middle. You will need to make good passes so that the person in the middle is unable to get the ball. We will play for 30 seconds. If the person in the middle gets the ball, just start again until you hear the signal to stop. We will then change the person in the middle. Ready, begin!
	Let's decrease the distance we are working in with our keep away games. Ready, begin!
Diagram:	**K** Kicker **D** Defender **K** Kicker
Cues:	Use the inside and outside of your foot.
	Use quick fakes.
Variation:	Vary the distance and vary ball.

MS ❸	**Kicking to a Moving Target**
Pacing:	*Externally paced*
Grade Level:	Typically upper elementary (3–5)
Content Focus:	*Mastering kicking to a moving target for accuracy*
Setup:	Groups of four are scattered in general space with one ball and one hula hoop. The thrower stands about 10 ft. from the two people who will be rolling the hula hoop. Refer to the diagram below.
Task:	In a group of four you will have one ball and one hula hoop. Two people will roll the hoop, while one will be the kicker and one the retriever. Let's see how accurately we can kick the ball, while the hoop is moving. The kicker's job is to time the kick so that the ball goes through the center of the hoop while it is moving. The retriever will stand on the other side of the hoop to stop the ball. Take five kicks before changing roles. Ready begin!
	This time, the retriever will roll the ball to the kicker before the hoop is rolled. The kicker must then redirect the ball through the hoop while it is moving. Again, take five kicks before changing roles. Ready, begin!
Diagram:	

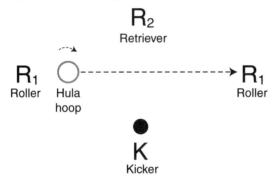

Cues:	Use the inside of your foot.
	Kick ahead of the target.
Variation:	Vary speed of roll and distance.

MS ❸	**Playing Modified Soccer**
Pacing:	*Externally paced*
Grade Level:	Typically upper elementary (3–5)
Content Focus:	*Mastering kicking while playing a modified game of soccer*
Setup:	Two groups of three children decide the playing area by defining it with the four cones.
Task:	Let's play a modified game (three-vs.-three) of soccer. Have one person from your group of six come and get four cones. You may determine the size of the space for your game. The key to this game is to pass and dribble the ball down the field in order to shoot for a goal (i.e., having the ball roll through the inside of the cones). We are going to play for about four minutes, and then we are going to change the teams we are playing against. OK, go find your space, and you may begin when you are ready.
Cues:	Keep your eyes forward.
	Use quick feet.
Variation:	Vary the size of playing field and width of goal.

MS Ⓓ	Guarding the Cone
Pacing:	*Externally paced*
Grade Level:	Typically upper elementary (3–5)
Content Focus:	*Mastering kicking while trying to hit the cone to score*
Setup:	Groups of four are scattered in a large outdoor space. There is one cone and one ball per group. Around the cone is a 3-ft. circle. Refer to the diagram below.
Task:	For this game, one person defends the cone while the other three people attempt to pass and kick the soccer ball in order to hit the cone. A point is scored each time the attacking team hits the cone with the ball. The defender and the offense must stay out of the 3-ft. buffer zone around the cone. Ready, begin!
Diagram:	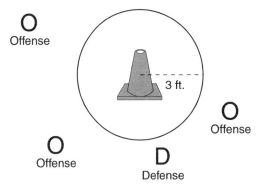
Cues:	Pass and move.
	Pass to open space.
Variation:	Vary the number of players and size of the ball.

Sample Learning Tasks for Punting

Punting is a manipulative skill using the foot to apply force to an object that begins in the hands and is dropped to the ground. This skill is more difficult for children than kicking, because the body must be coordinated to contact a ball that is dropped before it hits the ground. Typically, when beginning to learn punting, students will toss the ball *up* instead of *dropping* it. This adds to the difficulty, because punting requires good timing, rhythm, and eye–foot coordination; and the height of the toss affects the other movements made to contact the ball. Box 12.4 highlights the progression for students learning the skill theme of punting. See Figure 12.7 for a graphic representation of sample learning tasks that follow this progression.

Developing Skills (Typically Grades K through 2)

Punting is a skill that begins with the ball in the hands; the punter must contact the ball before it hits the ground. In developing this skill, students will need to learn to drop the ball before they learn to punt it. Using lightweight large-sized balls is the first step in this process. Once children can make good contact, they can start punting for distance, height, and accuracy.

BOX **12.4** ■ Progression for Children Developing Punting Skills

Punting

1. Work on dropping the ball in front of the body.

2. Punt while stationary.

3. Catch a ball, take preparatory steps, and punt.

4. Punt a ball while on the move.

5. Punt against opposition.

DS Ⓐ	Dropping the Ball
Pacing:	*Self-paced*
Grade Level:	Typically lower elementary (K–2)
Content Focus:	*Exploration of dropping the ball for punting*
Setup:	Children are scattered in general space, each with a playground ball.
Task:	On my signal, get a foam ball from the cart and find your own space. Practice extending your arms and dropping the ball right in front of you. If it is a good drop, the ball should come right back to you. So we are just going to drop and catch for this task. Remember the ball should bounce right back into your hands. Keep practicing dropping and catching until you hear the signal to stop. Ready, begin!
Cues:	Drop the ball rather than toss it.
	Keep your arms straight in front.
Variation:	Vary the type of ball dropped.

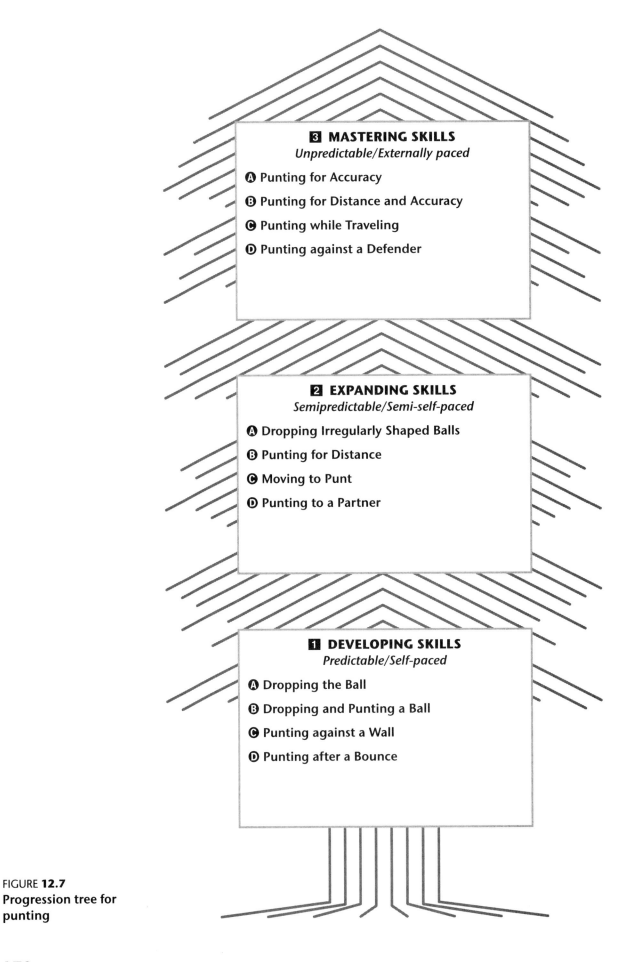

3 MASTERING SKILLS
Unpredictable/Externally paced

Ⓐ Punting for Accuracy

Ⓑ Punting for Distance and Accuracy

Ⓒ Punting while Traveling

Ⓓ Punting against a Defender

2 EXPANDING SKILLS
Semipredictable/Semi-self-paced

Ⓐ Dropping Irregularly Shaped Balls

Ⓑ Punting for Distance

Ⓒ Moving to Punt

Ⓓ Punting to a Partner

1 DEVELOPING SKILLS
Predictable/Self-paced

Ⓐ Dropping the Ball

Ⓑ Dropping and Punting a Ball

Ⓒ Punting against a Wall

Ⓓ Punting after a Bounce

FIGURE **12.7**
Progression tree for punting

DS ❸	**Dropping and Punting a Ball**
Pacing:	*Self-paced*
Grade Level:	Lower elementary (K–2)
Content Focus:	*Exploration of dropping then punting a ball*
Setup:	Children are scattered in general space, each with a balloon.
Task:	Stand on your spot in general space. On my signal, drop the balloon and punt (kick it while it is still in the air) it to yourself. Use the shoelace part of your shoe to contact the balloon. Catch the balloon and punt it again. Keep punting and catching the balloon until the signal to stop is given. Ready, begin!
Cues:	Use the shoelace.
	Drop the ball rather than toss it.
	Keep your head down.
Variation:	Vary the size and weight of the ball.

DS ❹	**Punting against a Wall**
Pacing:	*Self-paced*
Grade Level:	Typically lower elementary (K–2)
Content Focus:	*Exploration of punting a ball against a wall*
Setup:	Children are scattered in general space, standing on a spot in front of a wall. On each spot is a foam ball. The spots are 10 ft. from the wall.
Task:	On my signal, go stand on one of the spots placed around the gym in front of the wall and begin punting the foam ball on the spot against the wall. Keep punting and catching the ball until I say, "Cut." Ready, action! Cut!
	This time, as you are practicing punting your ball against the wall, make sure that you punt the ball above the blue line that is on the wall. Remember to use those shoelaces for good contact. Ready, action!
	We have been practicing punting against the wall at a close distance. This time, move your poly spot back a couple of steps and continue punting and catching until I say, "Cut."
Cues:	Contact using the shoelaces.
	Keep your head down.
Variation:	Vary the ball, distance, target, and height.

DS ❺	**Punting after a Bounce**
Pacing:	*Self-paced*
Grade Level:	Typically lower elementary (K–2)
Content Focus:	*Exploration of punting a ball after a bounce*
Setup:	Children are scattered in general space facing a wall. On each spot is a foam ball. The spots are 10 ft. from the wall.
Task:	As you are practicing punting against the wall, drop your ball and let it bounce once before you try to punt it. You must really concentrate on making good contact. What part of the foot do we use for good contact? That is right, the shoelaces. OK, let's begin practicing. Remember, it is drop, bounce, and punt. Retrieve your ball and continue practicing. Ready, action!
	As you continue to drop, bounce, and punt, this time make sure that your punt goes above the blue line as you are practicing. Make sure that you have a good drop. Keep practicing until I say, "Cut." Ready, action!

continued

Punting after a Bounce, continued

You may continue practicing with the ball you are working with or you can choose any of the balls that are in the cart. Once you have made your choice, continue practicing dropping and punting the ball against the wall. Ready, begin!

Cues:	Keep contact with the shoelaces.
	Drop, bounce, punt.
	Keep your eyes on the ball.
Variation:	Vary the balls, distance, and height.

Expanding Skills (Typically Grades 1 through 3)

As students learn to consistently make contact on their punts with the foot (not the leg or knee), they start the transition into the expanding phase of punting. In this phase, they can work on distance, accuracy, and height on their punts. Students can punt heavier and irregularly shaped balls (footballs) while taking preparatory steps for punting.

ES Ⓐ **Dropping Irregularly Shaped Balls**

Pacing:	*Semi-self-paced*
Grade Level:	Typically elementary (1–3)
Content Focus:	*Expanding dropping to include irregularly shaped balls*
Setup:	Children are scattered in general space, each with a foam football.
Task:	On my signal, go stand by one of the foam footballs placed in general space. Begin extending your arms and dropping the ball right in front of you. If it is a good drop, the ball should come right back to you. So we are just going to drop and catch for this task. Remember, the football should bounce right back into your hands. Keep practicing dropping and catching until you hear the signal to stop. Ready, begin!
Cues:	Use the right hand as a cradle under ball (for right-handed people).
	Keep your head down.
Variation:	Vary the height of the drop.

ES Ⓑ **Punting for Distance**

Pacing:	*Semi-self-paced*
Grade Level:	Typically elementary (1–3)
Content Focus:	*Expanding punting for distance*
Setup:	Children are standing side by side in a large outdoor space, facing the four punting zones. Refer to the diagram below.
Task:	Today, we will be working on punting for distance. As you can see there are four punting zones increasing in distance. On signal, go stand on one of the spots that I already have laid out. Pick up the ball that is on your spot and wait for my signal to begin punting. See if you can punt the ball so that it lands in the first zone. Wait for my signal to retrieve the ball. Ready, punt! Retrieve!
	This time, punt the ball to any one of the four zones. Remember to make a good drop and use your shoelaces. Ready, punt! Retrieve!

continued

ES Ⓑ   *Punting for Distance, continued*

Diagram:

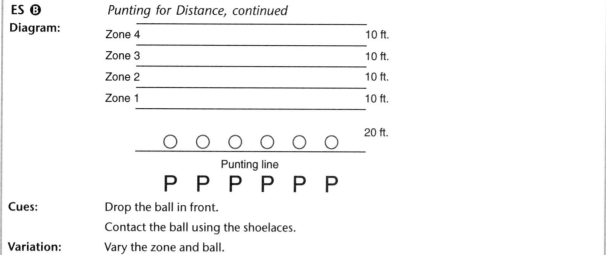

Cues: Drop the ball in front.

Contact the ball using the shoelaces.

Variation: Vary the zone and ball.

ES Ⓒ   **Moving to Punt**

Pacing: *Semi-self-paced*

Grade Level: Typically elementary (1–3)

Content Focus: *Expanding punting by using preparatory steps*

Setup: Children are standing side by side behind a punting line in a large outdoor space. Refer to the diagram below.

Task: We have been working on dropping the ball and punting it before it hits the ground. Now let's work on using an approach to help gain momentum and force on your punt. We will start with a two-step approach. For a right-footed punter the steps should be right-left-and-punt. For a left-footed punter the steps should be left-right-and-punt. OK, go to your spot. Wait for my signal to retrieve the ball. Ready, begin! Retrieve!

Let's use the two-step approach to help us gain distance on our punt. Try to punt your ball as far as you can. Remember to wait for my signal before retrieving your balls. Ready, begin!

Diagram:

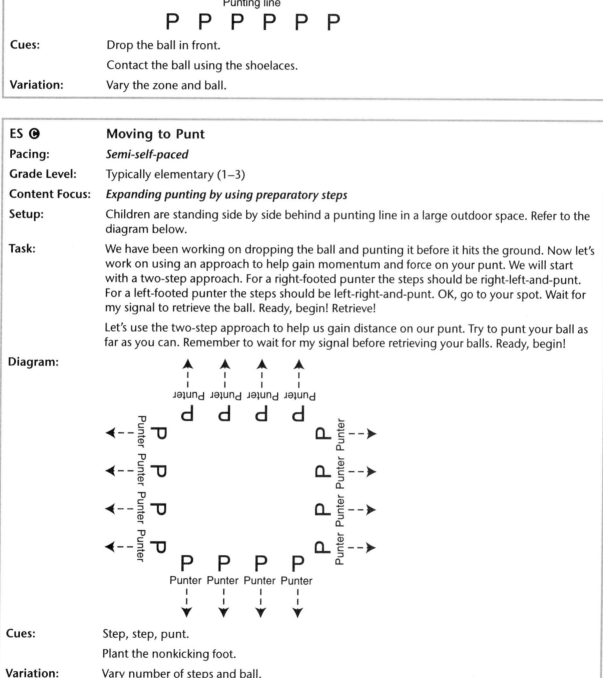

Cues: Step, step, punt.

Plant the nonkicking foot.

Variation: Vary number of steps and ball.

ES ⓓ	**Punting to a Partner**
Pacing:	*Semi-self-paced*
Grade Level:	Typically elementary (1–3)
Content Focus:	*Expanding punting by using preparatory steps*
Setup:	Partners are scattered in general space with one ball per pair. Children decide their working distance.
Task:	Stand across from a partner. On my signal, punt the ball right back to your partner. Punt the ball so that your partner does not have to move to catch it. Keep punting back and forth with your partner until I say, "Cut." Ready, action!
	This time, increase the height of your punt as it goes to your partner. Remember, he or she should not have to move to catch the punt. Ready, action!
Cues:	Follow through with your toe in the direction of the target.
	Keep the back of ball in line with step.
Variation:	Vary approach, distance, and height.

Mastering Skills (Typically Grades 3 through 5)

As students move into the mastering phase of punting, they can punt for distance, yet are still working on accuracy. They are punting in more dynamic and gamelike situations, while on the move, to a moving target, or against a defender.

MS ⓐ	**Punting for Accuracy**
Pacing:	*Externally paced*
Grade Level:	Typically upper elementary (3–5)
Content Focus:	*Mastering punting for accuracy*
Setup:	Partners are scattered in general space with one ball and two boxes or milk crates.
Task:	Everyone is to get with a partner, then get one ball and two boxes from the cart. Find a space where you can work with your partner. I want you to place the boxes directly opposite each other and at a distance that is challenging for you both. Your task is to punt the ball so that it lands in the box. Your partner will retrieve the ball and punt it toward the other box. Keep practicing until you hear the signal to stop. Ready, begin!
Cues:	Plant your nonkicking foot.
	Keep your head down.
Variation:	Vary targets and balls.

MS ⓑ	**Punting for Distance and Accuracy**
Pacing:	*Externally paced*
Grade Level:	Typically upper elementary (3–5)
Content Focus:	*Mastering punting for distance and accuracy*
Setup:	Children are scattered in general space, standing behind the punting line. There are four punting zones 10 ft. apart with the first zone 20 ft. from the punting line. Boxes are scattered throughout the zones. Refer to the diagram.
Task:	I have placed a large number of boxes out in the punting zones. On my signal, decide on one box you want to try to hit and see if you can punt your ball into the box. This will require distance and accuracy in your punting. Go stand on one of the spots I have placed on the ground, and you may begin punting. Wait for the signal to retrieve the balls. Ready, begin! Retrieve!

continued

MS ⓑ
Diagram:

Punting for Distance and Accuracy, continued

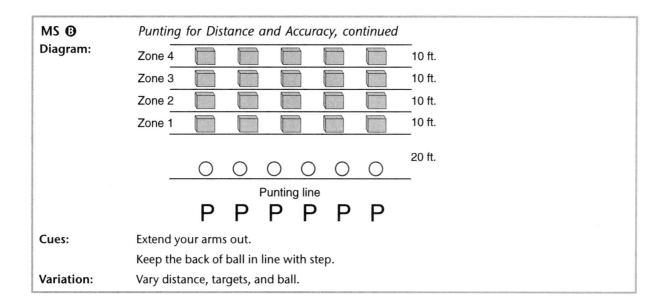

Cues: Extend your arms out.

Keep the back of ball in line with step.

Variation: Vary distance, targets, and ball.

MS ⓒ **Punting while Traveling**

Pacing: *Externally paced*

Grade Level: Typically upper elementary (3–5)

Content Focus: *Mastering punting while traveling*

Setup: Partners are scattered and moving in general space.

Task: On the signal, travel in general space and punt the ball back and forth to your partner while moving. You are going to have to make controlled punts to be able to keep moving while punting accurately. Ready, begin!

Cues: Keep your eyes forward.

Use quick feet.

Variation: Vary the ball and speed.

MS ⓓ **Punting against a Defender**

Pacing: *Externally paced*

Grade Level: Typically upper elementary (3–5)

Content Focus: *Mastering punting against a defender*

Setup: Groups of four are scattered in general space with one ball per group. Children choose the workspace. Refer to the diagram.

Task: In your group of four, there will be one punter, one center (person who tosses the ball underhand to the punter), one person who rushes the punter, and one receiver. The punter will receive the ball from the center and punt it to the receiver. This time the rusher will just raise his or her hands to try to stop the punt. Take three punts before changing roles. Remember to choose a responsible workspace. You may begin when I say, "Action." This time, we are going to let the rusher run forward. Once the center releases the ball, the rusher must count to two before rushing the punter. The rusher cannot go past the rush line. Again, take three punts before changing roles. Ready, begin!

continued

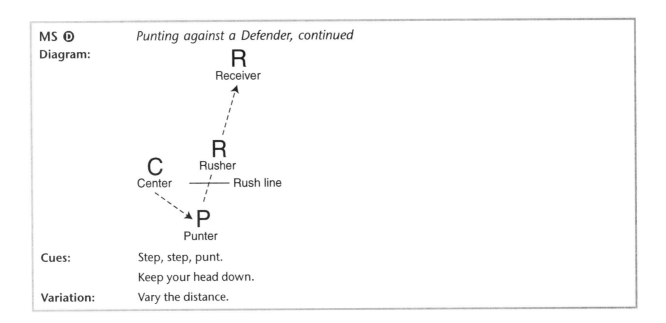

MS ⓓ

Punting against a Defender, continued

Diagram:

R
Receiver

R
Rusher

C ———|——— Rush line
Center

P
Punter

Cues: Step, step, punt.

Keep your head down.

Variation: Vary the distance.

DRIBBLING WITH THE HANDS AND FEET

Dribbling is the art of maintaining control of a moving ball with the hand or the feet while remaining in place (see Figure 12.8) or advancing with it (see Figure 12.9). Students often spend a lot of time practicing different ways to manipulate and control a ball with the hands or feet (see Figure 12.10). In two very popular sports, soccer and basketball, learning to control the ball by dribbling is a large part of the game. Fortunately, these skills can be easily practiced alone.

dribbling
Maintaining control of a ball with the hands or the feet while either advancing with it or, at times, remaining in place.

Source: Reprinted with permission from Queensland Studies Authority.

FIGURE **12.8**
Here you see the progression for dribbling in place.

Source: Reprinted with permission from Queensland Studies Authority.

FIGURE **12.9**
Here is the progression for dribbling on the move. Notice that the ball is further out in front and the body leans forward more than when dribbling in place.

Source: Reprinted with permission from Queensland Studies Authority.

FIGURE **12.10**
Here is the progression for dribbling with the feet. Notice that in this skill the aim is to keep the ball as close as possible to the feet.

More skillful dribblers can dribble, stop and change directions, dribble in different pathways, and dribble successfully against an opponent. The ultimate dribbling experience is for the student to dribble without watching the ball. They will then have mastered the whole purpose of dribbling: to move with the ball to create space to shoot at the goal or pass to a teammate who can shoot at the goal.

Sample Learning Tasks for Dribbling with the Hand

Dribbling with the hand involves striking the ball downward so it bounces continuously. The goal is either to advance the ball or to maintain control or possession of the ball. To do this well, students must be able to use both hands

Dribbling with the Hand

1. Bounce and catch in self-space.

2. Dribble continuously in place.

3. Dribble while moving in general space.

4. Dribble around various obstacles and change direction on signal.

5. Dribble against a defender.

6. Dribble in a gamelike activity.

interchangeably and dribble without looking at the ball. Box 12.5 highlights the skill progression for children learning the skill theme of dribbling with the hand, and Figure 12.11 gives a graphic representation of sample learning tasks that follow this progression.

Developing Skills (Typically Grades K through 2)

Students in the developing phase of dribbling with the hand are just starting to establish control over the ball instead of letting the ball control them. They are trying to establish a rhythmic dribbling pattern (dribbling continuously). Tasks where the student is able to dribble while stationary, with different hands, or around different body parts facilitate this process. As they make the transition to the expanding phase, students begin to dribble while moving, although at a pace where they can maintain control of the ball.

DS ❹	**Bouncing and Catching**
Pacing:	*Self-paced*
Grade Level:	Typically lower elementary (K–2)
Content Focus:	*Exploration bouncing and catching in self-space*
Setup:	Children, each with a ball, are scattered in general space either in an indoor or outdoor (with a blacktop) area.
Task:	In your self-space, bounce the ball one time with two hands and catch it. Continue practicing until I say, "Freeze."
	This time, try to bounce the ball twice before you catch it. Let's see if we can keep the time between bounces low. Ready, begin!
Cues:	Use your finger pads.
	Watch the ball.
Variation:	Vary the distance or object.

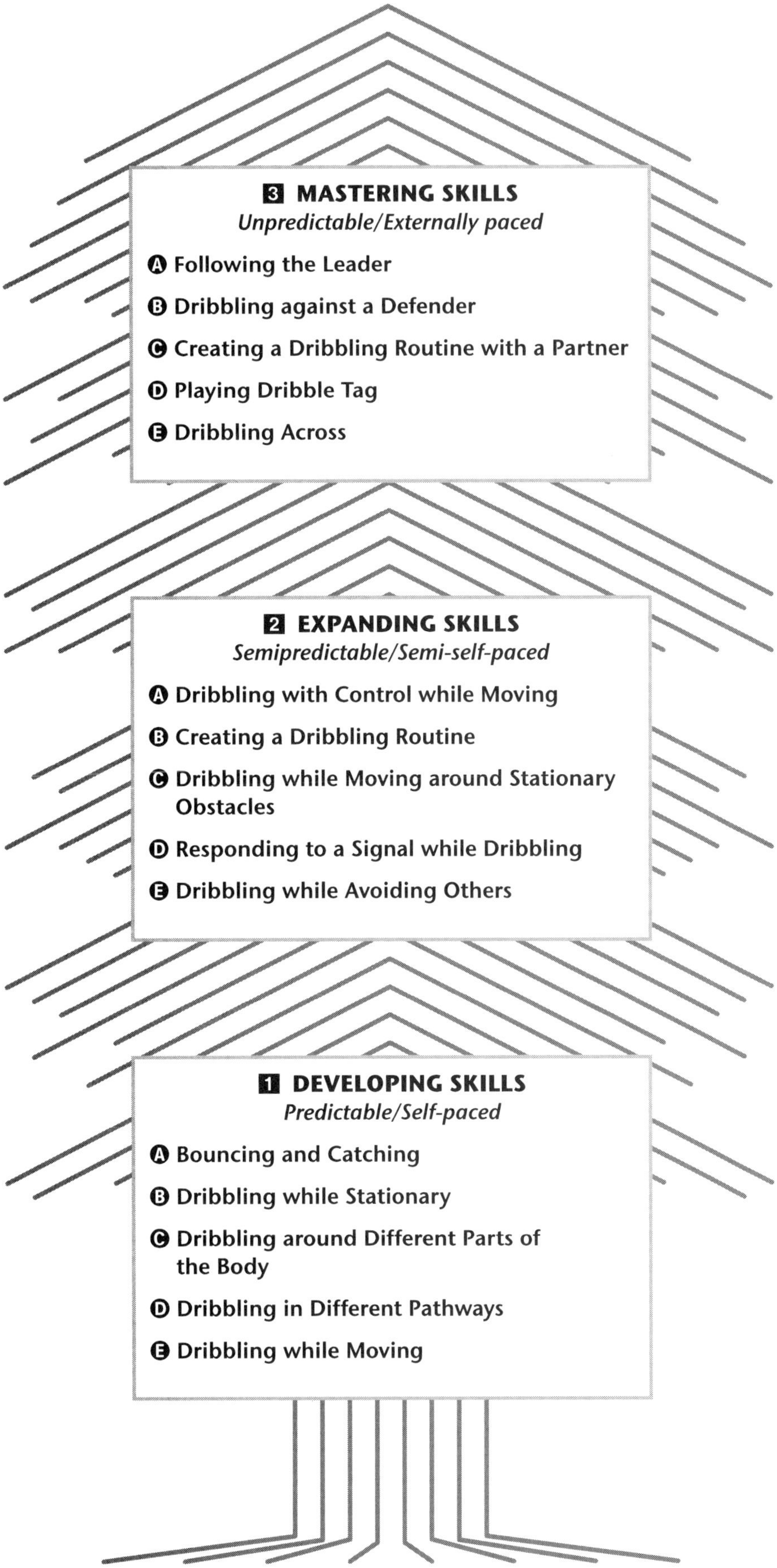

3 MASTERING SKILLS
Unpredictable/Externally paced

Ⓐ Following the Leader

Ⓑ Dribbling against a Defender

Ⓒ Creating a Dribbling Routine with a Partner

Ⓓ Playing Dribble Tag

Ⓔ Dribbling Across

2 EXPANDING SKILLS
Semipredictable/Semi-self-paced

Ⓐ Dribbling with Control while Moving

Ⓑ Creating a Dribbling Routine

Ⓒ Dribbling while Moving around Stationary Obstacles

Ⓓ Responding to a Signal while Dribbling

Ⓔ Dribbling while Avoiding Others

1 DEVELOPING SKILLS
Predictable/Self-paced

Ⓐ Bouncing and Catching

Ⓑ Dribbling while Stationary

Ⓒ Dribbling around Different Parts of the Body

Ⓓ Dribbling in Different Pathways

Ⓔ Dribbling while Moving

FIGURE **12.11**
Progression tree for dribbling with the hand

DS B	**Dribbling while Stationary**
Pacing:	*Self-paced*
Grade Level:	Lower elementary (K–2)
Content Focus:	*Exploration of dribbling while stationary*
Setup:	Children, each with a ball, are scattered in general space either in an indoor or outdoor (with a blacktop) area.
Task:	On my signal, stand on your spot and begin dribbling the ball at a low level (use the hand you write with). Place your other hand behind your back. Continue dribbling. Every time you hear the drumbeat, stop, change the level (low, medium) of your dribble, and continue dribbling.
	This time we will do the same thing, except let's change our dribbling hand. Ready, begin!
Cues:	Stand in stride position (nondribbling side foot in front).
	Use the finger pads.
	Push the ball down.
Variation:	Vary the level and hand, dribble around different body parts.

DS C	**Dribbling around Different Parts of the Body**
Pacing:	*Self-paced*
Grade Level:	Typically lower elementary (K–2)
Content Focus:	*Exploration of dribbling around various parts of the body*
Setup:	Children, each with a ball, are scattered in general space either in an indoor or outdoor (with a blacktop) area.
Task:	On my signal, see if you can dribble around one leg. Keep practicing until I say, "Freeze." Action!
	This time, see if you can dribble the ball around the entire body while remaining still. Action!
	This time, stand in a stride position (one leg forward/one back), and dribble the ball between your legs continuously (alternate hands—left, right, left, right). What part of the body should we use to contact the ball? Right, the finger pads. Keep trying until you hear the signal to stop. Action!
Cues:	Push the ball down.
	Use the finger pads.
	Keep one leg forward and one back—stride position.
Variation:	Dribble around different body parts or while looking up.

DS D	**Dribbling in Different Pathways**
Pacing:	*Self-paced*
Grade Level:	Typically lower elementary (K–2)
Content Focus:	*Exploration of dribbling in different pathways*
Setup:	Children, each with a ball, are scattered in general space either in an indoor or outdoor (with a blacktop) area. Pathways are placed on the floor using floor tape.
Task:	There are various pathway patterns (curved, zigzag, straight) made with floor tape, spread throughout general space On the signal, go stand at the start of one of these pathway patterns, pick the ball up, and start dribbling the ball from the start to the end of the pathway. Make sure your ball stays on the line. Action!
	Put your ball back on the start spot. On the signal, you have three seconds to go to a new pathway and start dribbling the ball on the new pathway pattern. Remember to try to look forward. Action!
Cues:	Look forward.
	Keep the ball to the side.
Variation:	Vary the pathway, speed, and dribbling hand.

DS ⒠	Dribbling while Moving
Pacing:	*Self-paced*
Grade Level:	Typically lower elementary (K–2)
Content Focus:	*Exploration of dribbling in general space*
Setup:	Children, each with a ball, are scattered in general space either in an indoor or outdoor (with a blacktop) area.
Task:	As you dribble in general space, keep your head up. Dribble at a speed where you can maintain control of the ball. When you hear the drumbeat, tell me how many fingers I am holding up. Action!
	This time, dribble in general space; every time you hear the drumbeat, I want you to change your dribbling hand. I want you to go only as fast as you can while maintaining control of your ball. Action!
Cues:	Keep your head up and eyes forward.
	Keep the ball close and low.
Variation:	Vary the dribbling hand and space for dribbling.

Expanding Skills (Typically Grades 1 through 3)

As students move into the expanding phase of dribbling, they can dribble with control (they control the ball instead of the ball controlling them) with either hand and while moving at different speeds. They are becoming more adept at dribbling in less predictable environments and can change direction on a signal or while avoiding obstacles.

ES ⒜	Dribbling with Control while Moving
Pacing:	*Semi-self-paced*
Grade Level:	Typically elementary (1–3)
Content Focus:	*Expanding dribbling with control while moving*
Setup:	Children, each with a ball, are scattered in general space, either in an indoor or outdoor (with a blacktop) area.
Task:	On my signal, start dribbling in general space at a slow speed. Every time you hear the drumbeat, I want you to go a little faster. Try to maintain control of your dribble at each speed. Remember to look up so that you don't run into others while you are dribbling. Keep dribbling until I say, "Cut." Action!
Cues:	Keep your head up.
	Keep the ball waist high.
Variation:	Vary the speed and dribbling hand.

ES ⒝	Creating a Dribbling Routine (Streetball or Harlem Globetrotters)
Pacing:	*Semi-self-paced*
Grade Level:	Typically elementary (1–3)
Content Focus:	*Expanding dribbling while creating a dribbling routine*
Setup:	Children, each with a ball, are scattered in general space either in an indoor or outdoor (with a blacktop) area.
Task:	In your self-space, I want you to work on a dribbling routine that includes a hand change, dribbling at different levels and speeds (dribble fast or slow), a directional change (ball going forward/backward or side to side), and a between the legs action. Your routine will be one

continued

ES **B**	*Creating a Dribbling Routine, continued*
	minute. I will beat the drum one time to let you know that time for working on your routine is over. Ready, begin!
Cues:	Use a smooth controlled dribble.
	Keep the wrist loose.
Variation:	Vary the routine requirements.

ES **C**	**Dribbling while Moving around Stationary Obstacles**
Pacing:	*Semi-self-paced*
Grade Level:	Typically elementary (1–3)
Content Focus:	*Expanding dribbling around obstacles while moving*
Setup:	Children, each with a ball, are scattered in general space, either in an indoor or outdoor (with a blacktop) area. A variety of cones and ropes are scattered in general space.
Task:	I have placed various cones and ropes around the gym. When you come to a cone, you are to dribble around it. When you come to a rope, you are to dribble over it. Go at a speed where you don't lose control of your ball. Keep your head up so that you don't run into your neighbor. Ready, begin!
	This time, the dribbling space will be smaller. We are going to use only half of the space we used before. You are to continue dribbling around and over the various objects that are placed in general space. Remember to watch out for your neighbor. Ready, begin!
Cues:	Look out for your neighbor.
	Push the ball forward.
Variation:	Vary the space, number of obstacles, and actions.

ES **D**	**Responding to a Signal while Dribbling**
Pacing:	*Semi-self-paced*
Grade Level:	Typically elementary (1–3)
Content Focus:	*Expanding dribbling while responding to a signal*
Setup:	Children, each with a ball, are scattered in general space, either in an indoor or outdoor (with a blacktop) area.
Task:	As you travel in general space, every time you hear the drumbeat I want you to stop as quickly as you can while maintaining control of the ball and dribbling at a low level. Ready, begin!
	This time, when you hear the drumbeat, use the behind-the-back or the between-the-legs dribble, change your dribbling hand, and continue dribbling until you hear the next drum sound. Ready, begin.
Cues:	Keep the ball close.
	Keep the ball low.
Variation:	Vary the time between drum beats; change dribbling action.

ES **E**	**Dribbling while Avoiding Others**
Pacing:	*Semi-self-paced*
Grade Level:	Typically elementary (grades 1–3)
Content Focus:	*Expanding dribble to avoid others*
Setup:	Children, each with a ball, are scattered in general space, either in an indoor or outdoor (with a blacktop) area.

continued

ES ❺	*Dribbling while Avoiding Others, continued*
Task:	As you dribble in general space, every time you pass by another person, I want you to turn and dribble in a new direction while keeping the ball at a low level. Ready, begin!
	This time, let's change our dribbling hand. Ready, begin!
Cues:	Keep the ball low.
	Keep the knees slightly bent.
Variation:	Vary direction, speed, and level.

Mastering Skills (Typically Grades 3 through 5)

In the mastering phase of dribbling, the environment becomes more complex, and children have to respond to others, including opponents trying to take away the ball they are dribbling. Challenges include more gamelike situations, where children can practice changing direction, speeds, and levels with control.

MS ❶	**Following the Leader**
Pacing:	*Externally paced*
Grade Level:	Typically upper elementary (3–5)
Content Focus:	*Mastering dribbling while playing follow the leader*
Setup:	Partners, each with a ball, are scattered in general space, either in an indoor or outdoor (with a blacktop) area.
Task:	I want you to face your partner. One partner will be the leader, the other the follower. We are going to work on mirroring and matching while being stationary. First, I want the follower to mirror the leader's actions. Remember that when we mirror actions we use opposite actions (i.e., the leader dribbles with the left hand, and the follower dribbles with the right). See how long you can mirror your partner's actions. Ready, begin! Now let's change roles. Ready, begin! This time I want you to match the actions of your partner (i.e., leader uses right hand and follower uses right hand).
	Now that you have a partner, I want you to play follow the leader dribble. Decide who will be the leader first and who will be the follower. The job of the follower is to walk behind the leader while dribbling. The follower should copy the leader's dribbling pattern without losing control of the ball. Use all the types of dribbles we have learned. If the leader loses the follower, start again. You will dribble throughout general space. When I say, "Freeze," you will stop and change roles. Ready, begin!
Cues:	Try to stay close.
	Keep your head up.
Variation:	Vary the speed and partners.

MS ❷	**Dribbling against a Defender**
Pacing:	*Externally paced*
Grade Level:	Typically upper elementary (3–5)
Content Focus:	*Mastering dribbling against a defender*
Setup:	Partners, with one ball per pair, are scattered in general space either in an indoor or outdoor (with a blacktop) area. A line made of cones is 30 ft. from where the dribbler starts. Refer to the diagram.
Task:	With a partner, one will be the dribbler, the other defender. The dribbler's job is to get the ball to the safe area while staying in his or her alley. A dribbler who gets to the safe area scores a point. A defender who steals the ball scores a point. Change roles after every point if scored.

continued

MS ❸   *Dribbling against a Defender, continued*

Diagram:

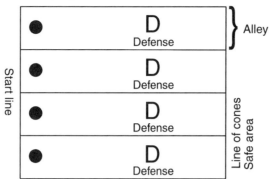

Cues: Keep your body between the ball and the defender.

Your fingers, wrist, and hand give with the ball.

Variation: Vary partners and distance.

MS ❹   **Creating a Dribbling Routine with a Partner**

Pacing: *Externally paced*

Grade Level: Typically upper elementary (3–5)

Content Focus: *Mastering dribbling in rhythm with a partner*

Setup: Partners, each with a ball, are scattered in general space, either in an indoor or outdoor (with a blacktop) area.

Task: With a partner, create a dribbling routine that includes a ball exchange between partners, a ball level change, a hand change, a directional change, and a position change.

Cues: Move in rhythm.

Look forward.

Variation: Vary the partner and number of requirements for the routine.

MS ❺   **Playing Dribble Tag**

Pacing: *Externally paced*

Grade Level: Typically upper elementary (3–5)

Content Focus: *Mastering dribbling while keeping away from taggers*

Setup: Children, each with a ball, are scattered in general space, either in an indoor or outdoor (with a blacktop) area. Four or more children are wearing yellow pinnies.

Task: Everyone should have a ball. This game is called dribble tag. Everyone with a yellow pinny on is "It." On the signal, everyone will travel while dribbling in general space. If you are tagged by someone who is It, you must stop, dribble in self-space, and wait for someone to come and dribble in a circle around you once to become unfrozen.

Cues: Bend the knees slightly.

Keep the ball low.

Variation: Vary the number of taggers and space.

MS ⓔ	**Dribbling Across**
Pacing:	*Externally paced*
Grade Level:	Typically upper elementary (3–5)
Content Focus:	*Mastering dribbling while playing a modified game*
Setup:	The class is divided into two teams (blue and red). Each person on the blue team is wearing a blue pinny and has a ball. Each person on the defending team is wearing a red pinny and doesn't have a ball. Teams start at opposite ends of the playing area. This activity can be played in an indoor or outdoor (blacktop) space. Refer to the diagram below.
Task:	There will be two teams, the dribbling team (blue pinnies) and the defending team (red pinnies). Everyone on the dribbling team has a ball. They are trying to get from one side of the gym to the other without having their ball stolen by the defending team or losing control of the ball (the dribblers have 30 seconds to get to the opposite side of the gym). If a person on the defending team steals the ball or causes the dribbler to lose control of the ball, the defender changes roles with the dribbler. Defenders start on the opposite side of the gym from the dribblers. The dribbler who gets across the gym successfully continues in that role. Once everyone has attempted to cross and time expires, the game will start again.
Diagram:	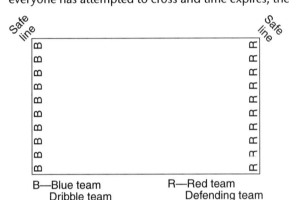
Cues:	Keep your body between the ball and the defender.
	Keep the ball close.
Variation:	Vary the number of players.

Sample Learning Tasks for Dribbling with the Feet

Dribbling with the feet involves a constant tapping of the ball to move it forward or sideways. As when dribbling with the hand, children need to use both feet equally well, as well as various parts of the foot (outside, inside, heel) to advance the ball and keep it away from opponents. Box 12.6 highlights the skill progression for children learning the skill theme of dribbling with the feet, and Figure 12.12 shows a graphic representation of sample learning tasks that follow this progression.

Developing Skills (Typically Grades K through 2)

In the developing phase of dribbling a ball with the feet, students learn to contact the ball using the feet and then to advance the ball while moving slowly. When teaching dribbling with the feet, it is difficult to create strictly predictable and

self-paced learning tasks. One way to do this is to have students dribble slowly using the inside of their feet until they learn to control the ball. Then as they move on to the expanding phase, they use other parts of the foot in dribbling and controlling the ball.

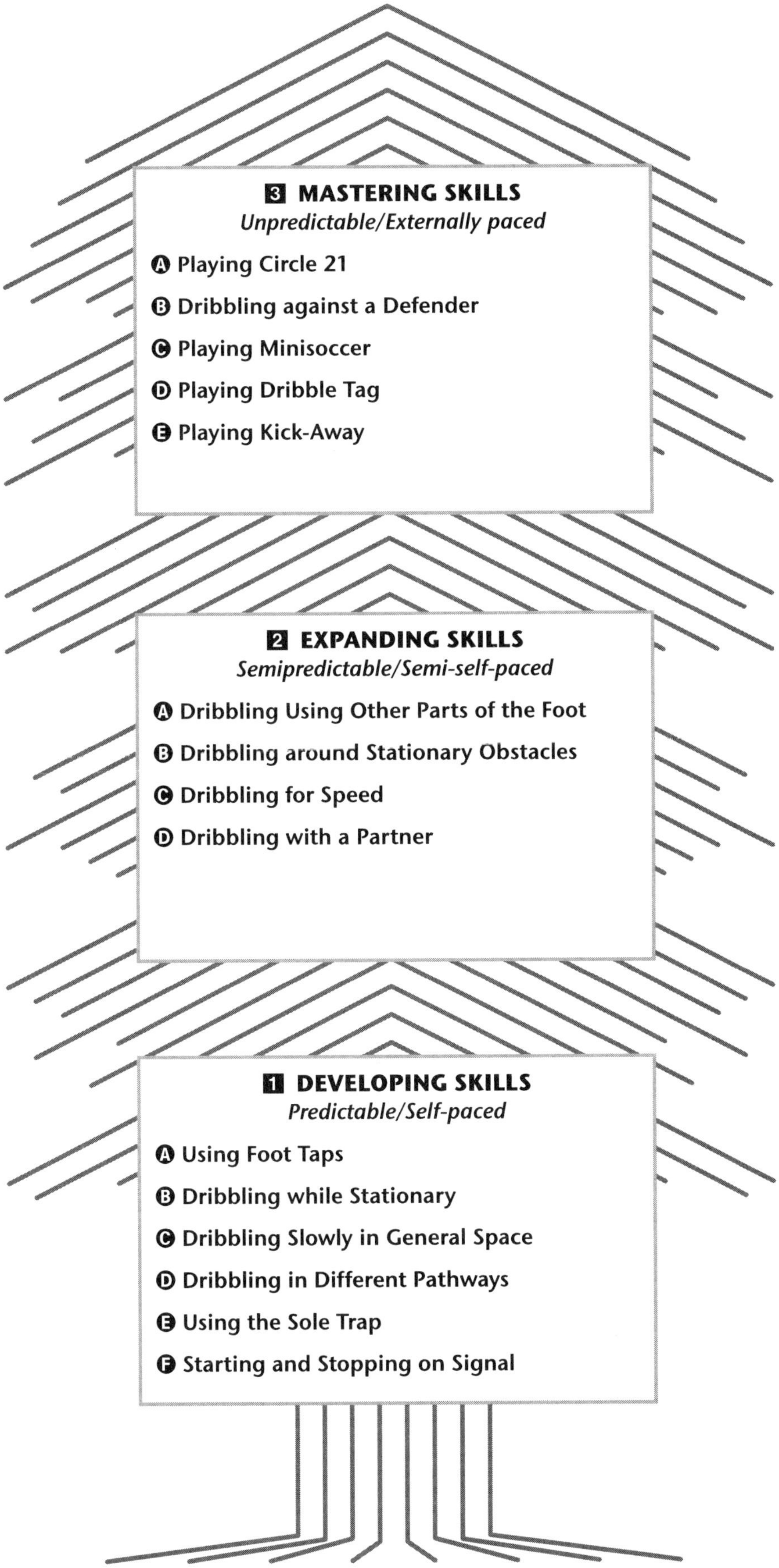

3 MASTERING SKILLS

Unpredictable/Externally paced

Ⓐ Playing Circle 21

Ⓑ Dribbling against a Defender

Ⓒ Playing Minisoccer

Ⓓ Playing Dribble Tag

Ⓔ Playing Kick-Away

2 EXPANDING SKILLS

Semipredictable/Semi-self-paced

Ⓐ Dribbling Using Other Parts of the Foot

Ⓑ Dribbling around Stationary Obstacles

Ⓒ Dribbling for Speed

Ⓓ Dribbling with a Partner

1 DEVELOPING SKILLS

Predictable/Self-paced

Ⓐ Using Foot Taps

Ⓑ Dribbling while Stationary

Ⓒ Dribbling Slowly in General Space

Ⓓ Dribbling in Different Pathways

Ⓔ Using the Sole Trap

Ⓕ Starting and Stopping on Signal

FIGURE **12.12**
Progression tree for dribbling with the feet

DS Ⓐ   **Using Foot Taps**

Pacing:	*Self-paced*
Grade Level:	Typically lower elementary (K–2)
Content Focus:	*Exploration of contacting the ball with quick feet*
Setup:	Children, each with a ball, are scattered in general space, either in an indoor or outdoor area.
Task:	Stand with your ball on one of the spots you see in general space. On my signal, touch the top part of the ball with the ball of your foot. Alternate feet right-left-right-left and so on until you hear the signal to stop. You must have quick feet. Remember that the ball should stay still while you move your feet. Keep practicing until the signal to stop is given. Ready, begin!
	As we practice our foot taps on the top part of the ball, let's see if we can move our feet a little bit faster than we did the last time. Ready, begin!
Cues:	Use quick feet.
	Keep the knees up.
Variation:	Vary the ball.

DS Ⓑ   **Dribbling while Stationary**

Pacing:	*Self-paced*
Grade Level:	Lower elementary (K–2)
Content Focus:	*Exploration of dribbling the ball slowly while in self-space*
Setup:	Children, each with a ball, are scattered in general space, either in an indoor or outdoor area.
Task:	On my signal, stand by your ball and begin gently tapping it back and forth between your feet using the inside part of your foot. Keep practicing until you hear the signal to stop. Ready, begin!
Cues:	Use the inside of foot.
	Use gentle taps.
Variation:	Vary the size of ball or speed of taps.

DS Ⓒ   **Dribbling Slowly in General Space**

Pacing:	*Self-paced*
Grade Level:	Typically lower elementary (K–2)
Content Focus:	*Exploration of dribbling slowly to maintain control in general space*
Setup:	Children, each with a ball, are scattered in general space, either in an indoor or outdoor area.
Task:	On my signal, dribble the ball with the inside part of your feet while traveling in general space. Go at a speed at which you can control the ball. Ready, begin!
Cues:	Keep the ball close.
	Gently push the ball forward.
Variation:	Vary the speed and directions.

DS Ⓓ   **Dribbling in Different Pathways**

Pacing:	*Self-paced*
Grade Level:	Typically lower elementary (K–2)
Content Focus:	*Exploration of dribbling in different pathways while moving in general space*
Setup:	Children, each with a ball, are scattered in general space, either in an indoor or outdoor area.

continued

DS **D**	Dribbling in Different Pathways, *continued*
Task:	On my signal, begin traveling in general space using a curved pathway. Action! In a straight pathway. Freeze. Remember to keep control of your ball. This time, move in a zigzag pathway. Ready, begin!
Cues:	Look over the ball.
	Keep the ball close.
Variation:	Vary the pathway and speed.

DS **E**	**Using the Sole Trap**
Pacing:	*Self-paced*
Grade Level:	Typically lower elementary (K–2)
Content Focus:	*Exploration of stopping the ball after dribbling*
Setup:	Children, each with a ball, are scattered in general space, either in an indoor or outdoor area.
Task:	Stand in front of your ball. On my signal, put the ball (sole) of your foot slightly below the top part of the ball. This is called the sole trap. You will use this trap when you need to stop the ball.
	On my signal, dribble your ball in general space and when I say, "Freeze," use the sole trap to stop your ball. Action! Freeze!
	This time, you will have three seconds to be able to trap the ball under control when I say, "Freeze." On my signal, begin dribbling in general space. Remember, you need to be able to trap the ball within three seconds. Ready begin!
	Let's do the same task, but move at a faster pace while you are dribbling. Remember, when I say, "Freeze," you need to be able to trap the ball within three seconds. Ready, begin!
Cues:	Place the ball (sole) of foot slightly below the top part of ball.
	Keep the heel down.
Variation:	Vary time to stop and speed of dribble.

DS **F**	**Starting and Stopping on Signal**
Pacing:	*Self-paced*
Grade Level:	Typically lower elementary (K–2)
Content Focus:	*Exploration of dribbling while responding to a signal*
Setup:	Children, each with a ball, are standing behind the start line, either in an indoor or outdoor area.
Task:	We are going to play red light, green light. Everyone line up behind the start line in your own space. When I say, "Green light," you are to dribble your ball toward the red line as fast as you can while maintaining control. When I say, "Red light," you must trap your ball within three seconds. If you don't have control of your ball or you are still moving, then you must go back and start again from the blue line. I will continue to say "red light, green light" until the first person makes it across the red line. Ready, green light! Red light!
	Let's continue playing red light, green light, but this time, when I say, "Red light," you must be stopped with your ball under control in one second. Ready, green light! Red light!
Cues:	Keep the ball (sole) of foot slightly below the top part of ball.
	Keep the heel down.
	Use the inside of the foot.
Variation:	Vary the time to stop the distance from blue to red line.

Expanding Skills (Typically Grades 1 through 3)

As students move into the expanding phase of dribbling with the feet, they can dribble slowly with control. As they expand on this skill, they start dribbling while looking forward and not at the ball. This will allow them to dribble faster in general space while avoiding others and obstacles. Because children can dribble with control in this phase, they can begin to work with a partner, making the skill less self-paced and predictable.

ES Ⓐ   **Dribbling Using Other Parts of the Foot**

Pacing:	*Semi-self-paced*
Grade Level:	Typically elementary (1–3)
Content Focus:	*Expanding dribbling with feet by using other parts of the foot*
Setup:	Children, each with a ball, are scattered in general space, either in an indoor or outdoor area.
Task:	We have been using the inside of our foot to dribble, but many times you will need to use the outside of your foot while you are dribbling. So this time, as you travel in general space, use the outside of your foot to keep the ball moving. Ready, begin!
	This time, use the inside and outside of your foot while you are dribbling and change direction quickly on the signal. The key is to maintain control of the ball so that you do not lose your momentum as you are dribbling. Ready, begin!
Cues:	Use short controlled steps.
	Dribble using the inside and outside to push the ball.
Variation:	Vary the speed, signal, and direction.

ES Ⓑ   **Dribbling around Stationary Obstacles**

Pacing:	*Semi-self-paced*
Grade Level:	Typically elementary (1–3)
Content Focus:	*Expanding dribbling to maintain control while avoiding obstacles*
Setup:	Children, each with a ball, are scattered in general space, either in an indoor or outdoor area. A number of cones and hoops are scattered in general space.
Task:	I have placed a number of cones and hoops in general space. Use the inside and outside part of your foot to dribble in general space. When you hear the drumbeat, I want you to dribble around the obstacle nearest to you. Once you have completed the circle, start dribbling in general space until you hear the next drumbeat. Ready, begin!
	This time, as you dribble in general space and move around obstacles, try to keep your head up to see where you are moving. It is good in soccer to be able to see your teammates so that you can pass them the ball. Remember, keep your head up. Keep dribbling until you hear the signal to stop. Ready, action!
Cues:	Keep your head up—eyes forward.
	Push the ball.
Variation:	Vary the number of obstacles and space.

ES ⊙   **Dribbling for Speed**

Pacing:	*Semi-self-paced*
Grade Level:	Typically elementary (1–3)
Content Focus:	*Expanding dribbling by working on controlling the ball while moving quickly*
Setup:	Three concentric circles are drawn on the playing surface. Children, each with a ball, are scattered in general space, standing around the outside of the largest circle. Inside the three circles are a number of cones. Refer to the diagram below.
Task:	Today, our working area is made up of three circles. Inside the three circles, I have placed numerous cones. On my signal, start dribbling on the outside of the largest circle. When you hear the drumbeat, I want you to dribble as quickly as you can to the cone nearest to you. Ready, begin!
	Let's continue dribbling on the outside circle. However, this time, when you hear me beat the drum once, try to get to one of the cones in the inner circle by the count of three. You must be at the cone with the ball under control by the time I get to three. Remember to watch out for your neighbor. Let's start dribbling. Ready, begin!
Diagram:	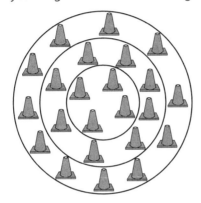
Cues:	Use short controlled steps.
	Keep the ball close when in traffic.
Variation:	Vary the space and number of cones.

ES ⊙   **Dribbling with a Partner**

Pacing:	*Semi-self-paced*
Grade Level:	Typically elementary (1–3)
Content Focus:	*Expanding dribbling while working with a partner*
Setup:	Partners are scattered and moving in general space with one ball per pair in an indoor or outdoor area.
Task:	Everyone is to get with a partner, then get one ball from the cart. Find a space where you can work with your partner. On my signal, start dribbling and passing with your partner in general space. As you are moving, make sure you give your partner a good pass. Make it so your partner is able to trap the ball and continue dribbling without having to stop. Keep practicing until you hear the signal to stop. Ready, begin!
	This time, as you travel back and forth with your partner dribbling and passing, increase the speed at which you are working, yet still maintain control of the ball. Ready, action!
Cues:	Lead your partner with the pass.
	Use inside and outside of foot while dribbling.
Variation:	Vary speed, partner and area.

WHAT'S WRONG WITH THIS PICTURE? Ms. Crabtree's brother is on the local university's golf team, and she has borrowed some clubs from the coach. She wants to teach her second grade children putting skills. Ms. Crabtree sets up a nine-hole miniature golf course on the outside basketball court. Students are grouped in fours, with two students having putters and two students with scorecards.

Mastering Skills (Typically Grades 3 through 5)

In mastering the skill of dribbling with the feet, students are ready to perform tasks requiring them to respond in more gamelike, uncertain conditions. They are going from being able to dribble in semipredictable environments, such as working cooperatively with a partner, to being able to control the ball to avoid defenders.

MS Ⓐ	**Playing Circle 21**
Pacing:	*Externally paced*
Grade Level:	Typically upper elementary (3–5)
Content Focus:	*Mastering dribbling while trying to score points*
Setup:	Three concentric circles are drawn on the playing surface. Children, each with a ball, are scattered in general space standing around the outside of the largest circle. Inside the three circles are a number of cones. Refer to the diagram below.
Task:	Today, our working area is made up of three circles. I have placed numerous cones inside the three circles. Cones in the inner circle are worth three points, cones in the second circle are worth two points, and cones near the outer circle are worth one point. Now, we are going to play a game called circle 21. On my signal, start dribbling your ball around the outside circle. When I say, "Go," you have three seconds to get to a cone with the ball under control. If you are still dribbling or you have lost control of your ball, you don't receive any points. This will be one round. If you were able to get your ball to the inner cone, you have three points for round 1. For each round, you will start on the outside of the circle dribbling, until I say, "Go." You will add up your points each round. Your job is to get 21 points as fast as you can. OK, everyone start dribbling on the outside of the largest circle. Ready, begin!
Diagram:	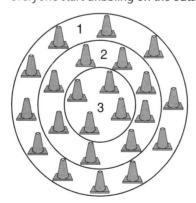
Cues:	Keep your eyes over the ball.
	Use short controlled steps.
Variation:	Vary the scoring system and size of the area.

MS Ⓑ   **Dribbling against a Defender**

Pacing:	*Externally paced*
Grade Level:	Typically upper elementary (3–5)
Content Focus:	*Mastering dribbling against one defender*
Setup:	Partners are scattered in general space with one ball and two cones per pair. The cones designate the playing area determined by the children. Refer to the diagram below.
Task:	This time, I want one of the partners to be the offensive player (one with ball) and one the defensive player (one who tries to take the ball). The offensive player's job is to dribble the ball from the yellow cone to the blue cone without letting the defense take the ball away. You change roles when either the defensive player takes the ball or the dribbler makes it to the blue cone. Change roles after each possession. Ready, begin!

Diagram:

 O   D

Offense / dribbler   Defense

Cues:	Keep your body in line with the ball.
	Keep the ball close.
Variation:	Vary partners and distance.

MS Ⓒ   **Playing Minisoccer**

Pacing:	*Externally paced*
Grade Level:	Typically upper elementary (3–5)
Content Focus:	*Mastering dribbling while playing a modified game of soccer*
Setup:	Groups of three are scattered in general space. Two cones, approximately 5 ft. apart, are set up as goals on either end of the playing area. Refer to the diagram below.
Task:	In groups of three, we will have two offensive players and one defensive player. The offensive players are trying to dribble and pass the ball to each other in order to score a goal through the two cones. In order to score a goal, the ball has only to roll inside the two cones on the other side of the playing area. If the defender takes the ball, then the offense starts over. The offense has three turns before you change defenders. Each player must take a turn at being the defender. Go to your designated area and begin play. Ready, begin!

Diagram:

O
Offense

D
Defense

Goal

O
Offense

Cues:	Keep your head and eyes up.
	Contact with the inside and outside of foot.
Variation:	Vary the number of players and playing area.

MS ⓓ　　　**Playing Dribble Tag**

Pacing: *Externally paced*

Grade Level: Typically upper elementary (3–5)

Content Focus: *Mastering dribbling while keeping away from taggers*

Setup: Children, each with a ball, are scattered in general space, either in an indoor or outdoor area.

Task: Everyone should have a ball. This game is called "dribble tag." Everyone with a yellow pinny on is "It." On the signal, everyone will travel while dribbling in general space. If you are tagged by someone who is It, you must stop, dribble in self-space (tap ball back and forth), and wait for someone to come and dribble in a circle around you once to become unfrozen. You cannot be tagged while in the process of freeing someone. Ready, begin!

Cues: Bend the knees slightly.

Keep the ball low.

Variation: Vary the number of taggers and space.

MS ⓔ　　　**Playing Kick-Away**

Pacing: *Externally paced*

Grade Level: Typically upper elementary (3–5)

Content Focus: *Mastering dribbling with the feet by maintaining control of one's ball while kicking away others*

Setup: Children, each with a ball, are scattered inside the playing area. Refer to the diagram below.

Task: In the space provided, we are going to play kick-away. On the signal, you will begin dribbling in general space. Your job is to keep possession of your ball while kicking the ball of one of your classmates out of the playing area. You cannot leave your ball to kick away another person's ball. You may only kick the ball away on the ground and not in the air. If your ball is kicked out of the playing area, quickly retrieve it and come back into the game. Every time you kick someone else's ball out of the playing area, you receive a point. For every time your ball is sent away, you have to take a point away from your total. The key to this game is to have the highest number of points after one minute of play. OK, everyone spread out. Ready, action!

This time, when we play kick-away, we are going to make the playing space smaller. You must be a really good dribbler to maintain possession of your ball while still being able to send someone else's ball out of the playing area. Ready, begin!

Diagram:

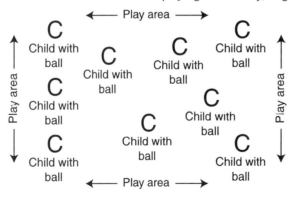

Cues: Push the ball.

Keep the ball close.

Variation: Vary the number of players and space.

VOLLEYING

Volleying is striking an object while it is in the air, using a variety of body parts. Although our most common conception of volleying comes from the game of volleyball itself, volleying is not limited to hands and a large ball. Volleying can be done with the feet. Think about those who are really skillful with a Hacky Sack or expert soccer players who can control a ball almost as though it were on a string.

Motor development experts tell us that volleying is one of the later manipulative patterns to develop. To volley successfully, one must make a number of critical adjustments as the ball approaches. The volleyer must track the path of the incoming ball (which is not the same each time) and needs good anticipation timing to know when to strike the ball (see Figure 12.13). While the timing skills of some children may have developed with practice, one of the most difficult challenges related to volleying is how much force to expend upon the ball to send it away. Even as adults, many of you may have struggled with accuracy when trying to volley.

Sample Learning Tasks for Volleying

Beginning volleying tasks should reduce some of the uncertainty implicit in the full skills. Striking balloons and lightweight objects without concern for the direction of the flight is a good beginning, as is letting students first practice using "volley-bounce-catch" tasks. Box 12.7 highlights the progression for students learning the skill theme of volleying, and Figure 12.14 shows a graphic representation of sample learning tasks that follow this progression.

volleying
Striking an object while it is in the air with a part of the body.

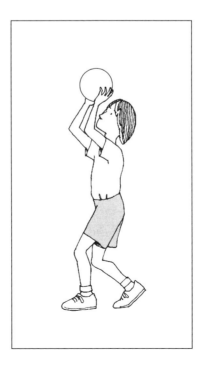

FIGURE **12.13**
Volleying overhand involves considerable skill in anticipation timing. The child has to move on the ball at the precise time to put the body in the best place.

Source: Reprinted with permission from Queensland Studies Authority.

BOX **12.7** ■ **Progression for Children Developing Volleying Skills**

Volleying

1. Volley to self once (use hands, knees, arms) and catch.

2. Volley to self continuously.

3. Volley a toss from an experienced tosser (stationary).

4. Volley while moving.

5. Volley back and forth with a partner.

6. Volley in a gamelike situation.

Developing Skills (Typically Grades K through 2)

In the developing phase of volleying, children learn to use a variety of body parts to contact an object in the air. They struggle with making contact and are far from the point where they can direct the ball effectively. Appropriate tasks at this place would include encouraging students to strike a variety of objects with different body parts while stationary. These students are able to master volleying only light-weight objects. As they move on to the expanding phase, they begin to have control of heavier objects in their volleys.

DS ❶	**Volleying Lightweight Objects while Stationary**
Pacing:	*Self-paced*
Grade Level:	Typically lower elementary (K–2)
Content Focus:	*Exploration of volleying lightweight objects to work on tracking the ball in flight*
Setup:	Children, each with a balloon, are scattered in general space.
Task:	On my signal, go to one of the spots and use your hand to volley (hit the balloon while it is in the air) the balloon above your head using a light force. Try to keep the balloon above your head without leaving your spot. Ready, begin!
	This time, volley the balloon above your head but jump up into the air and meet the balloon as it drops, thus giving your balloon a high five. Remember to try to stay on your spot. Ready, begin!
Cues:	Keep the hand flat.
	Watch the ball.
Variation:	Vary the object, height of volley, and body part.

DS ❷	**Volleying and Catching**
Pacing:	*Self-paced*
Grade Level:	Lower elementary (K–2)
Content Focus:	*Exploration of volleying by catching the ball after one or two contacts*
Setup:	Children, each with a lightweight foam ball, are scattered in general space.

continued

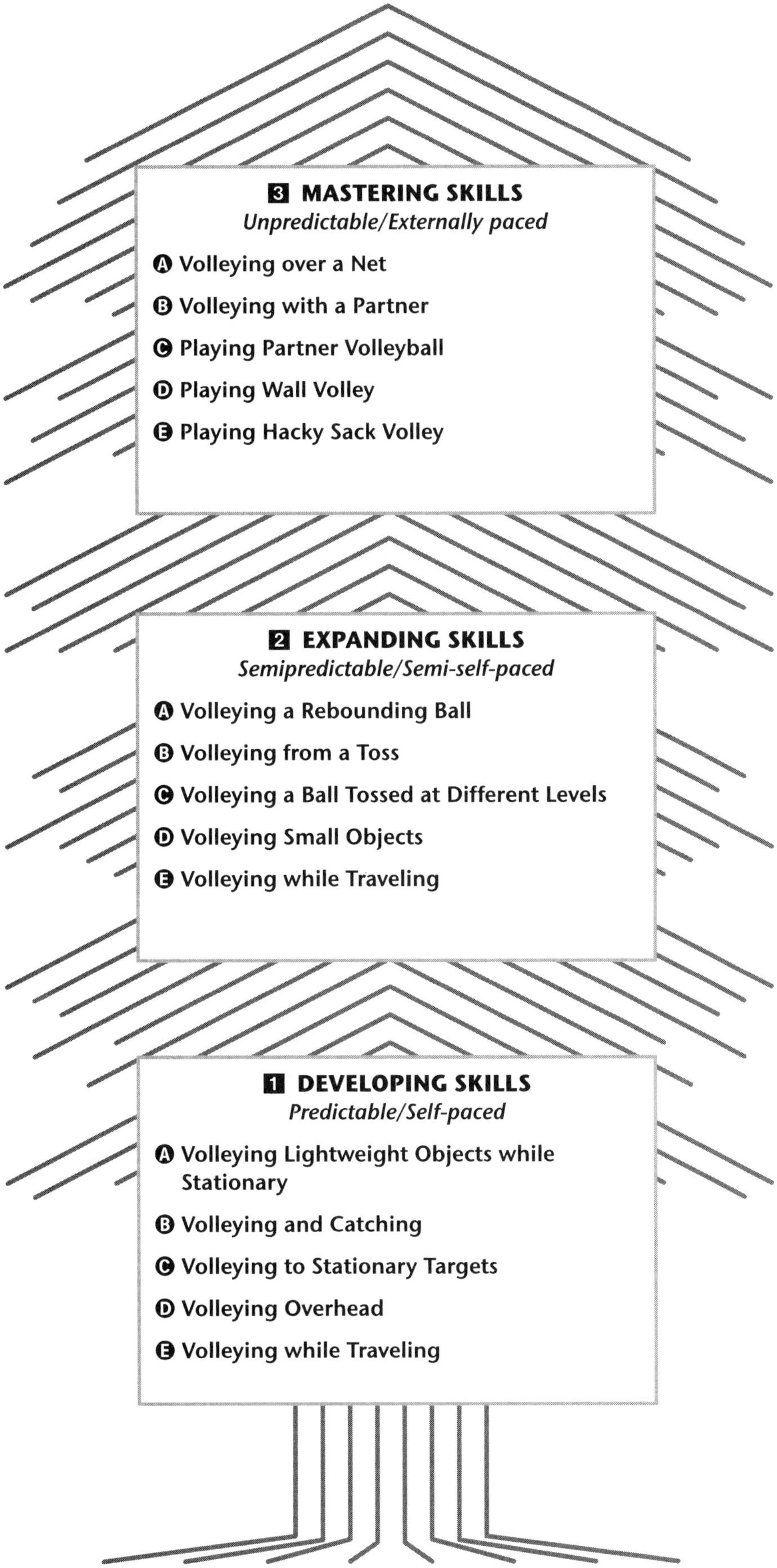

3 MASTERING SKILLS
Unpredictable/Externally paced

Ⓐ Volleying over a Net

Ⓑ Volleying with a Partner

Ⓒ Playing Partner Volleyball

Ⓓ Playing Wall Volley

Ⓔ Playing Hacky Sack Volley

2 EXPANDING SKILLS
Semipredictable/Semi-self-paced

Ⓐ Volleying a Rebounding Ball

Ⓑ Volleying from a Toss

Ⓒ Volleying a Ball Tossed at Different Levels

Ⓓ Volleying Small Objects

Ⓔ Volleying while Traveling

1 DEVELOPING SKILLS
Predictable/Self-paced

Ⓐ Volleying Lightweight Objects while Stationary

Ⓑ Volleying and Catching

Ⓒ Volleying to Stationary Targets

Ⓓ Volleying Overhead

Ⓔ Volleying while Traveling

FIGURE **12.14**
Progression tree for volleying

DS **B**	*Volleying and Catching, continued*
Task:	Choose a ball from the bin and go to one of the spots that are placed around the gym. On my signal, volley the ball once, using your knee, and then catch it. Ready, begin!
	This time, see if you can volley the ball with your knee at least twice before catching it. Ready, begin!
	This time, I want you to try a body part other than your knee. Ready, begin!
Cues:	Keep the volleying surface flat (knee).
	Keep the knee stiff.
Variation:	Vary the height, object, level, and body part.

DS **C**	**Volleying to Stationary Targets**
Pacing:	*Self-paced*
Grade Level:	Typically lower elementary (K–2)
Content Focus:	*Exploration of volleying to a target*
Setup:	Children, each with a ball, are scattered in general space, standing on a spot facing the wall.
Task:	Go stand on one of the spots you see in front of the different targets that have been placed on the wall. While standing on your spot, I want you to bounce the ball once and volley the ball (using an underhand pattern—hand below the waist to hand above the waist) to one of the targets on the wall. Ready, begin!
	This time I want you to take your ball, toss it to yourself and volley the ball using your hand so that it hits the high target at a high level.
Cues:	Keep the hand below the waist to above the waist.
	Follow through toward the target.
Variation:	Vary the bounce, body part, ball, and target.

DS **D**	**Volleying Overhead**
Pacing:	*Self-paced*
Grade Level:	Typically lower elementary (K–2)
Content Focus:	*Exploration of volleying using an overhand pattern*
Setup:	Children, each with a ball, are scattered in general space, standing on a spot facing the wall.
Task:	Go stand on one of the spots you see in front of the different targets on the wall. On my signal, toss the beach ball to yourself; and, using the overhead pattern (looks like a volleyball set with two hands using the pads of your fingers), volley the ball to one of the targets on the wall. Volley it once, catch it, and volley it again. Keep practicing until I say, "Cut."
Cues:	Extend arms to the target.
	Keep the hands above the head.
Variation:	Vary the height, target, and distance.

DS **E**	**Volleying while Traveling**
Pacing:	*Self-paced*
Grade Level:	Typically lower elementary (K–2)
Content Focus:	*Exploration of volleying while traveling in general space*
Setup:	Children, each with a ball or balloon, are scattered in general space.

continued

DS ❸	Volleying while Traveling, continued
Task:	After you get a balloon or beach ball from the basket, spread out in general space. On the signal, I want you to start volleying your ball above your head while traveling around the gym. Remember to keep the ball close to you so that you don't lose control of it.
	As we continue moving around the gym with our ball, this time I want you to volley the balloon or beach ball using your knee only. Ready, begin!
Cues:	Keep the volley surface flat like a pancake.
	Keep your eye on the ball.
Variation:	Vary the ball and body part.

Expanding Skills (Typically Grades 1 through 3)

As students move into the expanding phase of volleying, they can volley the ball continuously with control while staying in their self-space. They can use this ability in less stable environments such as working with a partner or volleying a ball after it rebounds from a wall.

ES ❹	Volleying a Rebounding Ball
Pacing:	*Semi-self-paced*
Grade Level:	Typically elementary (1–3)
Content Focus:	*Expanding volleying by working on volleying a ball after it rebounds from a wall*
Setup:	Children, each with a ball, are scattered in general space, standing on a spot facing the wall.
Task:	Stand on one of the spots you see in front of the wall. On my signal, pick up the ball on the spot and, using an underhand striking pattern, volley it against the wall. Use the pattern: volley, bounce once (on return from wall), volley, bounce once, and volley. Keep this pattern going until you hear the signal to stop.
Cues:	Stay behind the ball.
	Use quick feet.
Variation:	Vary the distance, volley pattern, and body part for contact.

ES ❸	Volleying from a Toss
Pacing:	*Semi-self-paced*
Grade Level:	Typically elementary (1–3)
Content Focus:	*Expanding volleying a ball from a soft toss*
Setup:	Partners are scattered in general space with one ball per pair.
	Children decide the working distance.
Task:	You have two seconds to stand by a partner. One person will be the tosser, the other the passer. The passer will volley the ball right back to the tosser using the forearms only. The tosser will catch it and toss it again. Take five turns then change roles. Ready, begin!
	This time, I want the passer to use only one arm to volley the ball back to the tosser. Change roles after five volleys. Ready, begin!
Cues:	The contact surface is flat.
	Extend your arms toward the target.
Variation:	Vary the number of volleys, the ball used, and the distance of toss.

ES ⓒ   **Volleying a Ball Tossed at Different Levels**

Pacing: *Semi-self-paced*

Grade Level: Typically elementary (1–3)

Content Focus: *Expanding volleying by contacting a ball that has been tossed as different levels*

Setup: Partners are scattered in general space with one ball per pair.

                   Children decide the working distance.

Task: With your partner, I want you to spread out in a space that you can work in responsibly. On my signal, the tosser is to toss the ball at a low level so the volleyer has to bend the knees in order to volley the ball. What part of the body do we want to use to contact the ball? Yes, the forearms. Tosser, make sure you toss it so that your partner doesn't have to move. Ready, begin.

Cues: Keep arms straight, elbows together.

                   Get the body in the path of the ball.

Variation: Vary the level of toss, and type of ball.

ES ⓓ   **Volleying Small Objects**

Pacing: *Semi-self-paced*

Grade Level: Typically elementary (1–3)

Content Focus: *Expanding volleying by working with small objects*

Setup: Children are scattered in general space standing on a spot. On each spot is a Hacky Sack.

Task: On the signal, I want you to go to one of the spots you see in general space, where you will find a Hacky Sack. While staying in your self-space, practice volleying the Hacky Sack with one foot. See if you can volley it continuously. Ready, begin!

                   Change the foot you are working with. Ready, begin!

                   This time, I want you to alternate between your right and left foot. Ready, begin!

Cues: Use quick feet.

                   The contact surface is flat.

Variation: Vary number of contacts.

ES ⓔ   **Volleying while Traveling**

Pacing: *Semi-self-paced*

Grade Level: Typically elementary (1–3)

Content Focus: *Expanding volleying while traveling to keep an object in the air*

Setup: Children, each with an object to volley, are scattered in general space.

Task: Choose an object that you feel comfortable volleying with from the ones you see placed around the gym (beach ball, foam balls, lightweight soccer balls) and then find your personal space in the gym. On the signal, start volleying your object while walking in general space. Use whatever body parts you need to keep the ball in the air while you are traveling. You may not use the same body part twice in a row. The pattern can be hand-knee-foot-knee-hand. The pattern cannot be hand-hand-foot-head.

Cues: Keep your eye on the ball.

                   Keep good posture.

Variation: Vary ball and pattern.

Mastering Skills (Typically Grades 3 through 5)

In the mastering phase of volleying, children can volley a ball with control and consistency to perform tasks in a more unpredictable environment. Students in this phase track the ball well with their eyes, get their body in good position to hit the ball, and begin to pass accurately. They begin to attend to other dynamics in the environment, such as volleying with a partner or volleying back and forth across a net.

MS ❶	**Volleying over a Net**
Pacing:	*Externally paced*
Grade Level:	Typically upper elementary (3–5)
Content Focus:	*Mastering volleying over a net to a partner*
Setup:	Partners stand across a net from each other. The net consists of two cones with a jump rope drawn between them. Refer to the diagram below.
Task:	With your partner, get a ball from the bin. Now, stand across the net from each other. One partner will toss the ball to the other. The second partner will use the two-handed overhead pass or the forearm pass to volley the ball over the net. Each person should have five tries and then change roles. Ready, begin!
Diagram:	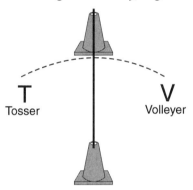
	T — Tosser V — Volleyer
Cues:	Keep your arms straight—elbows together (forearms).
	Keep both hands above the hairline (overhead).
Variation:	Vary the distance, the ball, and height of the net.

MS ❷	**Volleying with a Partner**
Pacing:	*Externally paced*
Grade Level:	Typically upper elementary (3–5)
Content Focus:	*Mastering volleying back and forth with a partner*
Setup:	Partners are scattered in general space.
Task:	There are red and blue poly spots scattered throughout the gymnasium. On the signal, go stand on one of the poly spots. You will notice that there is a ball on each blue spot. The person standing directly opposite of you on the red spot is your partner. With your partner, volley the ball back and forth continuously without losing control. You may use any body part for this task except the head (i.e., hands, knees, feet, and arms). Action!
Cues:	Get your body in the path of the ball.
	Watch the ball.
Variation:	Vary partners, distance, and type of ball.

MS ⓒ   **Playing Partner Volleyball**

Pacing: *Externally paced*

Grade Level: Typically upper elementary (3–5)

Content Focus: *Mastering volleying while working with a partner to keep the ball in play*

Setup: Groups of four are working at one net. The net is approximately 5 ft. high.

Task: This activity will require groups of four. There will be two people on each side of the low nets you see around the gym. At each net you will find a balloon, a beach ball, or a playground ball. Your group may choose one of the items with which to practice. Your task in your group is to try to keep the item up for as many volleys as you can. Each person must hit the object before it can count as one cycle. See how many cycles your group can get through before you lose control of the ball. Ready, begin!

Cues: Keep the contact surface flat.

                 Move to the ball.

Variation: Vary the partner, type of ball, and number of hits.

MS ⓓ   **Playing Wall Volley**

Pacing: *Externally paced*

Grade Level: Typically upper elementary (3–5)

Content Focus: *Mastering volleying against a wall to keep the ball going*

Setup: Partners standing at one of the play areas in front of a wall. Refer to the diagram below.

Task: In pairs, find one of the play areas marked on the wall around the gym. This game is called "volley wall ball." The object is for you and your partner to keep the ball from striking the ground. The first person will volley the ball to the wall above the dotted line, and the second person will try to return it above the line before the ball hits the ground. Keep alternating hits until the ball hits the ground. Any part of the body may be used to volley the ball. Ready, begin!

                 This time, you may choose to score your game. The person who fails to return the ball above the dotted line loses a point. Ready, begin!

Diagram:

Cues: Use quick feet.

                 Watch the ball.

Variation: Vary the space and ball.

MS ⓔ   **Playing Hacky Sack Volley**

Pacing: *Externally paced*

Grade Level: Typically upper elementary (3–5)

Content Focus: *Mastering volleying a small object within a group*

Setup: Groups of three or four are scattered in general space.

Task: On my signal, one person in your group of three or four will come get a Hacky Sack from the crate. Your group is trying to keep the Hacky Sack from hitting the floor. You may use only your feet. Ready, begin!

continued

MS ❸	*Playing Hacky Sack Volley, continued*
Cues:	Keep the contact surface flat.
	Use quick feet.
Variation:	Vary number of players and body parts for contact.

STRIKING WITH RACKETS AND PADDLES

Striking uses a piece of equipment to hit a ball or other object, moving it through the air or along the ground. To successfully strike a moving object, children need hand–eye coordination, visual tracking skills, and good timing. Because hand–eye coordination is more difficult for children when the object is further from the body, beginning striking tasks should use either the hand or short-handled paddles (see Figure 12.15).

Sample Learning Tasks
for Striking with Rackets and Paddles

In the early stages, students will focus on striking with one and two hands into open space and then explore paddle striking by hitting the ball with the face of the paddle. In this phase, students should be using larger paddles and slower or larger balls. Later they will challenge themselves to keep striking a ball individually and in cooperative partnerships that will progress to striking objects over a net or a rope. Once partnership play has been established and students can achieve some form of continuity, the focus of striking becomes hitting the ball *away* from the

striking
Using a piece of equipment to hit an object, making it move through the air or along the ground.

FIGURE **12.15**
Children find it easier to begin striking tasks with short-handled paddles rather than longer-handled rackets.

Source: Reprinted with permission from Queensland Studies Authority.

BOX **12.8** ■ **Progression for Children Developing Striking with Rackets and Paddles Skills**

Striking with Rackets and Paddles

1. Balance object on racket or paddle.

2. Strike stationary objects (if possible: suspended objects like balls or shuttlecocks).

3. Strike lightweight objects into the air once and then catch, staying in self-space.

4. Strike lightweight objects into the air continuously while staying in self-space.

5. Strike objects against a wall one time.

6. Strike heavier objects continuously into air.

7. Strike objects continuously against a wall.

8. Strike objects back and forth with a partner.

partner. Box 12.8 highlights the progression for students learning the skill theme of striking, and Figure 12.16 shows a graphic representation of sample learning tasks that follow this progression.

Developing Skills (Typically Grades K through 2)

One of the hardest aspects of learning to strike with a racket or paddle is for the student to develop a feel for the implement in the hand and work on eye–hand coordination. In developing this ability, students work on balancing balls on the racket or paddle and striking the ball once and catching it. Gradually, they learn to strike lightweight balls or objects continuously while staying in self-space and while traveling.

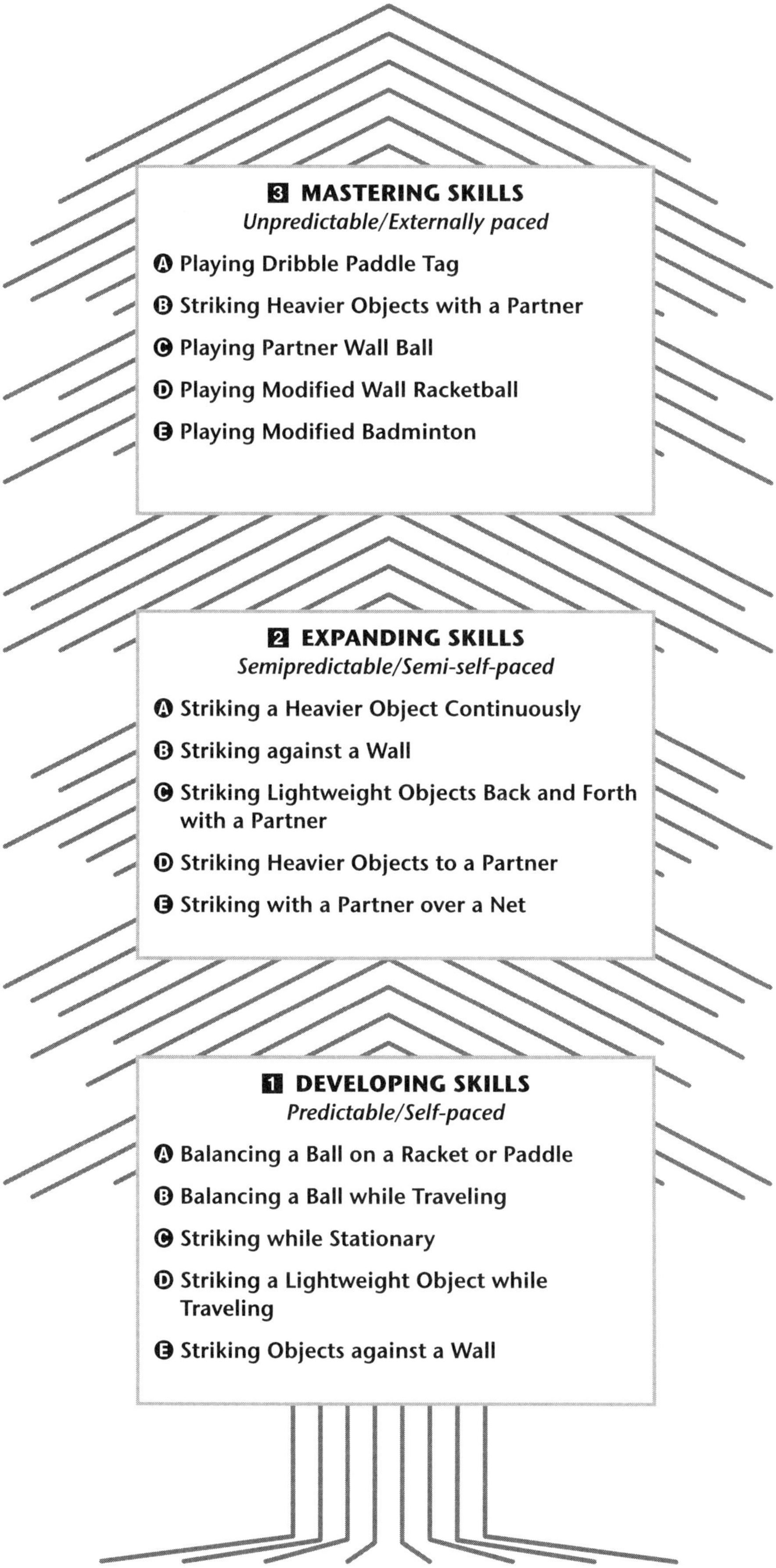

3 MASTERING SKILLS
Unpredictable/Externally paced

Ⓐ Playing Dribble Paddle Tag

Ⓑ Striking Heavier Objects with a Partner

Ⓒ Playing Partner Wall Ball

Ⓓ Playing Modified Wall Racketball

Ⓔ Playing Modified Badminton

2 EXPANDING SKILLS
Semipredictable/Semi-self-paced

Ⓐ Striking a Heavier Object Continuously

Ⓑ Striking against a Wall

Ⓒ Striking Lightweight Objects Back and Forth with a Partner

Ⓓ Striking Heavier Objects to a Partner

Ⓔ Striking with a Partner over a Net

1 DEVELOPING SKILLS
Predictable/Self-paced

Ⓐ Balancing a Ball on a Racket or Paddle

Ⓑ Balancing a Ball while Traveling

Ⓒ Striking while Stationary

Ⓓ Striking a Lightweight Object while Traveling

Ⓔ Striking Objects against a Wall

FIGURE **12.16**
Progression tree for striking with rackets and paddles

DS Ⓐ

Balancing a Ball on a Racket or Paddle

Pacing:	*Self paced*
Grade Level:	Typically lower elementary (K–2)
Content Focus:	*Exploration of striking by learning to get the "feel" of having the racket in the hand*
Setup:	Children are scattered in general space with a yarn ball and a paddle.
Task:	Everyone stand in general space with your yarn ball and paddle. On my signal, the first thing I want you to do it try to balance the yarn ball on your paddle while you are standing still. Ready, begin!
Cues:	Keep the paddle flat.
	Keep the wrist stiff.
Variation:	Vary the ball.

DS Ⓑ

Balancing a Ball while Traveling

Pacing:	*Self-paced*
Grade Level:	Lower elementary (K–2)
Content Focus:	*Exploration of getting the "feel" of the racket while balancing a ball while traveling*
Setup:	Children, each with a yarn ball and a paddle, are scattered in general space.
Task:	You are doing a good job balancing the yarn ball while standing still. On my signal, continue to balance the ball on your paddle as you move in general space. Go slowly at first, just to make sure you can maintain control of the ball on your paddle. Keep traveling until you hear the signal to stop.
Cues:	Keep the paddle flat as a pancake.
	Keep the wrist stiff.
Variation:	Vary the ball, speed, and level of paddle or racket.

DS Ⓒ

Striking while Stationary

Pacing:	*Self-paced*
Grade Level:	Typically lower elementary (K–2)
Content Focus:	*Exploration of striking a lightweight object while staying in self-space*
Setup:	Children, each with a paddle and a balloon, are scattered in general space.
Task:	As you stand in your self-space with your paddle and balloon, use an underhand motion to hit the balloon once into the air and then catch it. I want you to remain in your self-space. Keep practicing strike and catch until you hear me say, "Cut."
	This time, still using our underhand motion, strike the balloon without catching it; instead of catching it, strike the ball again until you hear me say, "Cut." Are you ready to start? Action!
Cues:	Keep your paddle flat.
	Swing upward.
Variation:	Vary the lightweight object, height, and level; use the hand.

DS Ⓓ

Striking a Lightweight Object while Traveling

Pacing:	*Self-paced*
Grade Level:	Typically lower elementary (K–2)
Content Focus:	*Exploration of striking lightweight objects while traveling*
Setup:	Children, each with a racket and a balloon, are scattered and moving in general space.

continued

DS ⓓ	*Striking a Lightweight Object while Traveling, continued*
Task:	On my signal, use the overhand (racket above shoulder) and the underhand (racket below waist) motion to keep the balloon going while you travel in general space. Remember to keep the paddle flat and your eyes on the balloon so that you can keep it going longer. Ready, action!
Cues:	Keep the paddle flat.
	Keep your eye on the ball.
Variation:	Vary the height, speed, motion, and object.

DS ⓔ	**Striking Objects against a Wall**
Pacing:	*Self-paced*
Grade Level:	Typically lower elementary (K–2)
Content Focus:	*Exploration of striking an object once against a wall*
Setup:	Children are scattered in general space, standing on a spot facing a wall.
Task:	After you get a foam ball or a yellow All Ball from the basket, stand on one of the spots you see in front of the wall. When I say, "Begin," strike the ball once against the wall and catch it. Ready, begin!
Cues:	Take the racket back.
	Keep your side to the target.
Variation:	Vary the ball, distance, height, and racket or paddle.

Expanding Skills (Typically Grades 1 through 3)

As students move into the expanding phase of striking with a racket or paddle, they can consistently strike a lightweight object. They can account for the length of the racket or paddle in their hand by moving their body into a position that lets them successfully hit the ball. In this phase, they are challenged by continuously striking heavier and irregularly shaped objects as well as balls that rebound from a wall or partner. Partner work at this level is cooperative.

ES ⓐ	**Striking a Heavier Object Continuously**
Pacing:	*Semi-self-paced*
Grade Level:	Typically elementary (1–3)
Content Focus:	*Expanding striking by continuously hitting heavier objects*
Setup:	Children, each with a racket and a whiffle ball, are scattered in general space.
Task:	While standing in self-space with your racket and your whiffle ball, try to hit the ball into the air and catch it once. Remember to use the handshake grip with the palm of your hand facing the sky. Ready, begin.
	This time, turn you hand over so that the palm of your hand is facing the ground. This is called the backhand grip. Remember to strike the ball once and catch it. Ready, begin!
Cues:	Your knuckles are on top of grip with your palm facing down (backhand grip).
	Keep the racket flat.
Variation:	Vary the object and grip.

ES ⓑ	Striking against a Wall
Pacing:	*Semi self paced*
Grade Level:	Typically elementary (1–3)
Content Focus:	*Expanding striking by hitting a ball against a wall from the rebound*
Setup:	Children are scattered in general space, each standing on a spot facing a wall.
Task:	On my signal, stand on one of the spots in front of the wall, where I have placed a racket and ball. Strike the ball against the wall and wait for it to bounce once before you strike it again. I want you to keep the ball going in this pattern until I say, "Freeze." The key is that you must use gentle taps to keep it going against the wall. Remember, the sequence should be strike, bounce, strike, bounce, strike, and bounce. Ready, begin!
	As you learn to control the ball as you hit it against the wall, increase your distance from the wall. You may choose the distance you would like to work from. The key is that you must be able to maintain control of the ball as you are striking. If you cannot control the ball, move closer to the wall. Ready, begin!
	I have placed a line about 3 ft. high on the wall. As you are striking the ball against the wall, I want you to make sure that it goes above the line each time. Ready, begin!
Cues:	Slant the paddle (hit the ball up).
	Stand sideways to the target.
Variation:	Vary number of bounce, ball, distance, and height.

ES ⓒ	Striking Lightweight Objects Back and Forth with a Partner
Pacing:	*Semi-self-paced*
Grade Level:	Typically elementary (1–3)
Content Focus:	*Expanding striking with a partner using lightweight objects*
Setup:	Partners are scattered in general space. Each child has a paddle and each pair has a balloon. The children determine the working distance.
Task:	As you stand across from your partner with your balloon, I want the two of you to strike the balloon with your paddle back and forth, keeping the balloon off the floor or ground. Ready, begin!
Cues:	Watch the balloon.
	Follow through to the target.
Variation:	Vary the object and distance.

ES ⓓ	Striking Heavier Objects to a Partner
Pacing:	*Semi-self-paced*
Grade Level:	Typically elementary (1–3)
Content Focus:	*Expanding striking by hitting heavier objects to a partner*
Setup:	Partners are scattered in general space. Each child has a racket, and each pair has a whiffle ball. The children decide the working distance.
Task:	As you stand across from your partner, I want you to bounce the whiffle ball once and strike it so that your partner is able to catch it. Remember to keep your racket flat and to control your strike. Your partner will catch the ball and then softly bounce it back to you, and you will strike it back to your partner. After five hits, change roles with your partner.
Cues:	Use a good tempo and gentle taps.
	Swing the racket from low to high.
Variation:	Vary the distance and number of hits.

ES ❸	**Striking with a Partner over a Net**
Pacing:	*Semi-self-paced*
Grade Level:	Typically elementary (1–3)
Content Focus:	*Expanding striking by working with a partner to keep the ball going over a net*
Setup:	Partners stand across a net (made with two cones and a jump rope) from each other. Each child has a racket.
Task:	With your partner, you may choose between a whiffle ball or a foam ball to complete the task. Stand across the net from your partner. On my signal, strike the object you chose back and forth over the net with your partner. The key is to keep the object going whether you have to hit it in the air or after it bounces. Keep practicing until you hear me say, "Cut." Ready, begin!
	This time, you can use a different object or the same one you originally chose to keep it going with your partner. Remember to keep your eye on the ball. Ready, begin!
Cues:	Keep your eye on the ball.
	Keep the wrist stiff.
	Slant the paddle.
Variation:	Vary partners, distance, and type of ball.

Mastering Skills (Typically Grades 3 through 5)

As students move into the mastering phase of striking with a racket or paddle, they have a good "feel" of the implement and can consistently strike heavier objects. They can do this in more unpredictable environments, including striking while moving or responding to an opponent trying to strike the ball away from them.

MS ❶	**Playing Dribble Paddle Tag**
Pacing:	*Externally paced*
Grade Level:	Typically upper elementary (3–5)
Content Focus:	*Mastering striking by manipulating the object while moving*
Setup:	Children, each with a paddle and a ball, are scattered in general space.
Task:	This game is called dribble paddle tag. Everyone should have a ball and a paddle. Everyone with a white shirt on is "It." On my signal, you are to spread out and begin dribbling your ball with the paddle. This should look like the dribble you use in basketball except that you are using a paddle. If you are tagged, you must continue to dribble the ball with the paddle while standing in place. Keep this up until you can touch paddles with someone who is unfrozen. Once you touch paddles, you become unfrozen. Ready, begin!
Cues:	Push the paddle down.
	Use a firm wrist.
Variation:	Vary the distance and ball.

MS ❷	**Striking Heavier Objects with a Partner**
Pacing:	*Externally paced*
Grade Level:	Typically upper elementary (3–5)
Content Focus:	*Mastering striking by hitting back and forth with a partner*
Setup:	Partners are scattered in general space. Each child has a paddle, and each pair has a ball. The children determine the working distance.

continued

MS Ⓑ   *Striking Heavier Objects with a Partner, continued*

Task: As you stand across from your partner, I want you to keep the ball going for as long as you can. If you miss, pick the ball up and continue practicing. For this task, the ball is to be struck in the air. No bounces are allowed. Ready, begin!

Cues: Stay behind the ball.

           Keep your paddle flat.

Variation: Vary partners, distance, and type of ball.

MS Ⓒ   **Playing Partner Wall Ball**

Pacing: *Externally paced*

Grade Level: Typically upper elementary (3–5)

Content Focus: *Mastering striking with a partner against a wall*

Setup: Partners are standing facing the wall. Each child has a paddle, and each pair has a ball. Children must stand behind line that is 3 ft. from the wall (no-volley zone). Children cannot enter this space to hit the ball. On the wall is a line 3 ft. high.

Task: Stand with your partner in front of the wall. We are going to work with our partner, alternating hits against the wall. You will need to work cooperatively in order to keep the ball going. Make sure each hit goes above the line I have placed on the wall and lands beyond the no-volley zone. Remember, I do not want the same person to hit the ball more than once before his or her partner strikes it. Ready, begin!

Cues: Move your feet.

           Follow through to the target.

Variation: Vary the partner, type of ball, number of hits, and space.

MS Ⓓ   **Playing Modified Wall Racquetball**

Pacing: *Externally paced*

Grade Level: Typically upper elementary (3–5)

Content Focus: *Mastering striking while playing against an opponent*

Setup: Partners are standing facing the wall. Each child has a racket, and each pair has a ball. Children must stand behind line that is 3 ft. from the wall (no-volley zone). Children cannot enter this space to hit the ball. On the wall is a line 3 ft. high. Refer to the diagram.

Task: This time we are going to play a game of modified racquetball. Each player must stay behind the line (no-volley zone) that is 3 ft. from the wall. The ball is served underhand above the line on the wall, and you and your partner alternate hitting the ball. Each time the ball is served, anyone can score a point. Any ball that does not go above the line on the wall or lands beyond the no-volley zone is no longer in play, and the opponent scores a point. The ball must stay in the playing area that is marked by the lines on the floor. The key to this game is to have more points than your opponent when time is called. Ready, begin!

    Let's keep playing modified racquetball. This time, if you had the most points stay where you are; if you had fewer points, find a new opponent from the ones staying in their spot. Everyone should be playing against a different person. Ready, begin!

continued

MS ⅅ
Modified Wall Racquetball, continued

Diagram:

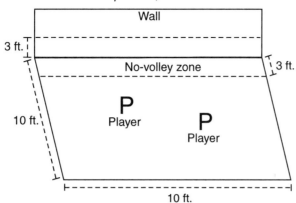

Cues: Use quick feet.

Watch the ball.

Variation: Vary the space and ball.

MS ⅇ **Playing Modified Badminton**

Pacing: *Externally paced*

Grade Level: Typically upper elementary (3–5)

Content Focus: *Mastering striking by playing a modified badminton game*

Setup: Partners are standing on the same side of net across from another pair. Each child has a racket, and each group of four has a shuttlecock or birdie. The net is approximately 2 ft. high. Refer to the diagram below.

Task: Stand with your partner. Now go stand on the same side of the net. Across from you will be two other people. I want you to work cooperatively with the other three people in your group in trying to keep the shuttlecock or birdie going back and forth over the net. Ready, begin!

This time you are going to try and score points with your partner against the two people on the other side of the net. The way you score points is for the birdie to hit the floor in the boundary area on the other side of the net. There must be at least two hits before a point can be scored. A different person must start the birdie each time. Ready, begin!

Diagram:

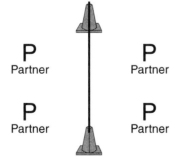

Cues: Snap the wrist on contact.

Watch the shuttle.

Variation: Vary the number of players, mode of scoring, and space.

STRIKING
WITH LONG-HANDLED IMPLEMENTS

Striking with a long-handled implement is a skill used in many games. Softball, baseball, and cricket players use the bat to send a ball into play, usually intending great force. Hockey players use the stick not only to strike the puck hard but also to control it and maneuver it in small spaces. Golf also requires a variation in force, with the objective of hitting the ball very long distances or tapping it into a small target.

Depending on the angle of contact, striking with a long-handled bat can move the ball either through the air or along the ground. The ball can also be struck from either side of the body and from different levels using one or both hands. With experience, the striking action can impart spin, increase or decrease power, affect placement, and improve control.

Striking happens in both the horizontal (sidearm) and vertical (underhand and overhand) planes. Horizontal examples include hitting with a softball bat and many strokes in the racket sports, while vertical examples are common in golf, hockey, and the various forms of polo.

Sample Learning Tasks
for Striking with Long-Handled Implements

Because learning to strike with a long-handled implement is complex, it is generally the last fundamental motor pattern learned. Several variables contribute to the difficulty in learning this motor skill, such as the length of the implement, the distance of the object from the body, and the need for fully developed visual tracking skills for eye–hand coordination. These factors can be overcome with practice and quality learning tasks. Figure 12.17 shows a graphic representation of sample learning tasks that follow this progression, and Box 12.9 highlights the progression for children learning the skill theme of striking with long-handled impements.

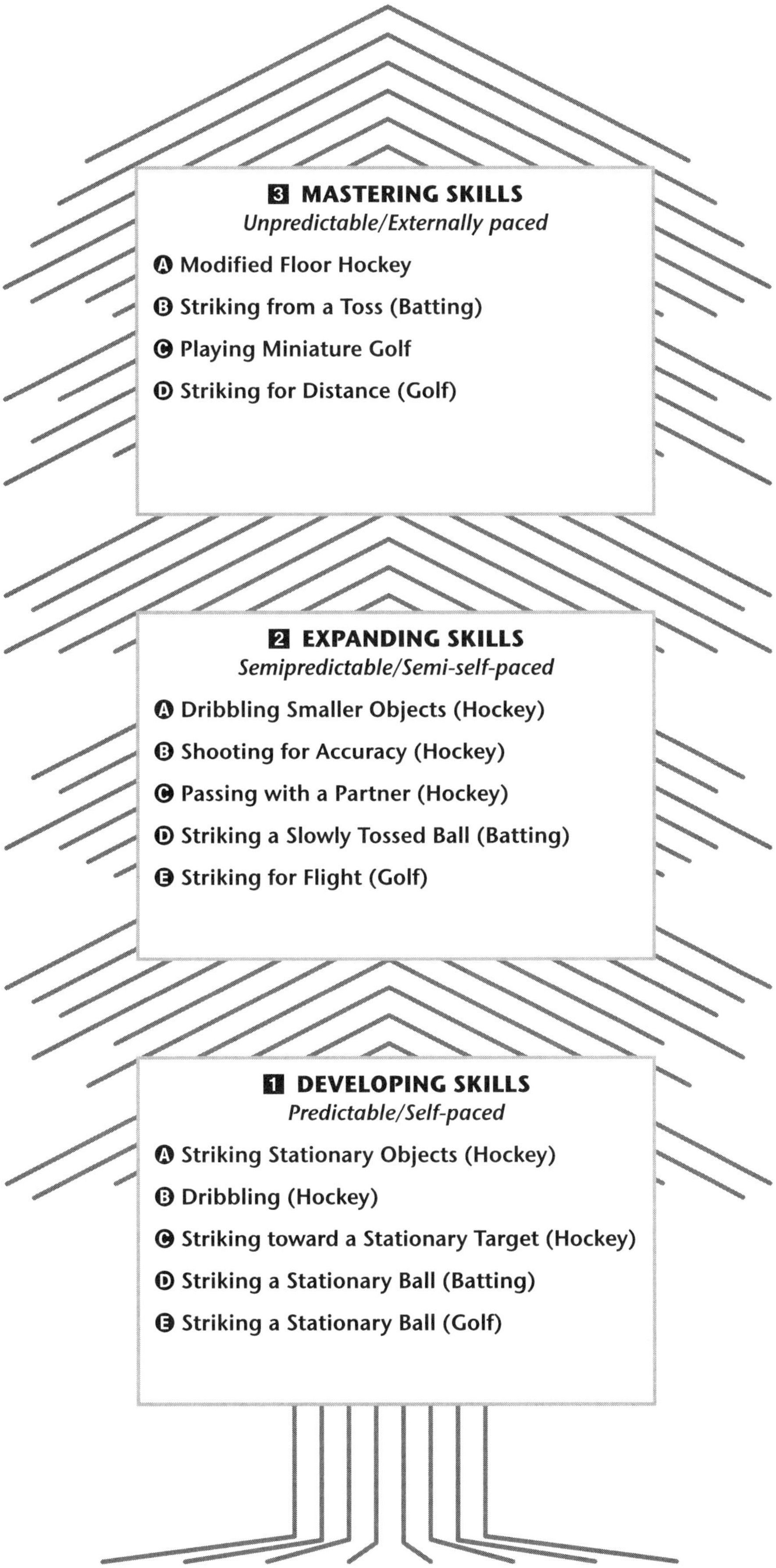

3 MASTERING SKILLS
Unpredictable/Externally paced

A Modified Floor Hockey

B Striking from a Toss (Batting)

C Playing Miniature Golf

D Striking for Distance (Golf)

2 EXPANDING SKILLS
Semipredictable/Semi-self-paced

A Dribbling Smaller Objects (Hockey)

B Shooting for Accuracy (Hockey)

C Passing with a Partner (Hockey)

D Striking a Slowly Tossed Ball (Batting)

E Striking for Flight (Golf)

1 DEVELOPING SKILLS
Predictable/Self-paced

A Striking Stationary Objects (Hockey)

B Dribbling (Hockey)

C Striking toward a Stationary Target (Hockey)

D Striking a Stationary Ball (Batting)

E Striking a Stationary Ball (Golf)

FIGURE **12.17**
Progression tree for striking with long-handled implements

FIGURE 12.18
For early experiences when hitting with long-handled implements, the ball should be stationary.

Source: Reprinted with permission from Queensland Studies Authority.

Developing Skills (Typically Grades K through 2)

The challenge of striking with long-handled implements is making contact with an object that is far away from the body. This is difficult, because the objects are closer in most other manipulative skills, even when striking with rackets and paddles. In the developing phase of striking with long-handled implements like bats and golf clubs, children need to strike large and stationary objects (see Figure 12.18). When using a hockey stick, children should explore striking toward stationary targets while remaining still and then begin to explore dribbling the ball or puck with the stick while moving.

DS Ⓐ   **Striking Stationary Objects (Hockey)**

Pacing:	*Self-paced*
Grade Level:	Typically lower elementary (K–2)
Content Focus:	*Exploration of striking a stationary object with a hockey stick*
Setup:	Children, each with a yarn ball and a floor hockey stick, are scattered in general space.
Task:	Everyone stand in general space with a hockey stick and yarn ball. On my signal, the first thing I want you to do is tap the stick lightly on the ground on each side of the ball. I don't want you to touch the ball. Ready, begin!
	I want you to move your stick a little more quickly this time. Ready, begin!
	This time I want you to use your stick to move the ball from side to side using quick taps. The taps should be so quick and light that I won't hear your stick touch the ground. Ready, begin!
Cues:	Place the hand you brush your teeth with halfway down the stick.
	Use quick taps.
Variation:	Vary the ball and speed.

DS Ⓑ   **Dribbling (Hockey)**

Pacing:	*Self-paced*
Grade Level:	Typically lower elementary (K–2)
Content Focus:	*Exploration of dribbling a ball with the hockey stick while traveling*
Setup:	Children, each with a yarn ball and a floor hockey stick, are scattered in general space.
Task:	On my signal, begin dribbling the yarn ball with your stick in general space. Let's start slowly so that we can maintain control of the ball while we are working. Be sure not to bump into your neighbor. Ready, begin!
Cues:	Use both sides of the blade.
	Push the ball forward.
Variation:	Vary the ball, speed, direction, and pathways.

DS Ⓒ   **Striking toward a Stationary Target (Hockey)**

Pacing:	*Self-paced*
Grade Level:	Typically lower elementary (K–2)
Content Focus:	*Exploration of striking toward stationary targets using a hockey stick*
Setup:	Children, each with a stick and a puck or ball, are scattered in general space standing on spots facing the wall. Refer to the diagram below.
Task:	As you stand on your spot in front of the wall, I want you to strike the puck or ball so that it hits the center target. Remember to follow through toward the target as you are shooting. Keep practicing until you hear the signal to stop.
	This time, aim so that your shot hits one of the side targets. Ready, begin!
Diagram:	

Target   Target   Target

5 ft.

_____

Shooting line

S

Shooter

continued

DS Ⓒ	*Striking toward a Stationary Target (Hockey), continued*
Cues:	Stay behind the puck.
	Drive the stick through the puck.
Variation:	Vary the target, distance, and ball.

DS Ⓓ	**Striking a Stationary Ball (Batting)**
Pacing:	*Self-paced*
Grade Level:	Typically lower elementary (K–2)
Content Focus:	*Exploration of striking stationary objects using a bat*
Setup:	Children, each with a bat, are scattered in general space, standing by a batting tee facing the wall. A foam ball is on each tee.
Task:	When I say, "Begin," use your bat to strike the foam ball on your batting tee toward the wall. Retrieve the ball and hit it again. Keep practicing striking the ball against the wall until you hear me say, "Cut."
	This time, concentrate on hitting the center of the ball with your bat. Are you ready to start? Begin!
Cues:	Start with the bat back.
	Start with your side to the target.
Variation:	Vary the distance.

DS Ⓔ	**Striking a Stationary Ball (Golf)**
Pacing:	*Self-paced*
Grade Level:	Typically lower elementary (K–2)
Content Focus:	*Exploration of striking stationary objects using a golf club*
Setup:	Children, each with a hula hoop, a golf club, and five balls, are scattered in general space.
Task:	Spread out in general space. You will not need your balls yet, so just place them on the ground beside you. The first thing I want you to do is take your golf club (i.e., children's size) and practice swinging the club back and forth like grandfather clock. Can you just skim the top of the grass with your club? Ready, begin!
	This time, get your whiffle balls; we are going to practice using the grandfather clock motion to put the balls into the hoop in front of you. You each have five balls. You may begin putting when you are ready.
Cues:	Keep your arms like a grandfather clock.
	Bend the knees slightly.
Variation:	Vary the ball.

Expanding Skills (Typically Grades 1 through 3)

As students move into the expanding phase of striking with long-handled implements, they start making consistent contact with a large stationary ball and can then be challenged by smaller balls (golf) or gently tossed balls (batting). In expanding their ability to strike using a hockey stick, they are challenged with smaller and heavier objects and shooting for accuracy. They now begin to work cooperatively with a partner in passing tasks.

ES **A**	Dribbling Smaller Objects (Hockey)
Pacing:	*Semi-self-paced*
Grade Level:	Typically elementary (1–3)
Content Focus:	*Expanding striking by dribbling a hockey puck while moving*
Setup:	Children, each with a hockey stick and a puck, are scattered in general space.
Task:	With your stick and puck, on my signal, I want you to begin dribbling the puck in general space. I want you to move at a speed that allows you to control the puck while dribbling. Ready, begin!
	As you are dribbling in general space, I am going to call out the pathway I want you to move in, such as straight, zigzag, or circle (i.e., curved). I want you to continue in that pathway until I give you a new one to perform. Spread out. Ready, begin!
Cues:	Use gentle taps, using both sides of the blade.
	Stay behind the puck.
Variation:	Vary the object, pathway, and speed.

ES **B**	Shooting for Accuracy (Hockey)
Pacing:	*Semi-self-paced*
Grade Level:	Typically elementary (1–3)
Content Focus:	*Expanding striking by shooting at stationary targets*
Setup:	Children are scattered in general space, standing on a spot facing the wall. Each has a ball and a floor hockey stick. Refer to the diagram below.
Task:	Let's play the game 11. If you hit that target (tennis can) in the center, you get one point, and hitting the target to the left or right of center is worth two points. You must shoot from behind the line that is 5 ft. in front of the targets. I will give you four minutes to try to accumulate 11 points. Ready, begin.
	Let's play 11 again. Remember the target in the center is worth one point, and the targets on either side of it are worth two points each. However, instead of shooting while stationary, we are going to begin dribbling from the first spot; when you get to the line 5 ft. from the wall, you can take your shot. Retrieve your ball and start again. Remember to keep your score. I will give you four minutes to try to accumulate 11 points. Ready, begin. I have placed a line about 3 ft. high on the wall. As you are striking the ball against the wall, I want you to make sure that it goes above the line each time. Ready, begin!
Diagram:	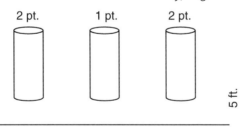

2 pt.   1 pt.   2 pt.

5 ft.

Shooting line

S
Shooter

Cues:	Drive the blade through the puck.
	Follow through to the target.
Variation:	Vary the time, distance, ball, and size of the targets.

ES ❻   **Passing with a Partner (Hockey)**

Pacing:	*Semi-self-paced*
Grade Level:	Typically elementary (1–3)
Content Focus:	*Expanding striking by passing with a partner*
Setup:	Partners are scattered in general space. Each child has a hockey stick; each pair has a puck.
Task:	Move with your partner to an area where you are standing about 10 ft. apart. On my signal, begin passing the puck back and forth. To receive the puck, gently "give" with the stick (bring the stick back slightly as the ball hits the stick). Keep passing and receiving until you hear me say, "Freeze." Ready, begin!
Cues:	Give or absorb the puck with the blade of the stick.
	Keep your side to the target.
Variation:	Vary the object and distance.

ES ❼   **Striking a Slowly Tossed Ball (Batting)**

Pacing:	*Semi-self-paced*
Grade Level:	Typically elementary (1–3)
Content Focus:	*Expanding striking by hitting heavier objects to a partner*
Setup:	Children are working with partners in a designated area in a large outdoor space. Each pair has a bat and several foam balls. Refer to the diagram below.
Task:	Your partner is going to slowly toss a foam ball in the air so that you can strike it with the bat. Take five swings before you retrieve the balls and change roles. Ready, begin!
	This time, as you work with your partner, see if you can strike the ball so that it lands farther than any of your previous five swings. Remember to retrieve the balls and change roles. Ready, begin!

Diagram:

Cues:	Watch the ball.
	Keep your hands together (writing hand on top).
Variation:	Vary the distance, height of toss, and tosser.

ES ❽   **Striking for Flight (Golf)**

Pacing:	*Semi-self-paced*
Grade Level:	Typically elementary (1–3)
Content Focus:	*Expanding striking by attaining height (chipping)*
Setup:	Children are scattered in general space, standing behind the chipping line. Each has a hoop about 10 ft. in front, a club, and five golf balls.

continued

<table>
<tr><td>ES ⓔ
Task:</td><td>Striking for Flight (Golf), continued
We are going to work on chipping today in golf. Spread out in general space with your five balls. We are going to try to get the ball in the air using a short backswing, still using the grandfather clock motion (straight back and straight forward). We want the balls to land in the hoops in front of you. Ready, begin!

Let's move the target (hoop) back further and try this again. Ready, begin!</td></tr>
<tr><td>Cues:</td><td>Swing the club like a pendulum (grandfather clock).

Use a baseball grip.</td></tr>
<tr><td>Variation:</td><td>Vary the height, targets, and distance.</td></tr>
</table>

Mastering Skills (Typically Grades 3 through 5)

As students move into the mastering phase of striking with long-handled implements, they consistently strike for distance and accuracy (golf and batting). Students need to be challenged by hitting a ball tossed from a pitcher and by work with a partner to score or avoid an opponent (hockey). In these tasks, the environment is neither stable nor predictable, thus adding to the difficulty of the movement.

<table>
<tr><td>MS ⓐ</td><td>Modified Floor Hockey</td></tr>
<tr><td>Pacing:</td><td>Externally paced</td></tr>
<tr><td>Grade Level:</td><td>Typically upper elementary (3–5)</td></tr>
<tr><td>Content Focus:</td><td>Mastering striking by using passing, dribbling, and shooting in a modified floor hockey game</td></tr>
<tr><td>Setup:</td><td>Partners are scattered in general space in one of the designated areas set up. Each child has a stick; each pair has a puck or ball. Two cones approximately 5 ft. apart serve as the goal area. Refer to the diagram.</td></tr>
<tr><td>Task:</td><td>With a partner, go to one of the designated areas. One player will be on offense, and one will be the defense. The offensive player's job is to keep the ball or puck away from the defender while making an attempt to score. The two cones in your area make up the goal. The puck must pass on the inside of the goal for it to count. The defense who takes the puck away immediately becomes the offense. Remember when shooting that the blade of the stick must stay below the waist. If I see the stick above the waist, you will get a warning. After one warning, you will have to go to the penalty box for 30 seconds before you can resume play. While you're in the penalty box, your partner will practice dribbling and shooting without a defender. We will play three-minute games. Ready, begin!</td></tr>
<tr><td>Diagram:</td><td> Goal

D
Defense

O
Offense</td></tr>
<tr><td>Cues:</td><td>Use gentle taps—dribbling.

Drive the blade through the puck—shooting.</td></tr>
<tr><td>Variation:</td><td>Vary the play area, goal, and ball.</td></tr>
</table>

MS **B**	Striking from a Toss (Batting)
Pacing:	*Externally paced*
Grade Level:	Typically upper elementary (3–5)
Content Focus:	*Mastering striking by hitting from a tossed pitch*
Setup:	Groups of four are spread throughout space. Each group has a bat and five balls. Refer to the diagram below.
Task:	We are going to practice our batting and fielding skills in groups of four. There will be a pitcher, batter, a fielder, and a catcher. The pitcher will toss the ball to the batter, who will hit it. If the batter misses, the catcher catches it and keeps it to put in the fielding basket later. If the batter hits the ball, the fielder retrieves it and puts it in the fielding basket until the batter has taken five swings. When the batter has taken five swings, the fielder will bring all five balls in the fielding basket to the pitcher. The batter becomes the pitcher, the pitcher becomes the fielder, and the fielder becomes the catcher. Change roles after the batter has taken five swings. Ready, begin!
Diagram:	
Cues:	Watch the ball.
	Swing through the center of the ball.
Variation:	Vary the number of pitches, and type of ball.

MS **C**	Playing Miniature Golf
Pacing:	*Externally paced*
Grade Level:	Typically upper elementary (3–5)
Content Focus:	*Mastering striking by working on consistency and accuracy when playing miniature golf*
Setup:	In a large outdoor space, nine hula hoops serve as the golf holes, and nine cones represent the start of each hole. The course is set up to maximize the available space. There is one golf ball and golf club per student and three students per hole, with each group starting at a different hole. Groups go through the holes in ascending order.
Task:	Have you ever played miniature golf? Well, today we are going to use our putting skills to play the miniature golf course that I have set up for you. Get your club, one ball, and your task sheet. Your job is to play the course with the fewest number of strokes. Get with your group of four and go to your designated start area. You may begin when you are ready.
	This time, we are going to play the course using both our putting and chipping skills. Remember you want to get the ball into the cup for each hole with the fewest number of strokes. Again, get your task sheet and go to your designated start area; you may begin when you are ready.
Cues:	Use a good tempo on the swing.
	Keep your feet, hips, and shoulders in line with the flight of the ball.
Variation:	Vary the course and ball.

MS ⓓ	**Striking for Distance (Golf)**
Pacing:	*Externally paced*
Grade Level:	Typically upper elementary (3–5)
Content Focus:	*Mastering striking a golf ball for distance*
Setup:	Children stand behind the driving line with three golf whiffle balls and a golf club per child.
Task:	We have been working on chipping and putting. Today, we are going to work on driving the ball for distance. Each person should have three whiffle golf balls. Stand behind the driving line, and on my signal strike the first ball as far as you can. Remember that distance doesn't come with how hard you swing but with the tempo and rhythm of the swing. Keep your head down throughout the swing. Now hit the second ball and the third ball. Go retrieve the three balls and return to the line. Let's try again.
	This time, I have placed various targets out on the driving range. As you are practicing hitting the ball far, I also want you to work on your accuracy. I want you to pick out one of the targets and attempt to hit the target with your three swings. You may begin when you are ready.
Cues:	Use good tempo.
	Keep your head down.
Variation:	Vary the ball and targets.

FINAL WORDS

This chapter is not meant to include all the skills and tasks that you might give students to help them develop their fundamental motor skills. However, it does highlight the progression that should be taken in skill development. As the progression tree highlights, students need to develop the skills in a predictable or stable environment, then expand their ability in environments that are less certain. Finally, these skills can be used in more dynamic and changing conditions. As the tree depicts, developing skills establish the basis for building skills that can be used for a lifetime of participation in sports and physical activity.

The tree also shows that even when learned skills are not used over time, they are not lost. Although there may be a decreased ability to use the skill effectively, with time and practice the skill level can be regained. Learning to ride a bike is a perfect example of this—once the skill is learned, it can be recalled even into adulthood.

OVER TO YOU

1. Explain the three levels of skill development on the progression tree and what a student might look like or need to practice at each of the different phases.

2. Explain the difference between punting and kicking, between striking with rackets or paddles and striking with long-handled implements, and between throwing and catching.

3. When developing learning tasks for students, what activities would you offer a beginning performer? An advanced performer?

PORTFOLIO TASKS

1. In your own words, write the important distinctions among the three phases of the progression tree. Use examples to support your case.

2. Write two additional learning tasks, not already listed in the book, for each progression phase for the skill of striking with long-handled implements (batting).

3. Place the nine manipulative skills discussed in the chapter in order of difficulty. Try not to look back at the chapter when attempting this task. Explain why you chose the order for the skills you listed. When you are done, check to see how closely your answers coincide with the information in the chapter.

CHAPTER

13

STRATEGIES FOR TEACHING GAMES

CHAPTER OUTLINE

GETTING STARTED

1. Think about a game you like to play. What features of that game make it fun?

2. How can you modify games like Simon Says to make them more active and so children will develop some skill?

3. When should children begin to play competitive games within physical education—if at all?

4. What's wrong with dodgeball? After all, children learn to throw accurately and develop quick movement and agility.

What is a *game*? In its most casual sense, a game can be any rule-driven activity done for entertainment or as a pastime, with an outcome determined by combinations of physical skill, strategy, and chance. Games are also usually activities involving competition, whether directed against others or one's own past performance. In this casual sense of the word, a game can involve any activity from soccer to gin rummy. In this chapter, however, a **game** is a rule-driven pastime involving physical activity that entails cooperation as well as competition (against others or oneself).

Why do people play games? What is so compelling about game-playing that it absorbs most people so intensely? Adults answering these questions say that playing games or sports allows them to:

- Release physical energy—as in marathon running, racquetball, or swimming

- Compete individually or collectively—as in basketball, football, or tennis

- Engage in thrill-seeking behavior—as in white-water kayaking or rock climbing

- Master precise movements—as in diving, archery, gymnastics, or dance

- Socialize with like-minded people—as in bowling, golf, or jogging

You might argue that some of these games could readily satisfy other needs and desires—for example, playing a spirited game of basketball certainly burns up a lot of physical energy, and it can be a joyously social event. But that's just the point! People find games so absorbing because games often fulfill many needs at once. In short, people play games or sports because they enjoy the challenges of (1) control, (2) manipulation, and (3) contest.

These notions of control, manipulation, and contest are equally important for children, too. Here is what two physical education specialists have observed in their own research:

Running, jumping and throwing seem to be three fundamental activities in which children like to engage in a competitive manner. They also derive great pleasure in becoming skillful with objects which can be set in motion, namely kicking cans or stones, or aiming and juggling with pebbles and striking at them in the air with a stick. Often these play activities lead to

game
Any rule-driven pastime involving physical activity that entails cooperation as well as competition (against others or oneself).

competition involving the making of rules and the scoring of points, whether against one or more opponents or individually attempting to beat one's own record. (Mauldon & Redfern, 1969)

Unfortunately, many children in elementary school encounter a physical education experience that does them the disservice of taking the spontaneous joy and inventiveness *out* of games. Worse still, some educators inadvertently perpetuate discriminatory practices that actually create a lifelong dislike of game playing.

THE PLACE OF GAMES IN THE PHYSICAL EDUCATION CURRICULUM

We teach games to children so they can move beyond simply executing isolated skills to combining skills with strategy to become competent and knowledgeable games players (Graham, Holt/Hale, & Parker, 2004). Children who feel competent in game play are more likely to continue a physically active lifestyle. Games also teach personal and social responsibility. Honesty, equity, and fair play can be discussed and taught in the context of cooperation and competition.

Games do not have to have inflexible, formalized rules. In the early grades, games might simply involve a situation where two students hit a ball back and forth over a net to see how many volleys they can do in a row. These tasks become game-like when we ask students to keep score (either competitively or cooperatively).

This chapter focuses on teaching motor skills–based games, building on the content about motor skill instruction in Chapters 11 and 12. We have four main objectives in this chapter. The first is to help you distinguish between games that are appropriate for an elementary school program and games that are not. The second goal is to introduce the concept of child-designed games, giving you strategies for helping children to design, critique, and play their own games. Third, we provide games suitable for your physical education curriculum, together with ways to present these games and organize your class for participating in them. By the end of this chapter, you will be able to confidently present these games to your class so *all* students have a positive educational experience. The fourth goal of this chapter is to give you a basic curriculum for creating a small tournament based on any of the games presented here. If you achieve these four objectives in your teaching, your students will get significant enjoyment from their participation, and you will produce confident and knowledgeable games players.

CRITERIA FOR SELECTING SUITABLE GAMES FOR ELEMENTARY SCHOOL CHILDREN

To begin, let's consider the qualities that make a game appropriate for an elementary school physical education program. Determining which games are suitable for elementary school children isn't necessarily a black-and-white issue. When we read the rules of a game, we usually come to one of three conclusions: (1) The game has no place in an elementary school physical education program; (2) the game may be suitable if modified; or (3) the game is suitable without modification.

Five criteria can help you decide which of these three categories a game falls into. These criteria are grounded on core principles discussed earlier in this book and include the focus of a game on motor skill development, its safety, whether it is inclusive, whether it offers a child frequent practice opportunities, and how much it truly challenges a child to improve his or her mastery of a particular skill.

Criterion 1: The Game Should Contribute to Motor Skill Development

If a game does not help students develop a motor skill (whether locomotor, non-locomotor, or manipulative), then consider it unacceptable. Physical education time is too short for it to be filled with games that are simply "fun." Recess is the time for students to play the games that are fun but develop no particular motor skills. Take musical chairs, for example. This game is one of the seven charter inductees into the "Physical Education Hall of Shame" because of its lack of skill development and focus on elimination. In this game, children walk around a circle of chairs to music and wait for the music to stop. When the music stops, children scramble madly for the nearest chair, knowing there is one less chair than the number of children. Clearly, there is no development of any skill in this game. Your goal should be to introduce your class to games that are both entertaining *and* educational.

Criterion 2: The Game Must Be Physically and Emotionally Safe

If a game is potentially harmful to children—physically or emotionally—it too is unsuitable for an elementary school physical education program. Many games, particularly those using projectiles, are physically unsafe for younger children. Dodgeball is an example of an unsuitable game. The object of dodgeball is to eliminate opposing players by getting them "out," hitting them below the shoulders with a thrown ball. Balls are sometimes thrown from as close as three or four feet, even when an opponent is not even facing the thrower and, therefore, can't take evasive action.

A child's emotional safety is as important as his or her physical safety. A game should not embarrass a student in front of the rest of the class. To highlight this point, let's examine another thoroughly unsuitable game for children called steal the bacon. In this game, two teams are chosen, and the members of each team are numbered. When the teacher calls out a number, the two players with that number from each side approach a central object (the "bacon") and then attempt to snatch it up and run back to their team without being tagged.

While steal the bacon may seem to provide opportunities for developing a child's reaction time, as well as his or her dodging, fleeing, and chasing skills, consider the experiences of the following children:

- A shy child who feels easily physically intimidated

- An uncoordinated child paired with the most physically skilled child in the class

- A low-skilled girl paired with a highly skilled boy

- A child with brand-new glasses his parents worked overtime to buy being paired with an aggressive, mean child

Can you identify emotionally with any of these children? Again, it is critical to consider the emotional safety of *all* your students before placing them in game situations.

Criterion 3: The Game Should Not Be Based on Player Elimination

Play elimination makes no pedagogical sense, because the first children eliminated are probably the very ones who have the least skill and need the most practice! Consider the following game: *Children form a circle and toss a Nerf ball from one to another. Whoever drops the ball sits down and takes no further part. The last person standing is the winner.* Does this encourage player participation? Of course not. The child with the least catching skill is likely to be eliminated first—once again, the very same child who needs the most practice.

Criterion 4: The Game Should Give Students Frequent Turns to Play

There is a clear association between how much a child practices a motor skill and his or her level of proficiency; you can predict a child's success in developing a motor skill by the number of successful practice trials he or she completes (Silverman, 1985). You should therefore choose games that give children frequent turns to play. Think of the game duck, duck, goose, where children sit in a circle while one student walks around the perimeter naming each person a "duck." A child who is named the "goose" instead of a duck must chase the tagger around the circle, trying to reach the home space first. Even if this game did foster motor skill development (and we dispute that it does), no more than two students can be active at any time.

Consider also relay games, whose very structure precludes high participation rates. In a relay, one child in a team is engaged in the content while the other children wait passively for their turn. Watching and waiting do not enhance motor skill development.

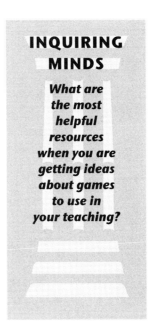

INQUIRING MINDS

What are the most helpful resources when you are getting ideas about games to use in your teaching?

You can modify some games with inherently low participation to meet the fourth criterion. The simplest option is to reduce the number of students in a group while adding more sections to the game. For example, students do not need to play a full nine-versus-nine game of softball to learn hitting, fielding and catching, and throwing accurately to a target. Setting up three separate three-versus-three softball games instead can give your students more practice opportunities to cultivate these motor skills.

The discussion above raises the questions: Is it ever acceptable to play games like baseball or track-and-field activities that may entail a lot of time sitting around waiting for a turn? Do these have any place in elementary schools? Are they sometimes acceptable in their original form, or only in a modified form?

Our answer is that in the forms played by adults, these games are *never* appropriate for elementary school children.

Criterion 5: Structure the Game so Children Feel Challenged

It goes without saying that a game is unsuitable if your students do not find it physically challenging. Although most children love challenging games, they usually need to have control over the level of difficulty. A suitable game lets children decrease or increase the game's challenge to match their current ability. A child who believes even before the game begins that he or she cannot achieve success will hardly feel enthusiastic. Consequently, we try to give children options when they first begin to play. We let them select from a variety of suitable balls; we give them choices in the type of equipment; and in many cases, we let them modify the dimensions of the playing area (like the distance between bases) to make the game more fun and challenging.

Modifying Games to Make Them Appropriate for Children

Games that do not develop motor skills and those that might cause physical or emotional harm to children should be rejected out of hand. But as the preceding discussion of game suitability criteria reveals, some games can be modified to encourage participation. A modified game that fits all five suitability criteria may well be pedagogically sound.

The game of tag is an example. There seem to be as many tag games as there are insects in the animal kingdom, most with names relating to the tag objectives or equipment used: clothespin tag, hula-hoop tag, caged-lion tag, and so forth. Tag games are notorious for their focus on player elimination. Tagged players are "out" and have to wait until the game is finished to re-enter. Tag games do not need to eliminate children, however. Numerous modifications can be made so all children are involved continually:

- Trading places with the tagger
- Joining the tagger as a second tagger (or joining the tagger's team)
- Using freeze and unfreeze tag methods

TABLE 13.1 ■ Freeze Tag Games

Fire Tag	Three or four students are chosen as taggers. Give those students a red sock stuffed with tissue paper. When the taggers tap the runners with the socks and say, "Fire!" the tagged runner must shout, "Stop, drop, and roll," and then perform those movements before continuing to play the game. After a few minutes, new taggers are selected, and the game continues.
Jack Frost Tag	One or more students are chosen to be Jack and/or Jill Frost (i.e., the taggers). They are identified by wearing a bright scarf. Two to four other students are the snow angels and carry the hand warmers (yarn balls/bean bags). Anyone Jack or Jill tags becomes a frozen snowman. To unfreeze the snowman, a snow angel must give him or her a hand warmer. An unfrozen snowman becomes a snow angel, and the person who gave him or her the warmer can now get tagged. Jack and/or Jill Frost cannot tag snow angels.
Beanbag Tag	One or two players act as chasers to tag the moving players. Two (or more) of the moving players have a beanbag to use as either a "safe" or a freeing device. The beanbag can be passed or thrown to other players who are frozen.
Ghostbusters	Six to eight students are designated as "slimers." The slimers are to tag (not throw) their classmate with soft foam balls. When tagged, a student must stop and stand with their legs in straddle position. To be deslimed, another student must run up and say, "Who ya gonna call?" The person who is slimed must say "Ghostbusters!" The student who approached the slimed student then goes through the slimed student's legs, and that person is then free to run again.

In freeze tag, a tagged child remains in place until freed by a classmate or until he or she performs a specific skill. Table 13.1 lists some tag games in which students stay in the game and resume active roles once freed.

An "Obvious" Conclusion: Adult Games Are Not Suitable for Children

The five game suitability criteria for children lead to this conclusion: *Full-sided, adult versions of games are clearly not appropriate for elementary school children.* In adult games, such as nine-versus-nine softball, too many players—like right fielders—spend time without engaging in the play, players get to bat only occasionally, and the skillful players in the dominant field positions get to perform most of the tasks.

Your take-home message: In elementary school game play during a physical education lesson, students should participate in small-sided games, using modified equipment, and only in conditions where the tactics don't overwhelm them so that only highly skilled players can achieve success (see Figure 13.1).

FIGURE **13.1**
In this two-versus-two game of beach ball volleyball, adjustments accommodate the developmental needs of the students. They are playing with a low net on a large area. Notice, too, that their lightweight ball travels more slowly through the air.

The reference list at the end of this chapter gives resources as a starting point for incorporating games into your teaching of skill themes. It is *vital,* however, that you cast a critical eye over the activities in these books or websites to determine whether they are suitable.

WHEN ARE ELEMENTARY SCHOOL CHILDREN READY TO PLAY GAMES?

To execute game tasks successfully, a child must display both bodily agility and the dexterity to manipulate objects in motion. And while the child is moving, she must adapt to the movements of teammates and opponents. All these demands typically overwhelm young children's ability to process sensory information and respond appropriately.

Successful participation in games also requires children to have reached certain physical, social, intellectual, and moral milestones. Weigh a game's competitive aspects against a child's intellectual and moral development. As Mauldon and Redfern observe, "Competition implies the understanding and voluntary acceptance of a code of rules governing methods of play and scoring, and if there is an independent umpire or referee, a readiness to abide by his verdicts—a degree of moral judgment" (1969, 10). Children begin to integrate these developmental aspects of game play only at the upper primary level (fourth and fifth grades). Elementary school children are what might be termed "emerging players" (Belka, 2000). As a result, you should expect children to make only a few carefully limited tactical decisions and employ a limited set of manipulative skills in games that have been considerably simplified from full game play.

Children can also play games in the younger grades (first through third). In fact, children at this age are motivated by self-competition ("Can you beat your own score?"), by working cooperatively to achieve a score ("See how long you and your partner can keep the ball going"), and by one-versus-one or two-versus-two competitive games ("Can you score more than your opponent?"). Thus, games for this group should focus on simple activities with a limited number of rules.

CHILD-DESIGNED GAMES

Many elementary education teachers have found that children learn significantly more by designing their own games, rather than playing games with rules predetermined by the teacher. Children who design games tend to engage actively with and explore the components of game play and may thus acquire a deeper understanding of skills and strategy. They will tend to think more critically about their experiences playing games. Child-designed games also teach children to learn cooperatively and to solve problems in groups. In many cases, children intuitively design games that meet the five game suitability criteria presented earlier in this chapter (see Figure 13.2).

Getting the Game-Design Process Started

Although children collaborate to create the rules of a child-designed game, they still work within certain limits you set as their teacher. In most cases, the fundamental limits relate to the game's goal. You will need to explain the *content* of the game and help your students focus on learning the smaller components of game play. For example, your limiting instructions might be, "Make up a game that focuses on dribbling in which you try to avoid having the ball taken away from you."

Ms Mullins is teaching throwing skills to her second grade class. She has a favorite game called not in my backyard. The rules are: Students are divided into two groups (one boys and one girls), and each group takes a position on either of the end lines of the gym. There is a large volleyball net in between. Under the net there are a large number of balls: gator balls, kick balls, yarn balls, tennis balls, and so on. On the whistle, both teams run to the center, retrieve the balls, and begin throwing them into the other team's yard. When the whistle is blown again, the children must stop throwing and collect all the "junk" on their side to be counted. The side with the most "junk" loses. Ms. Mullins's class is also studying Spanish, so she often gets them to count in Spanish with her as she keeps score.

In guiding your students through the game-design process, first ask them to determine the following three features of the game:

1. *Rules:*

   How many players are involved?

   What is the aim of the game?

   What are players allowed to do (e.g., with and without the ball)?

   What are players *not* allowed to do?

2. *Boundaries:*

   Where are the boundaries?

   What do the boundaries mean (e.g., safe, out, unplayable)?

3. *Penalties:*

   What happens if a player breaks one of the rules?

Typically, game-design lessons follow a format of *play-discuss-play*. This pattern is useful because many children don't understand the reason for rules or how rules can affect game play. Children also sometimes don't know how to change a rule to make their game fairer. By playing, then discussing, and then replaying the newly modified game, children learn how to make it a "good game." In this sense, *good* means that the game "works," and that it's meaningful, educational, and fun for both teams (Rovegno & Bandhauer, 1994).

Game Focus

Sometimes children will design competitive games, while at other times their games will be cooperative. For example, a game that involves throwing a rubber ring over a net may have a goal of landing the ring in the opponent's court (competitive) or of seeing how many consecutive throws a pair of players can make before missing (cooperative).

Because competition and cooperation are inherently neutral attributes (one isn't intrinsically better than the other), why do children design games that are competitively or cooperatively focused? Some researchers think children make this decision because of their view of the meaning and desirability of competition (Rovengo & Bandhauer, 1994). Children who are socialized to view games as being about "winning" tend to design games with a competitive focus that may go so far as to deliberately penalize cooperation. Because this "competition-means-winning" bias is prevalent in Western culture, you may have to help your students appreciate that competition means learning how to play a "good game." *This does not mean forcing children to change a competitive game into to a cooperative one!* What it may mean, for instance, is showing them how to design a competitive game in which the team trying to score and the defending team have equal opportunities for success.

Here is where the play-discuss-play instructional strategy is particularly useful. Box 13.1 has some sample questions to ask children when their games do not seem to be working.

The OKs of Child-Designed Games

As this discussion makes clear, creating child-designed games involves more than giving your students some equipment and telling them to improvise a game. You need to (1) describe and qualify the game content and (2) actively guide your students as they collaborate to perfect a "good game." In addition, let's consider two additional points you may find useful as you guide students in designing their own games.

Point 1: It's OK to tell children what to do. It is sometimes entirely proper for you to stop play in a child-designed game. For example, you should intervene whenever necessary to ensure safety. You should also intercede to be sure that students treat each other with respect. Child-designed games do not eliminate arguments, which typically involve rule disputes, but they do tend to lessen them. Your role is to help your students learn to work out the underlying cause of the

FIGURE **13.3**
This teacher is working with a group during the "discuss" part of their *play-discuss-play* sequence of game design. She is using questioning techniques to direct instruction.

argument. It's also OK to stop play from time to time so students can critique and modify their games, but this requires questioning and listening attentively to students' explanations rather than direction (see Figure 13.3).

Point 2: It's OK if the game looks like an existing sport! Inventing something new and unique is *not* the object of having children design their own games during physical education. Like adults, children create things on the basis of what they already know. Hence, it's understandable—and OK—for children to design games that mimic familiar sports such as soccer, football, or baseball. In fact, if you give your students footballs and some boundary markers and ask them to design a game that involves throwing to a moving target, don't be terribly surprised that the result looks like a close cousin of football (Rovegno & Bandhauer, 1994)!

GETTING ORGANIZED FOR TEACHING GAMES

While the above sections have discussed the *selection* of appropriate games to include in physical education, we now turn to *organizing* your class for instruction. As you will have read in Chapter 4, an effective daily physical education lesson plan identifies how to organize and structure the class. When introducing a game, four key features are necessary: players, equipment, rules, and organization. *Players* refers to the number on each team, which will then affect how many games you will need to organize depending on your class size. *Equipment* refers to the type and amount of equipment you will need, including both implements of play (such as bats and balls) and other equipment to act as boundary markers (such as cones or domes) or bases. *Rules* provide players with the key information as to what they have to do to win and also the limits on what they are allowed to do to win. *Organization* refers to how you will set out not only one game, but also the total number of games required to actively involve all children in your class. Recall from Chapter 10 that safety is a priority in teaching motor skills, and careful planning of your play area is critical. This chapter includes diagrams of ways to safely conduct a number of games simultaneously without the danger of children being accidentally hit with balls from other games.

We find that the best way to organize all four of these elements is with a **game sheet,** which is in effect a recipe for putting together a game. It provides you with all the ingredients necessary to prepare for a game, as well as those that inform children of their responsibilities as players. If you follow a game sheet in your planning process, your resulting game-based lesson should run smoothly and be enjoyed by all involved.

Game sheets for five different games suitable for the upper grades (third through fifth) are found in Applications 13.1 through 13.5 (pages 344–349), while Applications 13.6 and 13.7 (pages 350 and 351) provide sheets for games suitable for the lower grades (K through second). These games involve little equipment, are easy to organize and explain, and keep students highly active. You will notice that we have stayed true to the goals of having small-sided teams playing modified games. You will also notice that we have not listed definitive dimensions for these games, such as court/field size or boundaries. This allows you to decide yourself, based upon your playing space (and whether you are indoors or outdoors), as well as the skill of your students. We have, however, provided some suggestions in the diagrams associated with each game.

Presenting a Game to Students

While the game sheet helps you in planning to teach a game, you now have to present the game to your students during a lesson. The following sequence is our most tried-and-true script. You can use the actual phrasing to instruct the students.

INQUIRING MINDS

What major factors influence when you play games in physical education and **what type of games you include?**

1. *Name the game:* "Today we will be playing a game called hoopball."

2. *State its purpose:* "Hoopball is a batting and fielding game that works on our hitting skills as well as our throwing and catching skills."

3. *Describe the rules:* "*Batting team,* your task is to hit the ball from the tee away from the fielders and then run around the three cone bases as fast as possible before you get out. You score one point for each cone you pass. A ball hit anywhere in front of the tee is a fair ball (in play). *Fielding team,* you can start anywhere you like in the field. It's up to you and your strategy. One of you will be holding the hoop that you will use to get the batting team members out. Your task is to collect the ball and then toss it from one team member to another through the hoop. So this involves three fielders; a thrower, a hoop holder and a catcher. When you catch the ball, yell out 'Catch,' and the batter then counts the bases made. If you drop the ball, you must throw it back through the hoop again until it is caught."

4. *Describe the organization:* "Each player on the batting team gets one turn, and you keep a tally of the total bases. Batting team, nominate your scorekeeper to count the bases as each batter goes up. The fielding team then becomes the batting team and has its turn. You will see we have three fields set up for you to play. I call these Yankee Stadium, Wrigley Field, and Fenway Park." [Point to appropriate field each time.]

game sheet
A plan for organizing students and equipment when teaching games.

This batting and fielding game reinforces the manipulative skills of throwing and catching, as well as striking. Two teams play a softball-like game in which the batter's aim is to hit the ball to open space in the field and run around a set of bases, while the fielders have to work as a team to throw the ball through a hoop to get an out. Teamwork is involved for the fielding team, which has to make sure their throws are accurate. Also, there is strategy involved, as the hoop can be carried by one of the fielders. Because an out can be made anywhere on the field, the players on the fielding team have to use good strategy in deciding where to start as each batter has his or her turn.

Game Name	Hoop softball
Number of Players	Four players per side (or three, for children at a higher level of skill with throwing and catching). Play as many games as needed so all students in the class are participating.
Equipment Needed	❑ Softball bat ❑ Tennis ball ❑ One hoop ❑ Batting tee ❑ Three cones as bases
Organization	The distance between bases can be modified according to the skill and experience of the players. Set up the fields so all batters are hitting outward from the center.

continued

5. *Announce the teams:* "Team 1: John, Jill, Thomas, Wendy [and so on]; you will be playing against Team 2: Patty, LaDerrick, Wee, Jack [and so on]." Remember, in selecting teams, the one strategy that you should avoid at all costs is allowing highly skilled players to conduct a "public auction" for team members in front of the class. To save time, you may put team lists on a notice board inside your classroom. (Please note: There is a range of issues to consider around picking teams, which we will discuss in detail later in this chapter.)

6. *Distribute the equipment:* "I'd like the first person on each team to collect the bat and ball and take these with you to your game area. You will also be responsible for returning this equipment at the end of class." Revisit Chapter 8 for the various ways to manage equipment.

Rules	Batting: ■ Hit from the tee—take as many turns as it takes to hit the ball. ■ A fair ball is anything hit in front of the tee. This can be on the ground or in the air. ■ Run counterclockwise around the three cones. Keep running until you are out (see below for how a player gets an out)—don't stop at a cone, or stop after you get home, keep running. ■ Every cone you pass before getting out counts as one point. Fielding: ■ Fielders can position themselves anywhere in the field of play. ■ Once the ball is hit, one player collects the ball and a second collects the hoop. ■ To get an out, the ball must be thrown from one fielder to another through the hoop. The ball must be caught. ■ If the ball is dropped, it must be rethrown through the hoop until it is successfully caught. ■ The person with the hoop is allowed to run with it. ■ Catching a fly ball does not constitute an out. The ball must be thrown through the hoop for an out. ■ After an out, place the hoop in its original position. Teams change roles after each batter has had a turn.
Variations	Allow batter to hit from a toss from a teammate rather than off the tee. Allow the fielding team to place the hoop anywhere they wish at the beginning of each bat. Do not allow fielders to run with the ball. Vary the distance between the bases.

7. *Send the students to the play areas:* "Teams 1 and 2 will be playing at Yankee Stadium, Teams 3 and 4 at Wrigley Field, and Teams 5 and 6 at Fenway Park. The first-named team will bat first while the second-named team will field first."

During play, remember the principles of active supervision discussed in Chapter 7. When children are playing the games, you should position yourself where you can see most of the class most of the time, move frequently from game to game, and provide students with feedback as to how they are playing. While the games may be running smoothly, this is not the time to sit in your chair and observe as a simple spectator.

This throwing and catching game reinforces the manipulative skills of throwing and catching a Frisbee rather than a ball. Players work in pairs to hit targets with the Frisbee in a designated time. Up to four pairs can play on the same field at the one time. Teamwork is involved; only one player can throw at the targets while the partner has to retrieve the Frisbee. The strategy lies in deciding whether to toss the Frisbee back to the thrower (faster, but more risky), or to run it back (slower, but less risky).

Game Name	Frantic Frisbee
Number of Players	Two players per team—up to four teams per game. Play as many games as needed, so all students in the class are participating.
Equipment Needed	❑ 4 Frisbees ❑ 5 hoops ❑ 5 domes or cones ❑ 5 beanbags per team
Organization	Each team begins on a different side of a square playing field. Squares can be any size and can vary according to the space available and the skill of the throwers. Set up enough fields to accommodate all students.
Rules	Each team consists of one thrower and one retriever. ■ On the "go" signal, the thrower attempts to either (a) land the Frisbee inside a hoop, or (b) hit a dome/cone with the Frisbee. ■ After the throw, the retriever runs into the field of play to collect the Frisbee. If the thrower is successful, the retriever places a beanbag either in the hoop or next to the dome/cone. The retriever can either toss the Frisbee back to the thrower or run it back. ■ The thrower may throw from any position along his or her team's side of the square. ■ Play for 30 seconds and then count the total bean bags for each team. ■ Repeat the game with thrower and retriever alternating roles.
Variations	Require a toss back of the Frisbee from the retriever rather than allowing them to run with it. Make each hoop/dome/cone unavailable as a target once one team has scored on it. Vary the length of time for each period. (*Hint:* We suggest you don't exceed 30 seconds.)

This court game reinforces the manipulative skills of throwing and catching and has a strong emphasis on the locomotor skills of moving quickly and dodging. Two teams play a basketball-like game in which the aim is to get a ball into a goal. In this game, however, a shot at the goal is unimpeded—that is, there are no defenders allowed. Teams must try to get the ball into a position on the court that will allow for a good shot, as any miss gives the ball to the other team. Players are limited to various sections of the court, and so teamwork is involved as no one player can dominate possession.

Game Name	Zone ball
Number of Players	Five players per side. Play as many games as needed so all students in the class are participating.
Equipment Needed	❏ Large playground ball or basketball ❏ 2 large buckets or open boxes
Organization	The size of each court can vary depending upon the skill and experience of the players. You could fit three courts side-by-side running the length of a basketball court. A_1 Attacker A_1 Attacker D_2 Defender D_2 Defender R_1 Rover R_2 Rover A_2 Attacker A_2 Attacker D_1 Defender D_1 Defender
Rules	The court is divided into two sections. Each team must have two defenders and two attackers. These players cannot cross the halfway line. Each team also has one rover, who can go anywhere on the court. ■ Progression of the ball is only by passing. There is no dribbling or running with the ball. ■ An attacker in possession has two options: (1) pass, or (2) shoot at the goal. The attacker who wishes to shoot at the goal must call out, "Shooting," and cannot make a pass to a teammate. ■ The rover can also be a shooter. ■ Once the attacker calls "Shooting," he or she cannot be defended and can take a clear shot at the goal. ■ After a shot attempt (whether successful or not), the opposing team takes possession of the ball from next to the goal. ■ No body contact is allowed, and no stealing/stripping of the ball from the player in possession is allowed. ■ After a designated time, all players must swap one position.

continued

Variations	Use varying size balls—this will change the way the ball is thrown.
	If you are inside, you may use a target on the wall instead of a goal.
	Success for younger students might be hitting the bucket or box, while for older students, the ball may have to remain *in* the bucket to be a goal.

APPLICATION **13.4** ■ Hand Tennis Game Sheet

This net game reinforces the manipulative skills of striking with the hand. Two players participate in a tennis like game in which the aim is to hit the ball over the net away from an opponent. Depending upon the skill of the players, different balls (slower or faster) can be used. The game can also be played in a cooperative manner, with the goal of making as many consecutive hits as possible.

Game Name	Hand tennis
Number of Players	Can be played as either singles or doubles
Equipment Needed	❑ *Choice of:* Small playground ball (4 inches or smaller), bouncing foam ball, or tennis ball
Organization	Court size can vary, depending on the skill and experience of the players. Courts do not have to be very large (12 ft. x 6 ft. is a good starting point). Set up as many courts as required to accommodate all students.
Rules	This game involves children hitting the ball with their hands over a line to land it in an opponent's space so that it is unreturnable.
	■ The server must begin outside the box.
	■ The serve consists of a bounce and then a strike of the ball.
	■ The ball must land inside the opponent's court to be in play. On the line is "in."
	■ Volleying (hitting the ball in the air before bounce) is allowed after the serve.
	■ There must be two hits before a point can be scored.
	■ The winner of a rally serves the next point.
	■ Points are scored on each rally.
Variations	Size and speed of the ball.
	Size of the court.
	Restrictions on how many hands can be used (one hand or both).
	Add a "net" (two cones with a jump rope between).
	Game can be cooperative instead of competitive.

This base-running game reinforces the manipulative skills of throwing and catching, as well as kicking and punting. Two teams play a softball-like game in which the aim for the batter is to kick to the spaces in the field and run between two bases, while the fielders have to work as a team to hit a cone target. Teamwork is involved for the fielding team, which has to make sure throws are accurate. Also, there is strategy involved, as the cone is small, and to shoot from far out and miss will mean the runner scores more points; and players will need to decide whether to run with the ball or throw it to a partner.

Game Name	Kicking rounders
Number of Players	Three or four players per side. Play as many games as needed so all students in the class are participating.
Equipment Needed	❑ *Choice of:* Large playground ball, large bouncing foam ball, or soccer ball ❑ Two domes or hoops as bases ❑ Cone
Organization	The distance between the bases can vary, depending on the students' kicking experience. For less skillful kickers, the bases can be closer. If the game involves punting versus kicking, move the bases further apart.
Rules	Kicking: ■ Kick the stationary ball into the field of play (running up to kick is allowed). ■ A fair ball is anything that goes forward. The foul line is just the horizontal imaginary line on which the kicker is standing. ■ After the kick, run back and forth between the two bases. Touching each base counts as one point. ■ Continue to run until the fielders make an out. ■ After each batter on a team has had a turn, the kicking and fielding teams swap over. Fielding: ■ Once the ball is kicked, the fielding team must collect it and knock down the cone to get an out. ■ A ball caught in the air after it has been kicked is also out, as is a ball caught with one hand only after it has bounced once. In these cases, the fielders do not have to knock down the cone. ■ Fielders may run with the ball, but there must be at least one pass made to a teammate before a shot at the cone is attempted. ■ After an out, reset the cone if necessary. ■ Teams change roles after each kicker has had a turn.
Variations	Different ball. Ball rolled to the kicker instead of kicking a stationary ball. Kicker may kick off the ground or punt. Vary the distances between the bases.

This net game reinforces the manipulative skills of volleying, similar to hand tennis. Players work in pairs to volley a large, slow-moving ball continuously across a net. The goal is to make the most possible passes between the two players. The game can be played in pairs or in fours, the latter being the equivalent of doubles.

Game Name	Beach ball volleyball
Number of Players	Two per group, as many groups as needed per class
Equipment Needed	❑ *Choice of:* One beach ball per pair, one balloon (helium quality) per pair, or one foam ball per pair ❑ Two cones and a jump rope that will form a net
Organization	Set up as many courts as required to allow all children to participate. P P Partner Partner
Rules	This game involves volleying the ball back to your partner. Children volley the ball to their partner, keeping track of how many times they can keep the ball going without it touching the floor. The ball must cross the "net" before it can be returned. Children may use either hand or both hands to hit the ball over the net. Children try to beat their best score each time.
Variations	Limit the type of hit (two hands or one hand). Form a partner pair with another student and play with another pair of students. Change the court dimensions.

MINITOURNAMENTS

If you are teaching in the upper elementary grades (fourth and fifth), you may sometimes like your students to concentrate on one specific game for an extended period. For example, you may have been teaching a series of lessons on striking, throwing, and catching and now wish to give your students a more holistic experience with a particular game. By *holistic* experience, we mean a complete experience of the game; your students will play this game longer than one lesson, and they will also play in competitive games where the scores actually count for something. A complete experience also means that the students will learn how to officiate and keep score, and they will become more aware of fair play.

This game reinforces the manipulative skills of dribbling with the hands. Played by children in the lower grades, the game involves children remaining in control of their ball while alternately progressing and stopping with it. What makes the game challenging is that the signal to dribble and stop dribbling is external to the students and comes as a surprise.

Game Name	Dribbling red light, green light
Number of Players	All students
Equipment Needed	❑ *Choice of:* One playground ball for each child (8.5 inches), or one basketball for each child
Organization	The distance between the caller and the dribblers can vary, depending on space as well as the skill of the dribblers. More skillful dribblers would require a greater distance.
Rules	This game involves dribbling and responding to the signal. ■ Identify one student to be the caller. This person stands facing away from the other students, who are waiting on the start line. ■ When the caller says, "Green light," all children start dribbling toward the finish line. When the caller says, "Red light," children must stop immediately. ■ The caller can face the students only after "red light" has been called. ■ Children moving after "red light" has been called must return to the start line. The caller and/or teacher can decide which students are still moving. ■ Children must return to the start line anytime they lose control of the ball. ■ The first person to cross the finish line is considered the winner.
Variations	Change the caller. Students work as partners or groups to get their team across the finish line. Change the mode of travel—walk, run, gallop.

One way to provide this holistic experience is for students to participate in a **minitournament.** A minitournament consists of five to eight lessons in which the students are split into teams playing against each other and also participate in the organization and administration of those games. That is, while two teams are playing against each other, a third team is officiating the game. Over the series of lessons, all teams get to play and officiate.

Minitournaments generally are broken down into three phases. Phase 1 is *getting ready to play,* phase 2 is *practice competition,* and phase 3 is *league play.* Phase 1 typically lasts either one or two days, while each of phases 2 and 3 last between two

minitournament
Between five and eight lessons in which the students are split into teams who play against each other and also participate in the organization and administration of those games.

and three days. The total time allocation will depend upon how much competition you wish to have and how long it takes for your students to learn the ins and outs of nonplaying tasks in phases 1 and 2, such as getting their teams organized and learning how to officiate.

If you chose to include a minitournament in your physical education curriculum, you must first be able to accept the four key principles. Based upon the curriculum and instruction model called "Sport Education" (see Siedentop, Hastie, & van der Mars, 2004), we believe these are essential if you are to provide a meaningful and quality tournament experience for your sudents. The four principles are:

1. *Players stick with the same team.* Unlike impromptu teams assembled for a game in a typical physical education lesson, teams stay together for the entire tournament, fostering a sense of unity and teamwork.

2. *Teams practice together, and make decisions about their team's tactics.* During each lesson, time is allocated for independent team practice, which can focus on the skills and tactics a team needs to counter its opponent's strengths.

3. *There is a formal schedule so teams know whom they're playing.* A schedule of matches is posted on a notice board listing the playing teams and the officiating teams. A set schedule allows each team to strategize ahead of time about effective competition against the specific strengths and weaknesses of the other team.

4. *There is formal record keeping.* Records and statistics are kept, and used to highlight individual and team performances.

Table 13.2 outlines the plan that you can follow when organizing a minitournament. To demonstrate this plan in action, let's look at how a teacher might use it to carry out a season of hoopball. As a quick reminder, however, before you commit to a minitournament: The students will need to have played the game and have some prior experience with the motor skills of that game. For hoopball, your students will have had to practice striking with either long handles or with paddles, and they will also need to have some skill in catching both balls hit in the air and those thrown from a partner. These experiences do not necessarily have to precede the participation in the tournament, but the students must have at least some mastery in these skills.

Phase 1: Getting Ready to Play

Much preparation for play can take place in the classroom. These tasks do not require moving out to the playing field. A detailed explanation follows of how you might proceed with each of the preparation tasks for a hoopball tournament.

Explaining the Tournament Format

It is important to explain to students how a minitournament is organized. The following dialogue provides a template of one way to explain how it works and what the children will be expected to do:

Boys and girls, in the next few lessons we are going to have a minitournament of hoopball. During this tournament, you will stay on the same team

TABLE **13.2** ■ Outline of a Minitournament

Phase	Activity	Components
One (1 or 2 Lessons)	Getting ready to play	Explaining the tournament format
		Allocating students to teams and having them develop a team identity
		Learning how to keep score and how to referee
		Learning about fair play—what it means and how to produce it
Two (2 or 3 Lessons)	Practice competition	Practicing games that *do not* count toward the class championship
		Practicing officiating
Three (3 or 4 Lessons)	League play	Competing formally in games that *do* count
		League play involves more than winning and losing, scoring includes fair play points and other teacher-determined point categories.

and play matches against other teams. When you are not playing, you will be the officials for a game between two other teams. That is, someone from your team will keep score, someone will be the referee, and someone will be the base umpire. We will play some practice games that do not count so you can learn all the jobs you need to get right before we start our league play. I will put the schedule of games on the notice board so that everyone can see the days on which they play or officiate.

Your team will also be given some time during each day to practice. The teams that take this time seriously will do the best during the competition.

Finally, the team that wins the championship may not be the team that wins the most games. Each team will get a score for its fair play, and I will also be giving teams points for how well they practice, set up their areas, and officiate.

Placing Students on Teams and Allocating Home Spaces

One of the most humiliating acts we can do to students is to subject them to the public cattle sale known as "picking teams." While having two captains call out players to be on their teams can be reasonably efficient, it is indefensible to subject the children picked last to the agony of being unwanted. There are even faster as well as fairer and more humane ways of placing students onto teams.

The most efficient of all team selections is for the teacher to complete the process prior to class. The teacher can then call out the students on each team, reinforcing the class ethic of "everyone can work with anyone in our class." Keep in mind that the teams should be evenly matched, with a balance of strong players and weaker players as well as girls and boys.

You may, however, wish to involve students in team selection. You should then provide the selectors with a quiet place away from the class and ask them to select even teams that can work together. The student selectors will then present their lists to the teacher.

One way a teacher can help develop even teams is to still use student selectors, but to allocate those selectors by lottery to the teams once they have been chosen. That is, John, Mary, Luis, Ramon, and Jackson have been asked to select five teams of four. They are reminded that each of them does not know of which team they will become a member. Only after the 20 other children have been placed onto teams will the selectors have their names placed in a hat and allocated randomly to the teams. In this way, Luis might become a member of the team selected by Mary, while she in turn might become a member of Ramon's team. This process helps to eliminate the stacking of teams with the friends of the selector.

It is important to note that *all* students should be considered as potential team selectors. Those with the highest skill are not automatically the best judges of talent. Less skillful children are still quite capable of rating their peers' skill and compatibility. The other key factor to remember when using students as selectors is to provide clear guidelines on the criteria they should use to make their decisions. The students need to know not only how many players are on a team, but what skills are critical for the upcoming game, and that the teams should be a balanced mix of boys and girls.

Once your children are in their teams, give them time to choose a team name and adopt team colors. Box 13.2 gives some suggestions for students to consider when selecting an appropriate team name. At this point, you will also want to allot each team a "home space" in the gym or on the playing field. This is the space where the team will meet at the beginning of each lesson and where it will complete its warm-up and practices.

Learning How to Keep Score and to Referee

You may wonder about the value of teaching students how to officiate games—after all, when they're officiating, they're not playing. However, to be complete games players, students should not just be competent in performing the motor skills but should also develop some literacy about the game. We believe that one way to do this is to become an official. Learning to referee and refereeing itself also

FIGURE **13.4**
Students enjoy taking the role of official. Here one student is acting as referee while a second is keeping score.

helps students understand more clearly the role of a referee in games: to help the game flow and to ensure fair competition. Elementary school students who have learned to officiate tell us that they enjoy taking these roles as well as watching other teams play (see Figure 13.4). These students learn about other teams, and in some cases, can identify certain strengths and weaknesses that they can use as tactics when they play against them. As an example from hoopball, a team officiating a game between the Eagles and Tigers may get to see who the Eagles have as their stronger batters, and they may notice who are the best throwers on the Tigers. Astute teams will take these opportunities to adjust their fielding and hitting strategies when they play these teams later.

All the games introduced in this chapter have simple officiating tasks. Most will need referees, scorekeepers, and base umpires/line judges. In hoopball, one student would become the referee, one the scorekeeper, and one the base umpire. The referee would be responsible for calling "stop" when the ball is successfully caught through the hoop and for being sure the hoop is returned to its starting place after each bat. The scorekeeper would call out whose turn it is to bat and record the number of bases against each batter. The base umpire would call whether the ball is hit fair or foul and make sure that the runner ran on the outside of the cones. These are simple tasks that give students an opportunity to take positions of responsibility. Having students as competent officials also frees you, the teacher, from having to referee and allows you to move between games, providing feedback to students about their skill or officiating or even completing some assessment tasks (see Chapter 6 for full details about assessment in physical education).

To teach officiating duties, set up a mock game (with six children playing and the rest of the class watching) and work through the roles of the various officials one by one. In hoopball, the first task is to call out the batter. You then play the game for just one batter and demonstrate the role of the referee in calling out "stop" and then replacing the hoop. One student can then take this role for the next batter. This process of a mock game with increasing student involvement effectively introduces officiating tasks to students.

Learning about Fair Play

It was mentioned earlier in this chapter that to successfully participate in games children require a degree of moral judgment and the understanding that competition implies acceptance of the rules governing methods of play and scoring. However, fair play is more than just following the rules. As Siedentop, Hastie, and van der Mars (2004) note, it includes respecting, participating with the right spirit and attitude, valuing equal opportunity, and behaving responsibly as a teammate and player.

Playing fair also has to do with making choices. As we interact in games, as either players or officials, we must regularly consider and define what we think is right and what is not. Box 13.3 lists a fair play creed you can use to help your students identify behaviors focusing on the positive social and behavioral aspects of playing games.

Note that fair play applies not only to players, but also those officiating. Giving a good effort means paying attention to one's job (be it scorekeeping or refereeing), while respect includes fairness to both sides (not cheating) as well as positive and friendly, rather than authoritarian, officiating.

You can teach fair play through posters, awareness talks, and having students sign fair play contracts, as well as by allocating fair play points within the points system used during league play (see page 359 for a more detailed discussion of points systems).

Phase 2: Practice Competition

practice competition
A series of unofficial games in which two teams play each other while a third officiates.

Phase 2 is **practice competition**, a series of unofficial games in which two teams play each other while a third officiates, designed to help the students learn to set up a game, begin a game, and practice officiating tasks. Your main responsibilities in this phase will be to help playing teams and officials learn their roles and

TABLE **13.3** ■ Outline of a Daily Games Lesson during a Minitournament

Time	Lesson Segment
Prior to Beginning Physical Education	Announce playing teams, officiating teams, and field numbers.
5 Minutes	Playing teams begin practice while the officiating team sets up the field and collects the scorecards.
15 Minutes	Games commence.
5 Minutes	End game and collect equipment. Officiating team fills in scoresheet and fair play sheet.
5 Minutes	Announce scores and hold lesson debriefing.

also to reinforce the notions of fair play with students who have difficulty getting the idea. It is important to reinforce to your students that this phase is simply practice and that game results do not count toward the final scoring of the tournament. This will go hand in hand with learning that refereeing is a new skill; and that in learning a new skill, people sometimes make mistakes. Remind students that one part of fair play is to understand that referees are not always perfect and to be courteous to their decisions. Table 13.3 gives a timeline of a day's practice competition.

Announce Playing and Officiating Teams

Before leaving the classroom, you will announce the games for each day:

> Girls and boys, today's games are as follows. The first team I name will bat first, the second team will field first, and the third team will be the officials.
> On field 1, Eagles, Tigers, and Devils. On field 2, Lions, Panthers, and Yankees; and on field 3, Dodgers, Jaguars, and Hoopsters.
> I need the officiating teams to collect the equipment and set up the fields while the playing teams are doing their skill warm-up. Playing teams, you must turn in your score sheets with your players' names before I give the signal to begin the games.

To save time, put the entire schedule of competition on a notice board in your classroom so the students can see on which day they will be playing and when they will be officiating. A visible competition schedule motivates students as the series takes on increased meaning. The notice board can be organized to identify the teams that bat and field first and also the officiating team.

Team Practice

On arrival at the playing area, teams should be given a few minutes to practice the skills used in the game (see Figure 13.5). In hoopball, they may throw and catch in pairs or practice other fielding skills, such as gathering a rolling ball. One player in each team might be responsible for leading this practice.

FIGURE **13.5**
Time should be allocated during each lesson for teams to practice independently of the teacher. Here, a team is practicing a move they will be using during their five-versus-five side flag football season, while a second team in the background is discussing strategy.

While the officiating team sets up the field, one member should also collect the score sheets from the playing teams. These score sheets list the team's batting order and will have space for recording their score (in hoopball, this will be how many bases they reach).

Practice Games Commence

Your first task is to be sure that each field is set up correctly and that the games get underway on time. You are then free to move about your class, spending most of your time helping the scorekeepers complete the score sheets and assisting referees where necessary. Your time can also be spent helping the playing teams with skills or reminding them to support and encourage their teammates.

End of Play

At the end of the designated time for play, you will tell the playing teams to collect the equipment while the officiating team finishes its paperwork, completing the score sheet, identifying the winner and the total score, and completing a fair play points sheet. All members of the officiating team should be involved in assigning the fair play points.

Announcement of Scores and Debriefing

An appropriate way to end games lessons is to announce the scores—both game scores and fair play points. The scorekeeper from each game can read these scores and also identify one highlight of the game (e.g., "Jennifer made an excellent catch to get Jakob out," or "Billy got the highest score. He made seven total bases"). The end of the lesson is also a suitable time for you to review the conduct of the day's organization and play. You may want to congratulate the teams that were practicing well or highlight an outstanding example of fair play. If you are using the "power ratings" version of a league scoring system (see the section on league scoring systems and power ratings), you might also use this time to announce those scores.

Phase 3: Competition Games

The lesson format for the competition games can be identical to that of the practice competition. The only difference is that, in competition, the scores for each game count. The following section outlines ways you can use the various components of a tournament (i.e., game play, student officiating, and a focus on fair play) to structure a league scoring system that takes the focus beyond simply winning and losing.

League Scoring Systems and Power Ratings

While most community-based or school-based sports only use a team's competition record to determine the final champion, we recommend using a scoring system that reflects more than win/loss totals. Although win/loss will certainly be part of this system, a team's dedication to fair play and its officiating performance should also be included.

To give a score for fair play, we usually ask the officiating team to ask itself three questions about each team. For each answer that is scored as a "yes," that team earns one point. Those questions are:

1. Did this team play by the rules and not try to cheat?

2. Did this team encourage one another?

3. Did this team respect the officials?

For scoring the officiating team, both participating teams can be asked similar questions, with a "yes" being scored as one point. The officiating team can thereby earn up to four points for doing its tasks well. Your two questions about them are:

1. Did the officials know the rules of the game?

2. Did the officials apply the rules equally to both teams?

Some teachers find that using a system of "power ratings" helps to reinforce critical components of a minitournament. **Power ratings** are points awarded by teachers to teams who successfully complete explicit tasks. Power rating points are usually a single point awarded on an all-or-none basis. Tasks that can earn power rating points include:

- A team gathers in its home space and has started its warm-up within two minutes of arriving at the playing area.

- A team returns all its equipment to the correct places at the end of a lesson.

- A team moves in a prompt and orderly fashion from its home space to the playing area and is ready to begin games on time.

- A team displays good sportsmanship at the end of matches by lining up and shaking hands with the opposition.

power ratings
Points awarded by teachers during minitournaments to teams who successfully complete explicit tasks.

Power rating points are added to a team's win/loss points and thus figure into the total score. An attractive feature of the power rating system is that *all* teams in a

FIGURE **13.6**
A sample league scoring table. Here you can see that teams are awarded points for winning, playing fair, and fulfilling other commitments as deemed necessary by the teacher. Note too, that the Devils, who have the most wins, are not the leading team.

		League Standings		
TEAM	WIN POINTS	FAIR PLAY	POWER POINTS	TOTAL
EAGLES	8	7	6	21
VULTURES	7	6	6	19
DEVILS	8	6	5	19
TIGERS	5	7	5	17
LIONS	6	6	4	16

class can earn the maximum number of points if they try. This has a tendency to keep league scores much closer together and thus more competitive than if only wins and losses were recorded.

Whatever the format of a league's scoring system, students must be able to see an up-to-date league scoring table. It's unrealistic to expect students to remain enthusiastic if they can't judge how well their team is faring in the competition. A public league table enhances a season's authenticity and encourages student commitment. One example of a league table is shown in Figure 13.6.

FINAL WORDS

The purpose of this chapter has been to help you select and teach your students games that contribute to their motor skill development. To do that, you cannot select just any game from a book, read students the rules, and let them play. You need to make sure the game actually *does* teach skill and that it challenges students in both fair and equitable ways. To do this, you must first cast a critical eye on a game to see if it achieves maximum participation and to examine ways to make it developmentally appropriate.

We have found that one of the most effective ways to present games to children is to have them design their own games. With guided practice, children can create games that provide them with challenge and success. By taking ownership of many of the rules and skill requirements of a game, children become more games knowledgeable and also often more tolerant of each other. The teacher-designed games described in this chapter also allow considerable flexibility in playing dimensions and the rules of play.

No matter what games you choose to incorporate in your lessons, and what skills those games help to develop, the bottom-line message is consistent and worth reading one more time: Elementary school game play during a physical education lesson should see students participating in small-sided games, using modified equipment, and playing under conditions where the nature of the game tactics doesn't overwhelm students so that the highly skilled are the only ones who can achieve success.

OVER TO YOU

1. How would you modify the game of chariot war to make it less exclusionary? Here are the rules: Students divide in groups of three. Two of the players link arms and become the "horses." The third player is the chariot driver and holds the horses by their belts. Each driver has a sock or rag tucked under his or her belt in the back that is able to come out easily if pulled. The teams are lined up, backs to the wall, around the room. On the cue "go," each team tries to steal as many tails as possible without losing its own. A team that loses its tail is out of the game. Only a horse may grab a tail.

2. How about this game? Evaluate it using the five criteria of game suitability. Would you make any modifications? Figure 13.7 shows the game's organization, and here are the rules: You will need a large open space for this activity. Divide your class into groups with no more than four players per group. Each

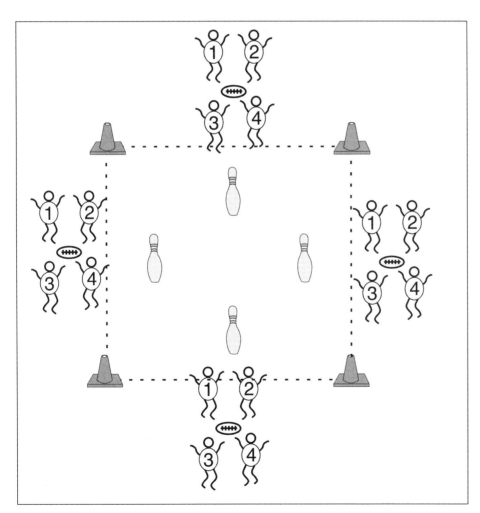

FIGURE **13.7**

group has a football. The game takes place on a large area designated by four cones. Each player is given a number, 1 through 4. When the teacher calls out a number, players with that number take the football and run clockwise around the cones and back to their group. The player then takes the football and throws it at the closest bowling pin. If he or she knocks the pin down before any other team does, the team scores one point. All the footballs are retrieved, and the pins are placed back in their original positions. The game continues with the teacher calling out another number.

3. What would be your major instructional challenge in incorporating child-designed games into your program? Compare your feelings with other members of your class to determine some solutions.

4. What are your opinions about competition? How would you describe "appropriate competition" to a group of students in an elementary setting?

PORTFOLIO TASKS

1. Find a book or website of children's games and evaluate the suitability of a selection of games for inclusion in an elementary physical education program according to the guidelines in this chapter.

2. Using the format of the game sheets provided in Applications 13.1 through 13.5, create your own game. Try the game out in a lab session of your class, or even with some friends, and analyze what worked and what didn't. Write a report showing your original rules and your final rules with some annotation justifying the changes.

3. Write the limiting instructions you would give students when asking them to create games relating to:

   - Shooting a soccer ball at a goal

   - Dribbling a basketball

   - Throwing a deck tennis ring over a net

REFERENCES

Belka, D. (2000). Developing competent games players: Rationale and tactics. *Teaching Elementary Physical Education, 11*(3), 6–7.

Dieden, B. (1995). *Games to keep kids moving: P.E. activities to promote total participation, self-esteem, and fun for grades 3–8.* West Nyack, NY: Parker Publishing Company.

Foster, D. R., Overholt, J. L., & Schultz, R. (1989). *Indoor action games for elementary children: Active games and academic activities for fun and fitness.* West Nyack, NY: Parker Publishing Company.

Graham, G., Holt/Hale, S. A., & Parker, M. (2004). *Children moving: A reflective approach to teaching physical education* (6th ed.). Boston: McGraw Hill.

Kirchner, G. (2000). *Children's games from around the world.* San Francisco: Benjamin Cummings.

Mauldon, E., & Redfern, H. B. (1969). *Games teaching: A new approach for the primary school.* London: Macdonald & Evans.

Physical Education Lesson Plan Page. Retrieved from http://members.tripod .com/~pazz/lesson.html

Physical Education & Health Lesson Plans, Ideas, and Activities. Retrieved from www.lessonplanspage.com/PE.htm

Rovegno, I., & Bandhauer, D. (1994). Child-designed games: Experience changes teachers' conceptions. *Journal of Physical Education, Recreation, & Dance, 65*(6), 60–63.

Siedentop, D., Hastie, P., & van der Mars, H. (2004). *Complete guide to Sport Education.* Champaign, IL: Human Kinetics.

Silverman, S. (1985). Relationship of engagement and practice trials to student achievement. *Journal of Teaching in Physical Education, 5,* 13–21.

14

STRATEGIES FOR TEACHING RHYTHMIC MOVEMENT

CHAPTER OUTLINE

1. Where is the best place in the elementary school curriculum to teach rhythms?

2. Why are many boys so reluctant to dance?

3. How comfortable are you with your rhythmic ability? Will this affect your decision or your ability to teach rhythmic movement?

For some children, the thought of dancing or moving to the beat of music inspires energetic feelings of joy and anticipation. For these children, moving skillfully to music is great fun! But other children feel they have "two left feet," and the thought of dancing may simply elicit intimidation and embarrassment. The same is true of teachers. When you teach movement and rhythms, your students will readily sense and mirror your own feelings about these activities, whether it's enthusiasm or awkwardness. This chapter presents strategies you can use to teach movement and rhythms. These strategies are intended to bolster your students' self-confidence (as well as your own!) and to demonstrate that rhythmic movement equally benefits both girls and boys.

THE PLACE OF RHYTHMIC MOVEMENT IN THE PHYSICAL EDUCATION CURRICULUM

In learning motor skills and applying them to game situations, the focus is on using the skilled movement to achieve a goal. The goal might be to run away from someone chasing you, kick a ball into a goal, or throw a ball to a partner. Rhythmic movement focuses on the movement itself, rather than on movement as a means to an end. To truly physically educate children, we need to stress rhythmic movement in the elementary physical education curriculum.

Children benefit in a number of ways from learning rhythmic movement. First, they expand their kinesthetic awareness of their body in motion and in stillness. Most physical activities have an inherent rhythm, and participating in specific rhythmic training helps sharpen awareness of the body in space. Second, children increase their coordination, balance, and stamina. All of these help develop other motor skills. Third, moving to percussive rhythms and music helps children develop multisensory integration.

Rhythmic movement may be defined as movement in time to individual sounds. **Dance**, a form of rhythmic movement, usually involves moving to music using prescribed or improvised steps and gestures. Rhythmic movement and dance are both formalized human movements focusing on style and beauty. In this chapter, we consider rhythmic movement to be the foundation of dance, which incorporates the movement into sequences and integrates it with music. While rhythmic movement focuses on the movement itself, dance can also be used to tell a story or express human emotions, themes, or ideas. Dance can also be performed with the aid of mime, costumes, scenery, and lighting.

rhythmic movement
Movement in time to individual sounds.

dance
Moving rhythmically, usually to music, using prescribed or improvised steps and gestures.

In this book we provide a strong focus on strategies for teaching rhythmic movement. We begin by building basic rhythmic competence and helping children become comfortable with movement. We revisit the nonlocomotor and basic locomotor movements introduced in Chapter 11, now linking these to external rhythms and music. Applying this foundation, we use the skills developed in Chapter 11 to learn and perform structured and student-designed rhythmic sequences and dances.

THE PROGRESSION TREE FOR TEACHING RHYTHMIC MOVEMENT TO STUDENTS

The chapter is structured to follow a progression tree similar to those used in Chapter 11 on motor skills. The base of the tree (developing a basic four-count rhythm) focuses on helping your students become more rhythmically competent so they can move in time to a beat and create their own small sequences. Further up the tree, we repeat the activities found at the base, except that now we introduce music to replace the percussive beat. Higher again (expanding rhythm skills), we broaden those rhythmic skills to include moving to more complex beats with whole (a whole note counts four beats), half (a half note counts for two beats), and quarter (a quarter note counts for one beat). Figure 14.1 explains the values assigned to the beats. The top of the tree (mastering rhythm skills) introduces line dances, folk dances, and tinikling skills that students can easily learn and perform, and it supplies you with strategies for helping students create their own rhythmic dance sequences. Figure 14.2 shows this progression.

Count	1	2	3	4
Notes	𝅝			
Action	Stomp			

Whole notes

Count	1	2	3	4
Notes	𝅗𝅥		𝅗𝅥	
Action	Jump		Jump	

Half notes

Count	1	2	3	4
Notes	♩	♩	♩	♩
Action	Step	Step	Step	Step

Quarter notes

FIGURE **14.1**
Values assigned to various notes. Whole notes count for four beats, half notes for two beats and quarter notes for one beat.

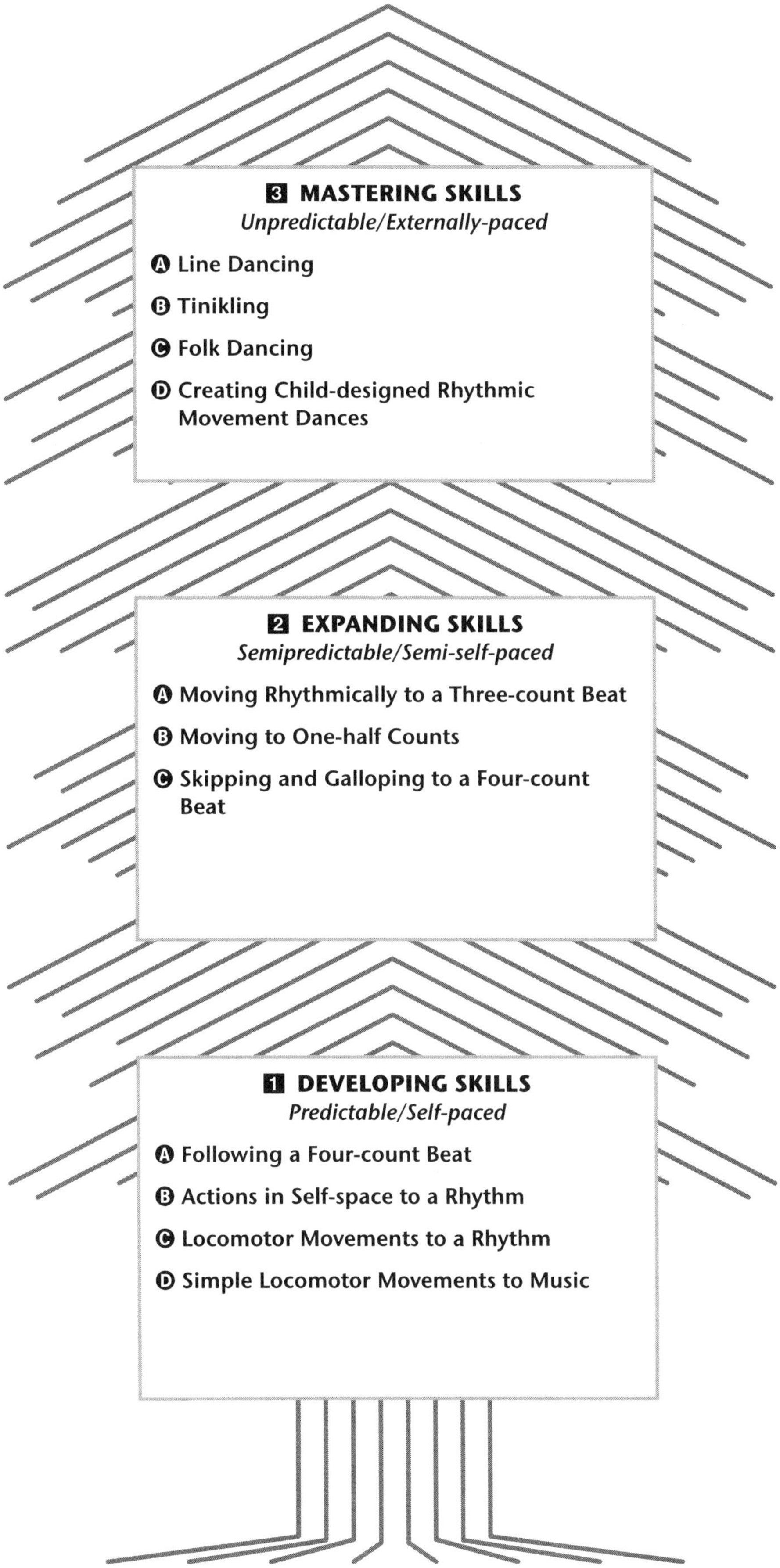

3 MASTERING SKILLS
Unpredictable/Externally-paced

Ⓐ Line Dancing

Ⓑ Tinikling

Ⓒ Folk Dancing

Ⓓ Creating Child-designed Rhythmic Movement Dances

2 EXPANDING SKILLS
Semipredictable/Semi-self-paced

Ⓐ Moving Rhythmically to a Three-count Beat

Ⓑ Moving to One-half Counts

Ⓒ Skipping and Galloping to a Four-count Beat

1 DEVELOPING SKILLS
Predictable/Self-paced

Ⓐ Following a Four-count Beat

Ⓑ Actions in Self-space to a Rhythm

Ⓒ Locomotor Movements to a Rhythm

Ⓓ Simple Locomotor Movements to Music

FIGURE **14.2**
Progression tree for teaching rhythmic movement

DEVELOPING BASIC RHYTHM SKILLS

As noted above, our first task in teaching rhythmic movement is to help students listen to and then move in simple ways to a beat. We then give a progression so all students can achieve mastery and gain confidence in their ability to develop rhythm.

Establishing a Four-Count Beat for Children to Follow

The first step in teaching rhythm is to establish a steady **beat** that students can hear and then follow. We suggest that a four-count beat is the easiest to produce and for students to copy; and because most dances follow this beat, it is also the most appropriate basis for eventually moving to music. You can represent the beat by counting aloud in a repetitive fashion; for example, 1-2-3-4, 1-2-3-4, . . . and so on. You may reinforce counting by clapping. While clapping is usually the chosen method of setting a beat, percussion or rhythm instruments such as tambourines or drums also make a clear distinguishable sound that is easy for the students to hear and work in synchronization.

Once you have established the beat, the task for students is to then follow it. At this time your primary focus is teaching the students to keep the beat; later we will describe how to add movement to their understanding of rhythm. First, they can clap with you, so that the whole class is in unison. Later, you might have children follow with their own percussion instruments. Many sporting goods catalogs have so-called rhythm kits, typically including sand blocks; tambourine sticks; crow

beat
The underlying pulse of a series of sounds that holds true throughout the entire piece (e.g., 1-2-3-4 or 1-2-3).

FIGURE **14.3**
Sample contents of a rhythm kit. These are commercially available from a number of sporting goods suppliers.

Maracas

Simple maracas can be made from many different types of household containers and an assortment of fillers. Different combinations will give different sounds. Suggested *containers* include two spray-can lids taped together at the rims with duct tape or empty 20 oz. water, juice, or soda bottles. The best *fillers* include beads, pebbles, and small dried peas. Avoid rice, as it attracts mice, and if it gets damp, it swells and becomes a great mess!

Wooden Sticks

Simple pieces of dowel cut to size (about 8 to 10 inches) are great for making rhythm sticks. You might also nail some bottle tops to the sticks to get a nice jangle each time they are hit together. Duct tape or pad the ends of the dowel with a piece of old tennis ball.

Handle Bells

Handle bells can be made by punching a hole in each end of a paper towel roll and tying two jingle bells to each side of the roll by running string or yarn through the holes and tying it off.

See http://www.rhythmweb.com/homemade/index.html for other great ideas.

sounders; two-tone sounders; cymbals; ankle, wrist, and handle bells; rhythm sticks; and triangles (see Figure 14.3).

You can also make your own equipment. Box 14.1 gives directions for making some very cheap homemade percussion instruments. The books by Banek and Scoville (1995) and Hopkin (1996) are also two excellent resources for making your own instruments.

Adding an Accent

Once students can follow a beat, you can include an **accent** (stress) on one of the counts. An accent increases the force of a rhythmic movement, such as applying an extra-heavy step versus a light step. The simplest and most common technique is to stress the first beat, called the *downbeat*. While accents can occur anywhere in a four-count rhythm, we recommend you begin by placing the accent on the first beat in a measure; thus, **1**-2-3-4, **1**-2-3-4. Clapping more forcefully or striking the drum hard on the first beat and then softly for three counts helps students get the idea of an accent. As we will see later, when *moving* to a beat or music, this accent could be stressed by different actions.

accent
An increased emphasis on a note, which can be through an increase in the force of a movement, such as an extra heavy stomp versus a light step, or perhaps through a marked gesture.

BOX **14.2** ■ Sample Nonlocomotor Action Words				
■ Rise	■ Jump	■ Stomp	■ Whirl	■ Shrink
■ Jerk	■ Explode	■ Collapse	■ Spin	■ Slither
■ Melt	■ Flop	■ Punch	■ Kick	■ Slash
■ Shake	■ Pop	■ Swoosh	■ Chop	■ Lower
■ Wiggle	■ Rattle	■ Pounce	■ Bounce	■ Squeeze

Actions in Self-Space to Rhythm

Once your students have mastered keeping a beat either with their hands or with instruments, they are ready to start moving their bodies to rhythms. Students can most easily begin moving to rhythms by completing nonlocomotor actions in self-space, rather than by performing locomotor movements. The teaching progression begins with you initiating the beat, followed by students keeping that beat with you, and then by the action.

Simple movement skills such as walking in place (marching) are useful starting points for moving to a rhythm. Following the cues of "right-left-right-left," students can move in time to a beat in a familiar action with easily followed directions. Commands such as "Stomp-2-3-4" or "Reach-2-3-4" allow students to achieve success quickly. Students can easily follow these activities by imitating a group leader.

You can incorporate a number of action words when students are moving in self-space. Action words are expressive verbs that, while not having an exact form (e.g., *wiggle*), are still clear enough for students to be able to dramatize. Box 14.2 lists words you can incorporate into simple sequences.

Action words can be used as one word that takes up the full four counts or whole note (e.g., "Melt-2-3-4"); or you can use the one word on all four counts or quarter notes (e.g., "Chop-chop-chop-chop"). You can also ask students to make up their own action words, first by telling and performing them and then later by allowing other students to interpret what words the movements could represent.

Locomotor Movements to a Rhythm

Once students can maintain a steady rhythm using simple movements or actions, you can gradually increase the difficulty by introducing various locomotor skills. As before, keep things simple by having a single locomotor movement equal a count of one. Walking, jumping, hopping, and stomping are examples of one-count movements. That is, each action takes place on one count. Compare this to skipping (step-hop), which requires two counts. Keep these first experiences simple by having students move in one direction. Initial sequences should be teacher directed, with all students moving in a straight line following the one call. For example, the first set of four beats could be "Hop-2-3-4," followed by "Jump-2-3-4." You can then continue introducing various locomotor skills.

TABLE **14.1** ■ Components of Movement Sentences

Verbs	Adverbs	Adjectives
Locomotor	**Force**	**Level**
Walk	Strongly	High
Run	Heavily	Low
Leap	Lightly	
Hop		**Pathway**
Slide	**Effort**	Straight
Gallop	Sharply	Curved
	Smoothly	
Nonlocomotor		**Shape**
Bend	**Speed**	Stretched
Twist	Quickly	Tucked
Stretch	Slowly	Curled
Tuck		
Curl		**Direction**
(any other action words from Box 14.2)		Upward
		Downward
		Forward
		Backward
		Sideways

Changing Directions, Levels, and Pathways

Once students have mastered moving rhythmically in a straight line, you can introduce changes in direction, levels, and pathways. The directions that we can move in are forward, backward, and sideways. The levels in which we can move are high, medium, and low. A pathway is the course traveled by a student when moving in each direction. Pathways include straight, curved, and zigzag. For example, you might ask the students to complete the following pattern: "Travel in general space in a forward direction, at a high level, and your pathway should be zigzag wherever possible." You now have myriad movements to combine when designing rhythmic sequences.

An effective way to help students incorporate these concepts into their rhythmic experiences is with *movement sentences.* As you know, sentences contain nouns, adjectives, verbs, and adverbs. In movement sentences, the verbs describe locomotor movements or action; adjectives describe levels, directions, and pathways; and adverbs like *forcefully, lightly,* and *quietly* can quantify effort.

To help students create movement sentences, create a series of cards of different colors, with each color representing a verb, adverb, or adjective (see Table 14.1). Ask your students to collect four verb cards, two adverb cards, and two adjective cards. The task will be to account for 16 beats (four beats per verb) that incorporate any combination of the cards.

WHAT'S WRONG WITH THIS PICTURE?

Ms. Benson remembers that the school's major fund-raising fete is only two weekends away. Because each class is expected to perform some activity during the open house, Ms. Benson decides to teach her third grade class a folk dance she found in a book of multicultural dances. Ms. Benson finds the appropriate CD and begins a four-lesson course to get her children proficient for the big day.

Let's look at the combinations of two students, Jack and Jill. Each chose the *stomp, shake, walk,* and *rise* cards as their verb cards, *high* and *backward* as their adjective cards, and *heavily* and *smoothly* as their adverb cards. Jack's sequence was:

Walk backward → Rise smoothly → Shake high → Stomp heavily

while Jill's sequence was:

Shake heavily → Stomp backwards → Walk smoothly → Rise high

Revisiting Accents

When students are proficient at simple locomotor movements to rhythms, you can add accents to allow for greater originality. Accents put an emphasis on a specific count (usually the first), so a student might use a stomp instead of a step. At this point, students should be able to interchange nonlocomotor actions with locomotor steps as another form of accent. For example, the rhythmic sequence might be "*Stretch*-step-step-step (all in a forward direction); *shrink*-step-step-step (backward)." Again, begin with all students completing the same sequence, then progress to some self-choice. Revisit the action words for options here.

Adding Props

As students become successful in following and maintaining a steady beat, applying accents, and moving in the proper direction, level, and pathway, they may enjoy adding hand movements. If a rhythm kit is available, each student could keep a beat with an instrument. Each instrument will create a different sound. The teacher may ask students with one type of instrument to accent the first beat, while those using another instrument accent the second or third beat only. This leads to many possible sound and rhythm combinations using hands while maintaining a steady beat using the feet.

Of course, the props do not necessarily have to contribute to making the beat. You might give students Rhythm Hoops, rhythm ribbons, or scarves (see Figure 14.4). You can also have students in the upper grades throw and catch to a rhythm. Using any size of ball, beanbags, or deck tennis rings, have students pair up and throw to each other keeping time with the beat. The count will usually be 1-throw, 2-catch; 3-throw, 4-catch. The students throw on a certain beat and catch on a cetain beat.

FIGURE **14.4**
Wands, ribbons, and scarves are useful accessories for students learning to move rhythmically.

Repeat the Above Steps with Music

So far, we have focused on instruction in rhythmic movement without music. To be able to dance, however, children will need to interpret an underlying rhythm *from* music. This is more challenging than moving to a rhythm from a percussive beat.

However, introducing music does not mean going straight into performing complete dances. Early experiences with music should simply repeat the sequences described above, but with the music, rather than the teacher, facilitating the beat. There is no limit to the music and rhythm choices and combinations; you must simply select music and put together the rhythms and movements to showcase your students' developmental levels. However, at first you can continue to count out loud or clap to help students move from pure beat to music.

What Is Appropriate Music?

Music selection should be based on the tempo, rhythm, and students' musical tastes, and be enjoyable to move to. The tempo must fit within the range of speed allowing for student movement, with 64 to 128 beats per minute acceptable for most elementary school children. As noted previously, rhythm should be based on a four-beat count. Four-beat counts are easier for children to follow, and many popular songs in the United States are written with a four-beat count.

Sources of Music

Children's music collections featuring hits from various artists can be found in most music stores. A series of CDs on the label Sugar Beats (www.sugar-beats.com) is particularly suitable. Sugar Beats's specialty is pop songs from the '60s, '70s, and '80s, remade especially for kids.

While many physical education equipment catalogues have some CDs, Nasco (www.eNASCO.com) appears to have the largest and most inclusive range, including the WB Dance Series of CDs. You should also feel free to select music from your own collection. Just time one of your songs for one minute and count the total number of beats.

EXPANDING RHYTHM SKILLS

After completing the activities and progression listed in the developing rhythm section, your students should be able to follow simple four-count beats either to a percussive instrument or to music. They should have experience following a beat using locomotor and nonlocomotor movements, with each movement taking up whole (four-count), half (two-count) or quarter (one-count) notes.

In expanding rhythm skills, we add two new rhythmic tasks. These are (1) moving to a three count, and (2) moving to eighth notes. These skills are necessary for progression to the mastering rhythms section, where the students focus more on complex movement combinations and working with partners.

Moving Rhythmically to a Three-Count Beat

To competently move to a three-count beat, students simply have to follow the same progression as for a four-count beat. Begin instruction with an external rhythm, having students clap or march in place to that beat. Follow this by other movements in self-space, moving on to locomotor movements and then a repeat of those activities to music. When incorporating an accent within a three-count beat, you should *always* stress the first note: 1-2-3, **1**-2-3.

Moving to One-Half Counts

Our counting to this point has been a very stable 1-2-3-4 or 1-2-3. To extend students' rhythmic skill, we can now change the rhythm to 1 & 2 & 3 & 4 &. The stress will still be on the numbers, but movement can occur on the "ands."

As a helpful hint, Figure 14.5 shows how to demonstrate the "1 & 2 & 3 & 4 &" rhythm to students. Upon each beat (i.e., 1-2-3-4), strike your hands on your hips and then move your hands forward to signify the "and" between the beats. The pattern of motion, then, for a four-count beat would be "strike & strike & strike & strike &."

To teach the "1 & 2 & 3 & 4 &," you simply follow the same progression as before. That is, you begin by having students clap (or play a percussion instrument) in time with the beat, followed by movements in self-space and then locomotor

FIGURE **14.5**
The actions for leading a one-half count. The hands slap the hips on "one" and then extended forward on "and."

movements. The key is that you will now have the possibility of eight movements in a count of four. You can also combine locomotor and nonlocomotor movements, with movement on the 1, 2, 3, and 4 and an action word on the "&" between each one.

When teaching the simple four-count beat, we encouraged you to use locomotor movements that involve one step per count (e.g., walking, hopping, or jumping). Skipping and galloping are locomotor movements that follow a 1 & count. From Chapter 3, you will recall that skipping is simply a combination of a step and a hop. As a result, the count for skipping will be "1 & 2 & 3 & 4 &" while the steps will be "step-hop-step-hop-step-hop-step-hop." Galloping also follows this pattern (step-together).

Revisiting Expanding Rhythms with Music

When introducing the skills in the developing rhythm skills section, the first experiences involve a percussive beat. Music is introduced only after students have learned to move to a solid count. This is also true for the expanding rhythm skills section. Practice moving to a three-count beat. Counts using eighth notes should begin using a percussive beat and then progress to music. For practicing movements to eighth notes, choose songs that follow a speed between 60 and 80 beats per minute. Even then, the students will be huffing and puffing if they have to move to each of the eight counts.

MASTERING RHYTHM SKILLS

This section focuses on how students can apply their rhythmic skills to formal dance forms, including line dance, tinikling, and folk dance. This section also includes a discussion on teaching students how to create their own rhythmic dance sequences. Line dances and tinikling are included because they reinforce the skills learned in the earlier sections of this chapter, but also because they have no rigid patterns. You and your students are free to create new and exciting routines involving steps that are true to the dance form or even to make up new ones. Folk dance offers an opportunity to learn about multiculturalism and diversity as well as being an entertaining way to work on key rhythm and dance skills.

Line Dancing

Line dances are very easy for students to learn, mainly because the steps are straightforward, and students do not have to coordinate their movements with a partner. Line dances also involve repeating series of steps, so a student who does get lost, can easily catch up with the rest of the class. Line dances are also perhaps the most popular dances now performed in elementary schools.

Because of its cowboy image, line dance is often thought to have originated in the Wild West. According to the *Wikipedia Encyclopedia,* line dancing in fact originated in the age of disco, though the concept goes back to folk dances such as the Virginia reel. Line dancing declined with the death of disco until it was more or less single-handedly revived by Billy Ray Cyrus with his hit "Achy Breaky Heart"—thus the cowboy image.

Line dances are both easy to teach and simple enough that your students can rearrange the basic steps to design their own dances. Numerous resources and websites offer examples of steps of line dances. Many resources come with accompanying music in the form of CDs or cassette tapes, and some dances are now available on video or DVD. This chapter's References list provides a number of print, audio, video, and web resources for expanding your line dance vocabulary.

When teaching line dance, begin with all students in self-space. Let them first listen, trying to detect the speed of the music and the underlying beat. Having students clap or march in place often helps in this early stage. A short dance (such as the bartender's stomp) can be taught as a whole, with students learning all the steps in one sequence. Longer dances might require learning in two or three parts. Once they have mastered the basic steps organized in self-space, you may then have the students form lines (usually six to eight per line). The challenge for each line is to move together with the music, forming a single unit of dancers.

To help you get started, we have included six line dances that are easy to teach and fun for all participants. The count, steps, and appropriate music for these dances are provided in Applications 14.1 through 14.6 on pages 377 through 382.

line dance
A choreographed form of popular dance incorporating a repeating sequence of steps identically performed by a group of dancers in one or more lines.

Count: 24
Music: "Honky Tonk Walkin'," by Kentucky Headhunters; "Homesick," by Travis Tritt; "God Blessed Texas," by Little Texas Daddy; "Laid the Blues On Me," by Bobbie Cryner; "Indian Outlaw," by Tim McGraw

Counts	Step Descriptions

Grapevine Right, Stomp Left (see diagram)

Beat 1	Step right foot (RF) to right
Beat 2	Step left foot (LF) to right behind left
Beat 3	Step RF to right
Beat 4	Stomp LF

Grapevine Left, Stomp Right

Beat 5	Step LF to left
Beat 6	Step RF to left behind left
Beat 7	Step LF to left
Beat 8	Stomp RF

Walk Back 3 Steps, Stomp Left

Beat 9	Step Back RF
Beat 10	Step Back LF
Beat 11	Step Back RF
Beat 12	Stomp LF

Forward Left, Stomp, Back Right, Stomp

Beat 13	LF step forward
Beat 14	RF together and stomp
Beat 15	RF step backward
Beat 16	LF together and stomp

Forward Left, Right Stomp, Hold, Stomp Twice Fast

Beat 17	LF step forward
Beat 18	RF together/stomp
Beat 19	Hold briefly on 19
Beat 20	Stomp twice fast on 20

Back Right, Touch, Left Forward, Hitch, and Pivot 1/4 Left

Beat 21	RF step back, touch LF
Beat 22	LF step forward
Beat 23	RF step forward
Beat 24	Pivot 1/4 turn left

Begin Again!

Alternate steps for 17–24.

Left Step Forward, Hold, Stomp Right Twice Fast

| Beats 17–18 | LF step forward, hold |
| Beats 19–20 | Step RF next to LF twice fast |

Back Right, Stomp Left, Forward Left, Pivot 1/4 Turn Counterclockwise Stomp Right

| Beats 21–22 | RF step back, stomp LF |
| Beats 23–24 | LF step forward while pivoting 1/4 turn left, stomp RF |

Count:	28
Music:	"Electric Boogie," by Marcia Griffiths
	"Bus Stop (Electric Slide)," by The World Class Wreckin' Cru

Counts	**Step Descriptions**

Grapevine Right, Stomp or Scuff Left

Beat 1	Step right foot (RF) to right
Beat 2	Step left foot (LF) to right behind left
Beat 3	Step RF to right
Beat 4	Stomp LF or scuff LF beside RF

Grapevine Left, Stomp or Scuff Right

Beat 5	Step LF to left
Beat 6	Step RF to left behind left
Beat 7	Step LF to left
Beat 8	Stomp RF or scuff RF beside LF

Walk Back 3 Steps, Stomp Left

Beat 9	Step back RF
Beat 10	Step back LF
Beat 11	Step back RF
Beat 12	Stomp LF beside RF

Straddle Jumps and Stomp

Beat 13	Jump up landing with feet shoulder width apart
Beat 14	Jump up landing with feet together
Beat 15	Stomp LF beside RF
Beat 16	Stomp RF beside LF

Step and Scuff

Beat 17	Step LF forward 45° to left
Beat 18	Scuff RF beside LF
Beat 19	Step RF forward 45° to right
Beat 20	Scuff LF beside RF

Step and Bump

Beats 21–22	Step LF forward and bump hips forward twice
Beat 23–24	Bump hips back twice

Bump and Hitch

Beats 25–26	Bump hips forward, bump hips back
Beat 27	Bump hips forward
Beat 28	Hitch (lift the knee) RF with 1/4 turn to left

Start Again!

Count: 32
Music: "A Little Boogie Woogie," by Shakin Stevens
               "You Drive Me Crazy," by Shakin Stevens
               "I'm Outta Here," by Shania Twain Dance Mix
               "Electric Boogie," by Marcia Griffith

Counts   **Step Descriptions**

Side, Slide, Side Shuffle RF, Side, Slide, Side Shuffle LF

Beat 1   Step RF to right
Beat 2   Slide LF together
Beat 3 &   Side shuffle RF stepping right and bring LF together
Beat 4   RF to side
Beat 5   Step LF left
Beat 6   Slide RF together
Beat 7 &   Side shuffle LF stepping left and bring RF together
Beat 8   LF to side

Forward, Together, Forward Shuffle, Back Together, Back Shuffle

Beat 9   Step RF foot forward
Beat 10   Step LF together
Beat 11 &   Shuffle forward RF-LF
Beat 12   RF together
Beat 13   Step back on LF
Beat 14   Step RF Foot together
Beat 15   Shuffle backward LF-RF
Beat 16   LF together

Back, Touch, Forward, Touch, Angle Forward RF and Hips RF-LF-RF,
Angle Forward LF and Hips LF-RF-LF

Beat 17   Step back on RF
Beat 18   Touch LF beside
Beat 19   Step forward on LF
Beat 20   Touch RF beside
Beat 21   RF foot steps forward slightly on RF angle while pushing hips forward
Beat 22 &   Then push hips back and forward (hips RF-LF-RF)
Beat 23   LF foot steps forward slightly on LF angle, pushing hips forward
Beat 24 &   Then push hips back and forward (hips LF-RF-LF)

Angle Back RF and Hips RF-LF-RF, Angle Back LF and Hips LF-RF-LF,
Side, Touch, 1/4 LF, Touch

Beat 25   Step back RF on back RF angle, pushing hips back
Beat 26 &   Push hips forward and back (hips RF-LF-RF)
Beat 27   Step back LF on back LF angle, pushing hips back,
Beat 28   Push hips forward and back (hips LF-RF-LF)
Beat 29   Step RF to side
Beat 30   Touch LF beside
Beat 31   Turn 1/4 LF and step forward LF
Beat 32   Touch RF beside

Count: 16
Music: "Achy Breaky Heart," by Billy Ray Cyrus
                     "Shake Your Groove Thing," by Peaches & Herb

Counts Step	Descriptions

Toe Touches

Beat 1	Touch right toe out to right
Beat 2	Close RF back to place (no weight change)
Beat 3	Touch right toe out to right
Beat 4	Close RF back to place (change weight)
Beat 5	Touch left toe out to left
Beat 6	Close LF back to place (no weight change)
Beat 7	Touch left toe out to left
Beat 8	Close LF back to place (change weight)

Heel, Touch, Heel, Touch

Beat 9	Touch right heel forward
Beat 10	Close RF back to place (no weight change)
Beat 11	Touch right heel forward
Beat 12	Close RF back to place (no weight change)

1/4 Turn, Touch, Side Step, Slide

Beat 13	Step forward on right with 1/4 turn to left
Beat 14	Close left next to right (no weight change)
Beat 15	Step left out to left side (long step)
Beat 16	Slide right over to meet left (no weight change)

Count: 22
Music: "Gonna Make You Sweat," by C&C Music Factory
                 "Jam," by Michael Jackson
                 "Put Some Drive in Your Country," by Travis Tritt
                 "I Like It, I Love It," by Tim McGraw

Counts	Step Descriptions

Right Side, Together, Side, Change Weight

Beat 1	Touch right toe to right side
Beat 2	Touch right toe next to LF
Beat 3	Touch right toe to right side
Beat 4	Step RF next to LF

Left Side, Together, Side, Change Weight

Beat 5	Touch left toe to left side
Beat 6	Touch left toe next to RF
Beat 7	Touch left toe to left side
Beat 8	Step LF next to RF

Turn/Tap Heel Twitch, Turn/Tap Toe Twice

Beat 9	Pivot 1/4 turn left on ball of LF and tap right heel forward
Beat 10	Tap right heel forward again
Beat 11	Pivot 1/2 turn right on ball of LF and tap right toe back
Beat 12	Tap right toe back again

Turn/Heel, Turn/Toe, Turn/Heel, Turn/Touch

Beat 13	Pivot 1/2 turn left on ball of LF and tap right heel forward
Beat 14	Pivot 1/2 turn right on ball of LF and tap right toe back
Beat 15	Pivot 1/4 turn left on ball of LF and step forward with RF
Beat 16	Pivot 1/4 turn right on ball of RF and touch left toe to left side

Cross, Point, Cross, Step Back

Beat 17	Step across in front of right leg with LF
Beat 18	Touch right toe to right side
Beat 19	Step across in front of left leg with RF
Beat 20	Step back with LF

Together, (Hop)-Hop

Beat 21	Step together with RF
Beat &	(Option) Jump forward with both feet
Beat 22	Jump forward with both feet

Count:	40
Music:	"Watermelon Crawl," by Tracy Byrd

Counts	**Step Descriptions**

Toe Points

Beat 1	Touch right toe to left instep
Beat 2	Touch right heel to left instep
Beats 3–4	Cha cha cha (step RF, LF, RF) in place
Beat 5	Touch left toe to right instep
Beat 6	Touch left heel to right instep
Beats 7–8	Cha cha cha in place

Kick and Clap

Beat 9	Step RF forward
Beat 10	Kick LF forward with a clap
Beat 11	Step LF next to right
Beat 12	Touch right toe back
Beat 13	Step RF forward
Beat 14	Kick LF forward with a clap
Beat 15	Step LF next to right
Beat 16	Touch right toe back

Grapevine to the Right with a Scuff

Beat 17	Step RF to the side
Beat 18	Step LF behind right
Beat 19	Step RF to the side
Beat 20	Scuff LF next to right

Grapevine to the Left with a 1/4 Turn to the Left and a Scuff

Beat 21	Step LF to the side
Beat 22	Step RF behind left
Beat 23	Step LF to the side with a 1/4 turn to the left
Beat 24	Scuff RF next to left

Step and Slide

Beat 25	Step RF forward (as far as you can, slightly diagonally right)
Beats 26–27	Slide LF up toward RF over two beats
Beat 28	Stamp LF beside right and clap
Beat 29	Step LF back (as far as you can slightly diagonally left)
Beats 30–31	Slide RF back toward LF over two beats
Beat 32	Stamp RF beside LF with a clap

Heel Shifts, Military Turns

Beat 33	Transfer weight to RF as you lift left heel
Beat 34	Lower left heel to the floor as you raise right heel
Beat 35	Lower right heel to the floor as you raise left heel
Beat 36	Lower left heel to the floor as you raise right heel
Beat 37	Step forward on RF
Beat 38	Pivot 1/2 turn to the left
Beat 39	Step forward on RF
Beat 40	Pivot 1/2 turn to the left

FIGURE **14.6**
Students enjoy mastering the rhythmic challenges provided by tinikling.

Tinikling

Tinikling (pronounced tee-NEEK-ling) is a rhythmic activity that involves individuals or pairs jumping in between, straddling, or standing outside of two long poles. Originating in the Philippines, tinikling actions imitate the movements of the tinikling birds as they walk between grass stems, run over tree branches, or dodge bamboo traps set by farmers. Tinikling provides an excellent application of basic rhythmic movements.

Tinikling is very similar to jump rope, with rhythmic jumping, but instead of a spinning rope, two long bamboo poles are used. Two people sit at either end of the poles, one pole in each hand. They hit the poles on a beater board, then raise them a couple of inches and hit the poles together. The performer(s) hops or jumps over and outside the poles when they are together, and in between them when they are apart (see Figure 14.6). If the polers sit cross-legged, their knees will be about the same distance apart as the poles should be when they hit the beater board. Some children may find it easier to kneel while they are playing the poles.

tinikling
A rhythmic activity that involves individuals or pairs jumping in between, straddling, or standing outside of two long poles.

BOX **14.3** ■ Directions for Making Tinikling Poles

Tinikling Poles

Two 5 or 6 ft. pieces of PVC pipe for a one-dancer set, or 8 ft. for a two-dancer set (a diameter of 1 inch works, but thicker is OK too).

Beater Boards

Two wooden blocks 24 inches long and 3 inches high. It is helpful to glue some no-mark rubber underneath them to keep them from slipping.

Tinikling can be performed with a three-count beat, where the poles are tapped twice on the boards and once together (with the dancer completing two steps inside the poles and then one outside) or a four-count, where the poles are tapped twice on the board and then twice together (two inside steps and two outside steps). Students more easily grasp a four-beat count, simply because they are familiar with songs containing a four-beat count. Some of the most basic steps are shown in Applications 14.7 and 14.8. More advanced and crossover steps can be found on many websites using tinikling and steps as the key search terms.

When first learning these steps, it may be helpful to practice jumping over stationary poles, jump ropes, or lines drawn on the floor. Practice using the poles before introducing dancers. You might help students keep the beat initially by playing a drum and counting aloud until the entire class is in sync. A useful cue for those using the poles is to "watch your partner, not the dancers"; this helps children focus on the rhythm rather than on all the activity of the dancer's feet (especially if they make a mistake).

PVC tinikling sets can be purchased from sporting goods manufacturers for between $60 and $75. Alternatively, you can make your own set for a considerably lower outlay (see Box 14.3 for directions). More recently, companies have developed stretchable 1-inch elastic bands with foot loops, so that instead of sitting less actively while playing the poles, two students perform continuous straddle jumps to provide the obstacle. These retail for between $12 and $17 per pair.

Folk Dancing

Folk dance is a style of dancing with grassroots origins, strongly integrated into the culture of those who perform the dances. It is called *folk* dance in contrast to dances that originated in the royal courts.

Almost every ethnic group has its own folk dances. Importantly, folk dance can be rural *or* urban; thus the traditional village dances of Europe, the Hawaiian hula, the Cajun dances of Louisiana, the Mexican hat dance, and the Argentine tango are equal members of the folk tradition.

folk dance
A style of dancing that originated among ordinary people and is an integral and anticipated behavior in the culture of those people.

Pole Pattern
Counts 1–2: Strike poles on beater boards twice
Counts 3–4: Strike poles together twice

Tinikling Steps

Steps on One Foot
When the poles are on the dancer's right side (right-foot lead),
the foot work of two one-foot steps would be

Beat 1	Hop on LF outside poles
Beat 2	Hop again on LF outside poles
Beat 3	Step with RF between poles
Beat 4	Step with LF between poles
Beat 1	Hop on RF outside poles
Beat 2	Hop again on RF outside poles
Beat 3	Step with LF between poles
Beat 4	Step with RF between poles

Steps on Two Feet Steps
The footwork for two two-feet steps (with right side next to poles) would be

Beat 1	Hop on both feet outside poles
Beat 2	Hop again on both feet outside poles
Beat 3	Hop on both feet between poles
Beat 4	Hop again on both feet between poles
Beat 1	Hop on both feet outside (straddling) poles
Beat 2	Hop again on both feet outside poles
Beat 3	Hop on both feet between poles
Beat 4	Hop again on both feet between poles

Hops on One Foot
The footwork for two hopping steps (right-foot lead) would be

Beat 1	Hop on LF outside poles
Beat 2	Hop again on LF outside poles
Beat 3	Hop on RF between poles
Beat 4	Hop again on RF between poles
Beat 1	Hop on LF outside poles
Beat 2	Hop again on LF outside poles
Beat 3	Hop on RF between poles
Beat 4	Hop on RF between poles

Pole Pattern
Counts 1–2: Strike poles on beater boards twice
Count 3: Strike poles together

Tinikling Steps

Basic Step

Beat 1	Step with RF into center of poles
Beat 2	Step with LF into center of poles
Beat 3	Step with RF to the right of poles, lift LF
Beat 4	Step with LF into center of poles
Beat 5	Step with RF into center of poles
Beat 6	Step with LF to the left of poles, left RF

Crossover Step

Beat 1	Start on left of poles; using left outside foot, cross over and step between the poles
Beat 2	Step RF to the right outside of the poles
Beat 3	Bring LF to the outside of the poles and place it beside the RF (two feet side by side outside the poles)
Beat 1	Bring outside RF, cross over and step between the poles
Beat 2	Step LF to the left outside of the poles
Beat 3	Bring RF to the outside of the poles and place it beside the LF (two feet side by side outside the poles)

Tinikling Step with a 1/4 Turn

Beat 1	Step with RF into center of poles
Beat 2	Step with LF into center of poles
Beat 3	Step with RF to the right of the poles, lift LF; quarter turn to right (back to the poles)
Beat 1	Step with LF to the side (SIDE)
Beat 2	Bring RF beside the LF (together)
Beat 3	Step with LF to the side; quarter turn to right (face opposite pole person ready to step between poles again)
Beat 1	Step with RF into center of poles
Beat 2	Step with LF into center of poles
Beat 3	Step with RF to the right of the poles, lift LF; quarter turn to right (back to the poles)
Beat 1	Step with LF to the side (side)
Beat 2	Bring RF beside the LF (together)
Beat 3	Step with LF to the side; quarter turn to right (face opposite pole person, ready to step between the poles again)

TABLE **14.2** ■ Sample Folk Dance Steps

Step	Description	Cues
Balance: also called the *pas de bas* or *three*	Consists of three steps executed either in place or while dancer is moving. It is a schottische step without a hop	Step, step, step, rest
Cherkissiya	A sequence of four weight changes executed in a forward and backward or in-and-out rocking motion	Step forward, step back, step back, step forward or step in, step out, step out, step in
Grapevine	A sequence of four or more movements executed sideways	Cross over, side, back, side or side, cross over, back, side
Polka	A sequence of four motions with three weight changes. It is often considered a two-step preceded by a hop	(Hop) step, close, step
Schottische	A sequence of three walking or running steps and a hop (or a kick brush, scoff, and so on)	Run, run, run, hop
Two-Step	Similar to the polka, but is done without the hop	Step, close, step
Waltz	Three even steps with an accent on the first	Forward, 2, 3; or down, up, up

When you introduce and teach folk dancing to children, students should understand these features. If you include folk dancing, you should also teach students about its customs or traditions—that is, the *context* of the dance. To expose students only to the steps of various dances leaves them shortchanged in the rich potential for multicultural instruction and discussions of diversity.

We also believe that children should have a strong grounding in basic rhythmic movement skills before attempting a folk dance. Because folk dances are more complicated and difficult than line dances or tinikling, don't try to teach a country's folk dance (just for the sake of cross-curricular teaching with social studies, let's say) without first grounding children in the skills they need to do it reasonably well. That would ill serve both the dance, which would be performed poorly and inaccurately, and your students, who would just get frustrated.

Some Basic Folk Dance Steps

Although there are many folk dances from all over the world, some common terminology of dance steps can be found across dances. Table 14.2 describes these common steps.

BOX 14.4 ■ Learning a New Dance

1. Read through the instructions and try to make the weight changes in place, saying the cues aloud as you do them. Each cue is the equivalent of one beat. A slash mark separating cues (step/step) means that two steps are done on one beat (e.g., count 1 &). Repeat this until you can shift your weight rhythmically to the cues.

2. Check the formation. If a partner is needed, practice with one.

3. Check for repetitions of steps or parts.

4. Listen to the music. Try to find the underlying beat and count the introduction.

5. If there is more than one part, master each one before moving on to the next.

6. Say the cues to the music without dancing.

7. Dance to the music until you can do the dance without any cues.

Tips for Teaching Folk Dance

When introducing a new folk dance to students you are faced with two challenges. You must first learn the dance yourself and then communicate the steps to the students. Boxes 14.4 and 14.5 give the progressions for these tasks.[a]

Resources for Teaching Folk Dance

Active Videos (www.activevideos.com) has a number of visual and audio resources for learning the most popular folk dances. In their Multicultural Folk Dance sets (two volumes of video, audio, and companion guides), each dance is taught by a native of the country from which it originated or by an expert in that particular dance form. After the instructors teach the dance, a group demonstrates it. Also available from the Active Videos series are resources for Cajun and zydeco dances, hula dances, and Irish dances. These videos can be valuable resources in discovering and learning new folk dances to teach to your class.

Creating Student-Designed Rhythmic Movement Dances

In the developing and expanding rhythms skills sections, your teaching style will be quite directed. You will be providing the beat to students (via an instrument or music) and asking all the students to complete similar movement tasks. While

---

a. The authors would like to thank Rosemary Slacks of the University of Texas at Austin for her kind permission in allowing us to use these valuable resources.

BOX 14.5 ■ Teaching a New Folk Dance

1. Thoroughly know the dance before presenting it to a class. Teach it to a friend to help you see potential problems.

2. Write the cues on an index card for reference. This should be a simple reminder that makes sense to you.

3. Try to teach it in the formation in which it is danced. If this seems too complicated, arrange the students so they are all facing the same direction that you are facing (free formation, lines, and so on).

4. If students have to mirror your movement, you must alter your directions (call "right," but move "left"). It is generally easier if you face away from the class. If teaching in a circle, you should be a part of the circle. Teaching from the center is too confusing.

5. Teach quickly, but by parts:
   a. Name the dance, give some background, and play a short piece of the music.
   b. Demonstrate the first step or phrase at a normal walking speed.
   c. Cue the class through this first step. Repeat until the majority can perform it at normal speed. Follow this method for the remaining parts.
   d. Give the class time to practice at their own pace. You might put them in groups of two or three to help each other.
   e. Walk the class through the entire dance without stopping (no music). Repeat this step until they are moving up to the tempo of the music.
   f. Teach any stylized arm, head, or body actions.
   g. Listen to music. Cue the introduction. Repeat this, having the class cue aloud through the dance (still not dancing).
   h. Have the class dance to the music. Cue as necessary. The class will have learned the dance when they no longer need to hear the cues or rely on you to lead them.

there is some flexibility for students in making choices (e.g., what action word to use), the main concern with your instruction is the development of a solid foundation upon which to build.

As they become proficient, students can also create their own rhythmic routines or dances. This allows them to both apply their skills and use their imaginations. As with student-designed games (see Chapter 13), the process of design may not only help students learn significantly more but also allow them to engage and explore rhythm and movement. Lessons with student-designed activities also give you feedback about what your students have learned and understand about rhythm.

Rhythmic Dance Scripts

We don't introduce student-designed games by giving children some equipment and telling them, "Go make up a game." We give them parameters in which to work. Likewise, we should give students some guidance for designing their own rhythmic sequences. We will call these guidelines a *rhythmic dance script*.

BOX **14.6** ■ A Rhythmic Dance Script

1. You are responsible for a dance that takes up a certain number of beats (e.g., 32 or 64).

2. How many people will be in your group?

3. You may use any of the equipment provided, or you can provide your own.

4. Are you going to exchange any of this equipment during your dance? (Students might pass a ball or balloon down a line of dancers in time to the music.)

5. What formation are you going to begin with? Does this formation change during the dance?

6. What is the spacing between your dancers? Does this change during the dance?

7. How are you going to highlight or contrast the dancers in your group (e.g., through changes in levels or directions)?

Very simply, a rhythmic dance script asks students to consider a number of questions from a list of options, including the number of beats, the use of props, the formation of the group, and the spacing between the performers. Details of specific questions for a script are given in Box 14.6. In Application 14.9 we show the steps and notes to a dance created by some fifth grade students.

Students may find it easier to create a script if they can use a familiar tune. They may also want to use only the chorus of a particular song. This activity lends itself to small-group collaboration and is excellent for including previously learned skills, movements, and steps. When students select their own music, preview the song to be sure its content is appropriate for everyone to hear.

Performing in Front of Others

Although some children are mortified by the suggestion, many dance teachers strongly believe that students should perform in front of others. For example, McGreevy-Nichols (1995) says that viewing live performances is vital to the learning experience. By both performing and watching, students learn to judge not only the technical qualities of rhythmic movement (i.e., are dancers keeping in time and performing the steps correctly?) but also the aesthetic qualities of performance.

McGreevy-Nichols (1995) suggests we use the specific cue, "Hold your concentration," when encouraging students to pay attention as dancers or observers. Holding concentration means not giggling or laughing (as either a performer or observer), talking, or losing focus in the performance. Remember, we usually ask

Beat 1	Side step right
Beat 2	Left slide right
Beat 3	Side step right
Beat 4	Left slide right
Beat 5	Side step left
Beat 6	Right slide left
Beat 7	Side step left
Beat 8	Right slide left
Beat 9	Right foot stomp
Beat 10	Clap
Beat 11	Left foot stomp, left foot stomp
Beat 12	Clap
Beat 13	Right foot stomp
Beat 14	Clap
Beat 15	Left foot stomp, left foot stomp
Beat 16	Clap
Beat 17	Left foot planted, 1/4 turn right
Beat 18	Left foot planted, 1/4 turn right
Beat 19	Left foot planted, 1/4 turn right
Beat 20	Left foot planted, 1/4 turn right
Beat 21	Right stomp
Beat 22	Raise right leg, clap under right leg
Beat 23	Right foot stomp, right foot stomp
Beat 24	Clap
Beat 25	Left foot stomp
Beat 26	Raise right leg, clap under right leg
Beat 27	Left foot stomp, left foot stomp
Beat 28	Clap
Beat 29	Left foot planted, 1/4 turn right
Beat 30	Left foot planted, 1/4 turn right
Beat 31	Left foot planted, 1/4 turn right
Beat 32	Left foot planted, 1/4 turn right

children to perform very short dance routines. They should learn sufficient control to be able to complete their sequences without distraction.

Students increase their levels of self-esteem and self-confidence partly through the discipline acquired from successfully participating in on-stage activities such as public speaking, singing, or acting.

The teaching of rhythmic movement can be an experience full of great pleasure. The key lies in helping students develop competence so they can be successful and therefore build confidence. The progressions described in this chapter assist *all* students in mastering moving to a structured and clear rhythm.

FINAL WORDS

Once students can move in time to obvious percussive beats, they find it easier to move in time with subtler musical beats. Line dances, tinikling dances, and folk dances all have easy-to-follow beats that let children begin to move rhythmically in elementary ways.

Any program in rhythmic movement should allow students to create their own dances. The strategies listed in this chapter allow for the creation of any number of simple rhythmic sequences. Students who have mastered the beginning steps of line dances and tinikling should also find satisfaction in being able to easily create their own dances.

Beginning in the earliest grades, progressive experiences teaching the essentials of rhythm should give students a solid basis for dancing to more complex musical beats. Students with experience and competence in movement should be more comfortable and less resistant to creating expressive rhythmic routines in later grades.

OVER TO YOU

1. Look at the music phrases in the three charts below. Where would you place each of these on a progression tree (e.g., developing, expanding, or mastering)? Justify your answer.

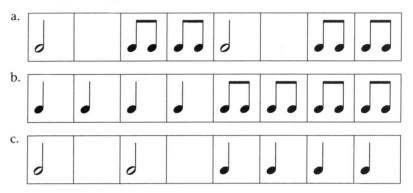

2. How much should student-designed rhythmic sequences be emphasized, as opposed to learning more formalized dances?

3. Should children have to perform their dances (of any form) publicly? Justify your answer. How could you make performance a more positive experience for reluctant students?

PORTFOLIO TASKS

1. Make a collection of inexpensive (costing less than $2) percussion instruments that could be used by children to help sound out various beats and rhythms.

2. Create a number of flash cards of the action words you could use when teaching rhythm sentences.

3. Develop a sequence of steps that create a new line dance. What teaching strategies will you use to teach this dance to your students?

4. Create a CD of music appropriate for teaching the transition from a percussive beat to following music. Remember to select music with a strong downbeat on the first note.

Banek, R., & Scoville, J. (1995). *Sound designs: A handbook of musical instrument building*. Berkeley, CA: Ten Speed Press.

Hopkin, B. (1996). *Musical instrument design: Practical information for instrument making*. Tucson, AZ: See Sharp Press.

McGreevy-Nichols, S. (1995). *Building dances: A guide to putting movements together*. Champaign, IL: Human Kinetics.

Wikipedia encyclopedia. (September, 2004). *Line dancing*. Retrieved from http://en.wikipedia.org/wiki/Line_dancing

Line Dance Resources

Package

Christy Lane's Complete Guide to Line Dancing (video, CD/cassette, book); can be purchased as a package or separately at www.christylane.com

Web Resources

MrHappyfeets' eDance Guide: Line Dance Basics Plus Five Line Dances: www.mrhappyfeets.com/home.html

Zip format dance step sheet collections: http://ourworld.compuserve.com/homepages/jgothard

Hundreds of line dance step descriptions: www.cwdancing.com/linedan.htm

Line Dance Fun USA: www.linedancefun.com

Dancin' Down Under: www.dancindownunder.com

Videos

MrHappyfeets' Dance Instruction—Line Dance Basics Series videos and DVDs
Hottest Line Dances: Country Fever USA II
Line Dancing the Country Way Two-Pack

CDs

Highliners, *Favorite Hits for Country Line Dancing*
Highliners, *More Country Line Dance Hits*

Physical education never stops. Your overarching goal is to help children develop the lifetime habit of physical fitness. As an elementary education teacher in training, you should learn a few "tricks" (actually time-tested strategies) to help children stay physically active and to help them see the relationship between physical education and the other subjects they study in school. Chapter 15 presents strategies for heightening children's general level of physical activity, both in school and at home. Chapter 16 shows you how to look for and apply the interdisciplinary connections between physical education content and other classroom topics.

PROMOTING PHYSICAL ACTIVITY THROUGHOUT THE SCHOOL DAY

UNIT V

"*My advice is to learn all the tricks you can while you're young.*"

STRATEGIES FOR PROMOTING PHYSICAL ACTIVITY AND FITNESS

GETTING STARTED

1. How fit and active are elementary school children?

2. Which is more important: activity, exercise, or fitness?

3. Do you think more children are overweight now than when you were in elementary school? Why?

4. What is an "activity prompt"?

5. How might pedometers be used in physical education?

6. Why do children hate fitness testing—and what can we do about it?

Since 1850, when physical training of students began, the emphasis of physical education in schools has expanded from physical training and calisthenics to a contemporary focus on health-related fitness and the behavioral competencies and motor skills needed for lifelong healthy, satisfying physical activity. As we reported in the first chapter of this book, the National Association for Sport and Physical Education (NASPE) appointed its Outcomes Committee to answer the question, "What should physically educated students know and be able to do?" The Outcomes Project defined five major focus areas, specifying that a physically educated person:

- *Has* learned skills necessary to perform a variety of physical activities
- *Is* physically fit
- *Participates* regularly in physical activity
- *Knows* the implications and benefits of involvement in physical activities
- *Values* physical activity and its contribution to a healthful lifestyle

This chapter focuses on the second and third components of that definition, discussing the concepts of physical activity and fitness. It also provides you with ways to present appropriate activities to your children. Along with the material from the four preceding chapters, this chapter discusses the fifth goal above—valuing physical activity and its contribution to a healthy lifestyle.

Before we begin, however, let us briefly discuss the other major contributor to a healthy lifestyle, diet. Of course, a child with an unhealthy diet is unlikely to be optimally fit, regardless of his or her level of physical activity. For this reason, your instruction and assessment during the health-related portion of your curriculum is critical in helping your students be physically active. Box 15.1 lists some resources you may find helpful in assessing and counseling children about their diet.

As we said, a physically educated person (1) has a physically active lifestyle, and (2) achieves and maintains a health-enhancing level of physical fitness. Your role as a teacher is to help children have regular participation in meaningful physical activity and connect what is done in the physical education class with their outside lives. The material in this chapter should provide you with a solid foundation of knowledge and associated resources to draw upon in achieving that task.

American Dietetic Association: www.eatright.org/Public/GovernmentAffairs/92_adap0199.cfm

Dietary guidance for healthy children aged 2 to 11 years.

Children's Nutrition Research Center: http://kidsnutrition.org/

Contains a free newsletter, Children's BMI calculators, Kids' Energy Calculator, and a number of free brochures and downloadable posters.

USDA Center for Nutrition Policy and Promotion: www.usda.gov/cnpp

Links to the Healthy Eating Index, Food Guide Pyramids, and other resources.

Kid's Health: http://kidshealth.org/kid

KidsHealth has separate areas for kids, teens, and parents, each with its own design, age-appropriate content, and tone. Each section contains in-depth features, articles, animations, games, and resources.

HOW DO WE DEFINE PHYSICAL ACTIVITY AND FITNESS?

You will notice two key terms in the NASPE goals, *physical activity* and *fitness*. As Figure 15.1 shows, **physical activity** is any pursuit that requires you to move your body. It can involve exercise, sports, dancing, and many other forms of leisure activities from fly-fishing to in-line skating. **Fitness,** on the other hand, is "a set of attributes that people have or achieve that relates to the ability to perform physical activity" (U.S. Department of Health and Human Services, 1996).

Physical fitness has two components: (1) **health-related fitness** and (2) **skill-related fitness.** Health-related fitness describes somatic qualities that promote optimum health and prevent the onset of diseases associated with inactivity. It includes cardiovascular (aerobic) endurance, muscular strength and endurance, flexibility, and body composition. Skill-related fitness components promote optimum performance of motor skills and include agility, balance, coordination, power, reaction time, and speed. Most activities presented in Chapters 11 through 14 develop skill-related fitness. This chapter focuses on developing cardiovascular fitness, muscular strength and endurance, and flexibility. It will also help you teach students awareness about becoming more physically active in their everyday lives.

As you can see from Figure 15.1, physical activity is a *process* that leads a child toward fitness, while fitness is a desirable *outcome* of that process. Why is this distinction important? First, as an elementary education teacher, one of your primary goals is to help your students develop the habit of becoming *physically active for a lifetime.* By teaching them motor skills and involving them in physical activities aimed at specific fitness goals, you help contribute to this process. Fitness-related exercises are not the be-all and end-all of this quest, simply a part of it.

physical activity
An umbrella term that includes exercise, sport, dance, and other leisure activities such as fishing or in-line skating.

fitness
A set of attributes that people have or achieve relating to their ability to perform physical activity.

physical fitness
A measure of a person's ability to perform physical activities that require endurance, strength, or flexibility; determined by a combination of regular activity and genetically inherited ability.

health-related fitness
Those components of fitness that promote optimum health and prevent the onset of diseases associated with a lack of physical activity.

skill-related fitness
Those components of fitness that promote optimum performance of motor skills.

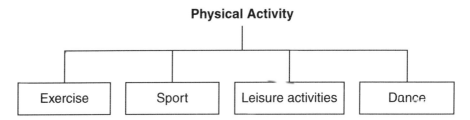

Physical Activity

| Exercise | Sport | Leisure activities | Dance |

FIGURE **15.1**
The Subcategories of Physical Activity.

Source: President's Council on Physical Fitness and Sports Research Digest, Series 3/9, March 2000. Retrieved from www.fitness.gov/activity/activity2/digest_mar2000/digest_mar2000.html

Second, one of your instructional goals is showing your students that physical activity contributing to fitness can indeed be fun and pleasurable. Recent research suggests that most children think exercises like push-ups are the only kind of physical activity that promotes fitness. This means that you need to help your students recognize that riding a bicycle, taking a brisk walk with the dog, or playing hopscotch can promote fitness too.

PHYSICAL ACTIVITY: HOW MUCH DO CHILDREN GET AND HOW MUCH DO THEY NEED?

Times have changed. After-school play was once an intrinsic and valued part of children's lives. Now, with less-safe neighborhoods, more working parents, and the attraction of sedentary pastimes such as video games, many children hardly spend minutes, let alone hours, playing outdoors after school. Consider:

- American children spend more time watching television and playing video games than they do on anything else except sleeping.

- Children watch an average of 25 to 27 hours of television a week. (Luepker, 1999)

- Many children spend less than 15 minutes a day engaged in physical activity. (Fry, 1999)

All these findings suggest that children are becoming ever less physically active. More worrisome still is research showing that physical activity among children steadily declines with age, with significant decreases in activity occurring between the fourth and sixth grades (see Hovell et al., 1999).

Except how much physical activity does a child typically need? The NASPE's Council for Physical Activity for Children (COPEC) has published guidelines on the appropriate amounts of physical activity for children:

1. At a minimum, elementary school aged children should accumulate at least 30 to 60 minutes of developmentally appropriate physical activity per day from a variety of physical activities.

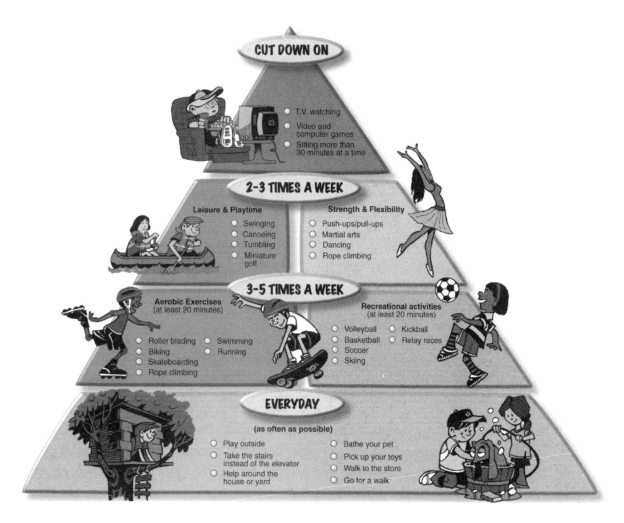

FIGURE 15.2
Physical activity pyramid for kids

Copyright 2003 University of Missouri. Published by MU Extension, University of Missouri–Columbia.

2. A child's daily physical activity should occur in periods lasting at least 10 to 15 minutes. This activity should involve moderate-to-vigorous physical activity that alternates with brief periods of rest and recovery.

3. Extended periods of inactivity are inappropriate for children.

4. A variety of physical activities are recommended for elementary school children (Corbin & Pangrazi, 1998)

Note two key terms in these recommendations. The first is *accumulate*. It is important to understand that the suggested 30 to 60 minutes of daily activity can be built up in 10- to 15-minute intervals. This abolishes the notion that physical activity has to be a lengthy workout. The other key term is *moderate-to-vigorous*. Just as physical activity does not have to occur in a single burst, it also does not need to be exhausting. Examples of moderate physical activity can include brisk walking or riding a bicycle.

The Physical Activity Pyramid

A practical way to help children fulfill the COPEC and NASPE recommendations is to introduce them to the activity pyramid shown in Figure 15.2 (Willenberg, 1999). You may recognize the activity pyramid's resemblance to the now-ubiquitous food

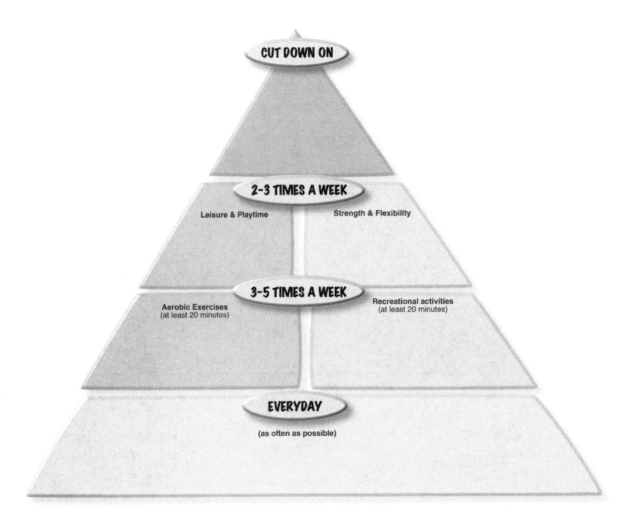

CUT DOWN ON

2-3 TIMES A WEEK

Leisure & Playtime

Strength & Flexibility

3-5 TIMES A WEEK

Aerobic Exercises
(at least 20 minutes)

Recreational activities
(at least 20 minutes)

EVERYDAY

(as often as possible)

FIGURE **15.3**

Blank physical activity pyramid

Copyright 2003 University of Missouri. Published by MU Extension, University of Missouri–Columbia.

pyramid created by the U.S. Department of Agriculture. In fact, both pyramids work the same way. Activities to be restricted or limited appear at the pyramid's narrow peak, while activities to engage in freely appear along the pyramid's broad base. In the activity pyramid, children are encouraged to cut down on the time spent watching television and playing computer games and are prompted to play outside or walk every day.

To help students understand the principle of the pyramid, first discuss each of its levels with your class and then ask each student to create a personalized activity pyramid by filling out the template provided in Figure 15.3. Start by having students list (or draw) their current activities in each space on the pyramid. Then ask them to plan new activities that they would enjoy to balance their pyramids.

FOSTERING HIGH ACTIVITY LEVELS DURING THE PHYSICAL EDUCATION CLASS

The activity pyramid acquaints students with structuring personally beneficial levels of physical activity, but it is ultimately up to them to follow through on its guidelines outside of school. Of course, you have much greater control of the

BOX **15.2** ■ Mission Possible Card

Mission 1: Complete the following:

- ❏ Gallop one lap.
- ❏ Do ten jumping jacks.
- ❏ Do ten curl-ups.
- ❏ Grapevine one lap.
- ❏ Do ten high jumps.
- ❏ Do 15 step-ups (on a stable bench or stairs).
- ❏ *V*-sit stretch left-right-middle (hold for ten seconds at each).

Your mission is complete!

Source: From www.pecentral.org/lessonideas/ViewLesson.asp?ID-683

quality and intensity of their physical activity during the physical education lesson. Use the strategies discussed below to maximize the opportunity for fitness-oriented physical activity during a typical physical education class.

Incorporate Instant Activities

Earlier in this book, we introduced instant activities—physical tasks that students start as they arrive at the work area before the actual physical education lesson. Some teachers choose to use task cards, such as the "mission possible" card shown in Box 15.2, to help students guide themselves through the instant activity. No matter how you script the activity, choose a series of activities that will physically prepare your students for the main tasks of the day's lesson.

Provide Activities for Students Who Are Waiting Their Turn

Equipment and space limitations are the most frequent reasons students spend time waiting rather than practicing a skill. In lessons designed around stations, for example, most of your class may be standing and waiting while a handful of students take their turn at each station. Rather than have students wait passively, have them jump rope or perform exercises with a resistance band. Such activities use inexpensive equipment and require little space. Box 15.3 gives examples of activities students can complete while waiting for turns.

Intersperse Activity-Oriented Tasks between Skill-Development Tasks

Many teachers find it helpful to break up skill-development tasks with activity-oriented tasks. The general idea is that activities should strengthen the body parts used during the skill-development phases of the lesson. For example, during a

FIGURE **15.4**
Pedometers are small devices that track the number of steps an individual takes.

volleying lesson, you might spend a minute or two on a whole-group activity centered on jumping. This also helps promote body awareness in younger students. The teacher's comment below shows another example of a brief physical activity within a skill-development lesson:

> Girls and boys, which body part have we been using to hit the ball? Right, our arms. Let's do an activity to strengthen our arms. I'd like each one of you to move over to the wall, and as a class we are going to try to push it over. Reach out to the wall and press hard against it while I count to five.

Use Pedometers to Promote Awareness of Activity Levels

Pedometers are small devices that fit comfortably on the wearer's hip and record each step as the hip rises (Figure 15.4). The number of steps is displayed on a small LCD panel. Simple pedometers cost less than $10. More sophisticated pedometers also calculate the number of miles walked (or run) and may even give an estimate of the total calories burned. Because pedometers provide direct feedback, wearing them during a physical education lesson can motivate children to increase their activity levels. Pedometers can also help children compare the levels of activity required to perform different skills (e.g., shooting a basketball versus playing three-on-a-side soccer).

The recommended targets for elementary school children are 12,000 steps per day for girls and 15,000 steps per day for boys. The President's Council on Physical Fitness has a program in which children can earn the Presidential Active Lifestyle Award for consistent accumulation of steps (http://fitness.gov/challenge/pala_fact _sheet/pala_fact_sheet.html). Note that these are daily targets which should occur at least five days a week for a total of six weeks. Use pedometers to motivate children to stay physically active after the school day and on weekends.

EXERCISE FOR STUDENTS WITH SPECIAL NEEDS

Some students in your class may have a disability that limits their physical activity. Some children's impairments create physical limitations on their activity, such as juvenile arthritis, cerebral palsy, cystic fibrosis, or musculoskeletal disorders such as spinal cord injury or scoliosis. Other children have *indirect restrictions* caused by conditions such as bronchial asthma, juvenile diabetes, hypertension, or obesity.

In both these situations, low energy, poor flexibility, minimal strength, and limited endurance can discourage youngsters from being active. The more sedentary they become, the worse their fitness becomes—and so it spirals, both alienating students further from physical activity and affecting their social interactions with more active peers.

We have two major goals for such children. The first is to improve their functional capacity, while the second is to increase their opportunities for habitual physical activity. We can achieve this by developing specific exercise prescriptions while modifying the learning environment. You will find a number of suggestions for these accommodations later in this chapter.

INQUIRING MINDS

What strategies do you use to keep children more physically active during each class period?

PROJECT POSITIVE MESSAGES ABOUT PHYSICAL ACTIVITY AND FITNESS

It's critically important that you project a consistently positive message about physical activity through your own attitudes and behavior. Here are some recommendations that can help you to serve as a positive role model for physical activity and fitness.

Stick to Your Physical Education Schedule

Your commitment to a regular schedule of physical education shows your students how much you value regular physical activity. Don't skip a physical education lesson because "it's too much trouble" or "another lesson is more important today." And don't keep children from physical activity as a form of punishment, denying physical education its place as a legitimate educational experience. And, as we stated earlier in this book, *never* use physical activity as a form of punishment!

Present Physical Education Lessons with Enthusiasm and Praise

A second way to advocate for physical activity is by presenting lessons energetically and with conspicuous enthusiasm. Enthusiasm is contagious, and if students see you—a primary role model—enjoying the lesson, this reinforces your positive message about the benefits of fitness-oriented physical activity. As this book has demonstrated throughout its skill-oriented chapters, it's also important to praise your students enthusiastically when they are doing their best to raise their level of physical activity or whenever they have met specific physical activity goals.

PROMOTING CARDIOVASCULAR FITNESS

Cardiovascular fitness is the capacity of the circulatory and respiratory systems to supply oxygen during sustained physical activity. High cardiovascular fitness means that your heart and lungs work well together to supply oxygen to your body during physical exertion. In kidspeak, cardiovascular fitness is your ability to "keep on doing stuff that makes you huff and puff."

Physical activity that strengthens cardiovascular endurance raises the heart and respiratory rates. This is also called **aerobic exercise,** meaning any physical activity that stimulates the body to use oxygen more efficiently (*aero*, air). Aerobic exercise decreases the risk of cardiovascular disease and diseases associated with a sedentary lifestyle by helping the heart and blood vessels (the cardiovascular system) work efficiently. Other benefits may include a reduced risk of developing some forms of diabetes mellitus. Your students can perform many physical activities to improve their cardiovascular endurance. Here are some that are effective with students at most developmental levels.

Jump Rope

One excellent activity for cardiovascular fitness is jumping rope. Each student should begin jumping solo with a short *beaded rope* rather than a lightweight cloth or plastic one; the beaded ropes are heavier and turn in a more consistent arch (see Figure 15.5). The rope should be long enough so that the ends reach to the student's armpits.

To teach the basics skills of the forward and backward jump rope, we suggest the following progression:

1. Jump an imaginary rope using the appropriate arm and wrist technique (see Box 15.4).
2. Turn the rope over the head and catch it with the toes.
3. Hold the rope to the side and swing it with both hands, jumping each time it hits the floor.
4. Turn the rope over the head and jump just before it hits the floor.

As a motivational strategy, have your children form a "jump rope club." In a jump rope club, students enter their names onto a chart as they master particular

aerobic exercise
Any physical activity that stimulates the body to use oxygen more efficiently.

FIGURE **15.5**
Beaded jump ropes are easier for beginners to turn than those made of cloth or plastic.

jumping criteria. These may be based on quality of performance (emphasizing skill development) or on duration alone (emphasizing endurance). For example, can students do 25 jumps without missing, 30 seconds forward, 30 seconds backward, one minute forward, two minutes forward, five minutes forward?

Designate certain times during a physical education lesson for jump rope skill testing. During these times, all students who wish to be tested enter a specific area and begin when instructed to do so. Students who miss return to the practice area, while those who still maintain control at the end of the period can write their names on the appropriate charts. Students in the higher grades (fourth and upward) can self-assess within the testing area.

During designated testing times, encourage students who aren't being tested to complete a series of jump rope task cards. Using self- or peer-evaluation, have children work toward mastery of a number of various jumps. Table 15.1 lists seven simple jump rope skills that all students should be able to master with practice. The American Heart Association's "Jump Rope for Heart" website also has many resources for the teaching of jump rope techniques and styles (www.americanheart.org/presenter.jhtml?identifier=2360).

TABLE 15.1 ■ Progression of Jump Rope Skills

Single Sideswing

1. Put your hands together, while holding the handles, and swing the rope from one side of your body to the other.
2. Keep repeating step 1.
3. When you are ready, open your hands. Swing the rope down and jump.

Skier

1. Jump side to side as if you're skiing.

Side Straddle

1. Pretend you're doing a jumping jack, using only your feet.

Front Straddle

1. Jump with one foot in front and the other in back.
2. Jump and switch the positions of your feet.

X-to-Straddle

1. Jump with your feet spread apart.
2. Jump and cross your legs.
3. Repeat steps 1 and 2.

Heel Exchange

1. Jump and touch your heel to the ground in front of you.
2. Switch feet and touch the other heel to the ground in front of you.
3. Keep repeating steps 1 and 2.

Toe Exchange

1. Jump and touch your toe to the ground behind you.
2. Switch feet and touch the other toe to the ground behind you.
3. Keep repeating steps 1 and 2.

Long-Rope Techniques

In addition to short-rope jumping, many students enjoy jumping a long rope turned by two other students. Rope turners should make sure the rope hits the ground on each rotation. At its peak, a long rope will be traveling either toward or away from the jumper waiting to enter (see Figure 15.6). A rope turning toward the waiting jumper requires a *front-door entry*. The entry cue is, "Go when you see the rope go down past you." A rope turning away from the waiting jumper requires a *backdoor entry*. This entry cue is, "Go when the rope goes up past you." A backdoor entry is typically more difficult for children to master because the jumper has to be ready to jump almost as soon as he or she enters.

Long-Rope Games

One advantage of long-rope jumping is that students can play (and invent) numerous games that are particularly motivating. One example is *chain jumping*. In this, the turners turn the rope front-door fashion, and the jumpers enter and exit one after the other. The aim is to reduce the number of jumps done by each jumper until they enter one after the other without any turns in between. Entering and exiting in one turn is known as *rapid fire*.

Children also enjoy rhyme or chant games. Well-suited to large or small groups, the aim of these games is to continue jumping, often as the rope is turned faster and faster. One such example that requires students to progress through a series of skills is the teddy bear rhyme:

FIGURE **15.6**
Children enjoy many games that involve a long rope.

Teddy bear, teddy bear, turn around,	[turn 360° while jumping]
Teddy bear, teddy bear, touch the ground,	[touch the ground while jumping]
Teddy bear, teddy bear, go upstairs,	[high knee lifts while jumping]
Teddy bear, teddy bear, say your prayers,	[clasp hands while jumping)
Teddy bear, teddy bear, turn off the light,	[reach up while jumping]
Teddy bear, teddy bear, say goodnight.	[exit the jump rope].

Another rhyme that requires students to go longer and longer, as well as faster and faster, is

Bubblegum, bubblegum, in a dish,

How many pieces do you wish?

One, two, three, etc. . . . [jump until you miss]

Running

While running is excellent for cardiovascular fitness, many students do not find it to be particularly fun, especially when they are required to "simply run" without specific goals or incentives. For that reason, running programs should be individualized, with you and your students collaborating to develop achievable and motivating lessons.

To make running goals meaningful, keep records of your students' distances. Most record cards have a series of symbols that are crossed out for specified distances. Two examples are shown in Figure 15.7. In the first, one foot is colored in for each mile run. In the second example, three laps of the school's running trail are equal to one mile, so one-third of a pie is colored for each lap run.

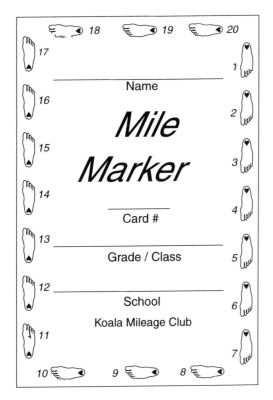

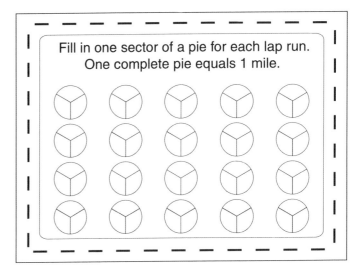

Fill in one sector of a pie for each lap run.
One complete pie equals 1 mile.

FIGURE **15.7**
Running record cards can chart the distances children run during class.

One popular way to motivate students to run is setting up a class marathon from your school's hometown to another city or state. All you need is a road map that indicates the distance between various points. For each lap or mile your class completes during a given lesson, you draw an equivalent mileage segment on the map in the classroom. As an interdisciplinary activity, have students research and report about the various towns and natural attractions that they "run" through along the way to their destination.

Instead of running the same course each day, use pedometers to translate steps into miles. Then your students can travel over different courses on successive days and still be able to calculate the total miles they have traveled. Your students can also find out how many steps they take per mile by walking a mile and counting their steps. They could also *run* a mile and count their steps and then compare their "mile walk" and "mile run" step counts.

Games That Promote Cardiovascular Fitness

You can use a number of games as instant activities to promote cardiovascular fitness. One particular favorite is called builders and bulldozers; another is called freeway racing.

In builders and bulldozers, divide students into two teams and place them on opposite sides of the play area. Between the teams are a number of cones, half of them lying on their sides and half of them upright. Team builders' task is to move in and turn upright the cones that are tipped over. Conversely, team bulldozers are to knock down as many cones as possible. Play lasts for a predetermined time (usually around 30 seconds or one minute). The team with the most success wins. Repeat the game with teams in their original roles or switching roles. As a safety precaution, teachers with younger children often require "fast walking" instead of running during this game.

In freeway racing, students move in one direction along the perimeter of a room or designated workspace. Their rate depends on "road conditions" that you call out at different intervals:

- Interstate—run as fast as possible, no speed limit
- School zone—slow
- Speed limit—walk
- Out of gas—stop

For added variety, you might add a number of additional road conditions:

- Bumpy road—skip
- Slippery road—slide
- Flat tire—hop on one foot
- Raining outside (so you need windshield wipers)—jumping jacks

Students who fail to adhere to the speed limit or cause traffic disruptions receive a citation and have to park their cars in the center of the area (a form of time-out consistent with the game). For children with hearing disabilities, you may hold up a series of colored cards or cards with diagrams as you call out the condition.

Cardiovascular Fitness Ideas for Students with Special Needs

Jumping rope is a great exercise, but many students will be unable to perform the full skill. Some may be in a wheelchair, others may lack the mobility to turn a rope, while still others may have difficulty coordinating a turned rope. Fear not; there are options. First, try a hoop instead of a rope; it will be easier to hold onto and still allows the child to jump. If this is still too challenging, place a rope on the ground so the student can jump side to side or over and back, without actually having to turn the rope. Have students with ambulatory difficulties mimic the action of the rope with their arms.

Children in wheelchairs can do marching exercises with their arms or various swimming strokes such as freestyle, breast stroke, or dog paddle. Avoid backstroke;

the arms go back over the head with one-arm full shoulder extension. Also avoid asymmetrical arm movements like windmilling.

Many students can take part in running exercises and games, but just at a slower speed. A student in a chair can move the chair in and out of an obstacle course set up with cones or move the chair up and down a ramp. For students with asthmatic conditions, be careful of planning activities that involve fast running on very dry or cold days. Let these students walk briskly rather than jog and always allow them to cool down slowly.

PROMOTING MUSCULAR STRENGTH AND ENDURANCE

There's a difference between muscular strength and muscular endurance. **Muscular strength** is the maximum force that a muscle produces against a resistance in a single, maximal effort, while **muscular endurance** is the capacity of a muscle to exert a force repeatedly against a resistance. In kidspeak, muscular strength is "lifting the heaviest weight you can budge," while muscular endurance is "when you can lift a weight over and over."

You should realize that both muscular strength and endurance are specific to particular muscle groups. For example, you can have muscular strength and endurance in your arms while lacking them in your legs. It is important to have strong muscles that can work forcefully over a period of time. Adequate muscle strength has a positive effect on physical appearance because it improves the muscles' shape and tone (the "tightness" of a muscle at rest).

Resistance training, or exercising with weights, is the basic way to build muscular strength and endurance. You do not need a gym full of barbells and dumbbells to develop this dimension of fitness in your students. They can work against gravity to create resistance. Jumping for height will help develop leg strength, while hanging from a bar and trying to lift the body will develop arm strength. If you can make strength and endurance activities fun, you are more likely to succeed in encouraging students to work at higher levels of resistance. The easiest way to help students build muscular strength and endurance is by focusing on one body region at a time.

Developing Arm Strength and Endurance

While push-ups are routinely assigned to develop arm strength, children do not have to begin by doing the traditional push-up. The easiest way to do push-ups is against a wall (so that the movement is more horizontal, rather than vertical against gravity) or a high bench (so more of your weight is on the feet), then moving to floor push-ups on the knees (the so-called girls' push-ups), and finally onto the toes for traditional push-ups. Box 15.5 describes how to do this full form. As well as this push-up progression, there are many activities similar to push-ups that your students may enjoy more. Table 15.2 lists some alternatives to standard push-ups suitable for students in the upper elementary grades.

muscular strength
The maximum force that a muscle produces against a resistance in a single, maximal effort.

muscular endurance
A muscle's capacity to exert a force repeatedly against a resistance.

BOX **15.5** ■ How to Do a Push-Up

Start position: The child lies face down on the mat in a push-up position with hands under the shoulders, fingers straight, and legs straight, parallel, and slightly apart, with the toes supporting the feet.

Action: The child straightens his or her arms, keeping the back and knees straight, then lowers the body until there is a 90-degree angle at the elbows, with the upper arms parallel to the floor. The picture in this box shows the extended position.

Cues: Head up, eyes up, body straight.

FIGURE **15.8**
Crab soccer is an excellent activity for promoting arm strength and endurance.

Push-ups are not the only activity that can develop arm strength. Activities in a crab position (i.e., bearing weight on hands and feet only, but with the back instead of the chest facing the floor) provide good resistance and require the arms to carry the body weight (see Figure 15.8). While in the crab position, students can walk, pass a ball in pairs or threes, or play four-on-a-side crab soccer.

In crab soccer, players try to kick an inflated ball into a goal to score points, and players other than the goalie must not touch the ball with their hands. But crab

TABLE **15.2** ■ Alternatives to Regular Push-Ups

Shoulder Touches

From a push-up position, students touch one hand to the opposite shoulder. Alternate shoulders.

Advanced: Pause on the touch for a count of 5.

Stacking

From a push-up position, students pick up small objects and either move them into piles, stacked one on top of the next, or simply change three objects from one side of their bodies to another.

Advanced: Stack and unstack the piles continuously.

Advanced: Tap a tennis ball back and forth between the hands.

Marching Push-ups

Begin in a push-up position with the hands on a line.

Place hands alternately over the line and back.

Advanced: Increase the speed, time, or number.

Macarena Push-ups (to the Macarena song)[a]

Begin in a push-up position.

Reach forward with the right hand with support on the left arm.

Return the right hand to the floor then raise the left hand while supporting with the right arm.

Right hand forward and turn palm up, return; left hand forward and turn palm up, return.

Right hand to left shoulder, return; left hand to right shoulder, return.

Right hand to right ear, return; left hand to left ear, return.

Right hand to left waist, return; left hand to right waist, return.

Right hand to right hip, return; left hand to left hip, return.

Quarter turn to your right and repeat the steps facing the next wall.

Partner Patty-Cakes

Two people in push-up position face each other.

Tap right hand to right hand and then left to left.

Continue alternating until too tired to go on.

Advanced: Increase distance between partners.

a. From www.pecentral.org/lessonideas/ViewLesson.asp?ID=686

soccer is different from the usual type of soccer in that players walk on all fours, face up, in motions that make them look like crabs. Crab soccer can be played either outdoors or in a gymnasium.

In addition to moving their bodies against gravity, your students can also work with resistance bands to build muscular strength and endurance. Resistance bands come in a variety of forms and are color-coded according to the level of resistance to pulling they offer. The most inexpensive come in continuous rolls you can snip

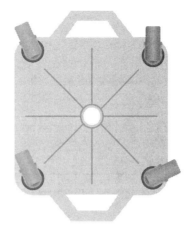

FIGURE **15.9**
Scooter boards come in many different sizes and shapes and can be used in pushing and pulling the body.

FIGURE **15.10**
Scooter swimming is excellent for promoting upper body strength and endurance.

to optimal lengths for your children's body sizes. But even bicycle inner tubes can be used as simple resistance bands. With these stretchy tools, children can explore movements that work different muscles. Upper body activities are particularly suited to resistance band exercises. Some specific examples are provided in Table 15.3.

Where budgets allow, gym scooters are popular physical education equipment and are a very useful and fun way for children to build muscular strength (see Figure 15.9). Children sit or lie on the scooter and propel themselves using their arms. Children lying on the scooter frequently use swimming strokes to move about. Scooters are well suited to strength-building activities such as negotiating an obstacle course. An obstacle course can be as simple as a number of cones placed as barriers in the work area. You can also design tunnels or low hurdles for your students to scoot under or have them mimic swimming strokes (see Figure 15.10).

TABLE **15.3** ■ Resistance Band Exercises

Stretch Band Biceps Curl

1. Grasp the stretch band in front of you with both hands, keeping your left hand slightly below waist level with palm facing down and your right hand just above it with palm facing up. Tuck your right elbow in close to your side.
2. Without moving your left arm, bend your right elbow and bring your palm up until it is facing the front of your left shoulder, with your thumb pointing out and away from the body.

Stretch Band Triceps Extension

1. Grasp the stretch band on either end, placing one hand behind your back and the other hand at the back of your neck with your thumb pointing down.
2. Keeping your bottom hand stationary, extend the top arm above your head by moving just the elbow; your shoulder should remain stable in order to isolate the triceps muscle.

Stretch Band Lateral Pulldown

1. Stand in an upright position with feet together. Hold your arms level with your chest.
2. Stretch the band apart and pinch your shoulders together. Hold this form for one second and return to starting position.

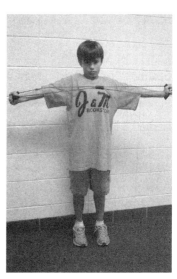

continued

TABLE **15.3** ■ Resistance Band Exercises, *continued*

Stretch Band Lateral Raise

1. Place one end of the stretch band under your left foot. Comfortably grasp the other end of your band in the left hand, maintaining a slight bend in your elbow. Position your left arm straight down from the shoulder with your thumb pointing forward.
2. Lift your arm laterally to shoulder height, keeping your wrist firm, thumb pointed up, and palm facing forward.
3. Repeat on the right side.

Chest Press

1. Grasp the ends of the stretch band in both hands and place it behind your back, under your arms, at chest level. Bend and raise your elbows to chest level.
2. Keeping your wrists firm and palms parallel with the floor, extend your arms straight in front of your body; do not lock out your elbows.

Developing Leg Strength and Endurance

Most activities that involve pushing the body off the ground also involve the legs. Jumping activities are particularly helpful in developing leg strength and offer many challenging variations. Students can jump for either height or distance and try to beat their previous result each time. You can also direct your students to jump over obstacles, such as hoops or low boxes.

A particularly useful exercise for developing leg strength is the lunge (see Figure 15.11). Perform a lunge by taking a large step forward on the heel and then the forefoot. Lower the body by bending the knee and hip of your front leg until the knee of your rear leg is almost in contact with floor. Return to original standing position by pushing up on the hip and knee of your front leg. Keep the back straight throughout.

FIGURE **15.11**
The lunge is a great exercise for developing leg strength.

Developing Abdominal Strength and Endurance

Abdominal strength and endurance are particularly important in promoting good posture and correct pelvic alignment. Strength and endurance of the abdominal muscles are also important in maintaining lower back health.

While there are many variations to the sit-up, all children should understand the basic technique. Effective sit-ups must pull the torso upward from a lying position toward the knees using only the abdominal muscle group. Bending the knees helps neutralize the action of the muscles that flex the hip, thereby making the abdominal muscles work harder. Straight-leg sit-ups also arch the back and may create overextension and strain. Sit-ups done rapidly and with momentum, whether or not knees are bent, do not work the abdominal group very much; rising slowly and only part way works the abdominal muscles best. While sit-ups are the most common form of abdominal exercise for adults, we prefer to help children learn the *curl-up*. (Box 15.6 provides details about how to do a curl-up.) Curl-ups involve sliding the fingers along the floor rather than raising the arms across the chest or placing the hands behind the head. The curl-up is both easier to teach and more commonly used for testing abdominal endurance in children.

Muscle of the Week

To reinforce the importance and relevance of muscular strength and endurance, bring the "muscle of the week" technique into your lesson plan. While your class is warming up, introduce the proper muscle name (e.g., quadriceps) and practice an exercise that strengthens and/or stretches that muscle (for example, using stretch bands to contract and lengthen it). Some teachers will actually draw the muscle on their bodies using washable markers. Muscles not readily displayed can be drawn on a T-shirt or shorts. Of equal importance, however, is helping your students understand how that muscle works in daily activities and what sports use it. Students can then be asked to identify activities *they* do that use this muscle. This

BOX **15.6** ■ How to Do a Curl-Up

Start position: The child lies on his or her back with the knees bent at 90° and the feet on the floor. Arms are extended to the sides with the fingers touching the ground. The picture in this box shows this start position.

Action: The child slowly lifts his or her shoulder blades off the mat by flexing the spine so that the fingertips reach forward a distance of about 5 inches. The child then slowly returns the shoulder blades to the mat by flattening his or her lower back.

Cues: Roll up with the chin first, fingers on the floor.

allows them to identify and explore a large range of muscles throughout a term or school year. Table 15.4 provides our list of "Top Ten Muscles in the Body."

Muscular Strength and Endurance Ideas for Students with Special Needs

The three major issues related to muscular strength and endurance for students with special needs are (1) the amount of weight they are expected to lift or move, (2) how they are able to hold the weight, and (3) the number of times they are required to repeat an exercise.

To address the first issue, it is useful to have students avoid lifting or pulling their body, giving them lots of opportunity to hang, climb, and crawl with some support. One exception here is for a student to lie on a scooter and pull him- or herself along a rope fixed at floor level. Some students benefit from doing "reverse" push-ups. That is, they begin sitting on the ground with their chest up, and push their bodies off the floor with their arms.

For difficulties holding a weight, plastic water bottles that are easy to squeeze are a cheap and effective solution. The child is able to hold the bottle as it squashed to conform to their grip. Another useful alternative is for a student to

TABLE **15.4** ■ Top Ten Muscles in the Body

Muscle Name	Location and Function	Simple Exercises and Activities
Biceps	Front of the upper arm Brings the hand to the shoulder	Chin-ups Any climbing activities
Triceps	Back of the upper arm Straightens the arm	Push-ups Throwing a ball or Frisbee
Quadriceps	Front of the thigh Straightens the knee	Any jumping activities Kicking or punting
Hamstrings	Back of the thigh Moves the hip backward	Lunges Bike riding
Rectus Abdominus	Stomach muscles Bends the trunk	Curl-ups Throwing overhead with two hands (e.g., like a soccer throw in)
Gastrocnemius	Calf muscle Points the toe	Hopping Kicking a ball along the ground with the shoelaces
Pectoralis Major	Chest muscles Used in pushing things away from the body	Push-ups Throwing a large ball with two hands from the chest
Deltoid	Large muscle on top of the shoulder Lifts the arm up when it's straight	Any hitting activity using straight arms (e.g., hitting a softball, hitting a hockey puck, playing tennis or badminton)
Trapezius	Large upper back muscles Shrugs the shoulders	Rowing actions Shrugging the shoulders
Gluteus Maximus	The muscles that make up the buttocks	Running Donkey kicks

hold milk jugs or containers with handles. In both cases, the weight of the bottle can be varied by its contents (i.e., nothing, or various amounts of water or sand). Remember that there are numerous levels of intensity for push-ups (see Table 15.2), and some students in chairs with handles may be able to push up and lower themselves.

In dealing with the third case, the key is to focus on intermittent, rather than continuous, work, by decreasing the total time a student spends on one exercise or decreasing the total number of repetitions. Allow students to work in their own time frames.

Mr. Chapman would like his fifth grade class to work toward a number of fitness awards. On the last Thursday of each month, Mr. Chapman has his class complete a push-ups test and a sit-ups test. Mr. Chapman has a notice board in his classroom that shows all students' scores and whether they have reached the standard for the "Presidential Champions Gold Award."

WHAT'S WRONG WITH THIS PICTURE?

Elastic resistance bands are excellent for strength development in children with disabilities. There are a few things to remember here, however. First, children with cerebral palsy, head injury, or incomplete spinal cord injury should exercise both sides of the body at the same time, while children with severe coordination and balance problems should complete exercises that work only one side at time. In both these cases, as well as with students in chairs who may lack strength, it is recommended that you wrap the stretch band around some fixed point, rather than having the student pull against his or her own resistance.

Students who have difficulty completing abdominal curls can benefit from doing them on an incline, so they do not have to lift their bodies so far. However, some students with spinal cord injuries may not be able to perform movements involving trunk flexion because they have no muscle control or have implanted spinal rods.

PROMOTING FLEXIBILITY THROUGH STRETCHING

Another component of physical fitness is **flexibility.** This is the ability of a joint to move through its full range of motion. Flexibility is related to the "stretchiness" of the muscles, ligaments, and tendons that help to operate and stabilize a particular joint's movement. Other things being equal, a joint is more flexible when the muscles, tendons, and ligaments surrounding it are fairly loose and stretchable.

Like muscular strength and endurance, flexibility is not a general quality but is specific to a particular joint or set of joints. It is not true that some people are "naturally flexible" throughout their entire body. Being flexible in one particular body region or joint does not necessarily imply being flexible in another.

Many muscular and skeletal problems result from poor flexibility. Flexibility is necessary for improving and maintaining postural alignment, for executing movements efficiently and gracefully, and for facilitating and developing motor skills. The more flexible you are, the more easily you can reach, bend, and stretch. You are also less likely to injure your muscles and joints. In kidspeak, flexibility is "being able to bend and reach really far."

flexibility
The range of motion around a joint.

Stretching as the Key to Developing Flexibility

The safest way to develop flexibility is through slow and sustained stretching, as opposed to bouncing movements. It is also important to warm up before stretching, so it is best to do these exercises at the end of a lesson rather than at the beginning. Think of a piece of cold taffy. It's hard and stiff. Trying to bend it is difficult, and it may even snap. Warm taffy is more pliable and easier to stretch. It's the same with muscles. Students should be taught this principle, together with the fact that the stretching does not have to *hurt.* When performing stretches, the key is to slowly stretch to a point of *discomfort* (not pain) and then hold that position for about 15 seconds.

While most pediatricians would suggest that children do not need to specifically perform stretching exercises, we believe that is it valuable to teach them about stretching. Then, when they reach adolescence, they will understand the key principles and have a repertoire of exercises they can perform. We feel you should regularly add various stretching exercises to your physical education lessons. Students should perform stretching activities daily for optimal flexibility, but at least three times per week.

Appropriate and Inappropriate Stretches for Children

Some stretching exercises are appropriate for children while others are not. Child-appropriate stretching activities:

- Should be performed slowly
- Follow a warm-up
- Are held for 15 seconds
- Are held in a comfortable position
- Are gentle (there is no pain)

Conversely, some stretching exercises and activities are inappropriate for elementary school children. Generally speaking, to ensure safe exercises, do *not:*

- *Bounce:* Using quick, jerking motions to stretch can tear muscles, tendons, or ligaments.
- *Lock or hyperextend:* Locking the knees or elbows overstresses the joints.
- *Perform fast exercises:* Sudden contractions cause tightening of muscles and do not strengthen the muscle correctly or help the muscle gain the ability to act in a slow sustained manner.
- *Swing:* Swinging motions can tear muscle fiber.
- *Overbend a joint:* The range of safe motion for the knee and elbow is limited.
- *Arch the low back or neck:* Hyperextension of the back or neck can damage the spine.

Table 15.5 lists stretches appropriate for students in elementary schools. When teaching one of the listed stretches, you can promote your students' body

TABLE **15.5** ■ **Appropriate Stretching Exercises**

Triceps Stretch

- Stand or sit and place your right arm over the top of your head, elbow bent.
- Place your left hand on the back of your right elbow, exhale and press, feeling a stretch in the back of your right arm.

Hamstring Stretch

- Sit down and straighten your left leg.
- The sole of your right foot should rest next to the inside of your straightened leg.
- Lean slightly forward and touch your foot with your fingers.
- Keep your left foot upright with the ankle and toes relaxed.

Calf Stretch

- Stand an arm's length from the wall.
- Lean into wall, holding the arms straight.
- Place one leg forward with knee bent; this leg will have no weight put on it.
- Keep your other leg back with the knee straight and the heel down.
- Keeping your back straight, move your hips toward wall until you feel a stretch.

continued

TABLE **15.5** ■ Appropriate Stretching Exercises, *continued*

Quadriceps Stretch

■ Stand erect, holding onto a wall for support.
■ Bend your knee behind you so that you can grasp your foot, holding your heel against your butt and your knees together.
■ Stand up straight and push your knee gently back as far as you can; the hand just keeps the heel in place.
■ Do not pull on your heel, just push the knee back.

Lower Back

■ Tighten your abdominal muscles to flatten your lower back.
■ Pull your right leg toward your chest.
■ If possible, keep the back of your head on the floor. Try to keep your lower back flat.

awareness by encouraging them to learn the names of the muscle groups associated with each stretch.

Games and Other Activities That Promote Flexibility

As well as having your students regularly perform stretching exercises, use games and activities that help promote flexibility. A few examples are discussed below.

Alphabet Stretching

In this game, students attempt to twist and stretch to form the shape of a selected letter of the alphabet. The letter might be one you call out, or students may select a letter from a deck of cards. The challenge is to hold the stretch for six seconds. Students may work in pairs or threes to form a certain letter (e.g., Q). Always focus, however, on the stretching and holding nature of the task.

Stretch Break

During any learning task, have students stop to do a quick stretch of the muscle that has been the dominant mover for that task. For example, stop and do some leg stretching during a lesson on punting. In a volleying lesson, do some arm stretches.

Pit Stop

A fun activity to include during the aerobic exercise we called freeway racing is the pit stop. When you call out "pit stop," students have to stop and check whichever part of the car the you designate. Examples include:[a]

- Check the brakes—calf stretch
- Check the engine—quadriceps stretch
- Check the wipers—triceps stretch
- Check the fan belt—hamstring stretch

Flexibility Ideas for Children with Special Needs

While able-bodied children may not need specific training for flexibility, some students with disabilities have a limited range of motion. Stretching is particularly important for children with cerebral palsy, because their muscles tend to contract. Stretching can also prevent the permanently shortened muscles (contractures) that may be problematic for children with spinal cord injury. These students should be able to do most of the activities that are being completed by their classmates. You can use bands to place under the legs of students in wheelchairs to help them lift their legs for hamstring stretches or pull their toes toward them for calf stretches. Likewise, you can tie the bands to their chair so they can pick them up as a substitute for triceps stretches.

INQUIRING MINDS

What do you see as the advantages and disadvantages of physical fitness testing for children?

PROMPT CHILDREN TO BE ACTIVE OUT-OF-SCHOOL AND DURING RECESS

Surprisingly, very few elementary education teachers prompt their students to stay active outside the physical education lesson time (McKenzie et al., 1997). A prompt needn't be particularly sophisticated and can take only a few seconds. What is important is the encouragement the prompt creates. Box 15.7 gives some examples of helpful out-of-class physical activity prompts.

FITNESS TESTING AND ITS ROLE IN PHYSICAL EDUCATION

Of anything about physical education, perhaps the bane of most students is "fitness testing." No other exam is approached with such dread. You might recall having to file out, one by one, in front of the rest of the class and attempt that one dreaded pull-up, a pull-up you knew perfectly well you couldn't do. From an educational perspective, what was more pointless was that the test results were

---

a. Modified from *Physical Best Activity Guide: Elementary Level,* by the NASPE, 2005, Champaign, IL: Human Kinetics.

Example 1: Today we worked on striking with a flat paddle, and I'm going to give you a challenge. I'd like to see if you all could ask your mom or dad to make you a paddle using an old coat hanger. I've given you the directions in your folders to take home. I am also going to give you each a balloon you can use to strike with the new homemade paddle. You can keep your paddle at home and use it to practice.

Example 2: Boys and girls, yesterday we practiced taking our arms way back when we were tossing underhand. Who asked someone to practice with them during recess?

Example 3: Today we practiced jumping for height. I wonder if everyone in the class has a place at home to practice after school. See if you can get three friends or brothers or sisters and find a place where you can all mark your highest jump. See if you can jump higher than your mom!

Example 4: Girls and boys, yesterday I scored 11,250 steps on my pedometer. Can anyone tell me what the target for adults is? That's right, it's 10,000 steps. Now, some of you indicated that your mom or dad had recently bought a pedometer. Would all of you children remember to check with them about their scores today, and even better, offer to go for a walk with them if they are under 10,000?

virtually meaningless. No one ever really got to see the scores and hardly any explanation was given about their purpose.

Fortunately, a more contemporary view of fitness testing is emerging. Thanks to a change in the way the major organizations such as the President's Council on Fitness and Sports perceive fitness, a number of tests are now available that compare a child's results with a particular *health standard*. These scores measure children against specific criteria rather than against others in a norm-referenced framework. The health standard gives minimum scores for children of various ages to have satisfactory levels of each fitness component.

The Role of Fitness Testing

Many factors other than physical activity can influence a student's performance on a physical fitness test: maturation, heredity, predisposition, and body composition. As Welk, Morrow, and Falls (2002) note, an overemphasis in the curriculum on fitness testing can send students the wrong message about physical activity. For example, some students who score poorly on fitness tests despite being physically active may get discouraged in physical education, while other students may incorrectly believe that they don't need to be active if their fitness levels are in the healthy zone.

Fitness testing, then, should be a self-monitoring tool for students' current health levels. Test results should work as feedback rather than being an end point

TABLE 15.6 ■ **Fitness Test Components**

President's Council Health Fitness Tests	FITNESSGRAM
Aerobic Capacity	**Aerobic Capacity**
■ Endurance run/walk	■ The pacer *or* one-mile walk/run
Muscular Strength and Endurance	**Muscular Strength and Endurance**
■ Right-angle push-ups *or* pull-ups	■ Curl-up test
■ Partial curl-ups	■ Trunk lift
	■ One of the following: 90° push-up, pull-up, flexed arm hang, or modified pull-up
Flexibility	**Flexibility**
■ *V*-sit reach *or* sit-and-reach	■ *V*-sit reach *or* back-saver *or* shoulder stretch

Source: President's Challenge: www.presidentschallenge.org/; FITNESSGRAM: www.cooperinst.org/ftginfo.asp#FITNESSGRAM

to be used as a grade. Fitness testing in schools, then, is an ongoing process, grounded in two essential objectives:

1. To help students become aware of their health status through self-testing activities of cardiovascular endurance, flexibility, muscular strength, and muscular endurance

2. To help students develop health-related fitness goals based on previous self-assessment

With these objectives in mind, teach your students the various fitness test protocols so they can self-administer these tests. You will also need to help them compare their scores with the age-related health standards and assist them in setting physical activity goals.

Fitness Tests and Health Standards

Table 15.6 lists the components measured in the fitness testing protocols of two major agencies. While the specific items and testing protocols differ, you can see that both tests measure aerobic fitness and muscular strength and endurance as well as flexibility. Protocols for the tests can be found at the websites provided in the table.

The health standards for the President's Challenge protocols are presented in Table 15.7. These should be the targets of all students in your class. Be sure to encourage them to set increasingly higher goals as they reach these health standards.

Administration of Fitness Tests

Again, fitness tests are not ends in themselves, but means through which your students learn about their fitness and health and how to set goals. Remember to administer fitness tests so that students are not singled out to perform in front of their peers.

TABLE **15.7** ■ Health Fitness Standards: *President's Challenge*

	Age	Partial Curl-ups (No.)	1 Mile Run (min.:sec.)	Distance Option or (min.:sec.) 1/4 mi.	(min.:sec.) 1/2 mi.	V-Sit Reach (inches)	Sit & or Reach (cm.)	Right Angle Push-Ups (No.)	Pull-or Ups (No.)
Boys	6	12	13:00	2:30		1	21	3	1
	7	12	12:00	2:20		1	21	4	1
	8	15	11:00		4:45	1	21	5	1
	9	15	10:00		4:35	1	21	6	1
	10	20	9:30			1	21	7	1
	11	20	9:00			1	21	8	2
	12	20	9:00			1	21	9	2
Girls	6	12	13:00	2:50		2	23	3	1
	7	12	12:00	1:40		2	23	4	1
	8	15	11:00		5:35	2	23	5	1
	9	15	10:00		5:25	2	23	6	1
	10	20	10:00			2	23	7	1
	11	20	10:00			2	23	7	1
	12	20	10:30			2	23	8	1

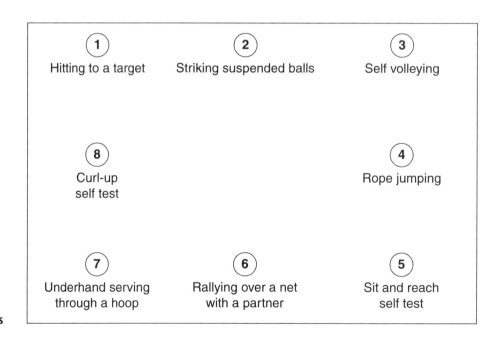

FIGURE **15.12**
Striking with paddles circuit incorporating fitness testing stations

Stations are an excellent way to include fitness testing within lessons. Whatever the content of the station, be it dribbling, striking, or volleying, one or two of the stations could offer a fitness test. Figure 15.12 gives an example of such a circuit.

There has been a major shift in thinking about exercise and fitness. The focus to-day is clearly on *activity*. We now realize that it is particularly important to help children and parents understand that *all* physical activity contributes to health and that physical activity is a process, while physical fitness is an outcome of that process. In the same fashion, fitness testing should be a guide to self-assessment and goal setting, rather than a once-a-year exercise. Children should target the specific health standards rather than compare themselves with others or national norms. At the same time, teachers should be encouraging students to be active outside school, accumulating the recommended 60 minutes a day of activity.

FINAL WORDS

1. How can you be more active in your own daily living? Take particular note of any strategies you could use to increase your activity level during a regular school day (e.g., parking a little further from the building and walking) and that you might use to reinforce activities to students.

2. Does your school have recess? How might you help your students become more active at recess?

3. A key factor in children's activity levels is the activity level of their parents. How might you involve parents to become more active themselves and become activity advocates for their children?

OVER TO YOU

1. Using hoops, mats, balloons, cones, and any other equipment you feel would be helpful, design an obstacle course that represents the circulation of the blood through the heart and lungs. Include the atria and ventricles, the valves that connect the heart's chambers; and, where possible, use the colors red and blue to represent the relative oxygenation of the blood.

2. Design a circuit of nine stations to encompass the three key areas of physical fitness. Have three stations dedicated to aerobic endurance, three to muscular endurance, and three to flexibility. Make a list of the equipment needed for each station of the circuit, and arrange the stations so that the fitness components are equally distributed.

3. Make a series of jump rope task cards, enough so that each student in your class can have at least three. Use color codes to designate the difficulty level of the jumping tasks. During lessons, students can randomly select three cards and put them together to create and then practice a routine.

PORTFOLIO TASKS

Corbin, C. B., & Pangrazi, R. P. (1998). *Physical activity for children: A statement of guidelines.* Reston, VA: NASPE Publications.

Fry P. L. (1999). From fat to fit. *World and I, 14,* 330–335.

Hovell, M. F., Sallis, J. F., Kolody, B., & McKenzie, T. L. (1999). Children's physical activity choices: A developmental analysis of gender, intensity levels, and time. *Pediatric Exercise Science,* 71, 158–168.

REFERENCES

Luepker, R. V. (1999). How physically active are American children and what can we do about it? *International Journal of Obesity and Related Metabolic Disorders,* 23 (Supplement 2), S12-7.

McKenzie, T. L., Sallis, J. F., Elder, J. P., Berry, C. C., Hoy, P. L., Nader, P. R., Zive, M. M., & Broyles, S. L. (1997). Physical activity levels and prompts in young children at recess: A two-year study of a bi-ethnic sample. *Research Quarterly for Exercise and Sport,* 68, 195–202.

U.S. Department of Health and Human Services. (1996). *Physical activity and health: A report of the Surgeon General.* Atlanta: U.S. Department of Health and Human Services, Centers for Disease Control and Prevention, National Center for Chronic Disease Prevention and Health Promotion.

Welk, G. J., Morrow, J. R. J., & Falls, H. B. (Eds.). (2002). *Fitnessgram Reference Guide.* Dallas: The Cooper Institute.

Willenburg, B. (1999). *Children's activity pyramid.* Columbia, MO: University Extension, University of Missouri–Columbia.

16

INTERDISCIPLINARY STRATEGIES FOR PHYSICAL EDUCATION

CHAPTER OUTLINE

1. How could you reinforce lessons learned in classroom subjects during physical education?

2. What material from physical education might be useful when teaching math, science, or social studies?

3. What significant social issues might best be learned through an integrated approach involving a number of different subject areas?

4. What is a "meaningful collaboration" in a discussion of teaching content across a number of subject areas?

L ife as you experience it doesn't happen in little clumps called "subjects." During a trip to the supermarket, for example, you use math, reading skills, and your knowledge of personal health to select foods that represent a balanced diet and fit your budget. Likewise, when you drive to another part of the country, you use communication skills and the map-reading skills learned in geography to successfully navigate from your starting point to your destination.

Some educators have advocated adopting interdisciplinary or integrated curriculum methods to help make the classroom experience reflect the "interconnectedness" of knowledge and experience in everyday life (Placek, 2003). In an **interdisciplinary curriculum,** the content of one subject is used to reinforce the learning of topics or skills in another subject. Asking your students to form the shapes of letters of the alphabet with their bodies is an example of a physical education task that reinforces knowledge from language arts. Likewise, having students plot column graphs to track their weekly running distance totals uses physical education content as the subject of a mathematics assignment.

An **integrated curriculum,** on the other hand, is organized around themes or what are sometimes called *big ideas* (Beane, 1990). These big ideas typically involve significant social issues such as conservation, technology, or justice. An integrated curriculum has a controlling purpose that shapes subjects' presentation. For example, if the big idea is social equality, physical education content may repeatedly stress team-based tasks to foster harmonious social interaction among students from various ethnic, racial, or socioeconomic backgrounds.

As the preceding examples demonstrate, you can use physical education lessons to complement classroom work in other subjects or vice versa. Alternatively, curriculum components usually taught during physical education can be made part of an integrated curriculum centered on some theme or larger purpose. Given that integrated curricula are typically developed by schoolwide curriculum committees, we will limit our focus in this chapter to the interdisciplinary side of the topic, the side that you as a teacher can plan and deliver yourself.

interdisciplinary curriculum
One in which activities taught in one subject are also used to reinforce knowledge and skill in other subjects.

integrated curriculum
One organized around themes, or "big ideas," rather than specific subjects.

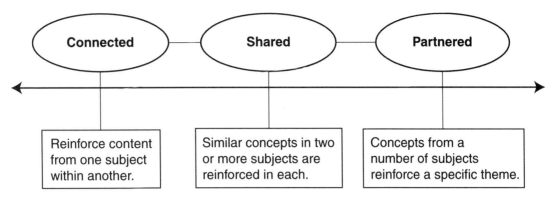

FIGURE **16.1**
Levels of Integration. As your move from left to right, the level of integration becomes more complex and usually involves more personnel and planning.

LEVELS OF CURRICULUM INTEGRATION

An interdisciplinary curriculum does not have to be developed in units or involve every minute of every school day. The key to success in implementing an interdisciplinary curriculum lies in identifying **natural links** among seemingly unrelated subjects. We can define natural links as ideas that flow together and make sense. Such natural links make the benefits of an interdisciplinary curriculum possible. Many authors suggest that the first places to seek these natural links are the curriculum guides you use in planning.

As Figure 16.1 shows, natural links among subjects exist along a three-part continuum of integration. The simplest method, *connected,* can be easily achieved by one teacher and involves making simple connections between two subject areas. An example from physical education would be showing your students the location of the Philippines when you first introduce tinikling (see Chapter 14 for a more detailed discussion on tinikling). As you move from left to right, the teaching process becomes more complex. In the *shared* level, you may continue to discuss the genesis of tinikling and its representation of the Philippine bird as it dances in the rice fields. In social studies, you (or another teacher if your students change classes) may teach more about agricultural societies and rice farming.

The most complex level, *partnered,* will probably involve a team of teachers focusing on a big idea. Here we might focus on sustainable agriculture, with students exploring how various forms of farming and pest eradication affect the environment. To revisit our example, the tinikling dances are said to mimic the movement of the tinikling heron as it dodges bamboo traps set by farmers. For a different option, you may also wish to read "Journey of the Flat People: A Fitness Adventure," by Napper-Owen and Day (1996), which describes a project integrating writing, math, spelling, reading, and art with personal fitness.

Is one of these linkage strategies "better" than another? No, but one strategy is likely to be more appropriate than the other two depending how much you want or need to make cross-curriculum comparisons a part of your teaching plan. At the connected and shared levels, your subject area will still have primacy, with the other content being used to enhance, extend, or complement learning. At the

natural links
Ideas that flow together and make sense.

partnered level, subject boundaries are less clear, as skills and topics across a number of disciplines are merged into an integrated theme (see Purcell Cone et al., 1998).

DEVISING YOUR OWN CROSS-DISCIPLINARY TOPICS

INQUIRING MINDS

What content at your grade level seems to have the most comfortable "fit" in terms of integration?

To help you think about cross-disciplinary studies so you can improvise your own topic connections, we have included a matrix listing major elementary school classroom topics down the left-hand column and major physical education skills along the top row (see Table 16.1). This tool will help you see where natural links occur. The classroom topics are from the performance standards found in state curricular goals and standards statements or courses of study. These documents describe the content standards and provide support to schools developing curricula. Use your own state goals and standards as a starting point.

Some links will come easily. Take, for example, body shape in physical education and shapes in geometry. You could easily develop a lesson plan in either math or physical education that reinforced these concepts. Similarly, concepts of force and various manipulative skills such as striking provide common themes, as do fitness concepts and energy. Reading and writing about movement topics are easily incorporated into both physical education and language arts lessons.

The remainder of this chapter will provide specific teaching examples for various subjects showing either connected or shared integrations possible between classroom-based subjects and physical education.

INTERDISCIPLINARY EXAMPLES: LINKING PHYSICAL EDUCATION CONTENT TO OTHER SUBJECTS

To start looking on your own for natural links among physical education and other topics, it's helpful to divide physical education content into some broad-but-useful categories. As shown in Table 16.1, these include:

- Body shape and awareness
- Movement concepts
- Locomotor and nonlocomotor skills
- Manipulative skills
- Fitness concepts
- Interpersonal skills
- Safety concepts

In the upcoming material, items from many of these categories are employed in suggestions for linking physical education content to other subjects.

TABLE 16.1 ■ Matrix of Major Elementary School Classroom and Physical Education Topics

Topic	Body Shapes	Movement Concepts	Locomotor Skills	Nonlocomotor Skills	Manipulative Skills	Fitness Concepts	Interpersonal Skills	Safety Concepts
Math								
Number								
Algebra								
Geometry								
Measurement								
Data Analysis								
Language Arts								
Reading								
Listening								
Writing								
Speaking								
Presenting								
Science								
Matter								
Forces								
Energy								
Living Systems								
Diversity and Adaptation								
Heredity								
Organisms and Environment								
Dynamic Earth								
Earth in Space								
Ordered Universe								
Social Studies								
Economics								
Geography								
History								
Political Science								

Linking Physical Education Content to Math Lessons

The National Council of Teachers of Mathematics (NCTM) suggests that mathematics teaching can be organized around five content standards: number and operations, algebra, geometry, measurement, and data analysis and probability.

Even just one physical education lesson can generate a lot of numbers. This quantitative content can include scores from games or worksheets, distances thrown or kicked, times spent doing various activities such as rope jumping or running, or the number of exercises completed. Here are just a few of many opportunities for using these data as well as other physical education content in math lessons. For each category we have included a list of activities and ideas written out in a scripted format for you to easily incorporate into your lesson.

Number and operations

- What percentage of your maximum heart rate did you reach after one minute of jumping rope?

- Express as a fraction the distance you threw the football compared to the distance that you kicked it.

- I see here that in one game today Kevin scored 3 points and Maria scored 2. Their team scored 12. I want you to express Kevin and Maria's scores as fractions of their team total. Then calculate their combined score as a fraction of the team total.

Algebra

- We have been exploring various shapes in physical education. Let's try to put these shapes into categories by looking at features that might be similar (e.g., color, size, or shape).

- As you know, during physical education we are running from here to Washington, D.C. Using the charts that you've been keeping, what percent of the total distance have we covered to this point?

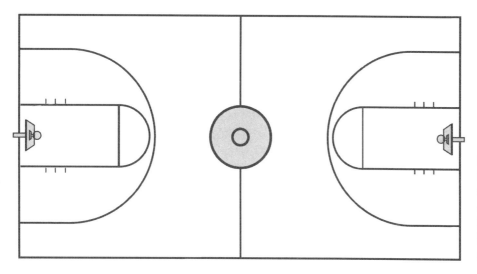

FIGURE **16.2**
Children can trace squares, rectangles, circles, semicircles, and hemispheres from the lines of a basketball court.

Geometry

- Take a look at the diagram of the basketball court. What shapes can you draw using these lines? (See Figure 16.2 for a basketball court.)

- Given the dimensions of our four courts (basketball, volleyball, tennis, and badminton), which has the greatest *perimeter,* and which has the smallest *area?*

- What is the difference in the area of the badminton court when we play singles versus when we play doubles?

Measurement

- Let's look at some of the equipment we use during physical education. I'd like you to complete the following sentences, with a piece of equipment at each end of the sentence and using these middle parts: *is longer than, is as long as, is shorter than, is heavier than,* and a tricky one— *holds more than.*

- In our last physical education lesson we focused on striking with long handles. That was yesterday at 9:30. How much time in hours and minutes has passed since that lesson, and if our next striking lesson is this Friday at 9:30, how long do we have to wait until that time arrives?

Data Analysis and Probability

- Today we completed that short putting circuit where your focus was on putting for accuracy. I'd like you to draw a pie graph that represents your scores on the four holes you played.

- On the board you can see a bar graph I made of the class totals from our recent basketball challenge. Which team scored the highest on free throws, and which team scored highest on total points?

FIGURE **16.3**
Physical education concepts can be reinforced in the classroom by teacher- or child-designed posters.

Cues for Heading

- Eyes open
- Use forehead
- Turtle neck
- Strong force
- Follow through

Linking Physical Education Content to the Language Arts

The National Council of Teachers of English suggests that the content of the English language arts curriculum should be based on two major goals for students: to comprehend meaning and to express meaning effectively. The strands of comprehension are reading, listening, and viewing, while the strands of expression are writing, speaking, and presenting.

Coverage of sports and movement-related topics is ubiquitous in today's news and entertainment media. You can have your students imitate various models of news media communication to write or speak about their experiences during physical education. In this section you will find numerous scripted ideas for creating links between physical education and language arts.

Reading

■ We have a lot of physical education words in our classroom. [Display the words associated with your current lesson content on the board.] Which of these words relate to locomotor and nonlocomotor skills, which are cues for manipulative skills, and which are fitness concepts? (See Figure 16.3 for a sample cue sheet for heading a ball.)

■ Here are a number of books that are based on movement or games. Reading any of these will help you make links with physical education. (Box 16.1 lists a number of books that use action words.)

BOX **16.1** ■ Action Stories That Incorporate Movement Verbs

Barton, Byron. (1981). *Jump, Frog, Jump!* New York: Scholastic, Inc.

Burleigh, Robert, & Johnson, Stephen. (1997). *Hoops.* New York: Silver Whistle/Harcourt Brace & Company.

Carle, Eric. (1996). *Little Cloud.* New York: Philomel Books.

Carle, Eric. (1997). *From Head to Toe.* New York: HarperCollins Publishers.

Cleary, Beverly. (1992). *Ramona the Pest.* New York: Harper Trophy.

Davis, Katie. (1998). *Who Hops?* New York: Harcourt Brace & Company.

Esbensen, Barbara Juster. (1995). *Dance with Me.* New York: HarperCollins Publishers.

Fleming, Denise. (1993). *In the Small, Small Pond.* New York: Henry Holt and Company.

Gillman, Alec. (1993). *Take Me Out to the Ballgame.* New York: Four Winds Press/Macmillan Publishing Company.

Hamanaka, Sheila. (1997). *The Hokey Pokey.* New York: Simon & Schuster Books for Young Readers.

Hayward, Linda, Korr, David, Moss, Jeffrey, & Muntean, Michaela—Children's Television Workshop. (1989). *My ABC's.* Mahwah, NJ: Funk and Wagnalls.

Holzenthaler, Jean. (1979). *My Feet Do.* New York: E. P. Dutton.

Hubbard, Woodleigh. (1990). *C Is for Curious.* San Francisco: Chronicle Books.

Jones, Bill T., & Kuklin, Susan. (1998). *Dance.* New York: Hyperion Books for Children.

Lerner, Sharon. (1970). *Straight Is a Line.* Minneapolis, MN: Lerner Publications Company.

Martin, Bill, Jr., & Archambault, John. (1989). *Chicka Chicka Boom Boom.* New York: Scholastic Inc.

Scarry, Richard. (1986). *Big and Little: A Book of Opposites.* Racine, WI: Western Publishing Company.

Seuss, Dr. (1963). *Hop on Pop.* New York: Random House Beginner Books.

Silverstein, Shel. [Any of his books.]

Source: From "Children's Books." List adapted from http://users.rowan.edu/~cone/childrensbooks.htm

Writing

■ I'd like you to write "I can" sentences that list the cues for various motor skills. Focus on legible letter formation and appropriate spacing and appropriate capitalization (e.g., proper nouns, first word of sentence, the pronoun *I*). A sample "I can" sentence would be "I can dribble well by using my finger pads, by keeping the ball below my waist, and by keeping

BOX **16.2** ■ Sample Cinquain Poem and Nouning and Acrostic Techniques

Cinquain Poem

Title in two syllables	*Volleyball*
Description of title in four syllables	*Big, white, and round*
Action in six syllables	*Trav'ling fast and downward*
Expression of feeling in eight syllables	*I hope I make an awesome save*
Another word for title in two syllables	*Great game*

Nouning Poem

Noun title	*Bat*
Two adjectives	*Long, slender*
Three verbs	*Smashing, crashing, hitting*
Phrase	*Powerful in its work*
Repeat noun	*Bat*

Acrostic Poem

Write a word vertically, then describe it, using each letter as a beginning to show attributes of that word.

Long

Extended

And

Powerful

my head up." (For students in older grades, focus on appropriate punctuation such as sentence ending marks—periods, question marks, and exclamation points—and the apostrophes in contractions and possessives.)

■ Create cinquain poems or use the nouning or acrostic techniques (see Box 16.2) to write a poem about a physical education topic.

■ Using the format found in our local newspaper—headline, byline, and story—write a news report about the game that you invented during games design lessons. Who were the teams that played, what happened during the game, and who won?

■ During many games units, we spend a lot of time discussing the idea of fair play. Write a one-page essay that compares the attributes of a "good sport" and a "bad sport."

- Write a letter to a brother, sister, or friend that describes the difference between muscular strength and muscular endurance. In the letter, describe the benefits of both of these forms of fitness to his or her health.

Speaking

- Prepare and orally present a news release headline or a slogan that reveals the key cues of dribbling a soccer ball or punting a football.

- Prepare and orally present a television advertisement that highlights the benefits of regular physical activity.

Linking Physical Education Content to the Study of Science

The science content of elementary schools can usually be organized according to three major areas: physical sciences, biological sciences, and Earth and space sciences. The physical science knowledge strands relating to elementary schools include properties and changes in matter, position and motion of objects/forces in motion, and energy/energy transfer. The life science knowledge strands include the structure and function of living systems, diversity and adaptations, heredity and reproduction, and organisms and environments. The Earth and space science knowledge strands include dynamic Earth, Earth in space, and ordered universe.

To relate to physical education: All physical activities operate under the laws of physics, particularly those that apply to motion. The human body itself is also the subject of scientific study. Finally, time and space are concepts fundamental to many movement skills. Use these script ideas to engage your students in making connections between the sciences and physical education.

Physical Sciences

- When we place a force (push or pull) on something we can create different effects. Let's look at some of the words we use in physical education: *fast, slow, forward, backward, sideways, straight, curved,* and *zigzag.* What forces do we need to make things go fast, slow, forward, and so on?

- All of us were practicing hopping today. When you hop up, why do you come back down to the ground? Why don't you just keep going higher and higher?

- Today in class you had a chance to throw baseballs and Ping-Pong balls. Which kind travels fastest and farthest? Why do you think that is so?

- We have been striking a number of balls with different long-handled implements during our physical education lessons. Let's look at this whole idea of "transformation of energy." What are some of the energy changes that take place when we hit (such as chemical to electrical, electrical to sound, mechanical to heat)? Think of your body's energy and the bat or stick, as well as the ball.

Life Sciences

- The general place or physical environment in which a population lives is called a *habitat*. Let's make a list of all the different places where we play games (including park, stadium, swimming pool, pond, school ground). What other animals or plants might also live in those places? What might be some of the natural homes of those animals or plants? Should we be careful where we play our games?

- What are some factors that affect the environment, both natural (as in weather, seasons, earthquakes or volcanoes), and human-made (such as pollution and conservation). How might some of these factors affect when and where we get to play?

- All of us were perspiring when we came in from our jumping circuit today. Is sweat good or bad for your body? How does sweat work?

- Today you worked in teams to capture the cone from the other team. Which of the animals that we are studying work in teams to get food?

Earth and Space Sciences

- We know the moon appears as different shapes (phases) at different times. What are those shapes? What are some of the shapes we have during our physical education activities that resemble these phases of the moon?

- What instruments do we use to measure the weather (rain gauge, thermometer, and the like)? What instruments do we use to measure things in physical education and sports? Would there be times when we would need weather instruments in a sport?

- If this tennis ball represents the size of Earth, what other ball would you choose to show the difference in size between Earth and other planets?

- We have been playing a series of hoopball games during our physical education classes. Let's list all the "components" of a hoopball game (such as balls, bases, players, field, and the like). The solar system is also made up of a number of components. Let's list some (such as planets, moons, asteroids, comets, sun, meteors). Now, can we draw any parallels in the roles of these components? What about the components of the universe (such as star systems, galaxies, black holes, nebulae)?

Linking Physical Education Content to Social Studies

The major focus on social studies in elementary schools involves using the strands of economics, geography, history, and political science. The underlying theme of social studies is often responsible citizenship. The scripts for these activities provide you with easy ways to incorporate concepts of physical education into your social studies lessons.

FIGURE **16.4**
Children in other countries play games that American children do not.

Economics

- Let's look at all the materials we used today during our dance lesson in physical education. Which of these were human-made, and which were natural resources? Do these cost more to produce?

- Participation in physical activity often involves both goods and services. What goods do you use outside of school to be physically active? Do you pay for any services (such as tennis lessons, karate club, or swimming pool entrance)?

- What are the differences between producers and consumers? How does this relate to our participation in physical education and activity outside of school? What about imports and exports? What games have been brought to the United States, and what games invented here have been taken to other countries?

Geography

- During physical education, we are practicing our punting and kicking skills. Let's look at other forms of football that are played around the world. Can you find the countries on our maps where these games are played?

- What recreational opportunities in our state and local communities are affected by the physical environment (such as beaches, lakes, or mountains)? What are some that we cannot do locally, but in our state? What are some that we don't really get the opportunity to do at all? Where would we have to go to have that opportunity?

- Look at these pictures of games children play in other countries (see Figure 16.4). How are these games similar to or different from the games that you play during physical education or at home?

- Right now in our social studies class we're studying different kinds of dances from all over the world. How are these dances similar to or

WHAT'S WRONG WITH THIS PICTURE?

Mr. Ulrich's fifth grade class has been practicing dribbling skills with rubber soccer balls. It's a cold day out, and many of the children are commenting that the balls are kind of flat. Mr. Ulrich tells them that he just pumped up the balls the morning. Following a series of two-on-two challenges, it is time to go inside. As the children resume their places in the classroom, many of them are still commenting about the state of the balls. "Quiet down now," instructs Mr. Ulrich, "It's time for science. We're continuing our unit on air."

different from the rhythmic dances we've been practicing in our physical education class?

History

- Some of the skills we have been learning in physical education date back a long way. Baseball, volleyball, and basketball were all played in the 1800s. How do you think teams might have communicated with each other in past times to report scores or arrange matches (letter, radio, rotary-dial telephone)? What are some of the different forms of communication we have now that those teams and players did not (e-mail, television, cellphone)?

- Think of the activities you do now after school. Which of these were not available to children 30 years ago (video and computer games)? What do you think your parents did when they got home from school? How do these compare in terms of physical activity?

- We have been keeping a lot of records during our physical education lessons recently. What are some of the primary sources our families and communities use as historical records (oral histories, vacation pictures in scrapbooks, videos, timelines)?

- All around the world countries hold celebrations: Children's Day in Japan, Thanksgiving in the United States, Bastille Day in France, Cinco de Mayo in Mexico, New Year celebrations in China. What are some of the physical activities or sports that are played on these days?

Political Science

- What are some of our civic responsibilities as members of a community and state (such as paying taxes and voting)? Can you connect these responsibilities to the ones you have as members of a team during a game?

- What are some of the similarities and differences between a referee in a game and a judge in a courtroom? Why do you think both are necessary?

■ When you have designed your own games during our lessons, you have listed the rules to that game. Let's compare game rules to laws; what makes them fair or unfair?

APPLYING CLASSROOM STUDY TOPICS TO PHYSICAL EDUCATION LESSONS

Just as you can bring physical education concepts into the classroom, you can incorporate classroom material into your physical education lessons. Recall that "natural links" between physical education content and classroom studies are those that make the physical education material *directly relevant to the classroom topic.* Likewise, when forging interdisciplinary connections during your physical education class, make sure that any classroom content you use *actually supports the aim of the physical education lesson.* As one specialist notes, it doesn't make your children any more physically fit to have them "run, skip, or gallop while counting, spelling words, or answering questions" (Allen, 1996):

> If students reflect on the day's physical education lesson and say it focused on spelling, George Washington, or how bears run, we have sacrificed a valuable opportunity to teach movement skills. After a lesson, students should be able not only to easily recognize the physical education objectives, but also see how the integrated concepts serve as a way to expand on that objective. (Allen, 1996, p. 12)

Many meaningful interdisciplinary connections achieve this overriding goal of staying true to the objectives of a physical education lesson. For instance, you can use simple foreign-language words on instant activity cards or as you direct students' behavior during a lesson (e.g., non-English words for "stop," "begin," and so forth). The foreign-language content need not interfere with the object of the physical education lesson.

The following section provides a more elaborate example of how a teacher might create interdisciplinary links while remaining true to the objective of a physical education lesson. This example bases a physical education lesson in movement and space on concepts from a science lesson on the states of matter.

1. Direct the students to invent a shape and a brief movement that represents the three states of water: solid (ice), liquid, and gas (vapor). Discuss the speed of movement of the molecules of water in each of these states so that the movements and shapes the students make are representative.

2. Revisit the definitions and processes of *evaporation, condensation,* and *precipitation.*

3. Have the students create a linking movement that represents these transitions—for example, how would they move from solid to liquid? Complete the transitions for evaporation, condensation, and freezing. The transitions should focus not only on movement but also on space. Ask children what kind of space they would need to complete these

movements. Decide which specific movements to use for each transition. Learn and practice these movements until everyone knows them.

4. Keeping a steady beat and starting in the solid state (ice), use a set number of counts for each phase:

- Remain solid for four counts.
- Melt for four counts.
- Remain liquid for four counts.
- Evaporate for four counts.
- Remain a gas for four counts.
- Condense for four counts.
- Remain liquid for four counts.
- Freeze for four counts.
- Remain solid for four counts

5. Practice this "water cycle phase" until everyone can move confidently from phase to phase in this sequence.

Math Content in a Physical Education Lesson

You can incorporate the five content standards of number and operations, algebra, geometry, measurement, and data analysis and probability into physical education lessons. Here is a range of activity ideas your students will enjoy:

- *Math wizards.*[a] Three students begin as taggers while three others begin as "math wizards," armed with cards that depict geometric shapes. The rest of the class finds an open space in the play area. On the music, taggers move around tagging people (the locomotor movements can differ at your request). A student who is tagged freezes in the shape of a star (hands above head and legs spread). A math wizard comes to the frozen student's rescue and shows him or her a card with a shape on it. To move again, the person must tell the wizard the shape and one thing about it. For example "Square, it has four sides and four angles." Have students change roles every minute so that everyone can be all parts of the game.

- *Card play:*[b] From a deck of playing cards, give each student two cards. (Take out the kings, queens and jacks if you do not need them, or have them count as a value of 10.) With students spread out in general space, explain that they must travel around the gym while controlling a soccer ball with a dribble. When the music stops, call out a number; students must then pair up with another student so their cards make an equation equal the number called out. (The number called should be from 2 to 20 so it's not too difficult. The ace equals 1.) Addition, subtraction, division, or multiplication can be used in this activity. For example, if you call out the number 6, students get together and examine their cards. If one

---

a. Adapted from www.pecentral.org/lessonideas/ViewLesson.asp?ID=2630
b. Adapted from www.pecentral.org/lessonideas/ViewLesson.asp?ID=4441

student has a 2 and a 9 in his or her hand and the other child has a 3, then they can either use the 2 and 3 by multiplying to get 6 or they can use the 9 and 3 and subtract to get the number 6.

- *Evens and odds:*[c] Explain the difference between dominant and non-dominant hands. Students use their dominant hand to dribble while reciting the even numbers, calling out one even number with each bounce of the ball. You can use a stopwatch to see what number they get to in 30 seconds. The students then switch to their nondominant hand and dribble while reciting the odd numbers for 30 seconds. Ask the students if they dribbled more even numbers or odd numbers.

- *Place values:* [d] This activity allows children to practice throwing while reinforcing the mathematical concept of place values. You will need a number of targets on a wall (for overhand throwing) or buckets (for underhand throwing) with different place values highlighted. For example, on each wall target or bucket, write 12,345.67 and highlight one numeral (e.g. 12,345.67). You will also need a variety of throwing objects (such as socks, newspaper balls, beanbags, or soft Nerflike balls). Divide the students into small groups (twos or threes) and have them stand about six to eight feet away from the targets. You will then call out a place value (e.g., hundreds or tenths), and the students throw to the wall target or bucket with that place value highlighted. Have students focus on different aspects of throwing each time, such as stepping with opposite foot, proper arm extension and so on).

Language Arts Content in a Physical Education Lesson

Given the emphasis in elementary education on teaching students reading skills, it is important to have strategies that can make reading more fun. One of these strategies is using *action stories,* incorporating movement verbs that can be explored within physical education lessons. Here is an example of a circuit that was developed from the book *Great Day for Up!* by Dr. Seuss. In this circuit, children complete a series of tasks that focus on the word *up* (see Figure 16.5).

A large number of topics are the subjects of poems or short stories that can be used to stimulate the development of short movement sequences and ultimately dances. Harrison, Layton, and Morris (1993) provide the following as but a few examples: weather, jungles, deserts, swamps, flight, trains, at the bus stop.

As Purcell (1994) notes, the connection of children's literature with movement presents an active and aesthetic opportunity for children to express their meaning and understanding of a literary experience. In her research, Purcell found that children, with practice, are able to spontaneously improvise movements and create variations to express their understanding and emotional response to stories. She also notes that children enjoy stories with an active dimension, especially humorous ones where objects or animals are personified and events presented contrary to logic.

---

c. Adapted from www.pecentral.org/lessonideas/ViewLesson.asp?ID=4283
d. Adapted from www.pecentral.org/lessonideas/ViewLesson.asp?ID=3908

Kick foam balls to wall

Foam balls in basketball net

Lollipop paddle and foam balls

Hit birdies up

Pogo ball

Lift weights up

Trampoline

Volley animal balls

Sit-ups and push-ups

Great Day for UP

Headstand and handstand

Hoppers

Jump on the states

Long jump rope

Red medicine ball

Pogo sticks

Jump up and touch numbers on the pole

Throw the tennis balls up and . . .

Throw playground ball so it hits the line on the wall

FIGURE **16.5**
Activity circuit to complement the book
Great Day for Up!

A good starting point for developing the connections between literature and movement is fairy tales. These stories are short, are often full of various emotions, have clear-cut plots, and provide numerous opportunities for expression and creativity. A website devoted to all things associated with the Grimm brothers (www.pitt.edu/~dash/grimm.html) has the complete text of all fairy tales collected by members of this famous family. Here are a number of specific examples of activities that bring language arts into the gym:

- Have your students read the book called *Ramona the Pest*. In the first chapter, Ramona learns all about jumping and running. You can then have your children do those very same activities during physical education. As noted earlier in this chapter, Box 16.1 lists books that incorporate physical activity. Reading these stories could be a classroom activity accompanying content work in gymnastics, fitness, dance, or various associated skills (e.g. striking or volleying).

- Simple poems can be used to reinforce motor skills. Any number of poems can also serve as starting points through which students can develop movement sequences and then dances. Consider this poem by Harrison (1993):

Shadows

Shadow, shadow curled up small

I can make you grow up tall

Now I'm jumping stretched and wide

Shadow, shadow at my side

Tiptoe slowly, shadow go!

I can't lose my shadow though.

This poem incorporates a number of dance elements (movement, time, space, body, energy) so students could create a sequence resembling the key features of the poem in ways that allow for individual creativity. Once the students have developed their movement sequences, you can incorporate a set beat with some percussive instrument and have them perform their dances to a beat. The poem itself fits very easily within a four-count beat. You might also have students perform their sequences behind a screen (see Figure 16.6) to accentuate the notion of shadows.

Science Content in a Physical Education Lesson

As noted, there is a strong connection between the physical and life sciences and physical education. Many mechanical concepts, as well as those from human anatomy, can be reinforced during physical education lessons:

- *Scooters:*[e] A push or a pull is needed for an object to be set in motion. The object moves in the direction of the force. Explore using pushing and pulling actions to move the scooter. Explore using force to propel the scooter forward, backward, right, and left. A push or pull action must be exerted to change the direction of a moving object. Explore following the

---

e. From the Flaghouse activity guide (see www.flaghouse.com)

FIGURE **16.6**
Children can design movement sequences to the poem "Shadows" and then perform these sequences using simple backlighting and a sheet to enhance the presentation.

path of a moving scooter and then applying a different force to change the direction of movement:

- Apply Newton's third law of motion. Explore the action/reaction concept of using the pull/push arm pattern for the freestyle swimming stroke. From a prone position on the scooter, use the arms alternately in the pull/push pattern. The final backward push of the stroke results in a forward motion of the body.

- Push an empty scooter with light force; watch the speed of travel and mark the spot where the scooter stops. Push an empty scooter with heavy force; watch the speed of travel and mark the spot where the scooter stops. Discuss the difference in speed and distance traveled with each type of force. Ask your students to repeat this activity while sitting on the scooter. Use the experiment listed above with a partner sitting on the scooter. Which force causes the scooter to travel fastest and farthest?

■ *Bone Hokey Pokey:* Using an instrumental version of the Hokey Pokey, you can follow the key concept of the dance ("Put your left
_____ in, put your left
_____ out, put your left
_____ in and shake it all about") but use the names of various bones instead of the more familiar body parts.

■ *Skeleton relay:* You will need cardboard cutouts of a number of bones for this activity. Create teams of three to five students. Using a dribbling skill from any number of activities (basketball, soccer, hockey) have one student dribble to the center circle and collect a bone. When that student returning to the home base, another player collects a bone, and students progressively build a skeleton.

Social Studies Content in a Physical Education Lesson

Social studies topics from history, geography, and political science lend themselves to connections to physical education. Some examples:

- *Tag games:* These can provide quick checks of understanding geographical or historical topics. A student who is tagged stays in place and raises his or her hand. "Tag releasers" (who themselves cannot be tagged) run to the tagged child and ask a question, which they carry on a card. Questions can relate to any geographical or historical topic. Have the answer written on the back of the card, so the tagged student can read it if he or she cannot provide the answer.

- *River game:* During lessons on chasing, fleeing, and dodging skills, you can also review social studies content using the "river game." In this game, students stand on either side of the river and have to cross over or remain on their side depending on the answer to the question. Taggers in this game stand in the river and attempt to tag their classmates as they cross. The following section shows an application of this concept to students' knowledge of state locations:

  1. Mark three lines across the width of your activity area: a centerline of one color and two lines of a different color that are 6 to 10 feet on each side of the centerline. The center line is the Mississippi River. The area between the other two lines, including the river, is a neutral zone. Students may be tagged in this zone.

  2. Two to three "taggers" start in the neutral zone but may move throughout the entire playing area.

  3. Half of the other students are located on the "west" side of the Mississippi River, and the other half are on the "east" side. The side of the river on which each child begins the activity is his or her "home side."

  4. Begin by calling the name of a state. Students who are standing on the opposite side of the Mississippi River from the state you call must cross the neutral zone to the correct side. That is, if Utah were called, all those on the east side of the Mississippi would attempt to cross to the west side without being tagged. Students on the west (correct) side who moved in error to the opposite side could also be tagged. A tagged student must spell the name of the state called. A student who does so correctly earns a life and rejoins his or her team. An incorrect student becomes a tagger.

  5. You should periodically have students return to their original sides in order to balance the numbers.

- *Landfill losers:*[f] When teaching various passes to a partner, you can review the content of environmental ecology using the game of landfill losers. To play this game, divide the class into three groups of about equal size. One group of players occupies a space between the other two groups. These players are known as the "landfill losers." You can reinforce the

f. www.pecentral.org/lessonideas/ViewLesson.asp?ID=1128

INQUIRING MINDS

How often do you collaborate with other teachers in your grade level to find connections among content areas?

How often does this connection involve physical education?

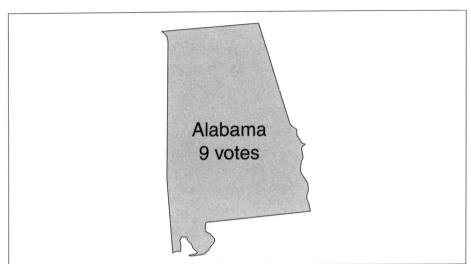

FIGURE **16.7**
During the game of Electoral College, students represent different states. This figure shows a task card of one such state and the college points it represents.

Alabama
9 votes

notion of how landfills take up valuable space and sometimes create groundwater pollution. The object of this game is to keep "recycling" balls by passing them back and forth to each other without the landfill losers grabbing them and putting them in the ground. The two groups on either side of the landfill losers will try to pass balls back and forth to each other without the losers getting them. Balls may be thrown or bounced to each other, but no ball may go above the heads of the losers. Balls that go above the heads of the losers become their property. Play for a certain time limit, and count the number of balls at the end to see which team has more.

■ *State boundary balance:* Have students create the outline of a particular state using jump ropes. The challenge is to then travel around that state's boundary while balancing on the jump rope.

■ *Electoral college:*[g] In this game, three students begin in the middle of the playing area. They are the presidential candidates. Each of the rest of the class is assigned a state and instructed to line up (in a spread out manner) at one end of the gym. Each student has a nametag with a number under the state name that represents the number of electoral votes that state casts in an election. When you begin the game, the students who are the states try to move past the candidates to the other end of the gym without getting tagged by the candidates. A state that gets tagged belongs to the candidate who tagged him or her. The state must then help its candidate capture more states until all are captured. Each candidate and his or her group of states will then add up their electoral votes to determine who will be the next U.S. President. Afterward, discuss electoral votes, populations, and the importance of each state's vote. Sample questions might include "Does it really matter which state each candidate wins in the electoral race?" and "How many votes are necessary to win the Electoral College?" See www.fec.gov/pages/elecvote.htm for the distribution of electoral votes across states. Figure 16.7 provides one sample card that students can use during this activity.

g. www.pecentral.org/lessonideas/ViewLesson.asp?ID=1128

Reinforcing classroom and physical education concepts in alternate settings is an exciting way to make the world come alive for children. Connecting content across disciplines reinforces learning through the kinesthetic, auditory, and visual modalities, as well as helping children's verbal and social skills. Teaching across disciplines does not mean that you have to sacrifice content or time. By seeking natural links and meaningful connections among subjects, you can actually strengthen learning in both domains. Start small, plan for simple connections between subject areas, and realize that the integration of ideas across curricula does not have to be a constant priority. Then, as you become more comfortable, expand the matrix that connects subjects to develop more shared levels of integration.

FINAL WORDS

1. In which subject area are you most creative? Does this creativity have an advantage in finding connections between different subjects? In what ways?

2. What resources could you use to find ideas about cross-disciplinary learning?

3. What might be some of the "big ideas" that could form the basis of an integrated unit using physical education as one of its learning areas?

4. In which *direction* do you think it will be easier to make connections: physical education into the classroom, or the reverse?

OVER TO YOU

1. Read three of the books listed in Box 16.1. Then design a circuit of physical activities that would complement the story or theme of one of these books.

2. Select one content area from your state's courses of study. Identify topics in three different grade levels that might be appropriate for a connected or shared level of integration with physical education.

3. Find the foreign-language translations to a number of "protocol" words you frequently use in physical education. First, identify this list and then the translations.

PORTFOLIO TASKS

Allen, V. L. (1996). A critical look at integration: Meaningful ways to incorporate cross-curricular content. *Teaching Elementary Physical Education, 7*(3), 12–14.

Beane, J. (1990). *A middle school curriculum: From rhetoric to reality.* Columbus, OH: National Middle School Association.

Harrison, K. (1993). Shadows. In K. Harrison, J. Layton, & M. Morris, *Dance and movement.* p. 84. Leamington Spa, U. K.: Scholastic Publications.

Harrison, K., Layton, J., & Morris, H. (1993). *Dance and movement.* Leamington Spa, U.K.: Scholastic Publications.

Napper-Owen, G., & Day, M. (1996). Journey of the flat people: A fitness adventure. *Teaching Elementary Physical Education, 7*(3), 16–17.

REFERENCES

Placek, J. H. (2003). Interdisciplinary curriculum in physical education: Possibilities and problems. In S. Silverman & C. Ennis (Eds). *Student learning in physical education: Applying research to enhance instruction.* Champaign, IL: Human Kinetics.

Purcell, T. M. (1994). *Teaching children dance: Becoming a master teacher.* Champaign, IL: Human Kinetics Books.

Purcell Cone, T., Werner, P., Cone, S. L., & Woods A. M. (1998). *Interdisciplinary teaching through physical education.* Champaign, IL: Human Kinetics.

Seuss, Dr. (1974). *Great day for up!* New York: Random House Beginner Books.

GLOSSARY

accent An increased emphasis on a note, which can be through an increase in the force of a movement, such as an extra heavy stomp versus a light step, or perhaps through a marked gesture.

accountability system The routines and procedures used by teachers for establishing and maintaining student responsibility for their work in the classroom.

active supervision A pattern of teaching that includes higher rates of interaction between students and movement.

aerobic exercise Any physical activity that stimulates the body to use oxygen more efficiently.

alternative assessment A type of evaluation instrument different from one-shot formalized tools such as written tests and skill tests.

application A task that challenges children to perform to a certain standard.

appropriate footwear Rubber-soled footwear that will not come off during activity.

assessment The process of gathering information on students (documentation) and making a judgment about the results (achievement).

authentic performance assessment An assessment requiring students to demonstrate the behaviors the teacher wants to assess in a real-world context.

back to the wall The strategy of standing on the periphery of the classroom or instructional session to better see what all students are doing.

balancing The skill of safely supporting one's body weight.

beat The underlying pulse of a series of sounds that holds true throughout the entire piece (e.g., 1-2-3-4 or 1-2-3).

callout Responding to a question simultaneously and immediately.

catching Receiving and controlling a propelled object.

cephalocaudal development The sequence of growth occurs from the head to the feet.

chasing Traveling quickly to overtake or tag a fleeing person.

closed skill A skill whose environmental demands are predictable or stable.

closure The strategy used to end or wrap up a lesson.

column format A lesson plan divided into sections of pertinent information.

competent bystander behavior Describes a child who appears to be engaged in the lesson but avoids participating.

congruent feedback Information related to the learning cue or critical feature of the task focus.

convergent problem solving A type of inquiry that uses a linear progression of questions to guide the student in discovering one single answer.

corrective feedback Information related to the performance that tells the performer what to do in future attempts.

cross-group feedback Feedback for students who are across the gym or work area from the teacher.

dance Moving rhythmically, usually to music, using prescribed or improvised steps and gestures.

discrete skill A skill with definitive starting and ending points.

divergent problem solving A type of inquiry in which the teacher presents the students with a problem and then challenges them to find multiple solutions.

dodging Abruptly shifting the body from one line of movement to another.

dribbling Maintaining control of a ball with the hands or the feet while either advancing with it or, at times, remaining in place.

educational gymnastics A form of gymnastics that develops skill within the ability and understanding of the individual student.

equipment managers Students who have responsibilities for collecting and returning specific pieces of equipment to and from the work area in which the lesson will be completed.

exercise Planned and structured physical activity, producing repetitive bodily movement that will improve or maintain one or more of the components of physical fitness.

extension An adjustment that makes an existing task easier or more difficult.

externally paced skill A skill initiated before the performer is ready, usually due to external stimuli.

fitness A set of attributes that people have or achieve relating to their ability to perform physical activity.

fleeing Traveling quickly away from a pursuing person or object.

flexibility The range of motion around a joint.

flight The act of traveling in the air.

folk dance A style of dancing that originated among ordinary people and is an integral and anticipated behavior in the culture of those people.

formal accountability System in which mechanisms such as tests or assignments are used to give students grades.

formation An arrangement or grouping of students for practice.

formative assessment Ongoing or continuous assessment used to show student progress toward meeting outcomes.

fundamental skills Basic motor actions with specific movement patterns.

game Any rule-driven pastime involving physical activity that entails cooperation as well as competition (against others or oneself).

game sheet A plan for organizing students and equipment when teaching games.

general feedback Comments that do not provide children with information on how to improve.

general space The space within the activity area that children can reach by moving.

guided discovery A teaching style in which the teacher uses a predetermined set of questions or movement problems to help students identify one correct answer or response.

health-related fitness Those components of fitness that promote optimum health and prevent the onset of diseases associated with a lack of physical activity.

inclusion A policy that lets all students successfully participate, develop skills, and have a sense of belonging in the class.

incongruent feedback Information not related to the cue or outcome of the lesson.

informal accountability System where the performance does not directly contribute toward a grade; examples include practice exams, active supervision, sitting out, public recognition, and teacher feedback.

instant activity A brief movement task children will begin immediately upon arrival at the work area.

instructional task system Those tasks relating to the subject matter.

integrated curriculum One organized around themes, or "big ideas," rather than specific subjects.

interdisciplinary curriculum One in which activities taught in one subject are also used to reinforce knowledge and skill in other subjects.

interskill variability The difference in students' performance among different skills.

intraskill variability The difference in students' performance within the same skill.

intratask variation A teaching strategy where the teacher changes or adjusts a task for a child or group of children.

inverted position Any body position that finds the hips higher than the head.

kicking Using the foot to apply force to an object on the ground.

knowledgeable practitioner A teacher with a thorough understanding of the content who knows how to teach the content to children.

landing The act of coming down to the ground or other surface (e.g., a mat).

learnable piece A physical act or behavior needed to perform a skill (or part of a skill) correctly.

least restrictive environment (LRE) The concept of placing children with special needs in the most inclusive environment they can handle.

line dance A choreographed form of popular dance incorporating a repeating sequence of steps identically performed by a group of dancers in one or more lines.

locomotor skill A movement that moves the body from one place to another within a vertical plane.

managerial task system Those tasks relating to the establishment and maintenance of appropriate behavior.

minitournament Between five and eight lessons in which the students are split into teams who play against each other and also participate in the organization and administration of those games.

motor skill development The quantitative and qualitative changes in children as they move to more complex versions of physical skills throughout the lifespan.

movement The teacher's constant changing of position around the physical education work area.

movement concept A word that describes how to perform a movement.

movement problems Tasks given to students asking them to explore a movement category in a way that encourages individual and developmentally appropriate engagement. These are frequently presented as "show me" or "find different ways" statements.

movement response Children provide answers to questions through movement rather than orally or by writing an answer. This could be prompted by asking them, "Show me a stable base that has only two body parts in contact with the floor."

muscular endurance A muscle's capacity to exert a force repeatedly against a resistance.

muscular strength The maximum force that a muscle produces against a resistance in a single, maximal effort.

natural links Ideas that flow together and make sense.

open skill A skill whose environmental demands are changing or unpredictable.

outcome What students should know and be able to do as a result of instruction.

passive supervision A pattern of teaching with little interaction between the teacher and students.

performance assessment Assessment requiring students to perform a movement or produce something.

performance task A performance assessment in which students physically perform a given task.

personal space All the space you can take up without moving from a particular point.

physical activity Any bodily movement produced by skeletal muscles and resulting in energy expenditure. This is an umbrella term that includes exercise, sport, dance, and other leisure activities, such as inline skating or fishing.

physical education A planned, sequential program of instruction designed to develop basic fundamental skills, sports skills, and physical fitness to prepare children for lifetime participation in physical activity.

physical fitness A measure of a person's ability to perform physical activities that require endurance, strength, or flexibility; determined by a combination of regular activity and genetically inherited ability.

pinpointing The act of directing the class to the work of two or more students to highlight a specific cue or outcome.

portfolio A collection of student work gathered over time and used to document progress.

portfolio task A performance assessment requiring students to perform a task that is cognitive or affective in nature.

power ratings Points awarded by teachers during mini-tournaments to teams who successfully complete explicit tasks.

practice competition A series of unofficial games in which two teams play each other while a third officiates.

protocols Commands that your students need to follow before or during the lesson.

proximodistal development The sequence of growth that occurs from the midline to the extremities.

punting Use the foot to apply force to an object that begins in the hands.

refinement A task that highlights the quality of student performance.

reliability A measurement issue related to consistency of scores.

rhythmic movement Movement in time to individual sounds.

rubric A rating scale used to judge student performance on a particular assessment item.

rule A stated expectation with regard to personal conduct.

scaffolding Linking students' previous knowledge, work, or experience with what will be covered in the present or future.

scripted format A plan showing word-for-word what the teacher will say during the lesson.

self-esteem The opinion you have of yourself.

self-paced skill A skill executed at a time decided upon by the performer.

self-space The area around the body that the student can reach without moving.

sequence A series of actions so skillfully aligned that all movements within the sequence fit together logically.

serial skill A combination of two or more discrete skills used to perform a movement.

set induction The beginning of the lesson that tells the students what they will be learning and why it is important.

skill-related fitness Those components of fitness that promote optimum performance of motor skills.

specific feedback Information given about a consistent aspect or result of a performance.

sports skills Proficiency in using fundamental motor skills in specialized and often competitive situations.

spotters Assistants who stand by a performer during gymnastics skills to prevent injury.

stations An instructional strategy in which children rotate from one learning task to another systematically throughout a lesson.

striking Using a piece of equipment to hit an object, making it move through the air or along the ground.

summative assessment Evaluation at the end of a unit or lesson used to determine a level of achievement.

takeoff The act of getting the body off the ground.

teaching by invitation A teaching strategy where the teacher invites students to change a task when they are ready.

throwing Accurately propelling an object away from the body.

tinikling A rhythmic activity that involves individuals or pairs jumping in between, straddling, or standing outside of two long poles.

traveling Changing location from one place to another.

validity The degree to which a test measures the attribute or characteristic it intends to measure.

volleying Striking an object while it is in the air.

working rules Rules giving children details about the number and type of actions that need to be involved, the equipment that may or must be used, and the number of people involved when solving a movement problem.

INDEX

Page references followed by *fig* indicates an illustrated figure or photograph; by a *t* indicates a table; by a *b* indicates a box.

CREDITS

Figures 12.1, 12.3, 12.5, 12.8, 12.9, 12.10, 12.13, 12.15, and 12.18 are reproduced with permission from Queensland Studies Authority, *Years 1 to 10 Health and Physical Education Sourcebook Modules* (originally published by the Queensland School Curiculum Council in 2000). For more information on these and other education publications, contact the Queensland Studies Authority via email at office@qsa.qld.edu.au or on the Internet at www.qsa.qld.edu.au.

Photographs supplied courtesy of:

Sheri Brock: pages 5, 20, 35, 61, 63, 81, 86, 89, 93, 102, 143, 150, 151, 154, 160, 188, 311

Charles Cooper: pages 8, 29, 39, 41, 74, 155, 189, 191, 195, 224 (top), 225, 247, 277, 320

Peter Hastie: pages 12, 13, 17, 21, 24, 27, 32, 45, 51, 56, 87, 97, 98, 105, 120, 143, 145, 154, 156, 157, 158, 162, 168, 169, 171, 174, 175, 177, 180, 186, 190, 201, 205, 213, 222 (top), 222 (middle), 222 (bottom), 223 (top, middle, bottom), 224 (bottom), 234, 235, 239, 240, 248, 259, 267, 284, 294, 303, 331, 338, 339, 342, 355, 358, 364, 368, 373, 375 (left), 375 (right), 377, 380, 383, 391, 397, 407, 409, 413 (top), 413 (bottom), 415, 416 (top), 416 (middle), 416 (bottom), 417 (top), 417 (bottom), 418, 419, 423 (top), 423 (middle), 423 (bottom), 424 (top), 424 (bottom), 431, 443, 450

Ellen Martin: 69, 71, 116